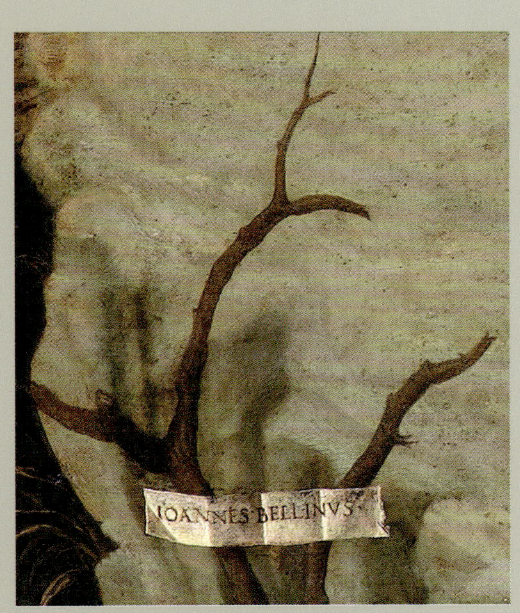

IOANNES·BELLINVS·

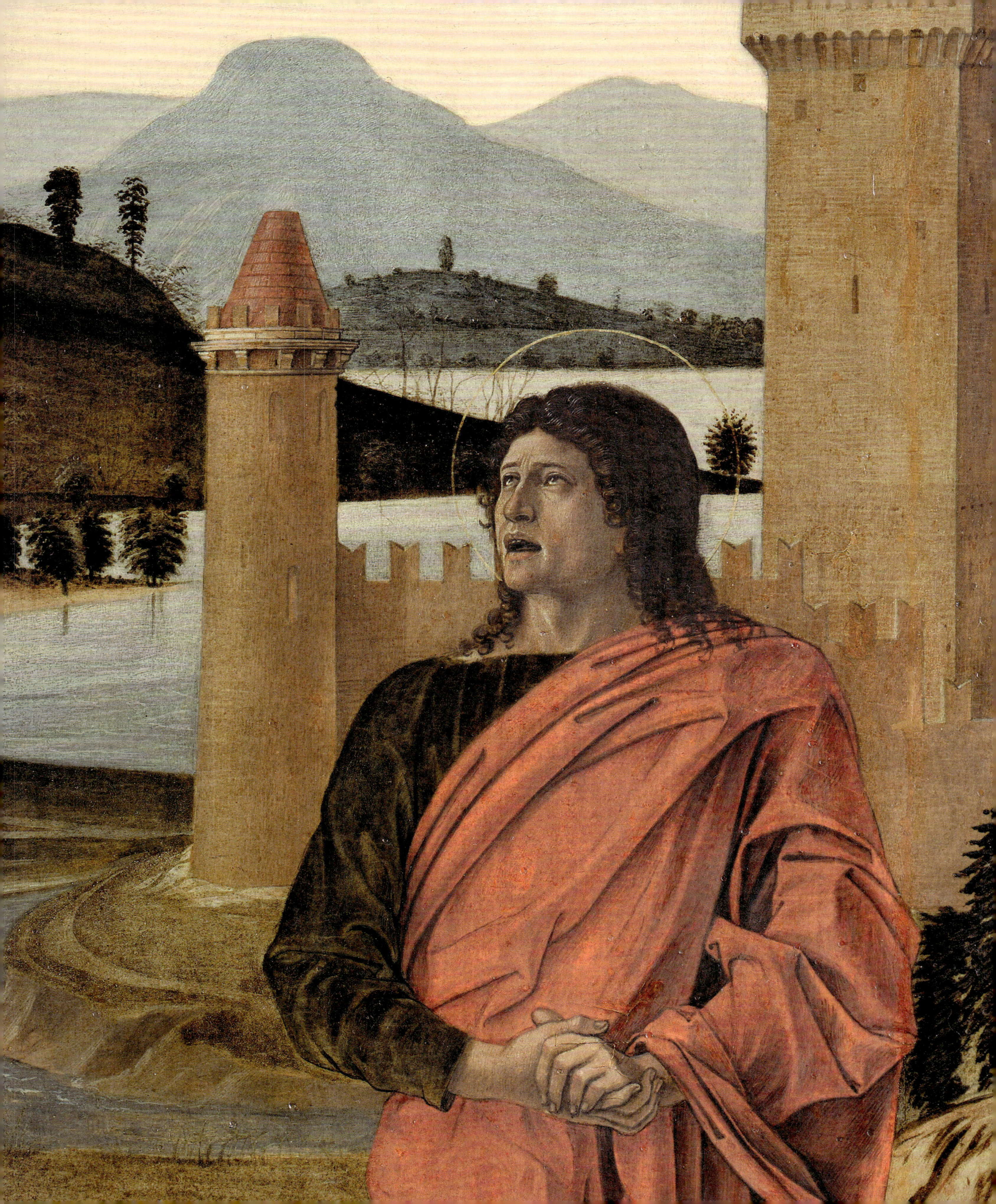

Giovanni BELLINI

LANDSCAPES OF FAITH IN RENAISSANCE VENICE

EDITED BY DAVIDE GASPAROTTO

With contributions by

Hans Belting

Keith Christiansen

Davide Gasparotto

Daniel Wallace Maze

Antonio Mazzotta

Susannah Rutherglen

Mattia Vinco

THE J. PAUL GETTY MUSEUM | LOS ANGELES

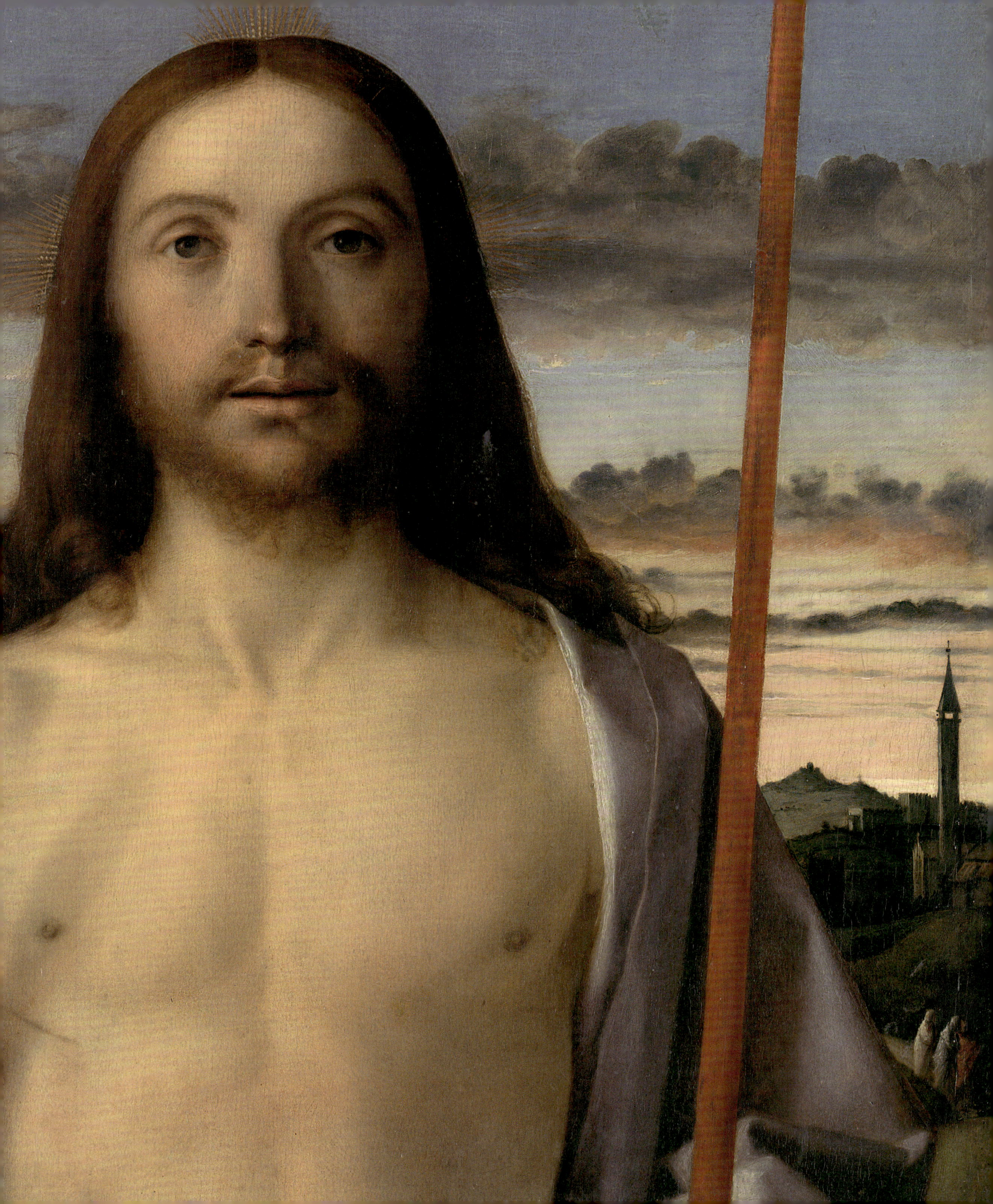

CONTENTS

Foreword   7
Timothy Potts

Acknowledgments   8

Note to the Reader   9

Giovanni Bellini and Landscape   11
Davide Gasparotto

Poetry and Painting:
Saint Jerome in the Wilderness   25
Hans Belting

The Life of Giovanni Bellini   37
Daniel Wallace Maze

Catalogue   57

References   131

Index   144

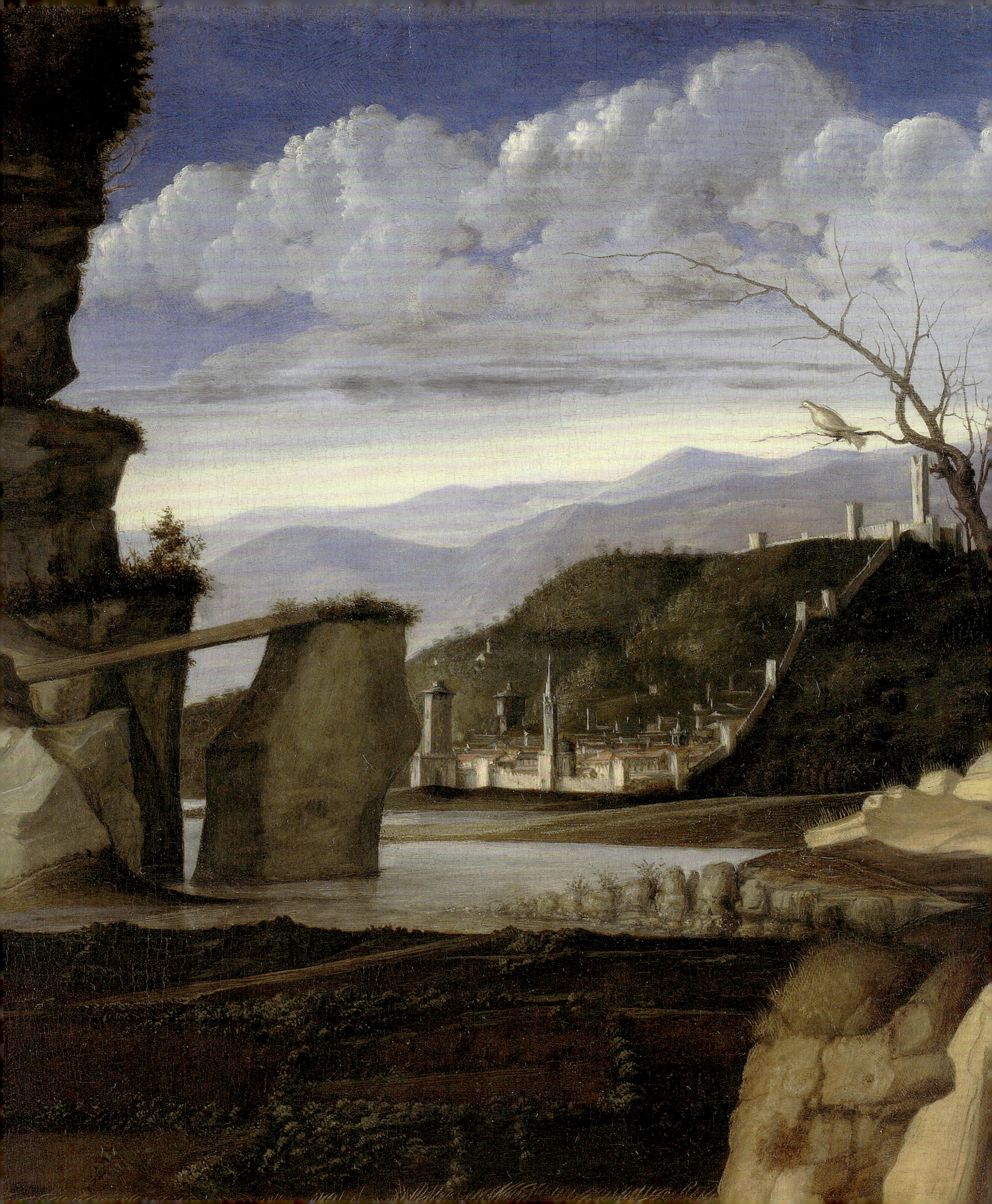

FOREWORD

Writing from Venice on February 7, 1506, to his dear friend the German humanist Willibald Pirckheimer, Albrecht Dürer praised Giovanni Bellini (ca. 1435–1516) as "still the best in the art of painting" despite the fact that the Venetian artist was in his seventies and a new generation of painters—among them Giorgione, Sebastiano del Piombo, and Titian—was already coming into its own. Indeed, it was thanks to him that the Venetian school was transformed during the later fifteenth century from one of mainly local standing to a center of international repute. In the mid-twentieth century, the eminent Italian art historian Roberto Longhi described Bellini as "one of the greatest poets of Italy," and he remains today the most illustrious Venetian painter of the quattrocento.

Remarkably, *Giovanni Bellini: Landscapes of Faith in Renaissance Venice* is the first monographic exhibition in America ever devoted to Bellini. Organized by the J. Paul Getty Museum, it brings together thirteen extraordinary and extremely delicate paintings and one drawing from the most prestigious museums in the world, selected to illuminate the role and significance of a particularly admired feature of Bellini's paintings—his landscapes. To a degree unmatched by any of his contemporaries, mountains, walled towns, castles, caves, rocks, trees, plants, flowers, sunrises, and sunsets are as much the protagonists of his work as are the human figures. Landscapes act as complements to religious subject matter and enhance the meditational character of his paintings, which were typically intended for the private devotion of highly sophisticated patrons. Bellini's paintings present characters and symbols from familiar sacred stories set in a realm of lived experience to an extent that was unprecedented in the Italian artistic tradition. Distinguished by his refined sensitivity to nature, Bellini was able to transform traditionally symbolic motifs into convincing yet poetic depictions of the Venetian mainland. Such innovations represent a crucial transition toward a novel consideration of the picture as not only a devotional tool but also an object worthy of aesthetic appreciation. In this way Bellini's work marks the beginning of a new chapter in the history of European painting.

We are grateful to Davide Gasparotto, senior curator of paintings, for conceiving and organizing *Giovanni Bellini: Landscapes of Faith in Renaissance Venice* and for editing the present catalogue, with contributions from an internationally acclaimed group of emerging and more established scholars. The landmark exhibition that occasioned this volume would have been impossible without the exceptional generosity of lenders across North America and Europe. The directors and owners of these public and private collections are especially deserving of our gratitude. We also acknowledge the generous support for the exhibition provided by John J. Studzinski CBE, Maria Hummer-Tuttle and Robert Holmes Tuttle, Álvaro Saieh, and Fabrizio Moretti.

Timothy Potts
Director
The J. Paul Getty Museum

Detail of cat. no. 7

To the memory of my father,
Erasmo Gasparotto (1929–2016)

ACKNOWLEDGMENTS

I would like to acknowledge the generosity and support of the institutions that lent works to this exhibition: Nicola Kalinski and Robert Wenley (Barber Institute of Art, Birmingham); Princess Lucrezia Corsini, Andrea Miari Fulcis, Francesca Franciolini, and Livia Branca (Corsini Collection, Florence); Eike Schmidt, Francesca De Luca, and Daniela Parenti (Galleria degli Uffizi, Florence); Eric Lee, George Shackelford, Nancy Edwards, and Claire Barry (Kimbell Art Museum, Fort Worth); Ernst Vegelin van Claerbergen and Ketty Gottardo (Courtauld Gallery, London); Gabriele Finaldi and Caroline Campbell (The National Gallery, London); Álvaro Saieh and Antonia Dittborn Bellalta (The Alana Collection, Newark, Delaware); Jean-Luc Martinez, Sébastien Allard, Dominique Thiébaut (Musée du Louvre, Paris); Paola Marini and Roberta Battaglia (Gallerie dell'Accademia, Venice); Gabriella Belli (Museo Correr, Venice); Gianni Mion, Fabrizio Viola, and Elisa Viola (Banca Popolare di Vicenza); Earl A. Powell III and David Alan Brown (National Gallery of Art, Washington, DC); and the following individuals: Ann Daley, Jan Meyer, and Timothy Standring.

I wish to thank my colleagues Hans Belting, Keith Christiansen, Daniel Wallace Maze, Antonio Mazzotta, Susannah Rutherglen, and Mattia Vinco for their contributions to this volume.

At the J. Paul Getty Museum, the exhibition and the book would not have been possible without the support of Timothy Potts, Richard Rand, Quincy Houghton, Carolyn Marsden-Smith, Amber Keller, Betsy Severance, Marit Coyman-Myklebust, Amy Weiss, Robert Checchi, and François Aubret. Anne Woollett, Scott Allan, Peter Björn Kerber, and Jill Hortz, my colleagues in the Paintings Department, never ceased to support me along the way. A special thanks is due to Laura Llewellyn for her precious help during the preparation of the exhibition and the catalogue.

Among friends and fellow scholars, the contributors and I would like to thank Giovanni Agosti, Malachi Beit-Airé, Guido Beltramini, Francesco Caglioti, Maichol Clemente, Evelyn Cohen, Jennifer Fletcher, Peter Humfrey, David Kerr, Rosella Lauber, Susy Marcon, Simona Pasquinucci, Debra Pincus, Francis Russell, Xavier Salomon, Menahem Schmelzer, Leo Schubert, Giuliano Tamani, Giovanni Carlo Federico Villa, Carolyn Wilson, Tom Whorten, and Ida Zatelli.

The publisher of Getty Publications, Kara Kirk, and the editor in chief, Karen Levine, played important roles in the genesis of this publication. I am grateful to our project editor, Nola Butler, for her guidance and diligence. Mary Christian improved the text in manifold ways. Kurt Hauser provided the elegant design of the book, Michelle Woo Deemer managed the complex production details, and Nina Damavandi's patient detective work ensured the quality of the imagery. I am also grateful to our excellent proofreader, Jane Bobko, and indexer, Theresa Duran.

My greatest debt of all, however, is to my wife, Silvia Ottolini, for her wise advice, constant encouragement, and love.

Davide Gasparotto
Senior Curator of Paintings
The J. Paul Getty Museum

NOTE TO THE READER

In this volume the reader will notice some discrepancies in the chronology of certain paintings. These discrepancies reflect the ongoing divergence of opinions that characterize the scholarship on Giovanni Bellini. In particular, since his first firmly dated work is from 1487 and there is no consensus on the artist's date of birth—with a range of proposals, from 1425 to 1440—the reconstruction of the beginning of his career and the sequence of his earliest works is still much debated. Even the new evidence provided by Daniel Wallace Maze in his stimulating and provocative biographical essay presented here is not definitive and reflects his interpretation of extant documentary evidence and early printed sources. The date of birth indicated in the individual catalogue entries (ca. 1435) represents the opinion of the editor of the present volume, an opinion that is not necessarily shared by the other contributors. This is also the case with the presumed date of certain works.

Regarding the technique used to execute the paintings: in the catalogue entries, only the material of the support—mostly wood panel—is indicated and not the binding agent. Bellini is known to have used egg tempera and oil throughout his career, sometimes even applying both in the same work of art, so identifying the medium of his paintings is a thorny issue. Since not all the works in the exhibition have undergone the relevant technical analysis that establishes the medium definitively, the decision was made to avoid conjecture.

During the production of this book, a masterpiece by Bellini was added to the checklist of works in the exhibition. The half-length *Saint Dominic* from a private collection in Denver (fig. 40), signed on the parapet and probably painted in 1501 for the Duke of Ferrara Alfonso I d'Este, has been known to specialists since 1926 but it has almost never been shown in public. We are fortunate to have the opportunity to present it alongside the nearly contemporary *Virgin and Child with Saint John the Baptist and a Female Saint in a Landscape* (cat. no. 10).

The catalogue entry contributors are:

Keith Christiansen	K.C.
Davide Gasparotto	D.G.
Antonio Mazzotta	A.M.
Susannah Rutherglen	S.R.
Mattia Vinco	M.V.

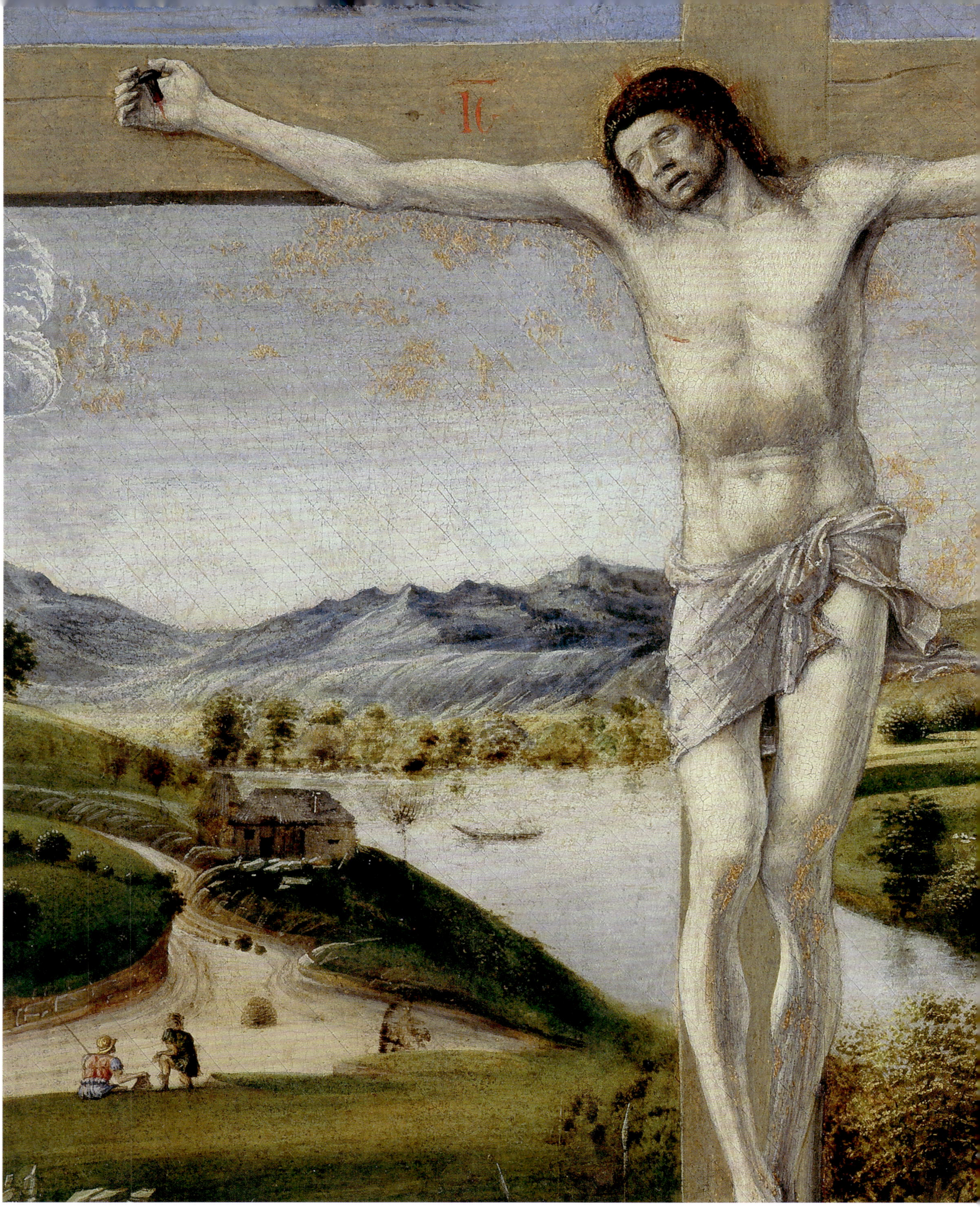

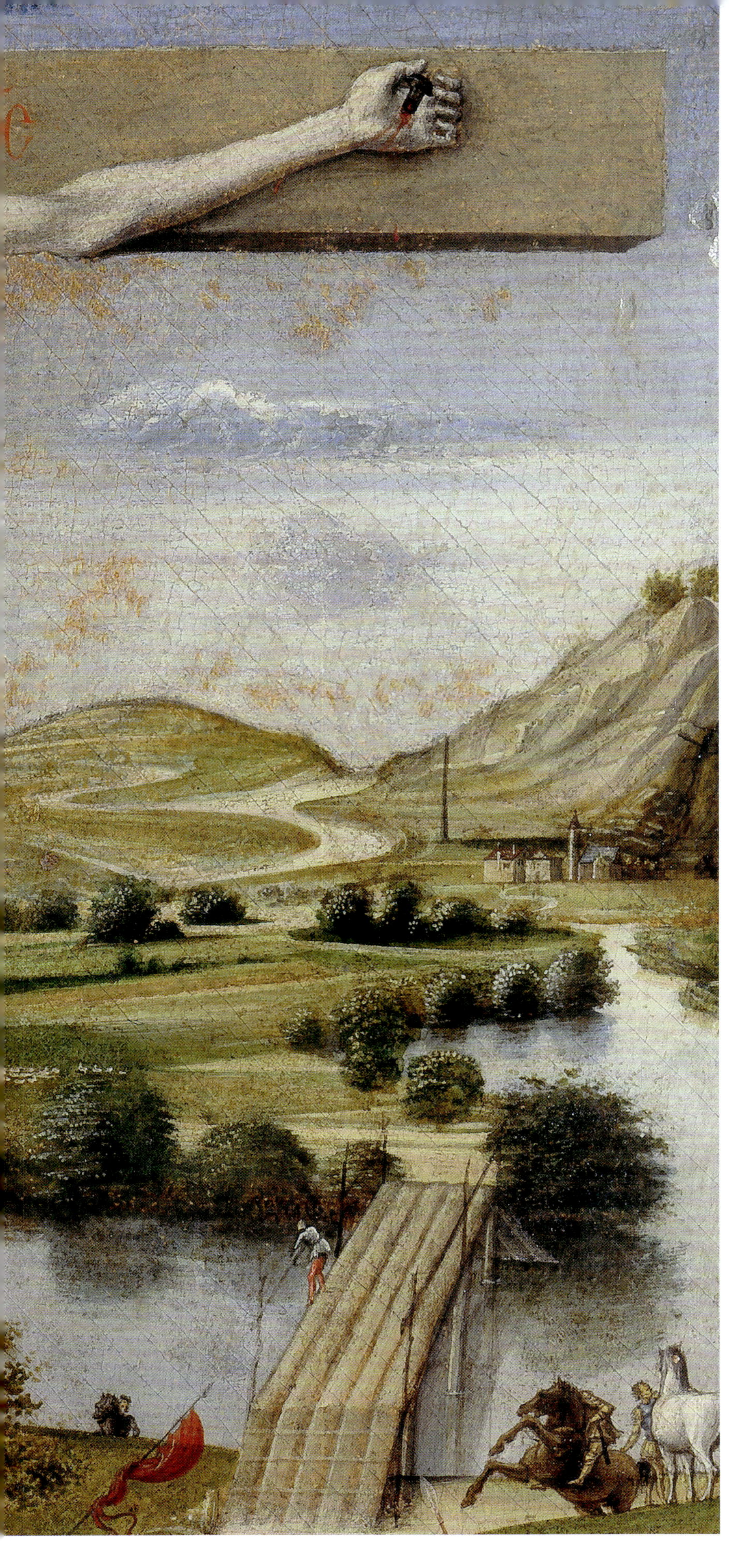

Giovanni Bellini and Landscape

DAVIDE GASPAROTTO

Zambelin se puol dir la primavera
Del mondo tuto in ato de pitura:
Perché da lù deriva ogni verdura
E senza lù l'arte un inverno giera.

Giovanni Bellini can be said to be the Spring
Of the whole world in the practice of painting:
Because all green scenery derives from him,
And without him art would have been a Winter.
—Marco Boschini[1]

Giovanni Bellini (ca. 1435–1516) is universally
acknowledged as being the founding father of Venetian Renaissance painting and one of the greatest
Italian artists.[2] There is arguably no more moving
homage to Bellini than that of Marco Boschini in
his *Carta del navegar pitoresco* (1660); of modern
historians, no one has summed up his remarkable
artistic career better than Roberto Longhi, who so
powerfully and suggestively captured the enchanting lyricism of his painting:

A man never tired of meditating, never satiated by evoking the antique or understanding the new and exploring them, he [Bellini] was everything that is said of him: initially Byzantine and Gothic, then Mantegnesque and Paduan, before following in the wake of Piero and Antonello, and lastly Giorgionesque. And yet he was always himself — passionate, with a sorrowful spirit, expressing the complete, deep harmony between man (the traces of man become history) and the mantle of nature: harmony between the prominent masses of human forms and the high, distant clouds, laden with narrated dreams; amidst the cloisters of the mountains, ancient apses, shepherds' caves, peasants' terraces, the dove-colored churches of the patriarchate, the flock's fold, medieval castles, and the brittle rocks of the Euganean Hills. There is a serenity that pervades the whole range of eternal human sentiments: cherished beauty, venerated religion, everlasting spirit, and keen senses; and a concerted pacification that merges and shades off feelings, from the pink dawn to the violet sunset, according to the hour of the day.[3]

Significantly, Longhi gives a good deal of room to the description of nature. And in fact landscapes appear with increasing frequency in Bellini's long career as he painted the many versions of the Madonna and Child and the suffering or blessing Christ (cat. no. 9), the half-length *sacre conversazioni* (sacred conversations) (cat. no. 10), the crucified Christ (cat. nos. 2, 3, 6, 8), or the various Saint Jeromes (cat. nos. 1, 7, 12). As Rona Goffen has remarked, the landscape in Bellini's paintings plays a key role, "visually, in the composition; emotionally, in establishing the mood of the scene — and of the beholder; and symbolically, as a metaphor for God's presence."[4] Mountains, hills, walled towns, castles, caves, rocks, trees, flowers, skies, clouds, sunrises, and sunsets are just as much the protagonists in Bellini's paintings as human figures. Always evoked with different nuances and details (as we will see below), the landscape becomes the vital complement to the figures. As he renders places in Andrea De Marchi's words, "in a world of caducity, accidental light, and the all-shrouding fleetingness of the hour,"[5] the principal characters and symbols in the sacred stories are set in a dimension of reality and lived experience to a degree that was unprecedented in the history of Italian painting.

Bellini initially experimented with the landscape in small paintings intended for private devotion, but the landscape soon also came to occupy a highly significant place in some altarpieces. In a key work in his career, the Pesaro altarpiece (ca. 1472–75; see fig. 13), Bellini for the first time sets a *sacra conversazione* against a sweeping background landscape, reminiscent of the inland hills of the Veneto and the Marches. A little later, between 1475 and 1480, he would even paint some radically new altarpieces, such as the *Resurrection* (ca. 1475–77; see fig. 4) or the *Transfiguration* (ca. 1478–79; see fig. 6), in which the landscape really does play as prominent a role as the human figures. In describing one of Bellini's greatest masterpieces, the *Saint Francis in the Desert* (see fig. 8) in 1525, the Venetian patrician and art connoisseur Marcantonio Michiel dwelled especially on the "wonderfully finished and refined landscape [*paese*] nearby," occupying practically the whole space of the composition.[6]

From a very early date, Bellini's landscapes had thus been greatly admired, and this exhibition, organized around a small but exceptional group of masterpieces, focuses on the role and significance of the landscape in his work. Can we establish how Bellini's contemporaries "saw" his landscapes (or how he himself considered them)? How did Bellini construct his landscapes? Are they the fruit of his imagination or do they reflect a specific direct experience of reality? What earlier works of art influenced his way of depicting nature? Can we see an evolution in his way of depicting landscape during his long career? What is the significance of the landscapes in relation to the subject matter of the paintings? The following pages are a response to these questions, to which others before us have also sought to provide answers.

Paesi and Lontani

The earliest known documented use of the Italian word *paesaggio* (landscape) appears in a letter sent by Titian to Prince Philip of Spain in 1552 to accompany the shipment of two paintings, one of which he described as a *paesaggio*.[7] Although there are no surviving paintings of "pure" landscapes by Titian (only drawings and engravings), the new word undoubtedly conveyed a technical concept that was part of a lucid awareness of a new pictorial genre. Landscape backgrounds in paintings had previously been described by using the word *paese*, often found in Vasari's *Vite* (*Lives*) (1550 and 1568), in which the term *paesaggio* never appears. In the foreword to the third part of the *Vite*, Vasari considered the skill in rendering "distance and the variety of landscapes [*paesi*]" to be a feature of modern painting not found in antiquity.[8]

In the mid-sixteenth century Vasari commented on the fashion for Flemish landscapes: "There is not a cobbler's house without German landscapes [*paesi*] in it."[9] Paolo Pino in his *Dialogo di pittura* (1548) points out that the northern European painters "imagine the landscapes [*paesi*] that they inhabit, which on account of their wildness are rendered very pleasingly," but remembers having seen "by the hand of Titian, miraculous landscapes [*paesi*] and much more graceful than those of the Flemish [artists]."[10] In Michiel's notes on Venetian collections, drafted from 1520 to 1540, the word used to identify landscapes is always *paese*, for paintings by both Flemish artists — such as "the many small panels of landscapes [*paesi*] by the hand of Alberto de Olanda" in the house of Cardinal Domenico Grimani — and Italian artists.[11] We have already mentioned how Michiel used the term *paese* to indicate the landscape dominating Bellini's *Saint Francis* and, in the same context, we are inevitably reminded of Giorgione's *Tempest* in the house of Gabriele Vendramin, described as "the small landscape [*paese*] on canvas."[12]

There is, however, some important evidence, only recently highlighted by Birgit Blass-Simmen, providing fresh insight into how Bellini himself described his landscapes.[13] She refers to the well-known negotiations that the Marchesa of Mantua, Isabella d'Este conducted with Bellini through her agents in Venice in an attempt to obtain a profane allegory for her Studiolo, to be hung beside Mantegna's paintings. Bellini initially tergiversated diplomatically before eventually firmly saying no. Behind this refusal there was obviously also a desire not to vie with his brother-in-law Andrea Mantegna in the field of allegorical-type antiquarian painting, in which Andrea excelled and toward which Bellini was not particularly well disposed.[14] Instead of "an ancient story or fable…with a fine meaning" that Isabella would have liked,[15] Bellini offered to do a painting on a sacred theme, which the marchesa would be able to hang in her bedchamber. Initially a *Nativity* was discussed and then the marchesa asked Bellini to add the figure of Saint John the Baptist to the scene. But since Bellini thought the saint was not appropriate for this scene, he suggested a painting of the Madonna and Child with Saint John the Baptist "and some distant views [*lontani*] and other fantasies."[16] We can thus imagine a work very similar to the almost contemporary Giovanelli *Sacra Conversazione* (cat. no. 10).

To indicate the background landscape — as recorded by Michele Vianello in his letter — Bellini used the word *lontani* (distant views), suggesting the elements in the background of the painting as opposed to those *vicini* (close up).[17] Although rather unusual, the use of the word *lontani* to indicate the background landscape of a painting is also found in various sixteenth-century sources: Pino recommended that painters should study nature "to gain experience and become skilled in distant views [*lontani*], in which the painters north of the Alps are particularly gifted";[18] in his *Ricordi* (1554), the humanist and connoisseur Sabba Castiglione praised Albrecht Dürer for "the figures, animals, perspectives, buildings, distant views [*lontani*], and landscapes [*paesi*]" and admired the wooden marquetry by Fra Damiano da Bergamo for his skill "not only in perspectives, like these other good artists, but in landscapes [*paesi*], buildings, and distant views [*lontani*]."[19] In *Dialogo d'amore* (1546), Sperone Speroni explicitly speaks of "paintings that we popularly call distant views [*lontani*], with landscapes [*paesi*] in which tiny figures can be seen walking."[20]

The *lontano* is thus what is seen in the background of the painting, and in general is characterized by the presence of *paesi*, small figures, animals, and buildings. We should not overlook the other term that Bellini employs in his reply to Isabella d'Este — *fantasie* (fantasies) — to indicate the possible inclusion of secondary elements for the purposes of building up the overall background of the painting. This word inevitably brings to mind the phrase that the great humanist and poet Pietro

Bembo puts in Bellini's mouth to explain to Isabella that the painter would be adverse to a program with too many detailed instructions for the commissioned painting: "The invention, for which Your Excellency wrote me to find a design, will need to be adjusted according to the imagination of the man executing it [Bellini], who is pleased when many stipulations do not limit his style, it being accustomed, as he says, always to wander at will in paintings, so that to the best of his ability they may satisfy whoever admires them."[21] This celebrated statement of artistic freedom helps us understand how Bellini constructed his landscapes, whose apparent naturalness is the result of a calculated blend of reality and imagination, of meticulous observation of the real world and invention, as he was inspired by and vied with tradition and the painting of his own age. The *lontani* are evidence that Bellini reserved a part of painting entirely for himself and his *fantasia*.

No Bellini landscape is an exactly identifiable place. For some time, however, it has been clear that in order to depict a series of buildings making up the towns in his paintings, he resorted when necessary to drawings and sketches made on the spot during trips outside Venice. Significantly, in 1497 Bellini refused to paint a view of Paris, requested by the Marchese of Mantua, Francesco Gonzaga, because he had not seen the French city firsthand ("per non l'haver io veduta").[22] His very probable journey to Pesaro in the early 1470s clearly seems to have made an impression on him: the background of the Pesaro altarpiece includes the Castle of Gradara (see fig. 13), and in several subsequent paintings he depicted buildings from nearby towns: the cathedral of San Ciriaco in Ancona, the late antique monuments of Ravenna (the church of San Vitale, the Mausoleum of Theodoric, and the bell tower of Sant'Apollinare in Classe), and the Bridge of Tiberius in Rimini.²³ The architecture of Vicenza, which he probably saw when he delivered the *Transfiguration* (see fig. 6), must also have fired his imagination: the cathedral facade, the pre-Palladian Palazzo della Ragione, and the Torre di Piazza are depicted in the background of the Niccolini *Crucifixion* (cat. no. 8) and the *Pietà (Donà delle Rose)* (see fig. 34).²⁴ Each time, all these buildings are combined in a different way, thus creating an ideal landscape—which gives the impression, however, of being a real place. But more generally speaking, the high mountains, at times snow-capped, behind green hills, and the walled towns and castles, typical of the countryside of the Veneto Alpine foothills, left a deep mark on Bellini's concept of landscape.

Evolution and Influences

One of the most striking aspects of Bellini's career is the evolution of his language and his capacity to assimilate a great variety of external stimuli, which he blended in his own unmistakably personal style. In this sense, arguably only Raphael can bear comparison with him in the history of Italian painting. Bellini's painting continually evolved, and on examining the landscapes in his works, we see that he obviously took into account a series of models—his father, Jacopo; Mantegna; the Flemish painters; and Antonello da Messina—as he gradually forged his own style. His landscapes are thus a good observation point to explore how his art developed.

In the Birmingham *Saint Jerome in the Wilderness* (cat. no. 1), now almost unanimously considered to be Giovanni's first known work, there is a very obvious comparison to be made with the models provided by his father Jacopo's sketchbooks and also with the Paduan works of his brother-in-law,

Mantegna. In the *Saint Jerome*, however, the mood of the landscape is already entirely Bellinian, characterized by the contrasts among the rocky wing in the foreground, the luminous verdant silhouette of the hills deep in the background, and the quiet, at times ironic presence of animals, such as the rabbit peeping out of its burrow in the foreground. In the subsequent *Agony in the Garden* (fig. 1), he continued the dialogue with his father, Jacopo, and with Mantegna:²⁵ the oblong composition is inspired by his father's drawing depicting Saint Jerome in the wilderness in the Paris sketchbook (fig. 2), in which we find the same rocky spur in the middle of the broad plain at the center. Giovanni paints the figure of Christ kneeling in prayer on top of this solitary rock. The horizontal arrangement dominates the scene. Christ and the Apostles all seem to be one with the rocky landscape, and the figures are separated by ample empty spaces. The viewer's gaze is not blocked by heaps of rocks, as in Mantegna. In Bellini's painting the open space prevails and we are directed to look beyond the plain toward the delicately rendered heights of the hills. But the real unifying element in the composition is light. The sun has already set, creating a strong contrast between the still-bright sky and the slopes now shrouded in shade. A second source of light is concentrated in the foreground, on the bare hollow between the sleeping Apostles and Christ, while shadows are also beginning to creep onto the rear side of the rock and the grassy carpet under his feet. The overall result is the first fully accomplished atmospheric landscape in Italian art.

Bellini's interest in phenomena of light and his attention to the tiniest detail must have driven him to a careful study of Flemish painting right from his early years. The importance of the Flemish element in the development of Bellini's vision of the

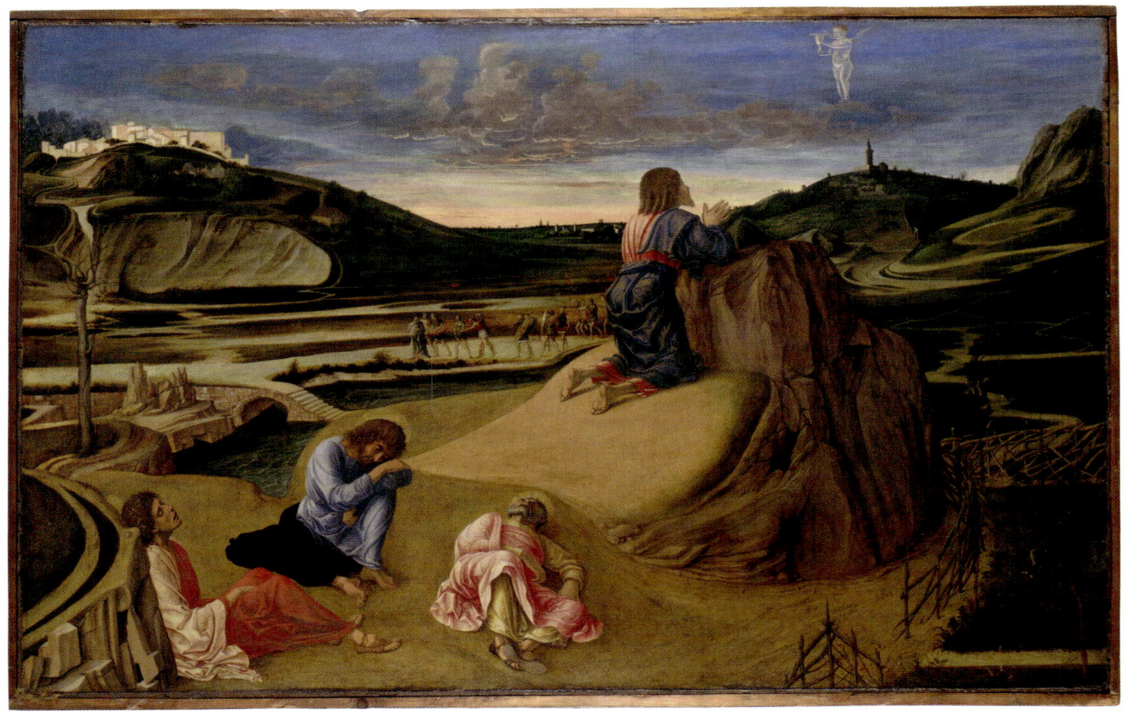

Figure 1
GIOVANNI BELLINI
The Agony in the Garden,
ca. 1460. Panel, 81.3 × 127 cm
(32 × 50 in.). London,
National Gallery, NG726

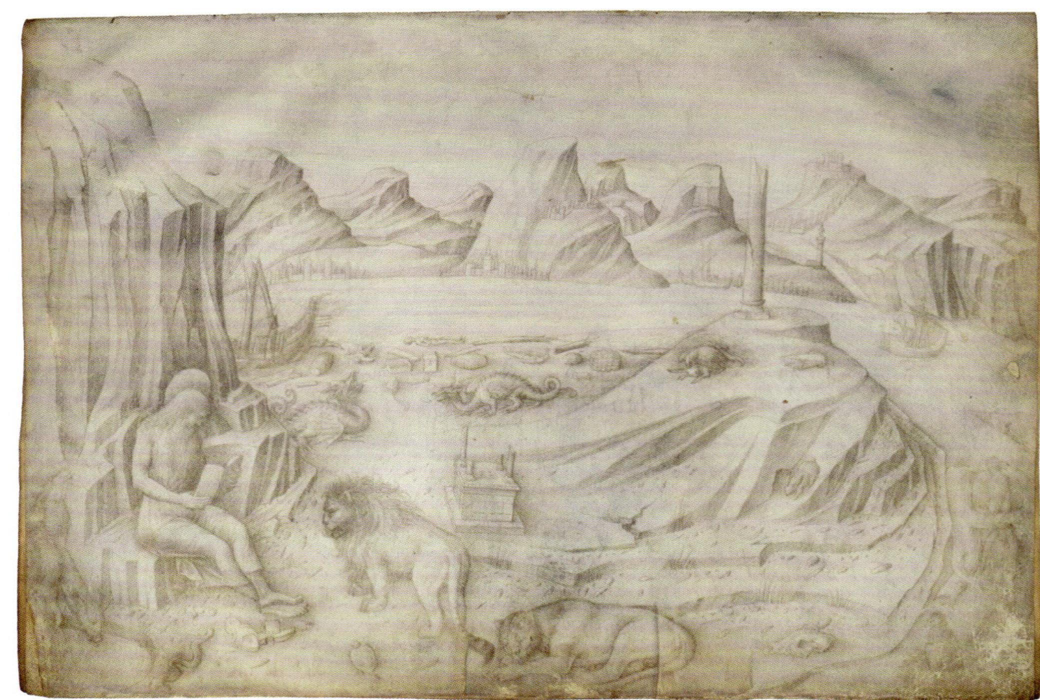

Figure 2
JACOPO BELLINI
(Italian, ca. 1390–95–
ca. 1470/71), *Saint Jerome in
the Wilderness* (Paris sketchbook, fol. 18v), ca. 1445. Silver-
point on gray chalk ground,
vellum, approx. 42.5 × 29 cm
(16¾ × 11⅜ in.). Paris,
Musée du Louvre, R.F. 1486

landscape cannot be underestimated. This influence goes beyond his use of the oil medium, which he favored over tempera with increasing consistency from the early 1470s.[26] Collectors in Venice eagerly sought Flemish paintings (a little later Michiel's notes were to offer emblematic evidence of this) and in some cases Flemish works could also be seen on the altars of Venetian churches.[27] An altarpiece by a certain "Pietro di Fiandra"—possibly Petrus Christus—already adorned one of the altars in the church of the Carità in 1451. That work must have been a familiar sight for Giovanni, who, together with his father, Jacopo, and brother, Gentile, made a series of triptychs for the same church in the early 1460s.[28] It is very likely that a complex polyptych made by Dieric Bouts the Elder in the 1450s, which included a series of paintings on canvas, now dispersed in various collections, could be seen in Venice at a very early date (the canvas support suggests that the work was meant for export right from its inception).[29] One compartment in the Bouts altarpiece, depicting the *Resurrection* (fig. 3), shows an elaborate background landscape at dawn. Its lasting impact on Bellini is clear from certain details in the landscape of the Berlin *Resurrection* (fig. 4) and much later from the memorable landscape view that appears on the right of the Kimbell *Christ Blessing* (cat. no. 9). But even an early work such as the exquisite *Crucifixion* in the Museo Correr, Venice (cat. no. 2), painted in the 1450s, has certain details that reflect an interest in Flemish style. While the rocky platform in the foreground is a Mantegnesque citation (from the predella with the same subject in the altarpiece of San Zeno), the landscape with the hills opening out into broad, deep rivers behind the figures, rich in lovingly described tiny details, are decidedly Flemish in taste. It was probably inspired by another work by Bouts, a

Crucifixion now in Brussels, which may have been part of the above-mentioned polyptych.[30] Another Flemish painting also had a profound impact on Bellini: Jan van Eyck's *Saint Francis of Assisi Receiving the Stigmata*, of which there are two versions, one in Philadelphia (fig. 5) and one in Turin.[31] In the fifteenth century one version belonged to a merchant called Anselmo Adorno, born in Bruges but of Genovese descent. In 1470–71 he set off on a pilgrimage to the Holy Land and evidently took this small painting with him.[32] In Florence the work was carefully studied by Botticelli, Filippino Lippi, and Leonardo da Vinci, but we can be certain that in Venice too (where Adorno stayed from February 10 to March 6, 1471), Bellini must also have had the opportunity to admire it. With its impassible optical precision and miraculous naturalism, its distant view of a city, crystal clear river, and imposing layered rock in the foreground, this work by Van Eyck had a lasting, deep influence on Bellini's painting:[33] works like the Frick *Saint Francis in the Desert* (see fig. 8) and the later Washington *Saint Jerome Reading in the Wilderness* (cat. no. 12) are inconceivable without this precedent.

From the mid-1470s to the mid-1480s, Bellini produced a series of masterpieces—the Berlin *Resurrection* (see fig. 4), the Frick *Saint Francis* (see fig. 8), the Naples *Transfiguration* (fig. 6), and the Contini Bonacossi *Saint Jerome in the Wilderness* (see fig. 7)—in which he fully realized his new poetics of the landscape and transferred to altarpieces (albeit of a smallish size) the innovative features that he had developed in paintings intended for private devotion. Take, for example, the *Transfiguration* commissioned for the chapel of the Archdeacon Alberto Fioccardo in Vicenza Cathedral by his brother and executor of his will, and painted between 1478 and 1479.[34] Bellini transforms Mount

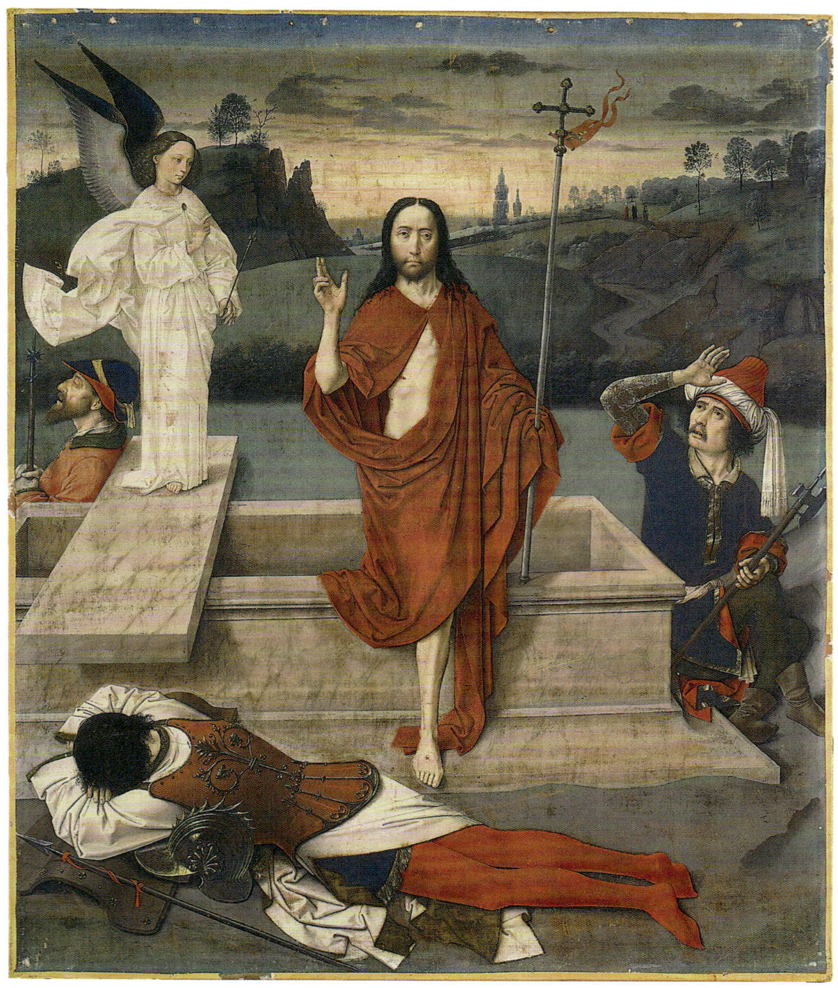

Figure 3
DIERIC BOUTS THE ELDER
(Netherlandish, ca. 1415–1475),
Resurrection, ca. 1450–60.
Linen, 89.9 × 74.3 cm
(35⅜ × 29¼ in.). Pasadena,
Norton Simon Foundation,
F.1980.1.P

Tabor into a broad, flattish area or plateau, as seems to be suggested by the rock face and the diagonal wooden railing in the foreground, typical of a mountain setting. Christ is depicted frontally and, wrapped in white drapery, he seems unapproachable. An invisible barrier separates him from the earthly figures and even from the two prophets—Moses and Elijah—who revere him at each side. Lower down in the foreground, three awestruck apostles (Peter, James, and John) crouch or sit on the grass, thus opening up the visual path

to the supernatural trio conversing behind them. The monumental figures dominate a landscape of autumnal colors, creating a lyrical counterpoint to the scene: the viewer's eye moves from the foreground rock to the broad, grassy expanses, the distant town, and the crown of hills and mountains with, above, a bright azure sky streaked by clouds, apparently heralding imminent rain.

The same harmonious, intimate fusion of humankind and nature, the same powerful poetic spirit, and the same sense of a silent, peaceful reconciliation permeating the scene like a miraculous fluid were to be the characteristic language of the large landscapes in Bellini's industrious old age: from the Niccolini *Crucifixion* (cat. no. 8) to the *Baptism of Christ* (see fig. 38), the sublime *Pietà (Donà delle Rose)* (fig. 34), and the melancholic *Madonna of the Meadow* (fig. 35). All these paintings are visions foreshadowing the idyllic, Arcadian landscapes of Giorgione and Titian.

Landscape and Devotion

Bellini was essentially a painter of sacred subjects and we should not forget that the overarching purpose of his paintings was devotional. However, they reflect an extremely sophisticated form of devotion, typical of new patrons, who not only perceived painted images as an aid to their prayers but also wished to use them as visual stimulus for individual meditation. A good deal has been written about the meaning of Bellini's landscapes, which are usually interpreted as the physical manifestation of the divine presence in nature.[35] Augusto Gentili, the most consistent advocate of the symbolic value of each tiny detail in Bellini's landscapes, authoritatively describes this idea: "The landscape that spreads out behind and around the protagonists of Bellini's devotional images is a container of symbols and metaphors, for allusions and quotations, constructed according to the demands of Christian allegory."[36] But let us look at a very emblematic painting in this sense, the Frick *Saint Francis*, commissioned by Giovanni (Zuan) Michiel around 1480. Its original use is still something of a mystery, and it is not known with any certainty whether it was originally intended for an altar in a small chapel in a Venetian church or for a private house.[37] The iconography of the painting has been described in detail by Millard Meiss, who, although noting the absence of the crucifix within a seraphim's wings and of Francis's confrere Leo, suggests that the scene depicts Saint Francis receiving the stigmata.[38] Standing alone, rapt in ecstasy and with his arms open, the saint receives the celestial vision that only

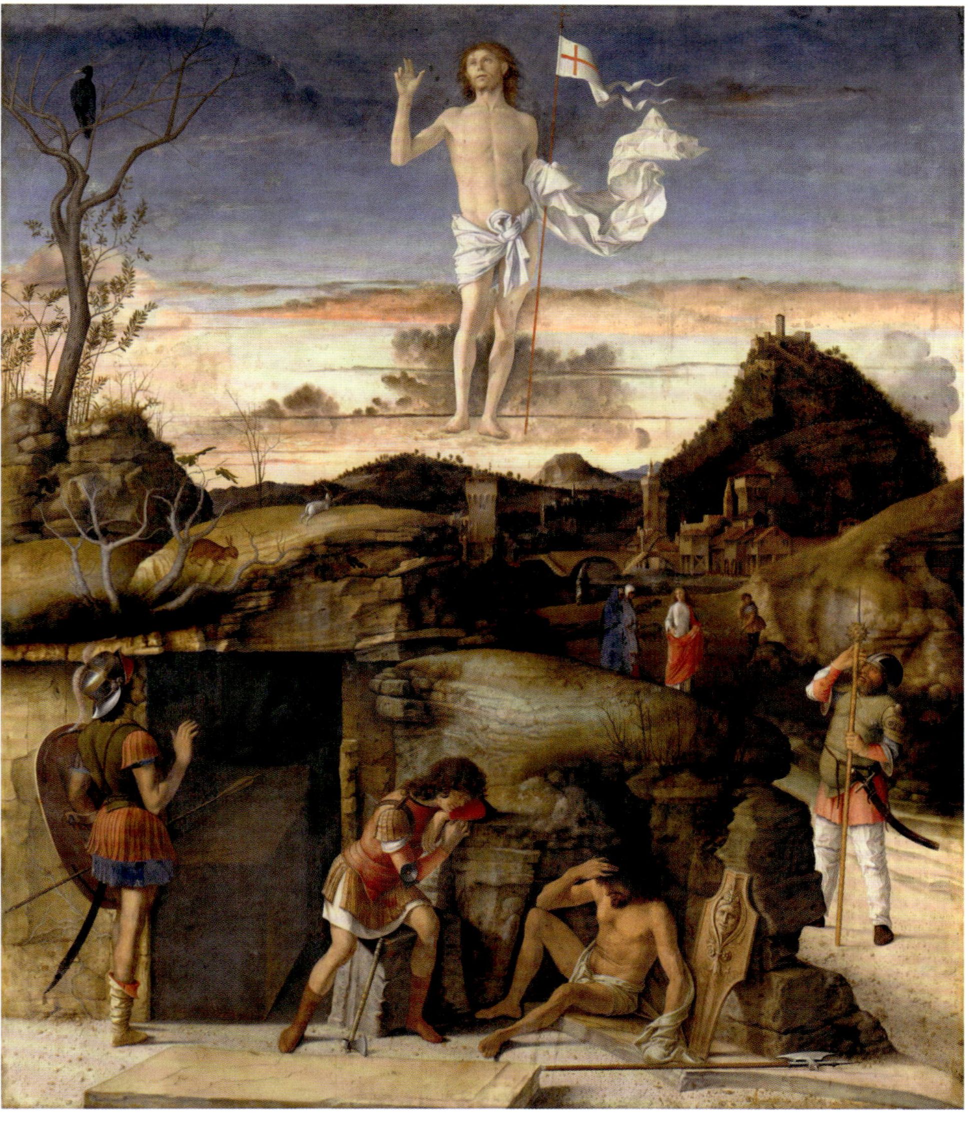

Figure 4
GIOVANNI BELLINI
Resurrection, ca. 1475–77. Canvas, transferred from panel, 150.5 × 128.8 cm (59¼ × 50¾ in.). Berlin, Staatliche Museen, Gemäldegalerie, 1177A

he can perceive. Two sources of light illuminate the scene: the divine light entering from the upper left and the natural light from the distant hills. The extraordinary natural setting has nothing ascetic about it. Indeed, warm and welcoming, it alludes to the saint's awareness of the full sensual wealth of the physical world. Bellini's relish in describing the details of the plants, depicted as identifiable individual species, also makes the painting a hymn to the beauty of the creation and obviously alludes to Saint Francis's own *Canticle of the Creatures*. According to Gentili, the landscape is a constellation of symbols, and "every single element has been predetermined in accordance with its symbolic function." The painting "is a masterpiece because everything is preimagined, predefined, and prearranged."[39] The constellation of symbols mentioned by Gentili,

however, tends to reduce the interpretation of the work to a host of details, thus overshadowing its extraordinary unitary dimension. Above we saw how Bembo explained to the Marchesa Isabella d'Este that the "invention" would have to be in accordance with the artist's "imagination," which he always left "to wander at will in paintings." Rather than a painting in which everything is predetermined, Bellini created a work aimed at arousing an intimate personal interaction with the deliberately allusive subject matter, and intended to stimulate comments and responses from a sophisticated, well-educated public. It is fascinating to think that in 1525 the *Saint Francis* hung in the house of Taddeo Contarini in Venice, alongside Giorgione's *Three Philosophers* (Vienna, Kunsthistorisches Museum), a work in some ways comparable in terms of scale,

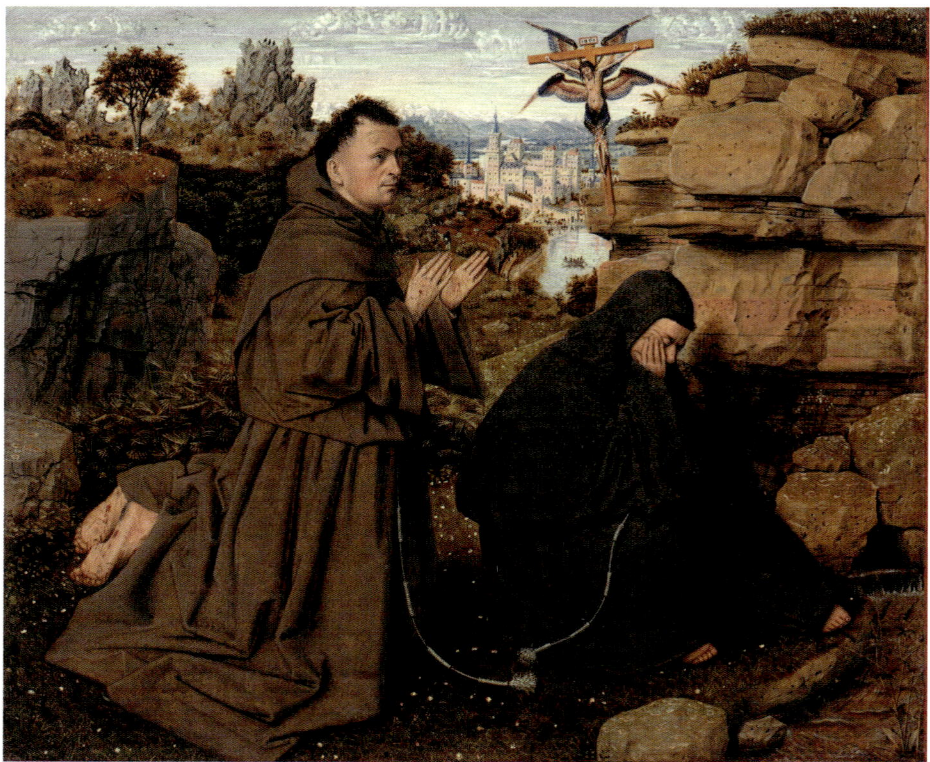

Figure 5
JAN VAN EYCK
(Netherlandish, ca. 1390–1441), *Saint Francis of Assisi Receiving the Stigmata*, 1430–32. Oil on vellum on panel, 12.7 × 14.6 cm (5 × 5¾ in.). Philadelphia Museum of Art, John G. Johnson Collection, 1917, cat. 314

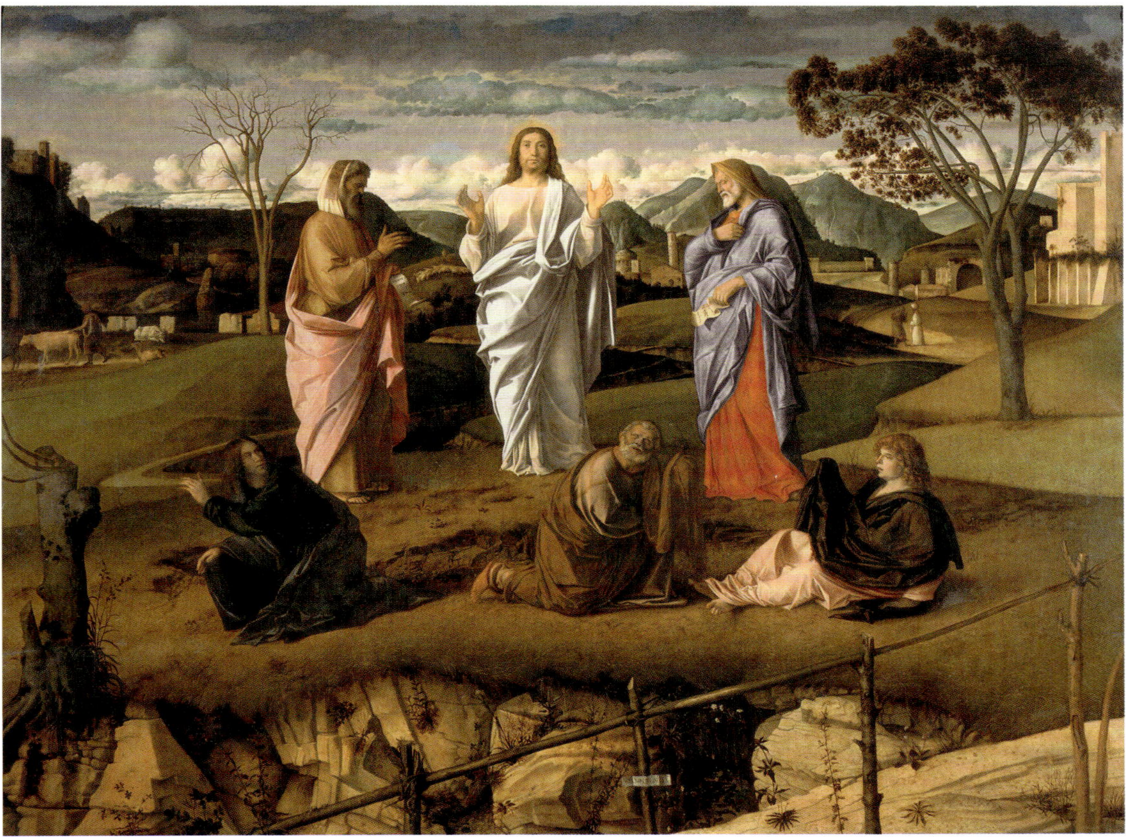

formal ambition, and the prominent role of the landscape.[40] In short, in this work Bellini invented a kind of "sacred poem" or "meditational *poesia*," to use the eloquent phrase coined by Keith Christiansen,[41] by creating a deliberately poetic language, in which the landscape becomes the main subject and for the first time the traditional hierarchy of figure and background is inverted.

The same poetics of silence and meditation are found in two of Bellini's subsequent works, which are landmarks in the creation of a completely new type of painting for private devotion. In the Niccolini *Crucifixion* (cat. no. 8), the scene is wholly unrelated to any narrative context. The crucifix is isolated, set in the foreground of the painting like a barrier between the physical space of the viewer and the imaginary space of the image, thus intensifying its physical presence in the eyes of the viewer. The landscape has been conceived as a poetic fantasy, a space for meditation extending from the top of the hill of Calvary, where the cross has been raised, to the Jewish cemetery in a meadow abounding with all kinds of plant species, minutely described in the middle ground, and then back to the imaginary Jerusalem in the distance, reinvented as a combination of real and fictitious buildings. Once again the landscape appears to be the supreme manifestation of the divine presence, and the wonder of nature is an invitation to strive for spiritual betterment.

Lastly, the *Sacred Allegory* (cat. no. 11), which still eludes scholars' attempts at interpretation, is arguably the climax of the new kind of painting for private devotion created by Bellini. The composition is very similar to that of a classic *sacra conversazione*, but rotated 90 degrees and moved to an outdoor setting—a vast, Flemish-like landscape.[42] The main characters are set on a terrace enclosed by a balustrade: on the far left is the Virgin's throne, protected by a baldachin, while a group of six saints is freely arranged here and there, both inside and outside the enclosed area. One of the four putti at the center, sitting on a cushion, is probably Christ (the Virgin's arms are empty); one of the other putti shakes fruit off a tree, which the others gather. The symbolic scene enacted by the four putti and the other episodes painted in the background beyond the enclosed area animate a landscape that has replaced, without losing any solemnity, the conventional austere interior architecture. In terms of size and subject, the painting could not have been intended for any purpose other than adorning the wall of a private house: this image, characterized by a sophisticated individual piety, was meant to foster meditative thought in the devout onlooker, as their gaze wanders from one figural motif to the next.

Around the time that Bellini was painting the *Sacred Allegory*, the word *quadro* first began to be used in Italian for a painting on various supports, as it still is today. A philologist, Gianfranco Folena, has studied the origin and use of the word in the late fifteenth and early sixteenth centuries.[43] The diffusion of the lemma *quadro* can be associated with a different form of erudite appreciation, typical of the Italian humanist circles in which a painting not only was an object for prayer and individual meditation but also became the subject of analytical descriptions emulating the classical ekphrastic tradition and assessing the painter's skill in rendering the subject and the details. The relationship with the *quadro* began to take on a typically individual and elitist intellectual dimension, paving the way for the rise of art collecting in the modern sense. The Uffizi *Sacred Allegory*—with its allusive subject, landscape as protagonist, and dreamy, enchanting atmosphere—must surely have been painted not simply for a devout patron but for a sophisticated, knowledgeable art lover, capable of grasping its refined artistic qualities, recondite meanings, and distance from traditional models. This work can thus be seen as a perfect candidate for one of the first-ever *quadri* of modern painting.

The notes for this essay have been reduced to the essential minimum. This reflects, on the one hand, a very personal selection from the vast Bellini bibliography solely for the purposes of the essay and, on the other, the fact that the most recent, updated bibliographic entry on a given theme is cited, and so from that source the interested reader can easily obtain any earlier bibliographies. Unless otherwise noted, all translations are mine.

1 Boschini 1660, 666.

2 Two brief accounts of Bellini's career, accompanied by large previous bibliographies, are in Pignatti 1970 and Humfrey 1996; more recently, see Humfrey 2004 and the catalogue for the monographic exhibition in Rome 2008.

3 Longhi 1946 (1978 ed.), 9–10: "Uomo di meditazioni instancabili, mai pago di evocare l'antico, d'intendere il nuovo e di provarli, egli fu tutto quel che si dice: prima bizantino e gotico, poi mantegnesco e padovano, poi sulle tracce di Piero e di Antonello, in ultimo fin giorgionesco; eppure sempre lui, caldo sangue, alito accorato, accordo pieno e profondo tra l'uomo, le orme dell'uomo fattosi storia, e il manto della natura. Accordo tra le masse umane prominenti e le nubi alte, lontane, e cariche di sogni narrati; tra le chiostre dei monti e le absidi antiche, le grotte dei pastori e le terrazze cittadine, le chiese color tortora del patriarcato e il chiuso delle greggi, le rocche medievali e le rocce friabili degli Euganei. Una calma che spazia fra i sentimenti eterni dell'uomo: cara bellezza, venerata religione, eterno spirito, vivo senso; e una pacificazione corale che fonde e sfuma i sentimenti, dall'alba di rosa al tramonto di viola, secondo l'ora del giorno."

4 Goffen 1989, 106; there are also some inspired pages

on Bellini's landscapes in Clark 1949, 23–25; Romano 1978, 61–67; and Zeri 1989, 17–18.

5 De Marchi 2012, 25: "nella dimensione della caducità temporale, degli accidenti luministici, della fuggevolezza avvolgente dell'ora."

6 [Michiel] 1884, 168: "paese propinquo finito et ricercato mirabilmente."

7 Folena 1983, 839–42; see also Venice 2012, 198–99, no. 163.

8 Vasari [1550, 1568] 1966–87, 4:6: "lontananza e varietà de' paesi."

9 Varchi [1549], as in Barocchi 1960, 61, Giorgio Vasari to Benedetto Varchi, February 12, 1547: "non è casa di ciavattino che paesi todeschi non siano."

10 Pino 1548, as in Barocchi 1960, 133–34: "fingono i paesi abitati da loro, i quali per quella lor selvatichezza si rendono gratissimi…di mano di Tiziano paesi miracolosi e molto più graziosi che li fiandresi non sono."

11 [Michiel] 1884, 195.

12 [Michiel] 1884, 218: "el paesetto in tela."

13 Blass-Simmen 2015, especially 77–81.

14 Barausse 2008, 345, doc. no. 64, Michele Vianello to Isabella d'Este, June 25, 1501.

15 Barausse 2008, 343, doc. no. 65, Isabella d'Este to Michele Vianello, June 28, 1501: "historia o fabula antiqua.…de bello significato."

16 Barausse 2008, 347–48, doc. no. 77, Michele Vianello to Isabella d'Este, November 3, 1502: "et qualche lontani et altra fantaxia." On the *Nativity* for Isabella d'Este, see

Fletcher 1971, 703–13.

17 Boschini 1660, 28, wrote that Bellini "worked by dividing the stories between the foreground and the background, in a fine, concerted way, and well positioned, distinguishing the close from the distant [views]" ("andava divisando sora i piani le istorie, con bel muodo concertae, benissimo a i so siti colocae, distinguendo i vesini dai lontani").

18 Pino 1548, as in Barocchi 1960, 133: "farsi pratico e valente nelli lontani, dil che ne sono molto dotati gli oltramontagni."

19 Castiglione 1560, 91 ("Ricordo 118"): "le figure, li animali, le prospettive, li casamenti, li lontani et li paesi"; and 57v ("Ricordo 109"): "non solo nelle prospettive, come questi altri buoni maestri, ma ne i paesi, ne i casamenti, ne i lontani."

20 Speroni 1546, 22: "dipinture, le quali noi volgarmente appelliamo lontani: ove sono paesi, per li quali si vedono camminare alcune picciole figurette."

21 Barausse 2008, 352, doc. no. 99, Pietro Bembo to Isabella d'Este, January 11, 1506: "La inventione, che mi scrive vostra signoria che io truovi al dissegno, bisognerà che s'accomodi alla fantasia di lui che l'ha a fare, il quale ha piacere che molto signati termini non si diano al suo stile, uso, come dice, di sempre vagare a sua voglia nelle pitture che, quanto è in lui, possano sodisfare a chi le mira."

22 Barausse 2008, 343, doc. nos. 54 (Francesco Gonzaga to Giovanni Bellini, October 4, 1497) and 55

(Giovanni Bellini to Francesco Gonzaga, October 12, 1497).

23 On Bellini's "topographic" landscapes, see Gibbons 1977.

24 On Bellini and the architecture of Vicenza, see Rigon 2003, 31–38.

25 There are some enlightening interpretations of this key painting in Fry [1899] 1995, 24–26; and Pächt 2003, 155–56.

26 On Bellini's relations with Flemish painting, see an important initial comment in Robertson 1968, 8–9; see also the excellent recent summary in Lucco 2004, 75–94.

27 On Flemish paintings in the Veneto, see the key work by L. Campbell 1981; for the Italian response to Flemish painting in the fifteenth century, see also Christiansen 1998, 39–61.

28 Lucco 2004, 78–80.

29 The surviving compartments are probably an *Annunciation* (Los Angeles, J. Paul Getty Museum), an *Adoration of the Magi* (private collection), a *Crucifixion* (Brussels, Musées Royaux des Beaux-Arts), an *Entombment* (London, National Gallery), and the Pasadena *Resurrection* discussed below. The altarpiece has been reconstructed by Koch 1988; see also Humfrey 1993, 159–60.

30 It is not completely certain that the *Crucifixion* now in Brussels was once part of the altarpiece; see the arguments for and against in Wolfthal 1989, 38–40; and Wolfthal and Metzger 2014, 46–87.

31 Cf. van Asperen de Boer 1997.

32 De Groër 1987.

33 As stressed in Christiansen

2004b, 40–41; and Lucco 2004, 83–85.

34 Tempestini 1992, 147–48, no. 50; there is an important clarification concerning the date in Dal Pozzolo 2003, 15–19; cf. also Dalhoff 1997.

35 Wilson 1977, 145–209; and Goffen 1989, 106–18.

36 Gentili 1991, 41; see also Gentili 2004, 167–81.

37 See Rutherglen and Hale 2015.

38 Meiss 1964; see also Fleming 1982; and Wohl 1999.

39 Gentili 2004, 173.

40 [Michiel] 1884, 168.

41 Christiansen 2015; Christiansen 2004b, especially 45–51; see also Grave 2004.

42 This was pointed out by Settis 1978, 121.

43 Folena 1983; Fry [1899] 1995, 47, speaks of the crucial importance of the *Sacred Allegory* "for its evidence of Bellini's unique position as pioneer of Cinquecento art."

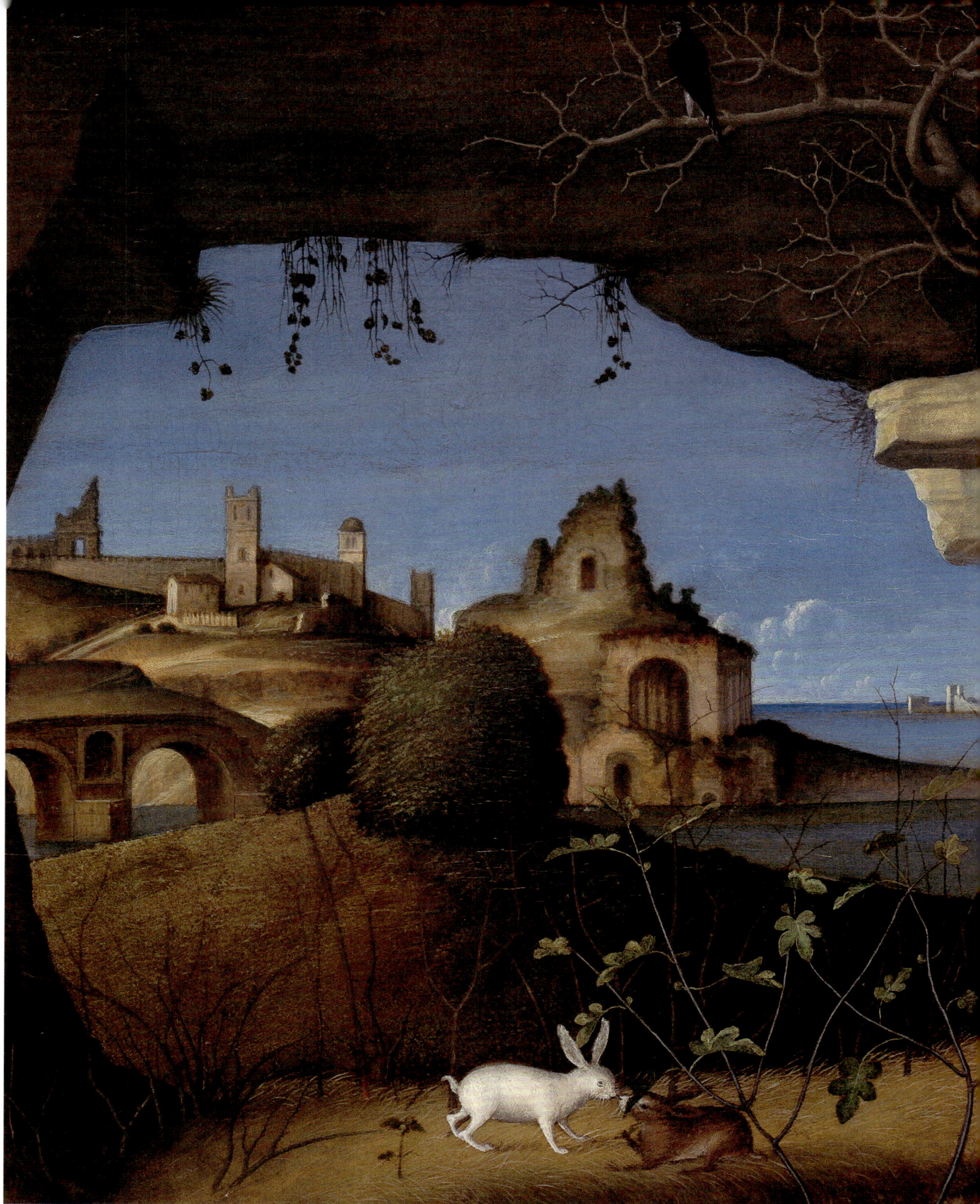

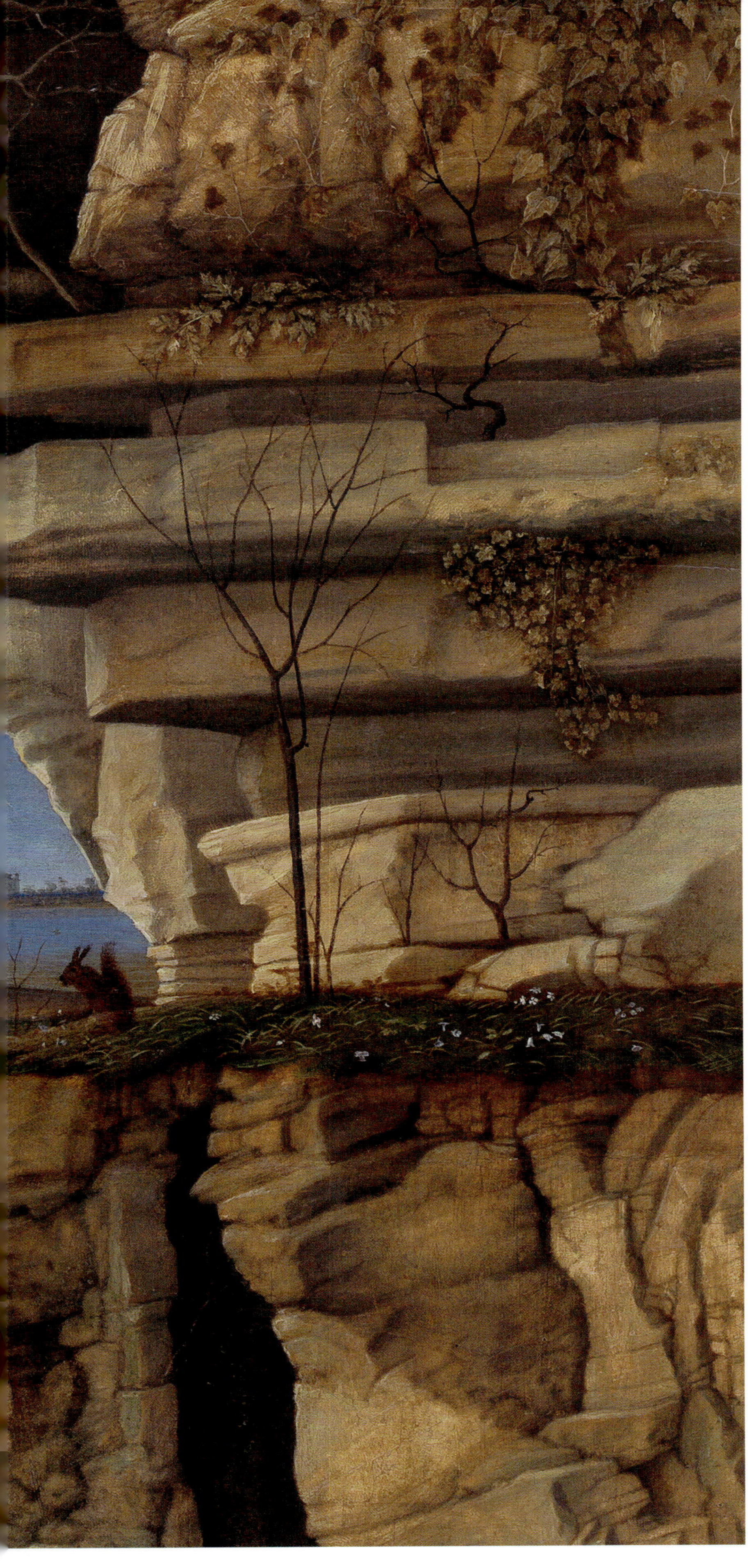

Poetry and Painting: Saint Jerome in the Wilderness

HANS BELTING

Giovanni Bellini's originality as an artist results
from his pictures of Saint Jerome in the Wilderness,
which, as will be seen, are entirely his invention
and differ from the mainstream iconography as
a variant with Venetian overtones. They seem to
have been destined for urban collectors, whom they
addressed with a dream of an alternative, solitary
life to be lived in nature. Thus they answered to a
current mood of melancholy and the desire to be
always ready to escape from the crowded city in the
lagoon. The general iconography of Saint Jerome
served many different functions that always had a
specific meaning for each given audience.[1] In this
way, the same figure mirrored diverse social and
religious milieus, which could each view the church
father as hermit, or penitent monk, or cardinal, or
humanist scholar who symbolized the union of
classical learning with Christian piety.

In Bellini's case, however, Saint Jerome represents the hermit as the model of a solitary life to
be lived in the bosom of nature. The masterpiece

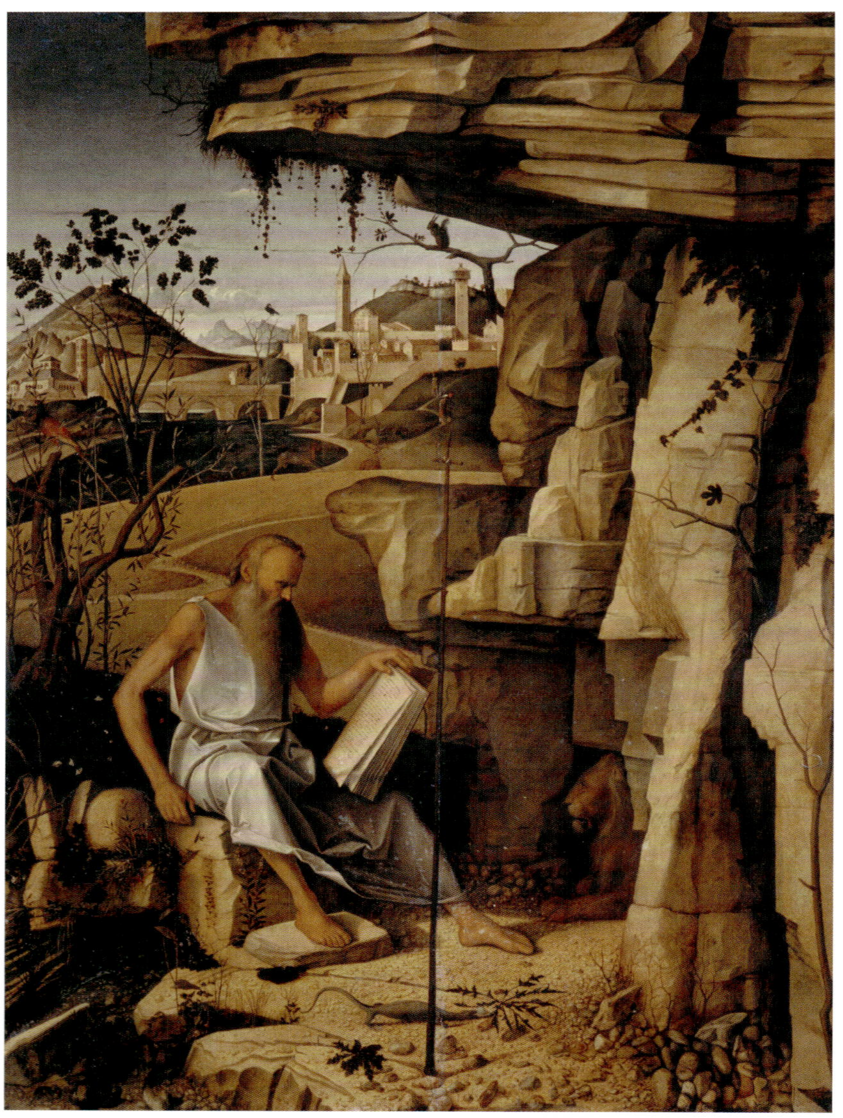

among his pictures of the saint is the panel in the Contini Bonacossi Collection in the Uffizi (fig. 7), which stands out for its high quality and truly monumental format.[2] Bellini here merged two different schemes of Saint Jerome's iconography, the humanist reading in his study and the penitent hermit in the desert. In Bellini's own invention, the saint is no longer the penitent shown beating his breast with a stone and kneeling contritely before the Crucified Christ. Instead, he quietly bends over a large book—one that would make sense in a library or study but looks out of place in the wilderness. The implied contradiction will lead us to Bellini's concept. The saint, as will become evident, lives in a solitary place, much as described in Saint Jerome's letters from the Middle East and echoed in Petrarch's *De vita solitaria*.

The contrast between nature and civilization, between the hermitage and the cityscape, the one visible in the foreground and the other in the back, is forcefully inscribed in the picture. Its precarious condition makes the dating a difficult task. Later interventions from its time on the art market have tampered with the original color scheme and obscured the contrast of bright and dark colors, such as that between the saint's skin and his white tunic. But even in its present condition, the richness of the original design comes through. The picture is a tour de force in its description of a rocky precipice that shelters the hermit and frames our sight. The large book, whose text is interrupted by red initials as in a manuscript of the age, rests on the saint's knee. His audience is restricted to the watching lion of his legend, whose presence we catch in the opening of a dark cave. The cross, which seems to have been twisted together from two thin branches by the hermit himself, looks here like a signpost for the holiness of the saint's dwelling.

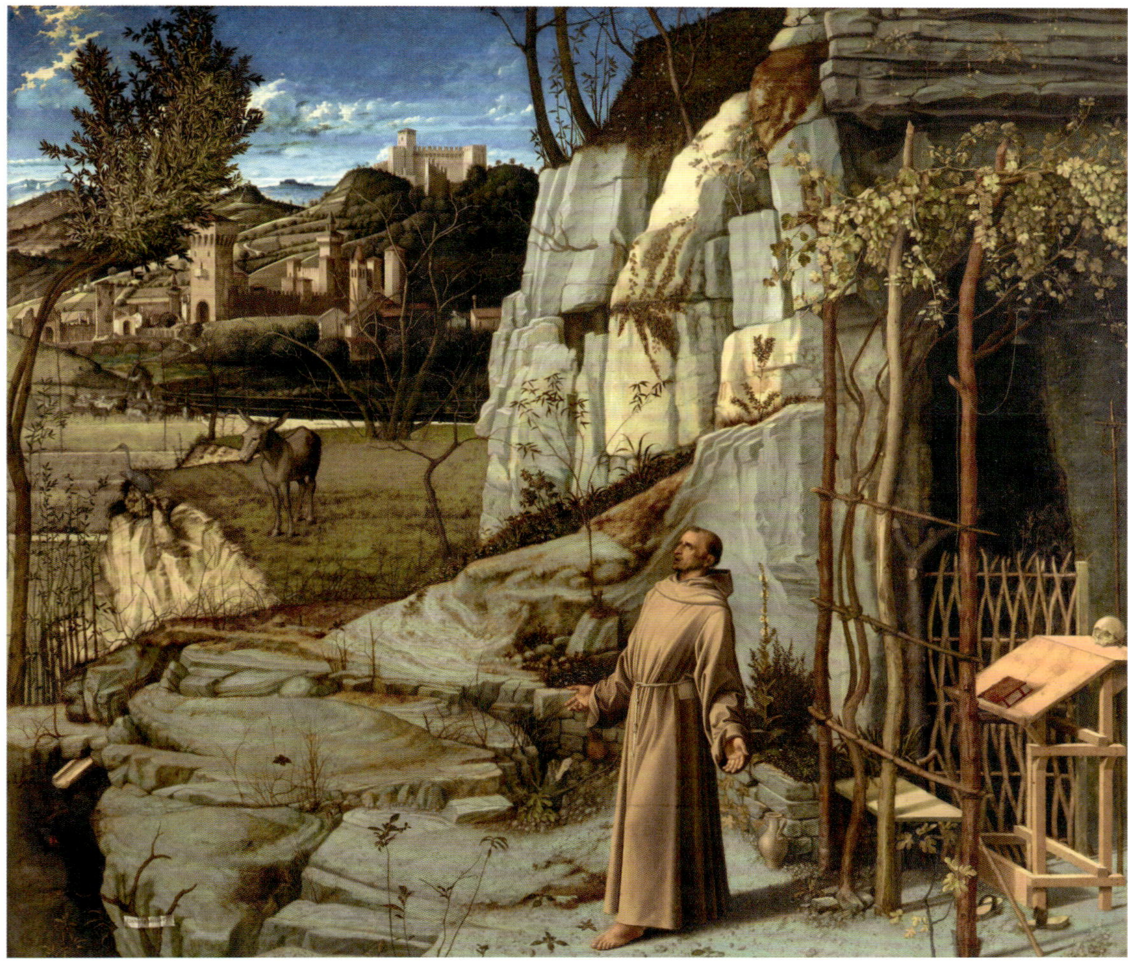

The plants and stones offer a rich still life of botanical and mineralogical observation. Beside a dark creek with pebbles, a lizard's movements seem to be suddenly arrested on the terrace at the feet of the saint. A pheasant sits on the twisted olive tree, which has produced verdant new shoots. The saint's attentive look captures the scene's total silence, interrupted only by the voices of birds and the running water. All this is, to use filmic language, a close-up of nature that had for a long time remained in the background of painting. The presence of physical nature constitutes the reality of the site. The same close-up rendering of nature pervades Bellini's *Saint Francis in the Desert*, today in the Frick Collection in New York (fig. 8). In this case, we have an almost contemporary description by Marcantonio Michiel, who saw the work in a private collection in Venice. In his notes he praises "the admirably finished and worked out landscape [*paese*] of the wilderness [*deserto*] that fills the whole panel up to the foreground [*propinquo*]."[3] Despite its different subject matter, the Saint Francis panel can be regarded as a companion piece to the Uffizi Saint Jerome in date and character. It exists in an

equally lyrical suspense, which has perplexed iconographic research, as it abandons any narrative from
the saint's life. Saint Francis is surrounded by an
unusually responsive nature that recalls the "solitary place" that Petrarch had chosen as a subject of
his book.

But our description of the Saint Jerome in the
Contini Bonacossi Collection is still incomplete.
Behind the hermit's dwelling opens a stretch of
land, which is the least distinct in the painting,
and yet for this very reason appears as an area
of transition between two places that represent
two different worlds. Alongside a river, a zone of
barren land puts the fortification of a walled city
into the farthest distance. It is crossed by a long,
winding path, which allows us to measure the journey to reach the solitary place. A hind and a stag
roam about freely in this depopulated land, while
humans appear only below the city walls. The
river is flanked by settlements, on one side, the city
or *castello* with a Venetian bell tower, and, on the
other side, some sort of fortified monastery that
resembles San Vitale in Ravenna. The topographical
allusions have found various interpretations, since
the cityscape is, in Felton Gibbons's words, "a curious potpourri of identifiable monuments."[4] Only
the ruinous bridge over the river, whose right end is
connected to the city gate by wooden planks, seems
to be a true portrayal of the old Roman bridge in
Rimini as it looked in Bellini's time. What matters
is the realism of the Venetian settlements in the
background and the contrasting view of a solitary
life in nature.

Landscape, with its seasonal colors and chang-
ing daylight, had been Bellini's unique contribution
to the history of painting from early on. Saint
Jerome is a key — and possibly the reason — for
reinventing a landscape in its own right, one that is
meant to attract a gaze of desire from a Venetian
collector, a landscape as a place of retreat from the
world and untouched by human intervention. The
saint justifies the depiction of a wild and secluded
and yet real place whose quiet peace he shares
with only animals and plants. This conclusion is
corroborated by a second and much smaller picture of Saint Jerome, in London's National Gallery
(cat. no. 7), where the figure of the saint is quoted
from the Contini Bonacossi panel literally, in every
detail, whereas the view into the distance has been
completely changed — or, better, reinvented.[5] The
resulting problem has been variously discussed,
either as a matter of attribution, with the suggestion that Marco Basaiti or an assistant in Bellini's
workshop was the painter of the smaller panel, or
with different dates proposed for the two pictures.

But these differences are also a result of an alternative *invenzione*. In this sense, the artist may have
created a new invention and another format for a
collector who already knew the Contini Bonacossi
version. The small panel represents a striking view
of the wilderness (*deserto*), where only a precarious
walkway along the precipitous cliffs allows access
to the saint's abode. The city across the water has
been removed even more deeply into the distance,
with the contrast between the two places powerfully enforced. Invention, the most appreciated
quality in painting, as in poetry, meant reinterpre-
tation and variation, and it is clearly the dual mode
of the landscape — nature and civilization — that
caught the eye of the beholder, as it fills almost the
entire panel, while the figure of the saint has been
reduced. In other words, the client requested or the
artist offered a new landscape for the same subject.
A small picture in the National Gallery of Art,
Washington, DC (cat. no. 12), dated 1505, which we
will discuss later, once again changes the invention

thoroughly,[6] and so does the altarpiece in San Giovanni Crisostomo (see fig. 10), dated 1513, where the poetry of a solitary landscape invades even official church art.

It is significant that Bellini retained the reading hermit in solitude, which he had created himself but which did not become the general fashion. He may have known a drawing of Saint Jerome reading in the sketchbooks of his father, Jacopo, although he did not own the books until late in his life, because of his illegitimate birth.[7] Jacopo had also painted a penitent Saint Jerome, as Giovanni Bellini did himself in his youth (cat. no. 1),[8] before he developed an altogether idiosyncratic representation of the same subject. It thus looks as if he even resisted any other iconography, despite the favor that other views of Saint Jerome—such as the penitent hermit in Giovanni Battista Cima da Conegliano's oeuvre—enjoyed in the new art collections of Venice. The most famous Saint Jerome picture in the city, even as late as the sixteenth century, remained the small panel that today is in London's National Gallery (fig. 9), which the Sicilian artist Antonello da Messina had created about 1475 during his stay in Venice. It represents the cardinal reading in his wooden study, which is fitted into the vast halls of a church-like building. This much-admired, even unparalleled masterpiece was part of the collection of Antonio Pasqualino in 1529, when Michiel recorded it in the longest description he left of any work he ever admired. Some fifty years after the execution of the painting he was still fascinated by the virtuosity of the Flemish manner that had caused a general discussion in the city about whether an Italian could have painted such a miracle at all.[9]

Bellini's paintings conveyed the message of the contrast between nature and civilization, between solitude and social life. But what did solitude actually mean? It could be understood both as a place for a radical hermit and as the retreat of a poet. Thus two different role models were inscribed in the same painting. Even Saint Jerome's letters themselves were exercises in a literary genre, as they described what was more an idea than reality. They could also be read through the eyes of Petrarch, who had introduced a more general concept of the significance of a solitary place. In fact, in *De vita solitaria*, written between 1346, when he lived in Vaucluse, and 1356, Petrarch celebrates solitude as the appropriate place for philosophers and poets, who had loved it even in pagan antiquity, before the saints would choose it in their search for God.[10] The author looks at nature with the eyes of a lyrical poet who seeks inspiration from a life of silence and freedom. The book is divided into two parts, of which the first describes a day in the busy cities and the second, a day in tranquility and peace, or *otium*, in solitude—the active life being a "negation" (*neg-otium*) of the contemplative one. Solitude, he insists, nourishes a state of mind that needs distance from "the crowd and the noise of cities."[11] He speaks of three kinds of solitude, that of place, that of time, and that of the soul, and he adds that his book treats mostly that of place.[12] Thus he connects such a place to saints and philosophers or poets alike.

In addition, the saints "illuminated the solitude with their sacred presence and condemned the cities when they decided to live a spontaneous exile."[13] This notion in a way anticipates the "voluntary exile" ("voluntario esilio") that Sannazaro describes for his hero in *Arcadia*, a pastoral poem that was immensely popular in Venice since its first publication in 1504. Sincero escapes his unhappy love in Naples and takes refuge in the solitude of Arcady, which he chooses as poet.[14] When it comes to the saints, Petrarch dedicates a long chapter to Saint Jerome, author of the letter on monasticism to Lady Eustochium, whose description of the desert as "a vast place under the burning sun" ("solis ab ardoribus exustam") he happily identifies as a quotation from Sallust.[15] He also introduces Saint Jerome as "witness" to the love of pagan philosophers for solitude, as "such an open place stimulates the genius…attracted by such considerations," and again quotes from Saint Jerome. "Many philosophers left not only the cities, as the seat of anxiety and distress, but also the suburban gardens, whose vicinity to noisy cities makes them suspect."[16] Petrarch summarizes his book with a self-quotation from a letter in which he wrote, "the woods appeal to the muses, whereas the city is the enemy of poets."[17]

The significance of Petrarch in general and of his book on solitude in particular in Bellini's lifetime can be exemplified by what we know of the library of Bernardo Bembo (1433–1519), father of the poet Pietro and himself a humanist of some reputation. He strove for a balance between his public career and his continuing interests in the humanities. When he acted as Venetian *podestà* in Ravenna, he commissioned the first chapel over Dante's tomb, inaugurated in March 1483, and composed an elaborate epitaph for it.[18] In recompense, he received a dedicatory copy of Cristoforo Landino's commentary on the *Divine Comedy*, including a personal letter of thanks by the author.[19] In his library he treasured two autograph manuscripts of Petrarch and a copy of *De vita solitaria*, which he regarded as an autograph. In a Latin annotation by his own hand, he encourages the reader to "overcome the fluent and all too uncertain condition of life.…In the midst

of the common people and its insane worries one should, as much as is possible for a mortal being, seek with a solid stance the happiest peace."[20]

He was not able to enjoy this peace himself, however, as for most of his life he was active in the service of the Venetian government. His son Pietro, the poet, in fact chose the freedom his father could only dream of, and experimented with an alternative life. He nevertheless suffered his father's accusations of wasting his life at the courts of Ferrara and Urbino, as he complained in a letter to the Duchess of Urbino in 1506.[21] Pietro, who, incidentally, annotated the same Petrarch manuscript with two epitaphs on Petrarch's image (*simulacrum*), was a driving force in canonizing Petrarch as the father of a common vernacular all-Italian language, as is generally known.[22] Even his life as what we would today call a freelance writer proved busy enough, and therefore he periodically retreated from his travels to his "villa" near Padua, where he also acquired a town house and brought together a substantial art collection. He thus shared the desire of many Venetians to live on the *terraferma* "in solitude." It should also be noted that he was familiar with Bellini's oeuvre and visited the painter in his studio, as he confirms in a letter from January 1506 to Isabella d'Este.[23] He could have seen the artist's Saint Jerome pictures but apparently he did not possess one. When Michiel visited his collection, he did not mention any Bellini painting at all, though we know from his letters that Bembo commissioned several portraits from the painter, including one of his beloved Maria Savorgnan.[24]

Petrarch's dream of a solitary life may even account for the unusual iconography, or lack of iconography, of Bellini's Saint Francis picture in the Frick Collection, which has perplexed all those who have studied the work. The view of Saint Francis

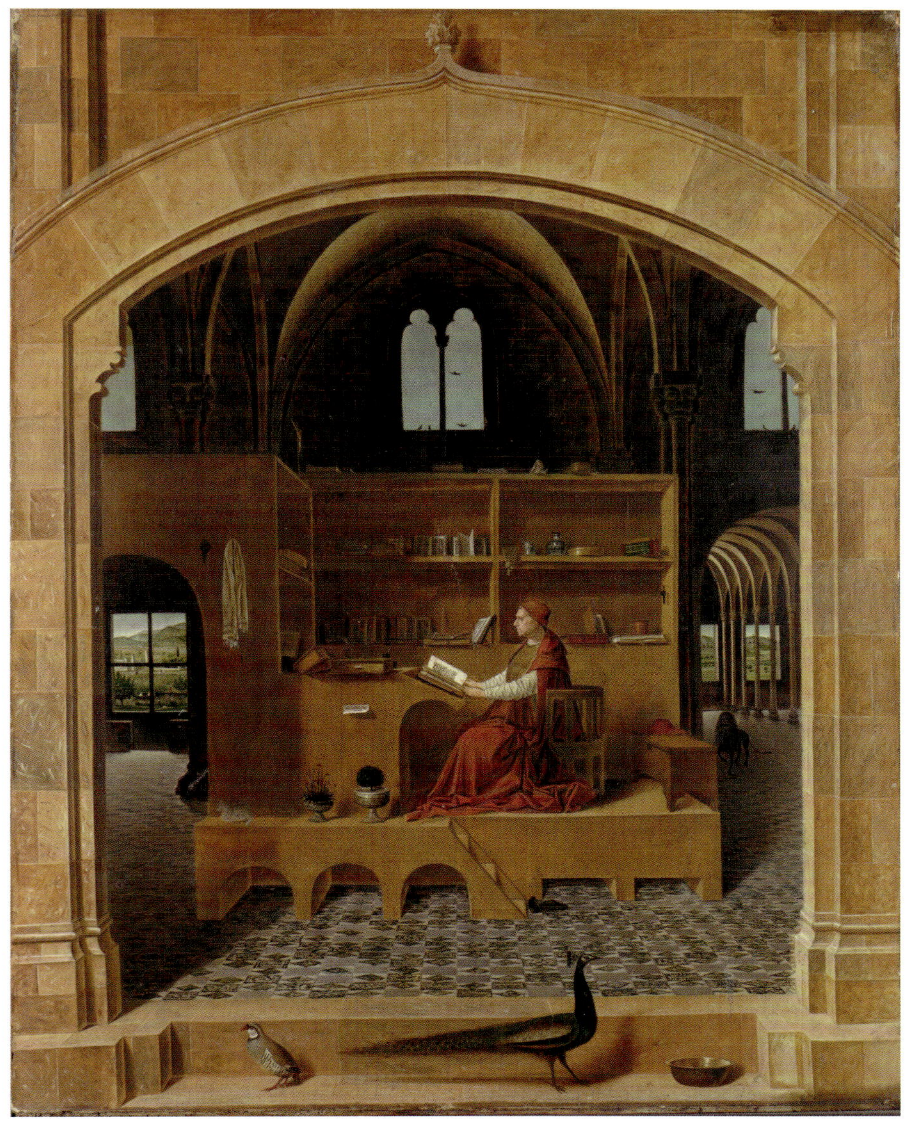

has given up all narrative features and represents the saint deeply immersed in contemplation, possibly on Mount La Verna, without clearly showing the marks of the miraculous stigmata on his hands and feet. Saint Francis stands in silent meditation in the middle of a beautiful hermitage (*eremo*) to which he had withdrawn from the world. The seductive charm of the painted solitude that so fascinated Michiel allowed a Venetian beholder to project his dreams to such an abode, while the topographical scenery of his own world remained in the distance. The whole body of Saint Francis is absorbed in a vision that we cannot see but happens only in his soul. The hermitage is clearly the focus of the composition as a place of meditation. If we again consult Petrarch's book, we discover that the

poet also includes Saint Francis, whom he calls a
"great lover of solitude" ("magnus amator solitudi-
nis") and an admirer of the eremitic life. Whenever
the saint retreated to a solitary place, as Petrarch
continues, he preferred Mount La Verna, which was
"perhaps the remotest place of all" ("quo non alius
fere uspiam remotior").[25] Bellini's picture, instead
of showing the miracle of the stigmata, creates a
landscape of dream and desire that turns the nar-
ration of religious rapture into lyrical suspense and
addresses the beholder's imagination.

Bellini's vision of solitary life also distinguishes
two late pictures that represent Saint Jerome. In
the small panel of the National Gallery of Art in
Washington, DC (cat. no. 12), dated 1505,[26] the saint
is reinvented as a very old man with a frail and
emaciated body whose "skin is burned and dried
up from the sun that gives him the look of a black
Ethiopian," to use Saint Jerome's own description in
letters to Lady Eustochium and to Nepotian.[27] The
landscape has gained complete dominance, and
the saint withdraws into a dark corner of his *eremo*.
Below the "rocky precipice," as the letters have it,
the hermit seems to be the only one who interrupts
the silence when he turns the pages of his book.
We also might hear the lizard occasionally rustling
over the pebbles. The modest walled fountain offers
drinking water, the cave shade from the burning
heat. A small fig tree grows behind the entrance to
the saint's sleeping place. Again, Bellini dedicates
all his love and attention to the still life of plants
and mineralogy.

The setting is tuned to the contrast of solitude
and civilization more forcefully than ever before.
The *eremo* does not offer any visible entrance but
is closed off by a high wall of stones. The plateau
behind is so deserted that a pair of hare play in
the open, undisturbed by humans. This time,

the backdrop is divided into two places that differ
strongly from each other. A Roman bridge leads to
an extended settlement, which, unlike Bellini's other
backdrops, has fallen into ruins. Do we see here
an allusion to Altinum, the sunken predecessor of
Venice on the *terraferma*, where Saint Jerome's friend
Heliodorus was bishop? Such a memory would
introduce the dimension of time, as the ruins would
take us back to antiquity, the saint's own era. Bellini seems to take up such an argument when the
scenery changes again and leads the gaze across
the Venetian lagoon, where the refugees of Altinum found a new home by building Venice. In the
far distance, a fortress bathed in the evening light
might represent contemporary Venice. The argument would also work in the sense that civilizations
come and go, while nature remains the same. The
landscape allowed for infinite variations according to
the artist's mood and the taste of a collector.

Bellini's last word in representing Saint Jerome
is the altarpiece that still keeps its original place in
San Giovanni Crisostomo in Venice (fig. 10).[28] In
his will (1494), the merchant Giorgio Diletti had
left instructions to install an altar and altarpiece
when the church was rebuilt. After the donor's
death (1503) and the new church's completion, the
widow deposited the necessary money in 1509 with
the Scuola Grande di San Marco, where Bellini
himself, like the donor, was a member. The same
confraternity commissioned the work in 1511, but it
was only in 1513 that Bellini, then more than eighty
years old, signed the finished altarpiece. The choice
of the three saints has caused some discussion. In
the place of Saint Christopher one would expect
the church's titular saint, the Greek church father
Chrysostom, but the church's priest, Ludovico
Talenti, may have proposed the Franciscan Saint
Louis of Toulouse.

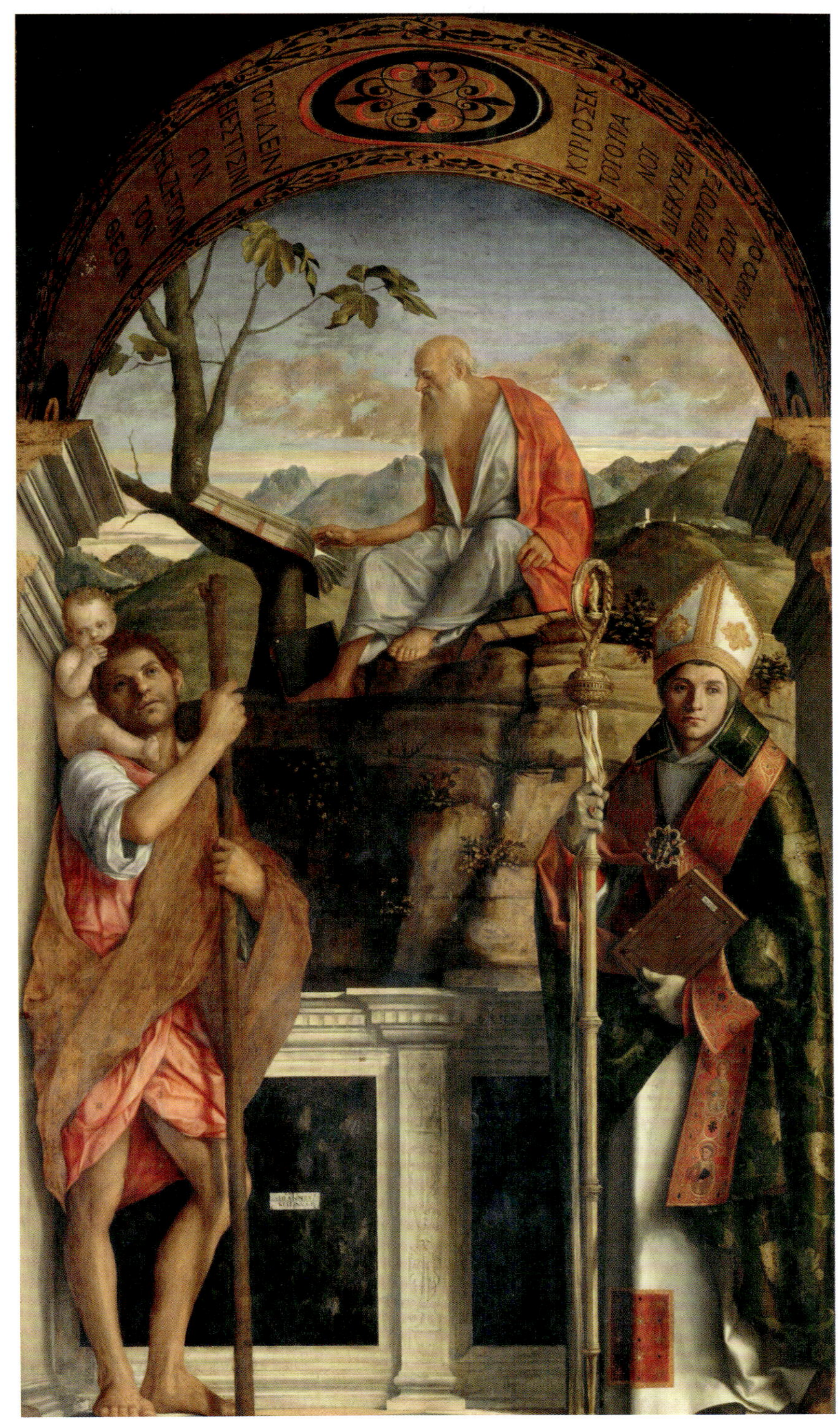

Figure 10

GIOVANNI BELLINI

Saint Jerome with Saint Christopher and Saint Louis of Toulouse, 1513. Canvas mounted on panel, 300 × 185 cm (118⅛ × 72⅞ in.). Venice, church of San Giovanni Crisostomo

The real surprise is the prominence of Saint Jerome, who represents a striking intervention in a conventional altarpiece. His view interrupts the interior painted architecture where we see the two other saints, as he sits in a self-forgetful position somewhere else, at a panoramic viewing point in an open mountainous landscape. The picture opens with an arch, where a Psalm verse (Ps 13:2) in Greek, the language of the church's titular saint, is written on the intrados. The arch, with its mosaics, is a clear reference to the church of San Marco, where such features are common, and thus introduces the Venetian patron saint, who was also the titular saint of the confraternity. In other words, we look out from Venice, symbolized by the interior space of San Marco's, toward a solitary place where the aged Jerome, sitting on rocks, is immersed in reading and deep meditation. He leafs through a folio-size book resting on the trunk of a fig tree, whose pages, if we consult the relevant parable in the gospels, announce the coming realm of God (Mt 24:32). The sunset behind the mountains, which changes the color of the clouds, is a metaphor that deepens the saint's solitude.

The contrast between civilization (Venice) and solitude (nature) that distinguishes all of Bellini's compositions with the saint returns here under the opposite premise. This time, we don't meet the saint in a close-up view that leaves civilization out in the distance; rather, we are positioned in Venice and look out at his solitude. The intimate view of a private beholder that we are given in the other Saint Jerome pictures turns into a collective view of the congregation at an official church site. In a quite literal sense the altarpiece addresses a beholder, who stands at the steps of the Diletti chapel. The feet of the indoor saints are situated at eye level and their shadows seem to be projected by

the real church window, while the light in Jerome's solitude has the setting sun as its source. The marble parapet strictly separates two places in the same altarpiece: the here, or interior site, and the there, or outdoor scenery. This dual space differs from Bellini's all-landscape altarpieces as much as from the all-indoor ones, where nature is admitted only by window-like openings. The parapet is prefigured by Bellini's Barbarigo picture in San Pietro Martire in Murano (1488), but there it does not create two independent sites.[29] Thus the altarpiece in San Giovanni Crisostomo reconfirms Bellini's meaningful strategy for constructing his pictures. It is one of his last words as a painter and already responds to the younger generation, among whom Titian has taken the lead.[30]

Here it is instructive to quote the beautiful description of the picture that Roger Fry, Bernard Berenson's friend, wrote more than a hundred years ago in his slender book on Bellini, which is still one the most intelligent attempts to capture the poetic character of Bellini's art. Fry speaks of

the strangest, most romantic enthronement ever conceived — an old hermit, who has grown by long years of secluded contemplation into mysterious sympathy with the rocks and plants and trees of his mountain solitude, sits in a scarlet robe, silhouetted upon a golden sunset sky, across which faint purplish clouds are driven by the wind; and below him there spreads a vast expanse of valley and mountain ridges. Bellini's intimate Wordsworthian feeling for the moods of wild nature finds here its remotest and sublimest expression.... In the consistent elaboration of a particular passing effect of atmosphere, Bellini has gone beyond what his pupils accomplished.[31]

Unless otherwise noted, all translations are mine.

1   Ridderbos 1984; Rice 1985; Russo 1987, 201–51; Aikema 2000; Wiebel 1988; "Être dans la solitude" 1987.

2   Today in Florence, Galleria degli Uffizi; see Tempestini 1997, 116–19, cat. no. 53; Tempestini, in Forlì 2005, 218–19, cat. no. 17; Bätschmann 2008, 115, fig. 102. For Bellini in general, see the magisterial work of Robertson 1968; more recently, Humfrey 2004; Finocchi Ghersi 2003–4; Grave 2004. For Bellini's color, see Venice 2000.

3   Marcantonio saw the picture in 1525 in the house of Taddeo Contarini, also the owner of Giorgione's *Three Philosophers*. See [Michiel] 1888, 88. For the Frick picture, see Meiss 1964.

4   Gibbons 1977, 180; Gentili 2004, 170–72; Grave 2004, 73–77.

5   Tempestini 1997, 116–19, 209, cat. no. 54; and Gentili 2004, 170–71.

6   Boskovits and Brown 2003, 70–74; Tempestini 1997, 226–27, cat. no. 107; Lucco, in Washington 2006, 132–35, cat. no. 22.

7   Grave 2004, 73n109; Degenhart and Schmitt 1990, vol. 7, fig. 18.

8   Russo 1987, fig. 37.

9   Aikema, in Venice 1999, 214–17, cat. no. 16. For the description, see [Michiel] 1888, 98.

10 Petrarch [1346–56] 1977, 122–23, 240–45.

11 Petrarch [1346–56] 1977, 12–13: "da turbis hominum urbiumque turbinibus."

12 Petrarch [1346–56] 1977, 170: "solitudo loci de qua maxime mihi nunc sermo susceptus est."

13 Petrarch [1346–56] 1977, 122 (book 2.1): "urbes spontaneo damnantes exilio."

14 Sannazaro [1504] 1926, 62; cf. Kidwell 1993, 9–36.

15 Petrarch [1346–56] 1977, 156–57.

16 Jerome, *Adversus Jovinianum*, in *Patrologia Latina*, vol. 23, col. 311; Petrarch [1346–56] 1977, 242–63.

17 Petrarch [1346–56] 1977, 246–47: "silva placet Musis, urbs est inimica poetis."

18 Giannetto 1985, 43, 156–57; Campana 1970, 2:710–13.

19 Giannetto 1985, 356–57.

20 Giannetto 1985, 321–23, about the contents of the MS Vat. Lat. 3357: "Quisquis humanae vitae conditionem ut est momentaneam fluxamque admodum, quasi e specula circumscrivere desideras, lege acuratius. [In the midst of the people and its] inanes curas..ad beatissimam illam quietem intentus quantum mortali praestare licet solido..pede calcaverit."

21 Bembo 1987, 216–20 (letter 231); Kidwell 2004, 114.

22 Bembo 1525; Kidwell 2004, 218–37.

23 Bembo 1987, 209 (letter 225).

24 See the report on his collection in [Michiel] 1888, 20–26. See the most recent study in Gasparotto 2013, 48–65.

25 Petrarch [1346–56] 1977, 170–73.

26 See note 7.

27 Jerome, 1949–63, 1:117 (letter xxii); 2:172 (letter lii).

28 See Venice 1978, 196; Lattanzi 1981, 29–38; Goffen 1989, 183–88; Tempestini 1997, 180–83, 231, cat. no. 119; De Luca, in Venice 2000, 164–66, cat. no. 37; Finocchi Ghersi 2003, 104; Bätschmann 2008, 176–81.

29 See *La Pala Barbarigo* 1983.

30 Compare Titian's altarpiece in Santa Maria della Salute, usually dated 1512: Joannides 2001, 148, fig. 135.

31 Fry [1899] 1995, 56–57.

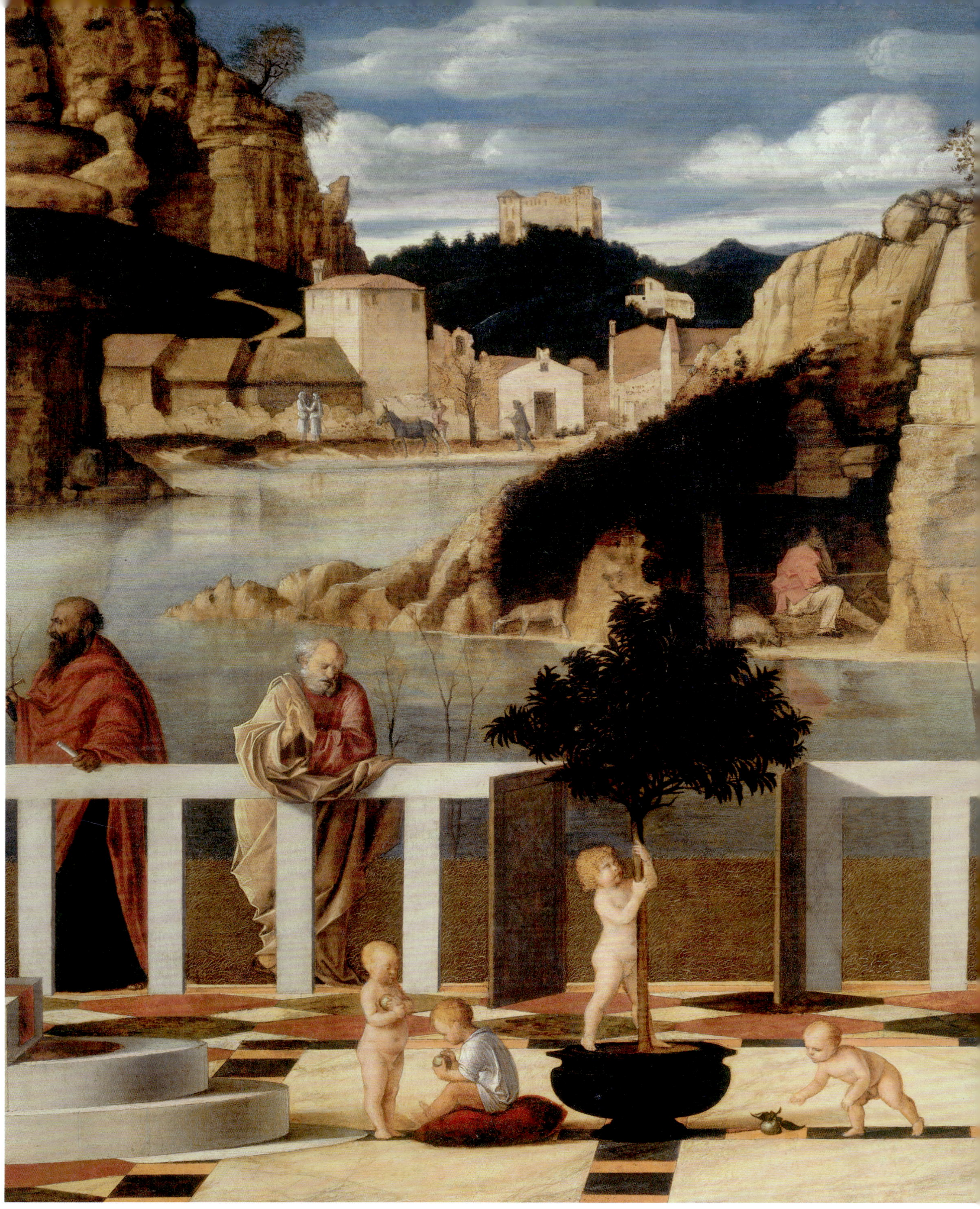

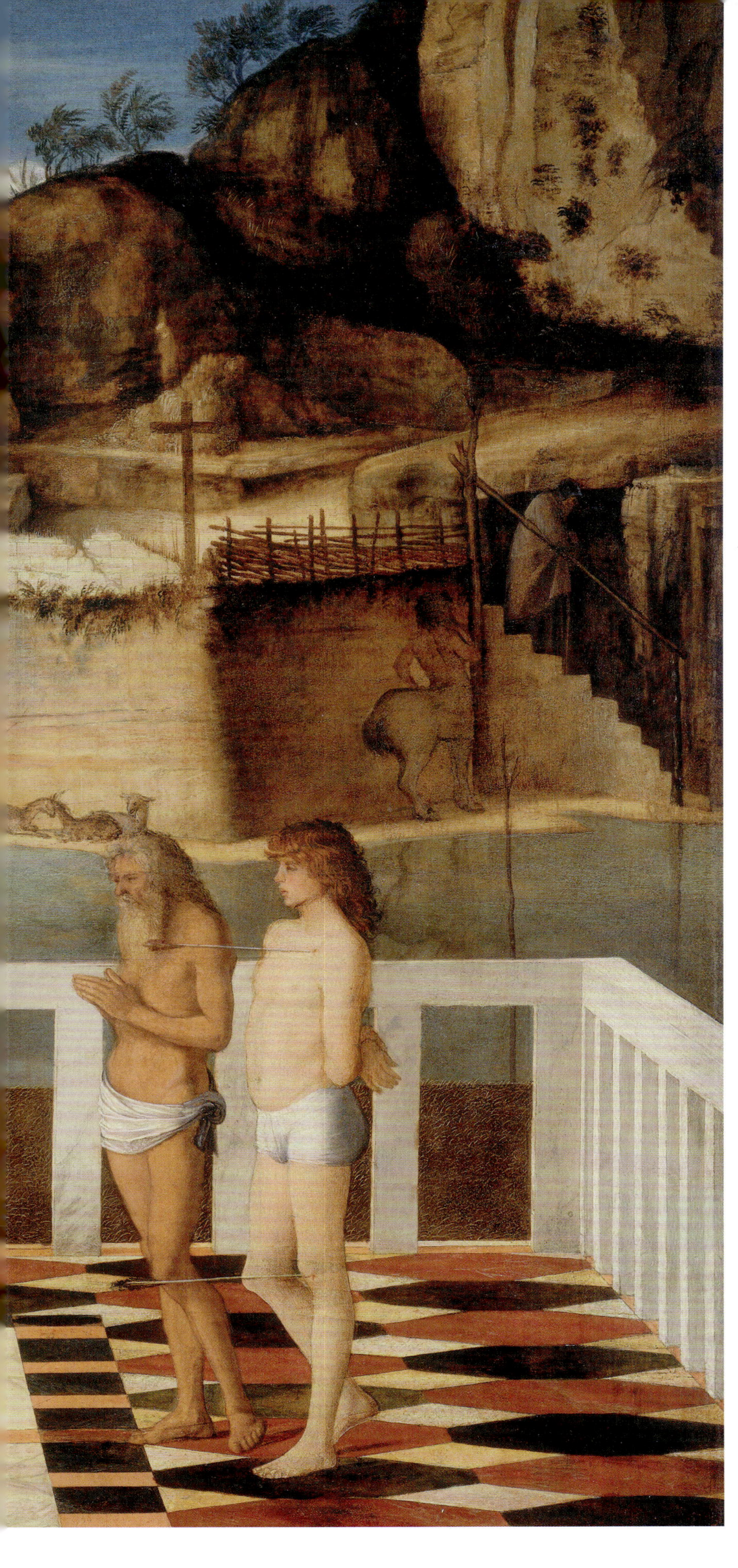

The Life of Giovanni Bellini

DANIEL WALLACE MAZE

An infant plays in the arms of his mother, who has
a premonition of the child's early death (fig. 11).
An impoverished hermit emerges from his wilderness cave to thank the sun for its light (see fig. 8).
A mother embraces her deceased son for the last
time before he is buried (fig. 12). With short, delicate brushstrokes and a remarkable depth of com-
passion, Giovanni Bellini transformed traditional
Christian subjects into transcendent images of
universal celebration and human suffering. These
works continue to elicit profound emotions from
observers today.

The current exhibition invites the exploration
of an essential aspect of many Bellini paintings: his
glorious landscapes. In his perceptive monograph
on Bellini (1968), Giles Robertson wrote that the
artist infused his landscapes with a spiritual light
that should be seen "as love, the divine element
permeating and binding nature and man together
in a single order."[1] The landscapes also evince Bellini's own gentle love, not least in the form of his

old, Bellini was "the best painter of all."[3] Still, none of Bellini's contemporaries recorded such fundamental biographical facts as his year of birth, whether he journeyed outside Italy or even visited Florence and Rome, or whether he was as pious and compassionate in life as his art would seem to suggest. This scant documentation, however, is to be expected: medieval and early Renaissance men of letters rarely expressed a biographical interest in visual artists, and the artists themselves left behind few memoirs or other personal documents.[4]

This essay seeks to bring into view the contours of Bellini's life and a faint image of the man. It revisits the scattered primary sources, explores major events in the artist's life, and considers various questions that scholars contest. It also highlights a number of Bellini's exceptional abilities: his skill in managing a large workshop and training younger artists, his sensitivity to the accomplishments of humanists, and, perhaps most impressive, his lifelong capacity to absorb into his own artistic style an extraordinary range of pictorial innovations by local, regional, and even international artists. In middle age, for instance, Bellini became among the first Italian artists to master the use of oils as revolutionized by Netherlandish painters;[5] and in Bellini's old age, Giorgione and Titian, some fifty or more years Bellini's junior, apparently inspired their former workshop master to participate in groundbreaking explorations of painting classical allegories and the female nude (see fig. 16).[6] Throughout Bellini's life, his ability to grasp the brilliance of another artist's work and incorporate some of its spirit into his own vision enabled him, arguably to an extent unsurpassed by other artists in the Renaissance, continually to replenish his creativity and develop an astounding diversity of styles across his long career.

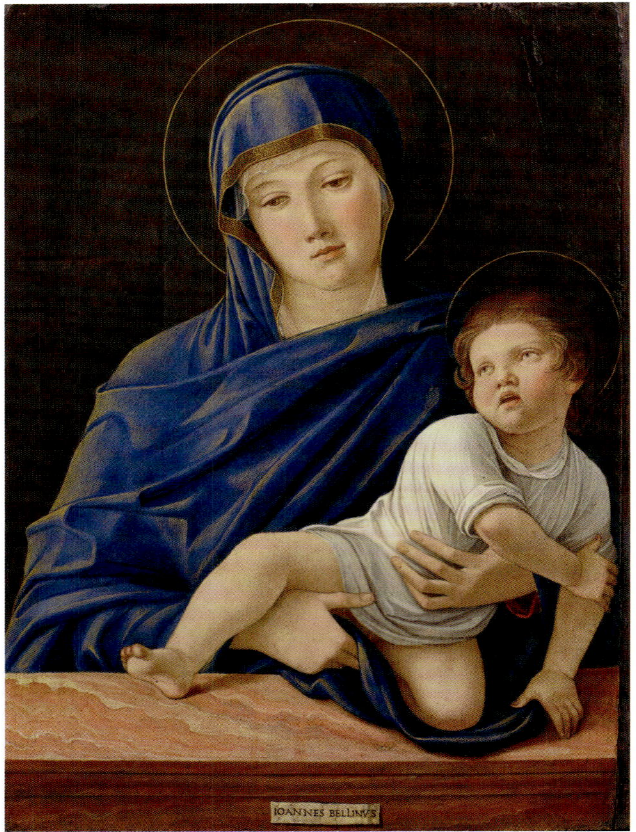

Figure 11
GIOVANNI BELLINI
Madonna and Child (Lochis Madonna), ca. 1470–75. Panel, 47.4 × 33.8 cm (18⅝ × 33⁵⁄₁₆ in.). Bergamo, Galleria dell'Accademia Carrara, 742

careful and tender observations, whether rendering the standards and falls of a blue iris or the bedrock outcrops and alluvial fans of a vast desert, illuminated by the dawn sun (see fig. 1).[2]

Art historians widely recognize Bellini as the greatest artist of fifteenth-century Venice and vital to the development of Venetian Renaissance painting, which plays a central role in the history of Western art. That no biography of the artist appeared during his lifetime was hardly due to his lack of fame: around 1474, the Paduan epigrapher and antiquarian Felice Feliciano described Bellini as "the most famous painter in the world," and in a letter of 1506, the supremely talented German artist and polymath Albrecht Dürer wrote that, although

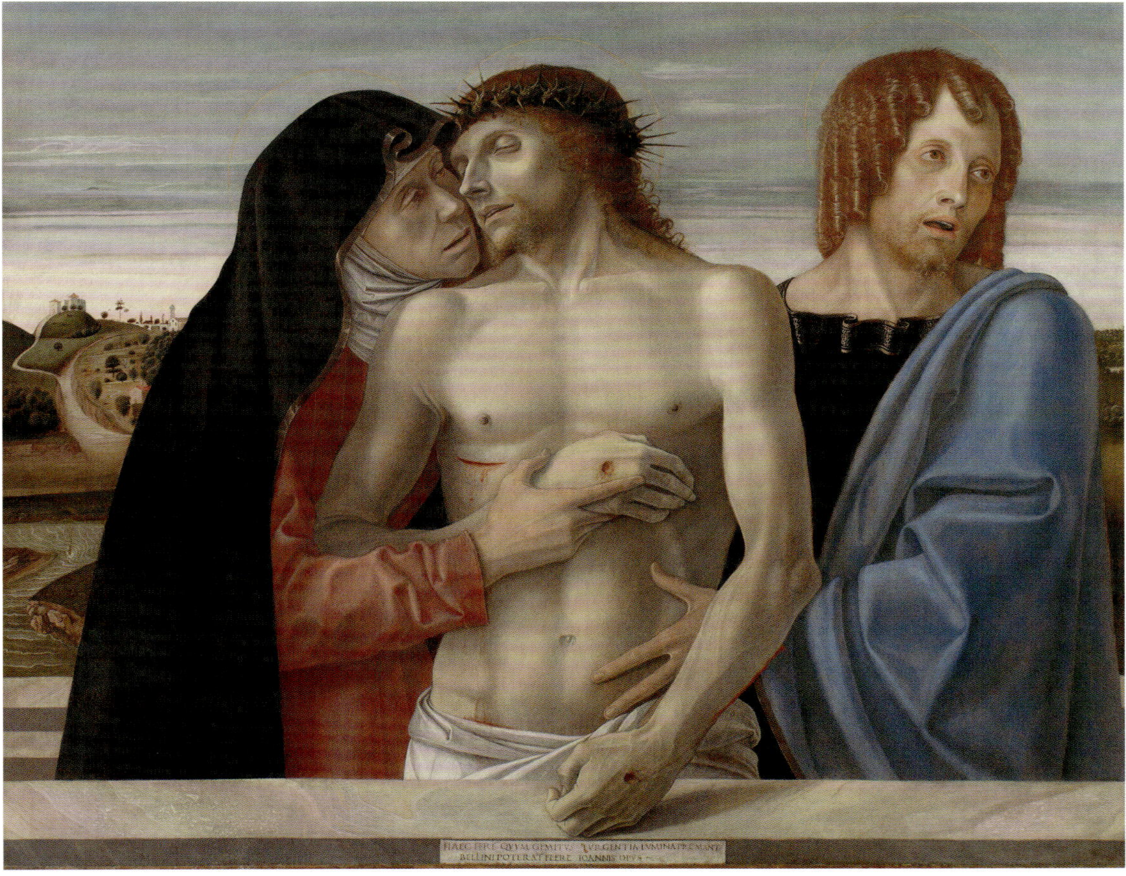

Figure 12

GIOVANNI BELLINI

Pietà, ca. 1465. Panel,
86 × 107 cm (33⅞ × 42⅛ in.).
Milan, Pinacoteca di Brera, 228

Birth

Among the most contentious questions in the
entire history of Renaissance art is Bellini's date of
birth. Scholars have long argued over whether he
was born circa 1425 (Longhi) or circa 1430 (Bellosi)
or circa 1435 (Christiansen) or circa 1440 (Lucco).[7]
Underlying these sometimes fiery disagreements are
historians' attempts not only to establish a chronology for Bellini's first works, which would underpin
an assessment of his early career, but to determine whether he was older or younger than the
Paduan-trained artist Andrea Mantegna (ca. 1431–
1506)—and hence, the argument runs, whether
Bellini principally originated, or was the recipient

of, the pictorial ideas in their early artistic dialogue.
At stake, then, is the direction of the lines of influence running between the two major artists of early
Renaissance northern Italy and therefore how the
history of art for the period ought to be written.[8]

The other long-standing mystery concerning
Bellini's birth is the identity of his parents. Until
recently, Giovanni was universally regarded as the
biological son of the Venetian artist Jacopo Bellini
(ca. 1390/95–ca. 1470/71). Extant documents record
that Jacopo was married once, to Anna Rinversi,
whose will of 1429 describes her as Jacopo's wife
and pregnant with her first child.[9] The puzzle,
however, has been Anna's deathbed testament of

November 25, 1471, in which she names as heirs her sons Gentile and Nicolò Bellini, but mentions neither her daughter, Nicolosia, nor Giovanni Bellini.[10] This omission suggests that by the winter of 1471, Nicolosia had already died; Giovanni, however, was still very much alive.[11] Some scholars have thus argued that Anna was not Giovanni's biological mother, and, remarkably, this century-old conjecture has recently received documentary support: in 2014 the last will of Samaritana Dominici née Vendramin, almost certainly Giovanni Bellini's maternal aunt, was identified and published in full, revealing that Giovanni's biological mother most likely also had the maiden name of Vendramin and therefore was not Jacopo Bellini's wife, Anna Rinversi.[12]

Research I published in 2013 argues that Jacopo Bellini was not the biological father of Giovanni Bellini but rather his much older half brother.[13] The pivotal evidence is a legal document (a *divisio*, or charter of division) drawn up on September 13, 1440, by the legitimately born brothers Giovanni and Jacopo Bellini to divide the estate of their deceased father, Nicolò.[14] This Giovanni, when understood in light of fifteenth-century Venetian civil law and other Bellini-related legal documents, was almost certainly the famous painter, who was therefore Nicolò Bellini's biological son and Jacopo Bellini's half brother. The document also helps determine Giovanni Bellini's birth date: by law, he must have been over age twelve to have agreed independently to the *divisio*, yet he also must have been born after his father Nicolò Bellini's testament of April 11, 1424, in which Nicolò was legally required to name all of his legitimate sons but mentioned only Jacopo and not Giovanni.[15] Thus Giovanni Bellini was born after mid-1424 and before September 13, 1428. Indeed, this range of dates accords with the earliest extant identification of

Giovanni's year of birth: in his *Lives of the Artists* of 1550, the art historian Giorgio Vasari wrote that Giovanni died at age ninety (in 1516).[16]

By integrating this legal analysis with the recently discovered will of Samaritana Dominici née Vendramin, undoubtedly Giovanni Bellini's aunt, the name of the artist's mother is almost certainly Franceschina Vendramin (published here for the first time).[17] She was Nicolò Bellini's second wife, who lived with Nicolò in the Venetian parish of San Salvatore near the Rialto Bridge.[18] (Nicolò's first wife, Giovannina, who was Jacopo's mother, died before 1424.)[19] Apparently Franceschina was not a noblewoman, for neither she nor her sister Samaritana can be located among the well-documented Vendramin line of patricians—which is not surprising, given her marriage to Nicolò, a tinsmith probably in his fifties.[20] Currently little else is known about Franceschina.[21] Circumstantial evidence, however, including Franceschina's absence from further recorded history and Samaritana's testamentary declaration that Giovanni "with love and kindness treated me always as a mother," suggests that Franceschina died young, perhaps during or shortly after Giovanni's birth or in the Venetian plague of 1427.[22]

One may thus conclude that as a baby or toddler Giovanni Bellini was orphaned: His father, Nicolò, is recorded as having died sometime prior to July 23, 1429, when Giovanni was age four or younger.[23] Apparently Giovanni's elder half brother, Jacopo Bellini, then in his early or mid-thirties, provided for the orphaned Giovanni and thereafter raised him as his own son. Indeed, apart from the *divisio*, which concerned Giovanni's legal inheritance as strictly determined by biological relations, Giovanni was known solely and accepted entirely as Jacopo Bellini's son and Gentile Bellini's brother, both in and outside the family, as when Jacopo signed the Gattamelata altarpiece of 1460 as a work by himself and his sons Gentile and Giovanni, or when Gentile, on his deathbed in 1507, appointed as an executor to his will "my dearest brother Giovanni."[24]

Childhood and Social Class

Whether one subscribes to this new Bellini genealogy or the traditional one identifying Jacopo as Giovanni's biological father, Jacopo undoubtedly raised Giovanni and trained him to be an artist. They lived in the Venetian parish of San Geminiano with Jacopo and Anna's children, Gentile, Nicolosia, and Nicolò, who were born no earlier than 1429 and whose birth order remains uncertain.[25] In 1431 Jacopo agreed to raise his sister Elena's son, Leonardo, the future miniaturist, "because of the demands of charity and kinship," as their later workshop contract stated, presumably because Leonardo's father, an oar maker named Paolo, had died (he was certainly deceased by 1443).[26] Giovanni, then, grew up probably as the eldest (if indeed older than Leonardo), in a house full of children and steps away from the basilica of San Marco—its Italo-Byzantine architecture and mosaics would come to inspire Giovanni's art—and doubtlessly with regular visits from his mother's side of the family and his aunt Samaritana.

The Bellini, Giovanni included, belonged to an emerging Venetian social class between the nobility and *popolo* (commoners), eventually called the *cittadini originari* (original citizens).[27] In the early fifteenth century, this was a loosely defined group of prominent non-noble citizens.[28] They were ineligible to sit on Venice's Great Council, participate in high government office, or collectively shape Venetian affairs of state, but a number of them became exceptionally wealthy; some became famous like the Bellini; and many aspired to more influential roles within the sociocultural fabric of their native city. To this end, they endowed and oversaw philanthropic institutions called Scuole Grandi (great confraternities), which provided alms to the destitute, medical care to the sick and elderly, dowries to poor women, including impoverished nobles, and lodging to many Venetians, especially the Scuole's own members who had fallen on hard times.[29] To honor God, the city, and their own members' escalating social status, the Scuole Grandi constructed elaborate administrative buildings with large meeting halls that required decoration.[30]

During Giovanni's childhood, Jacopo frequently executed paintings for patrons outside Venice—in Padua, Brescia, Verona, Bologna, and Ferrara—perhaps bringing along Giovanni, when old enough, as his assistant. In 1437 Jacopo became a member of the Scuola Grande di San Giovanni Evangelista and in 1441 served on its board.[31] This social positioning helped Jacopo secure his most important painting commission to date, a now-lost cycle of some seventeen New Testament scenes decorating his Scuola's vast central meeting room, the Sala Capitolare.[32] Jacopo also executed a series of paintings, destroyed by fire in 1485, for the *albergo*, or board room, of the Scuola Grande di San Marco.[33] In a period when even the greatest Italian artists were often forced to itinerancy in search of employment, Jacopo's Scuole commissions constituted years of continuous work, all within a short walking distance of his home-workshop in the parish of San Geminiano. For Giovanni, the narrative cycles in the Scuole Grandi were his training grounds, and in these years he would have become expert in the technique of preparing walls for fresco and grounds for panel and canvas, mixing glues and paints, and applying gilding and glazes.[34]

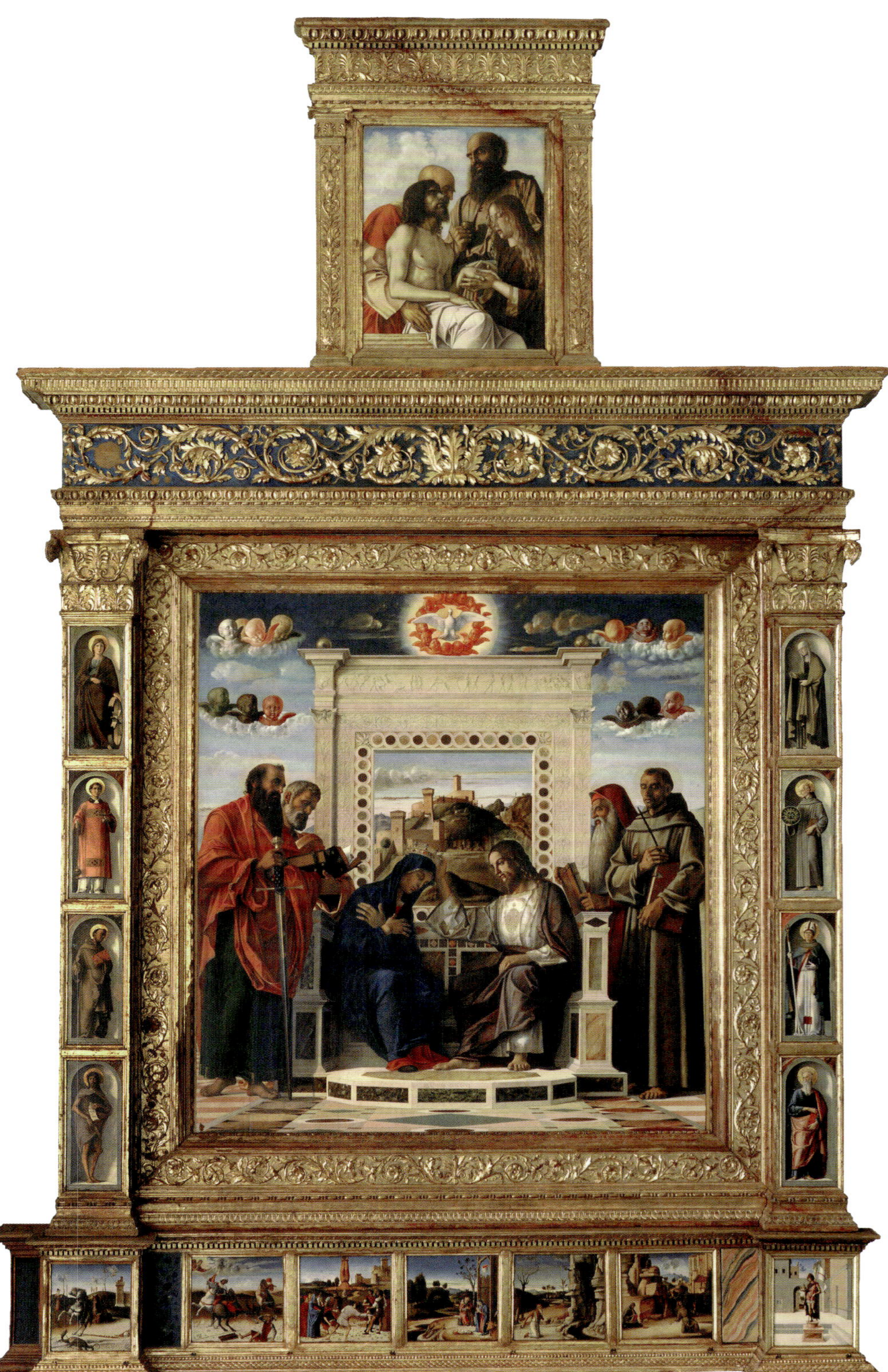

Figure 13

GIOVANNI BELLINI

Reconstruction of the Pesaro altarpiece, ca. 1472–75. Top: *Lamentation over the Dead Christ*. Panel, 107 × 84 cm ($42\frac{1}{8}$ × $33\frac{1}{16}$ in.). Vatican City, Musei Vaticani, 40290; main image: *Coronation of the Virgin*. Panel, 262 × 240 cm ($103\frac{3}{16}$ × $94\frac{1}{2}$ in.). Pesaro, Museo Civico

Formative Outlook

From youth through early adulthood, Giovanni's foremost artistic influence was Jacopo. Through Jacopo, Giovanni received a rich artistic heritage passed down from Jacopo's master, Gentile da Fabriano (d. 1427), among the most celebrated Italian painters of his day. Inspired by the artist-illuminators at the Visconti court in Milan, Gentile's art emphasized personal observation over formulaic constructions, especially in the portrayal of flora and fauna and the effects of light. In Italy this novel approach resulted in a new kind of naturalism, so critical to the history of Western art that some scholars have dubbed it "the Other Renaissance"—because it was arguably no less consequential than the appropriation of ancient Greek and Roman artistic models or the invention of drawing in linear perspective.[35] For over twelve years Jacopo assisted Gentile, but it was Giovanni, more than Jacopo or any other artist in fifteenth-century Italy, who would prove ideally receptive to this Gentilesque vision.[36] Together with Leonardo da Vinci, Giovanni Bellini became the Italian Renaissance's most observant and lyrical renderer of flora, fauna, and the ethereal qualities of light as it modeled objects, sculpted faces, and irradiated verdant valleys—as the landscapes in this exhibition illustrate.

Jacopo's own artistic interests also flowed into Giovanni's art. Jacopo owned ancient sculpture, recorded classical inscriptions and medals, and drew the antique, both real and imagined, in the form of monuments, pagan statues, bacchanals, and fanciful temples.[37] This antiquarian enthusiasm also possessed Giovanni, who painted classicizing friezes, constructed his signature with Roman imperial capitals, and occasionally employed antique models.[38] In the 1430s Jacopo sought the secrets to the new art of drawing in linear perspective, unraveling them in the 1440s.[39] Giovanni advanced these discoveries, undergirding his paintings with seamless perspectival systems that are nonetheless so complex, they have only recently begun to be elucidated.[40] Most tangibly, in some 220 drawings spread across two invaluable sketchbooks now at the Louvre and the British Museum, Jacopo experimented in fusing artistic genres and formulating rich, expressive compositions that anticipated much of the Venetian Renaissance in art. When embarking on a painting commission, Giovanni routinely returned to the wellspring of ideas contained in Jacopo's notebooks, even long after Jacopo's death, employing the drawings as compositional points of departure and mining them liberally for settings, motifs, and even overall tone.[41]

The Venice and nearby Padua of Giovanni's youth attracted an array of artists and art representing more diverse styles and far-flung geographies than at any previous point in Venetian history. Raised within Veneto-Byzantine pictorial traditions articulated foremost by the mosaics of San Marco, Giovanni absorbed the styles of local late Gothic painters such as Giambono, who collaborated with Jacopo, and Giovanni d'Alemagna and Antonio Vivarini, who headed Venice's most successful painting workshop of the 1440s. Giovanni assimilated perspectival innovations and monumental figure types of central Italy, brought north by artists such as Andrea del Castagno, Filippo Lippi, and, most influentially, Donatello, who worked in Padua during 1443–53 and whose sculptural reliefs Giovanni occasionally used as models for his devotional paintings and Madonnas. From the Netherlands arrived astounding landscapes and intimate three-quarter-view portraits executed in oils, exposing Giovanni to stunning new compositional and material possibilities.[42]

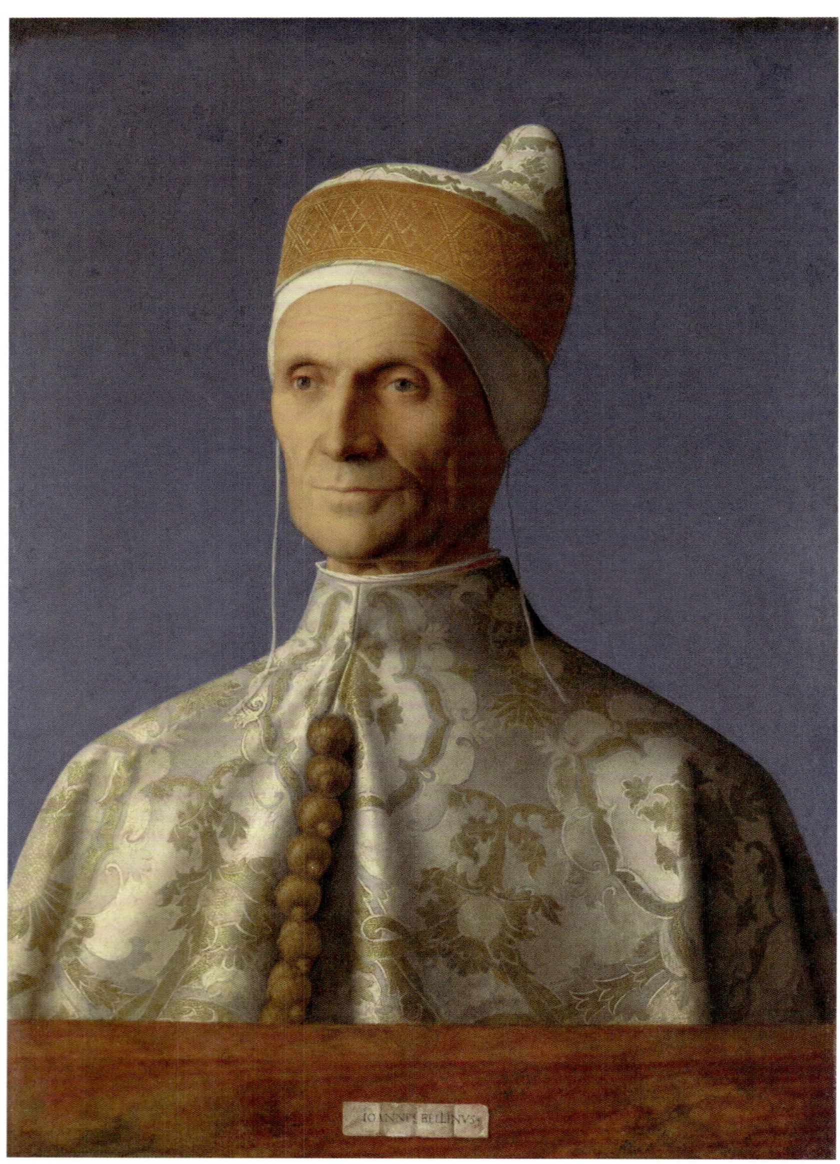

Figure 14
GIOVANNI BELLINI
*Portrait of Doge Leonardo
Loredan*, 1501–2. Panel,
61.6 × 45.1 cm (24¼ × 17¾ in.).
London, National Gallery,
NG189

Early Career: 1450s–60s

If Giovanni's principal occupation in the 1440s
and much of the 1450s was assisting Jacopo, he
nonetheless found time to execute independent
paintings, mostly manuscript illuminations and
small-scale devotional panels for the home (apparently Bellini received early training as an illumi-
nator; Keith Christiansen, following Robertson,
observed that his youthful paintings reveal "the
exquisite touch of a miniaturist").[43] In many early
pictures, Bellini represented traditional Christian
iconographies—such as the Virgin and Child or
the Suffering Christ—as quiet, spiritual, and aes-
thetically pleasing images, which often included
landscapes inspired by Jacopo's notebook experi-
ments and Netherlandish art. These compassionate
portrayals of Christian subjects helped elicit pious
emotions from the viewer and thus augmented the
works' religious functions. Bellini's early paintings
include the Birmingham *Saint Jerome in the Wilderness* (cat. no. 1), the Marcello Manuscript Illuminations (1453, Paris, Bibliothèque de l'Arsenal), the
Bergamo *Pietà* (ca. 1453–54, Accademia Carrara),
the Correr *Transfiguration* (ca. 1455, Venice, Museo
Correr) and *Crucifixion with the Virgin and Saint
John the Evangelist* (cat. no. 2), the Davis *Virgin and
Child* (ca. 1455, New York, Metropolitan Museum
of Art), the *Imago Pietatis* (1457, Milan, Museo Poldi
Pezzoli), and his masterpiece of the decade, the
National Gallery's *Agony in the Garden*, a work that
features the earliest-known depiction of dawn in
Italian art (see fig. 1).

Andrea Mantegna's entrance into the lives of
the Bellini was a milestone in Giovanni's career and
in the development of northern Italian Renaissance
art. Born around 1431 or perhaps a few years earlier,
Mantegna was trained in Padua by the artist and
early antiquarian Francesco Squarcione (ca. 1395–

after 1468).[44] In 1452 or 1453 he married Jacopo Bellini's only daughter, Nicolosia.[45]

Giovanni's fascinating and much-debated artistic duologue with Mantegna—in which the two artists shared pictorial ideas, motifs, compositional strategies, and aspects of their styles—begins with Giovanni's earliest extant painting as an adult, which most scholars identify as the Birmingham *Saint Jerome in the Wilderness* (cat. no. 1). The artists' cross-fertilization of ideas continued through the 1450s, their work often so stylistically similar that several paintings and drawings by each were first attributed to the other.[46] According to some, Bellini in these years was under the influence of Mantegna, while others argue that Bellini originated the pair's most significant innovations.[47]

After 1460, when Mantegna departed nearby Padua to become court painter to Marchese Ludovico Gonzaga of Mantua, their artistic interchange appears to have slowed.[48] It did not cease altogether, however. Bellini's *Presentation in the Temple* of the mid-1460s (Venice, Fondazione Querini Stampalia), for example, reproduces the central composition of Mantegna's earlier work of the same subject, adding to it lateral figures.[49] Since recent scholarship has cast doubt on whether Bellini was indeed younger than Mantegna, as has long been believed, their artistic relationship, crucial to our understanding of the development of northern Italian Renaissance art, undoubtedly will receive much scholarly attention in the coming years.

Maturity and Family

Remarkably, only one extant document from either the 1450s or 1460s directly records Giovanni Bellini's activity: on January 30, 1459, Bellini witnessed the will of a woman named Margarita, the wife of Angelo de Comitibus, a physician.[50] The artist's signature indicates that he lived in the Venetian parish of San Lio, a brisk five-minute walk from Jacopo and Gentile Bellini's home-workshop in San Geminiano, meaning that Giovanni had moved into his own residence while continuing to work with Jacopo.

Indeed, Bellini bridged two worlds in the 1460s: he developed beyond his early influences toward a more mature, early Renaissance style featuring naturalistic depictions of nature and the human body, delicate modeling, geometric perspective, and carefully observed, sweeping landscapes, yet he also painted in a more conservative style when assisting Jacopo.[51] That Giovanni consciously adapted his hand to Jacopo's somewhat *retardataire* approach seems evident in four triptychs for the church of Santa Maria della Carità in Venice (1460–1464), where Giovanni's presence is discernible in various full-length figures, such as the central Madonna and Saint Anthony Abbot.[52] The Bellini must have been sensitive to the idea that a work of art should appear as if harmonized by a single hand in a single style: years later, when Giovanni ran possibly the largest painting workshop in Italy, he apparently would assign one assistant to each commission—rather than, say, a landscape specialist to execute the workshop's *lontani*, or distances—and would collaborate with that assistant to complete each painting in what seemed like a fluent hand.[53]

The 1460s also witnessed Giovanni's branching out into large-scale church altarpieces, with his masterful *Saint Vincent Ferrer* triptych (ca. 1460–65, Venice, basilica of Santi Giovanni e Paolo) into narrative painting; with his now-lost scenes from the Life of Saint Jerome (1464); and into marriage.[54] His wife's name was Ginevra Bocheta and her dowry brought a respectable 500 ducats (about 62.5 ounces of gold), which typically would have been invested in the husband's business while remaining the wife's

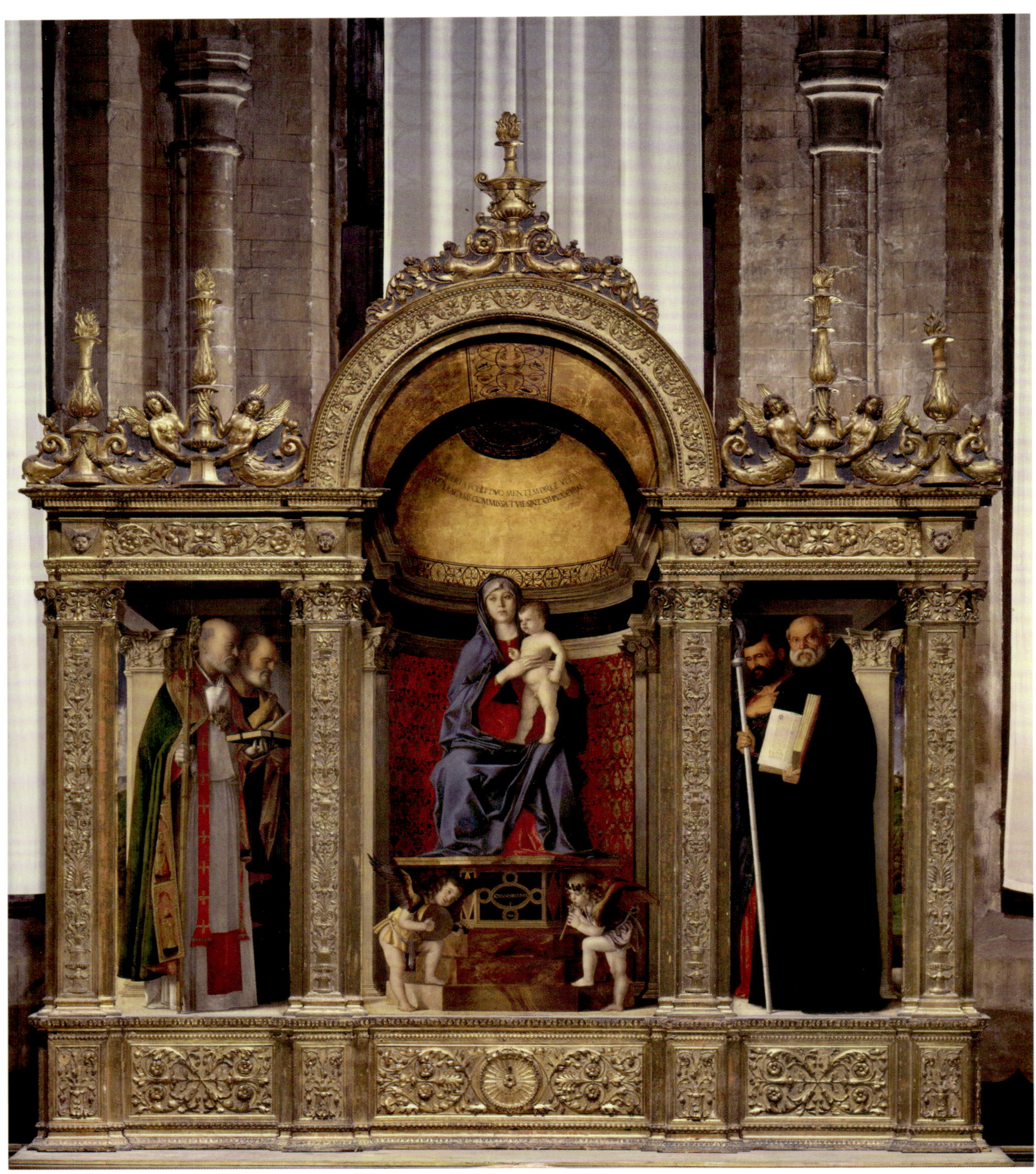

share.[55] Ginevra's brother, and probably also her father, were members of the Scuola Grande di San Marco and could have met Giovanni while he was assisting Jacopo in the Scuola's decoration.[56] Giovanni and Ginevra had one child, Alvise, who was likely born in the middle to late 1460s and did not become a professional artist.[57] Instead, in 1486 Giovanni (presumably) secured for Alvise a highly coveted place in the Ducal Chancery school. Alvise would learn fluent Latin and perhaps Greek, and receive a humanist-based education far more scholarly than Giovanni's. The expectation was that Alvise would become a government notary and, hopefully, chancery secretary, a prestigious and well-paid position reserved for non-noble *cittadini originari*. Indeed, by 1496 Alvise was stationed in Apulia, at the heel of Italy's boot, serving as the government secretary to a Venetian diplomat.[58]

Middle Career: 1470s–90s

Jacopo Bellini died in 1470 or 1471, his wife Anna followed in 1471, and Gentile Bellini, as Jacopo's legitimate son, inherited the Bellini workshop and its contents, including Jacopo's famous sketchbooks of drawings.[59] In a letter dated May 11, 1471, Elisabetta Morosini Frangipani, writing from the Adriatic island of Veglia (now Krk), asked her brother Marco in Venice whether "the painters Gentile and Giovanni Bellini" would teach the "foundations of drawing [*rason del desegno*]" to "our Father Domenico," so that Domenico might incorporate these new methods when returning to Veglia.[60] The letter suggests not only that Gentile and Giovanni shared a workplace but also that their followers (the *Belliniani*) were spreading the workshop's style to other regions.

Written sources track Giovanni's escalating fame during the 1470s. The evidence begins with a sonnet by Giovanni Testa Cillenio of circa 1470 that celebrates "the great Giovanni" and "the good Gentile."[61] This is rather modestly followed in 1473 by a letter from Pera (Istanbul) in which Antonio di Choradi wrote his brother-in-law in Venice, the stonemason Nicolò Gratto, to commission a painting of Christ from Lazzaro Bastiani, and if Bastiani was unwilling or dead, to employ instead Giovanni Bellini.[62] Rarely, if ever again, would Bellini play second fiddle to Bastiani or any other painter. Soon several humanists, those classically educated cultural tastemakers of the Renaissance, began lauding Bellini (invariably in platitudes governed more by rhetorical convention than original critique).[63] Felice Feliciano's letter of circa 1474 has been mentioned, and about that same year, the Triestine poet Raffaele Zovenzoni wrote a poem likening Giovanni, "a painter of the utmost fame," to Alexander the Great's acclaimed painter Apelles, the artist of antiquity most often invoked by humanists to eulogize a contemporary painter.[64] The prolific poet Piattino Piatti, probably writing from Urbino in late 1474, praised "the excellent Venetian painter Giovanni Bellini."[65]

This cluster of panegyrics likely responded to two magisterial church altarpieces Bellini had recently executed: his *Madonna and Child with Saints Thomas Aquinas and Catherine* (ca. 1472, destroyed in a fire of 1867 but known, at least compositionally, from an engraving of 1858) for the church of Santi Giovanni e Paolo in Venice, and his *Coronation of the Virgin* (ca. 1472–75) for the church of Saint Francis (now Santa Maria delle Grazie) in Pesaro (some twenty miles northeast of Urbino) (fig. 13).[66] In the *Madonna and Child with Saints Thomas Aquinas and Catherine*, Bellini arranged the attendant saints to either side of a centralized, elevated, and enthroned Madonna within a unified architectural space; this format, the so-called *sacra conversazione*, became, along with the single-field narrative scene, the Venetian model for the church altarpiece, ultimately supplanting the polyptych format. The Pesaro *Coronation*, considered among the greatest paintings of the Italian Renaissance, may have been the first Italian altarpiece executed principally in oils. (Some argue Piero della Francesca influenced Bellini here and elsewhere, but this is unclear.)[67] These two altarpieces seem to have propelled Bellini into the upper echelon of artists across Italy, even if he rarely departed Venice: though never documented outside the Veneto, Bellini must at least have traveled along the Adriatic coast to Pesaro to assess the architecture, windows, and light of the high altar of the church of Saint Francis, for which his *Coronation* altarpiece was designed.[68]

Antonello da Messina

Prior to the arrival of Antonello da Messina (ca. 1430–1479) in Venice in late 1474 or early 1475 (see figs. 10, 30, 31), Bellini had already begun to implement linseed oil to bind his color pigments in works such as his portrait of the German merchant *Joerg Fugger* (1474, Pasadena, Norton Simon Museum) and the Pesaro *Coronation of the Virgin* (ca. 1472–75; see fig. 13).[69] Nonetheless, early writers such as Vasari and Ridolfi viewed Antonello's Venetian sojourn as marking the origins of a revolution in Italian painting, the rejection of egg tempera in favor of oil paints.[70] Antonello came to master the oil medium probably as an apprentice in the Neapolitan workshop of Niccolò Colantonio (ca. 1420–after 1460), an experimenter in oils at the court of King René I of Naples.[71] Bellini apparently experimented for himself by studying Netherlandish works in and around Venice.[72] While it is unknown whether Bellini and Antonello shared a friendship, it is certain that Antonello's examples encouraged Bellini to deploy oils in new ways and to stunning effect.

Bellini had executed few independent portraits before Antonello's visit. The genre was simply not popular in Venice.[73] Antonello, a highly sought-after portraitist, represented his sitters gazing directly at the viewer against a black background, capturing their subtle facial expressions and facets of personality with a bravura mastery of oils.[74] Bellini, though about age fifty, consciously altered his technique to absorb Antonello's innovations—though Bellini usually placed his sitters against a sky background and rarely, if ever, represented them engaging the viewer.[75] Portraiture soon became enormously popular in Venice (due to Bellini, according to Vasari), and Bellini was its greatest local practitioner;[76] his *Portrait of Doge Leonardo Loredan* (1501–2; fig. 14) is generally considered among the finest portraits of the Renaissance.[77] Antonello, for his part, adapted Bellini's compositions when executing devotional paintings, and drew inspiration directly from Bellini's destroyed *Madonna and Child with Saints Thomas Aquinas and Catherine* (ca. 1472) to execute his famous San Cassiano altarpiece (1475–76)—indeed, the combination of these two altar paintings established a Venetian model for church altarpieces for decades to come.[78]

Giovanni Bellini's most enduring relationship, however, was with Gentile Bellini (1429/35–1507), his younger biological nephew according to the new Bellini genealogy, but who was raised as his brother.[79] When the two were compared, Giovanni was consistently described as the preferred artist.[80] Yet in 1474 it was Gentile who received arguably the most prestigious Venetian commission of the century: to "renew and restore" (in reality to execute anew) the large-scale history paintings and portraits of doges for the Great Council Hall of the Ducal Palace, among the largest rooms in Europe, and to receive as remuneration a *sansaria*, or broker's patent, at the German trading warehouse (Fondaco dei Tedeschi), which paid the substantial annual income of about one hundred ducats for life.[81]

In 1479 Giovanni took over Gentile's work in the Great Council Hall after the Venetian Senate dispatched Gentile to the Ottoman court for his famous rendezvous with Sultan Mehmet II. Perhaps surprisingly, Giovanni might not have been entirely comfortable in the genre of large-scale narratives. In a period when artists were loath to reject commissions, he uncharacteristically failed to complete for the Scuola Grande di San Marco a large-scale narrative depicting the Flood and Noah's Ark, commissioned from the artist in 1470 and reassigned to Bartolomeo Montagna in 1483.[82] The Scuola, perhaps in response, did not admit Giovanni until 1484, even though his wife's relatives were members and Gentile Bellini had joined by 1466.[83]

For his continued work in the Ducal Palace, Giovanni was likewise promised the next available *sansaria*, of which there were thirty, and was paid a salary while waiting at least fifteen years to receive

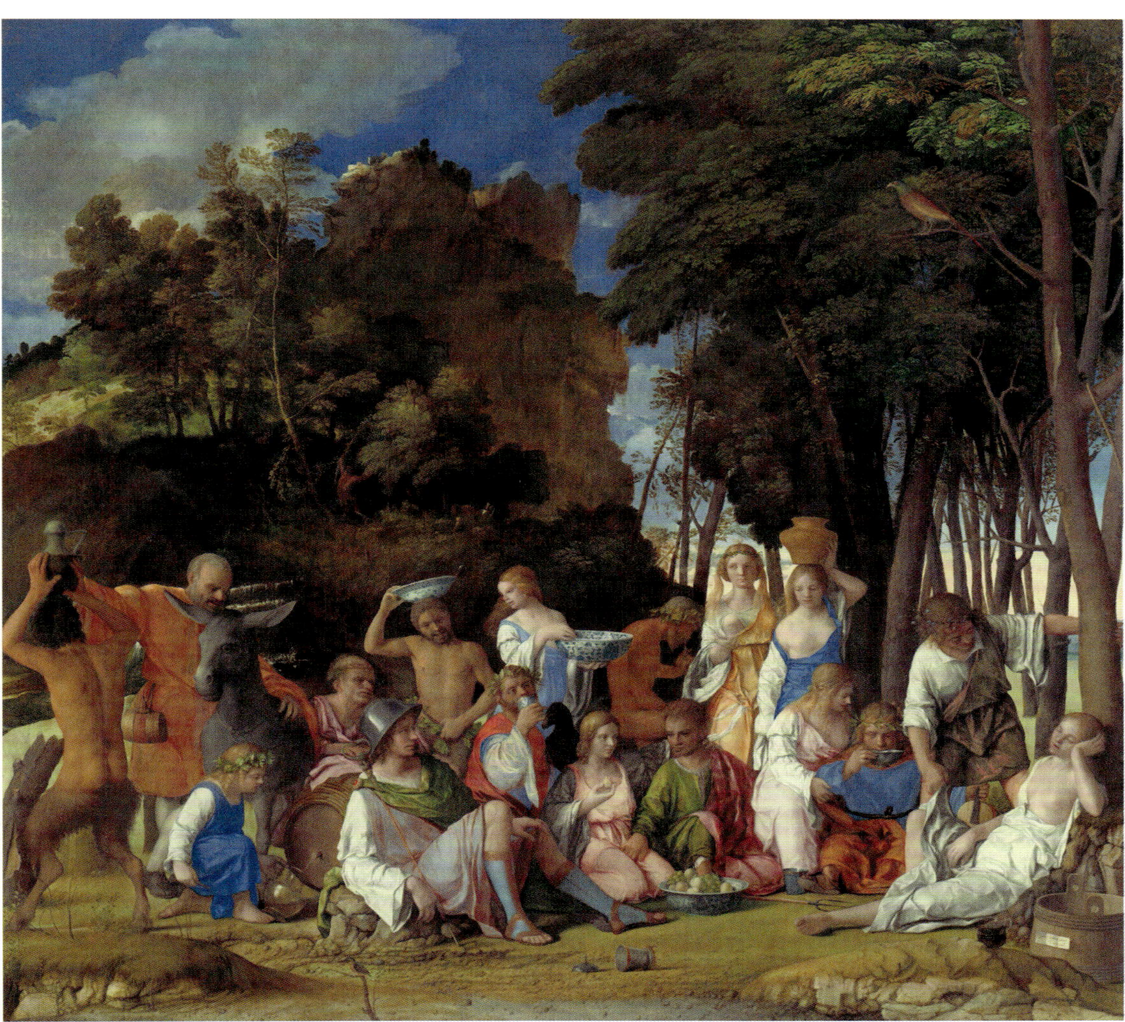

Figure 16
GIOVANNI BELLINI
and TITIAN
(Italian, ca. 1488/90–1576),
The Feast of the Gods, 1514/29.
Canvas, 170.2 × 188 cm
(67 × 74 in.). Washington,
DC, National Gallery of Art,
Widener Collection, 1942.9.1

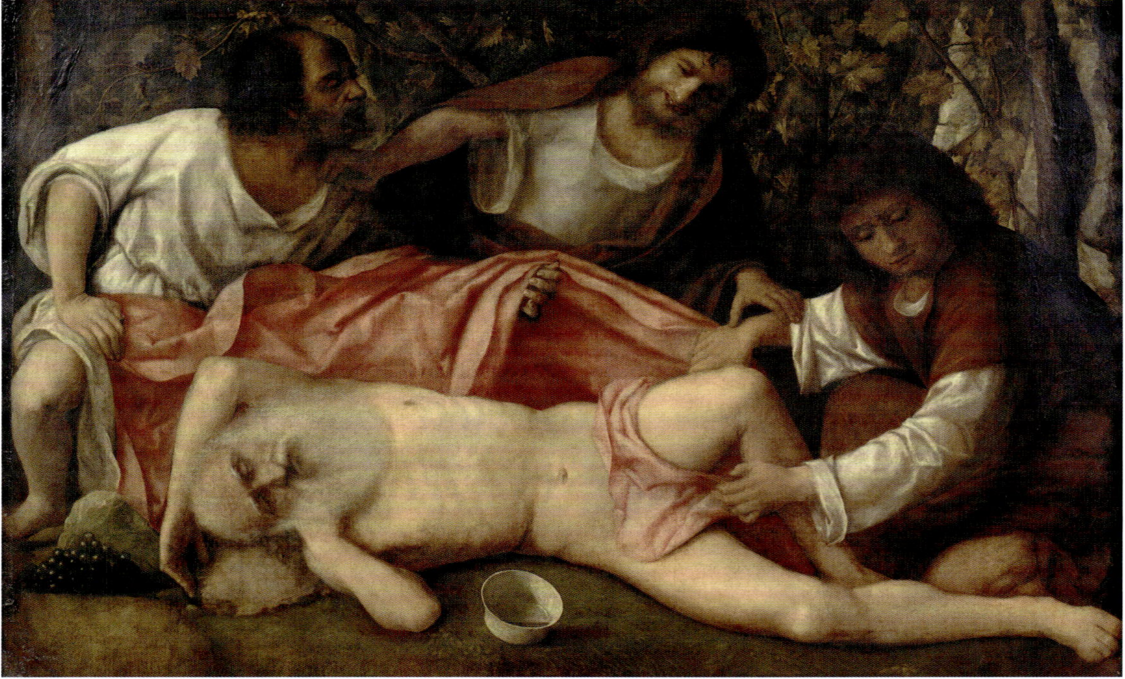

his.[84] Though the government named him a painter of the Republic ("pictor nostri Domini"), the tradition that Venice appointed a single official painter, who held the *sansaria*, largely began with Titian in the next century.[85] When Gentile returned from the Ottoman court, both he and Giovanni continued their work in the Great Hall, where they were eventually joined by other artists, including Alvise Vivarini (ca. 1442/1453–1503/1505), who were paid salaries.[86] Though Gentile was known primarily for his large-scale narrative paintings—his *Miracle during the Procession in Piazza San Marco* (ca. 1496, Venice, Accademia) is his masterpiece in the genre—the diarist Marin Sanudo called Giovanni's pictures in the Ducal Palace "the more beautiful" and Vasari also considered them "truly most beautiful."[87] Unfortunately, the Great Hall's paintings were destroyed in a fire that swept through the Ducal Palace in 1577.

Expanding His Workshop

Giovanni's responsibilities in the Ducal Palace and the increasing demand for his devotional paintings, portraits, and church altarpieces meant the artist had to expand greatly his workshop and oversee a large number of assistants—from lesser-known artists, such as Francesco Bissolo, Rocco Marconi, and Niccolò Rondinelli, to better-known ones, such as Andrea Previtali, Vittore Belliniano, and probably Vincenzo Catena, Sebastiano del Piombo, Giorgione, and Titian.[88] In 1483 the Signoria, desiring Bellini to concentrate on completing his paintings in the Ducal Palace, officially freed the artist "from all offices and related commitments in the brotherhood, or guild, of painters," an unprecedented privilege.[89] Though Bellini was not exempted from mandatory obligations such as paying the *luminaria*, or annual dues, his partial independence from guild oversight might have facilitated the expansion of his atelier.[90] Some scholars believe it soon became Italy's largest painting workshop, producing, for instance, at least eighty variants of the Virgin and Child alone, many of which were then replicated.[91]

Documents in these middle years record Giovanni's close contact with humanists, such as the Pesarese poet and historian Pandolfo Collenuccio.[92] In paintings deploying numerous Christian or classical symbols, such as the Frick Collection's *Saint Francis in the Desert* (see fig. 8) or the Uffizi's *Sacred Allegory* (cat. no. 11), Bellini must have relied on humanist friends or learned ecclesiasts for guidance, or at least to translate Latin source texts.[93] A number of wills in this period register how some wealthy Venetians, concerned about their afterlife, turned to Bellini to execute altarpiece paintings for their funeral chapels.[94] One can imagine certain patrons not wishing to spend such extravagant funds for a Bellini picture in life, but finding the costs far more reasonable in death, especially if the artist's beautiful painting would induce visits to the patrons' chapels, bestow honor on their families, and perhaps elicit prayers for their souls.

By the end of the fifteenth century, Bellini found himself the leading master in nearly all genres of Venetian painting. The extant masterpieces of his middle period include the San Giobbe altarpiece and Frari triptych (fig. 15), the smaller-scale Frick *Saint Francis* and Naples *Transfiguration* (see fig. 6), the *Votive Picture of Doge Agostino Barbarigo* (1488, Murano, San Pietro Martire), and a number of portraits, Madonnas, and other devotional works for the *casa*. Bellini, however, was bereft of both wife and child. Ginevra had died prior to 1498 and probably soon after she drew up her will of 1489; his son, Alvise, died, presumably of an illness, within weeks of making his will in

late 1498.[95] Apparently Bellini never remarried or fathered other children.[96] While it may be hard to imagine that an artist as sensitive as Bellini would not in some form channel the anguish of the loss of his wife and child into his art, it is difficult to relate these deaths directly to any change in his style.[97]

Final Years: 1500–1516

Remarkably, Bellini continued to absorb pictorial innovations that were redefining art in High Renaissance Venice. In 1506 Albrecht Dürer visited the city. "Giovanni Bellini praised me highly to many gentlemen," Dürer wrote to a friend in Nuremburg. "He came himself to me and commissioned me to do something for him, and said that he would pay well for it, and everyone tells me what an upright man he is, so that I am really friendly with him."[98] Later, Vasari wrote that Bellini was a kind master to his pupils — many continued to sign their names as his disciples long after becoming independent masters — and that he was directly influenced by Dürer, especially in the German "sharpness in the style of the draperies" in Bellini's *Feast of the Gods* (1514) (fig. 16).[99] But undoubtedly it was the example of Giorgione, some fifty years Bellini's junior, that must have encouraged the artist to take on the challenge of the humanist *istoria*: besides *Feast of the Gods*, Bellini's extraordinary allegories include *The Drunkenness of Noah* (ca. 1510–15; fig. 17) and *Venus at Her Toilet* (1515, Vienna, Kunsthistorisches Museum), each to some extent experimental and departing significantly from the devotional Christian subjects in which Bellini had specialized since youth.

Perhaps the best-recorded episode in Bellini's life is his revealing correspondence with Isabella d'Este, the famous Marchesa of Mantua.[100] In 1501 Bellini agreed to execute an allegory for Isabella's Studiolo in the Castello, but after reading the text — probably by the poet-astrologer Paride da Ceresara, who supplied the conceit for Perugino's convoluted *Battle of Chastity and Lasciviousness* in the same room—Bellini refused, saying he "could not make anything beautiful out of it," especially if his painting "would be compared with those by Mantegna," also in the Studiolo.[101] Isabella and Bellini then agreed that Bellini would execute a classical subject of his own choosing, but a year passed and he had not begun, and after much hounding and further negotiations—Giovanni's lone extant autograph letter is a response to Isabella dated July 2, 1504—the artist ultimately provided only a religious painting for the marchesa's bedroom, probably a *Nativity* for which he had refused her request to include John the Baptist.[102]

Isabella was not satisfied and continued trying to extract a "poetic invention" from the artist, using the Venetian poet Pietro Bembo as her agent.[103] Bembo responded: "The invention, for which Your Excellency wrote me to find a design, will need to be adjusted according to the imagination of the man executing it [Bellini], who is pleased when many stipulations do not limit his style, it being accustomed, as he says, always to wander at will in paintings, so that to the best of his ability they may satisfy whoever admires them."[104] The artist never did execute an allegory for Isabella's Studiolo.

The correspondence portrays Bellini a world away from his beginnings. Giovanni the teenager, whom Jacopo likely brought to Ferrara in 1440 to assist on a commission for Marchese Niccolò III d'Este—one imagines the youth's awe and awareness of his own servant-like status at court—is now the old Bellini, famous and sought-after, and displaying the laxest of interest in obliging Niccolò III's granddaughter, Isabella d'Este, the Marchesa of Mantua.[105] (On at least one occasion, when Isabella's agent attempted to visit Bellini, he was told the artist was at his villa, away from Venice.)[106] The young Bellini often employed artistic models, whether Jacopo's drawings or finished works by Donatello or Netherlandish artists. The middle-aged Bellini painstakingly executed detailed underdrawings with such "extreme diligence" that in 1548 Paolo Pino described them as "wasted labor, since it is all to be covered over with the colors."[107] The old Bellini, according to Bembo, has freed his brush and his creativity, so that his art pleases himself first. Indeed, according to infrared analyses, in his late works Bellini painted with minimal or no underdrawing.[108]

The art historian Neville Rowley recently described Bellini's quasi-industrialized workshop, producing large numbers of variants based on Giovanni's prototypes and founded on Jacopo's strategy of continually striving to innovate, as "the premise for a more modern conception of art."[109] If modernity can be defined as a movement away from tradition to new technologies that must be constantly updated, in an economic environment of capitalism and industrialization, then Bellini's late workshop practice, artistic process, and even behavior seem precociously modern. But modernity also implies an "autonomy of art" and the possibility of artists expressing personal experiences and psychological states.[110] Isabella's difficulties with Bellini testify to his autonomy. Still, he was principally bound to the well-defined subjects of Christian art. For Bellini, painting might have been a cathartic act, but art cannot yet express Bellini's own personal catharsis. An exception to this may be *The Drunkenness of Noah* (see fig. 17), a late and mysterious work not universally attributed to the artist, in which an inebriated, naked Noah is covered up by two of his three sons, the other of whom laughs.[111] The figure of Noah "might almost be taken for a self-portrait," Rowley observed.[112] The picture displays free and visible brushwork, spontaneity, a break with conventional compositions, and a deep sense of personal expression, such that the art historian Roberto Longhi (1890–1970) declared it "the first work of modern painting."[113]

Bellini died on November 26, 1516, an event recorded by the Venetian diarist Marin Sanudo, who wrote that he was "the best of painters ... famous throughout the world."[114] When Mantegna died in 1506, Giovanni had continued Andrea's partially executed Scipio cycle, and when Gentile Bellini died in 1507, Giovanni had completed Gentile's *Saint Mark Preaching in Alexandria* (1504–7, Milan, Pinacoteca di Brera).[115] Now it was Vittore Belliniano's turn to complete Giovanni's unfinished *Martyrdom of Saint Mark* (1515/1526, Venice, Accademia).[116] Bellini was buried in the family tomb at Santi Giovanni e Paolo in Venice.[117] He left no known will or immediate family. The Bellini workshop that had brought Venice into a new age of painting closed its doors.[118] Jacopo's sketchbooks, once blueprints for the future of Venetian Renaissance art, became collectors' items, the Paris sketchbook almost certainly gifted by Gentile to Sultan Mehmet, and the London version recorded in the collection of Gabriele Vendramin in 1530.[119] By the mid-sixteenth century, art critics, followed by many later scholars, identified not Bellini but Titian as the greatest painter of the Venetian school. In the next centuries, Bellini's *fortuna critica* rose and fell.[120] John Ruskin, the leading art critic of nineteenth-century England, revitalized interest in the artist by naming as "the two best pictures in the world" Bellini's San Zaccaria altarpiece and his Frari triptych (see fig. 15). "In that estimate of them," Ruskin wrote, "I of course considered as one chief element, their solemnity of purpose—as another, their unpretending simplicity."[121]

I thank Davide Gasparotto for his invitation to write this essay. I am grateful to Jenifer Maze, Debra Pincus, Susannah Rutherglen, Carolyn Wilson, Joanna Woods-Marsden, and Tom Worthen for their helpful comments on earlier drafts. Research was made possible through the support of an American Council of Learned Societies Fellowship and a Fulbright Fellowship at the University of York. The Venetian year began March 1, but unless otherwise indicated, dates are not in *more veneto* (m.v.). Owing to limitations of space, from a vast bibliography I have selected representative references and accessible transcriptions that indicate archival sources. Please consider "with further references" to be appended to the citations below. Translations mine unless otherwise noted.

1   Robertson 1968, 33.

2   Eisler 2015, 21–25.

3   Fiocco 1926, 193: "Famosissimo in orbe pictori Joanni bellino"; Rupprich 1956–69, 1:44: "Er jst ser alt vnd jst noch der pest jm gemoll."

4   The principal exception is Ghiberti [ca. 1447] 1988.

5   In the twelfth century, Theophili 1847, 34–35, described the use of linseed oil to bind pigments. The Netherlandish accomplishment, aspects of which Bellini absorbed, was not in the discovery of oil paints but in techniques of their deployment. For a recent discussion, see Whitehouse 2012, especially 22–26; for references, see Rutherglen and Hale 2015, 196n7.

6   Anderson 2006, 172–75; Ferino-Pagden 2006, 219–23, cat. no. 41; and McHam 2008.

7   Longhi 1949, 277–78; Bellosi 2008, 103–9, 120–21; Christiansen 2004c, 53; and Lucco 2008, 21.

8   For example, contrast Longhi 1949, 274–83; Christiansen 2004c, 48–74; and Bellosi 2008, 103–9.

9   Barausse 2008, 330–31, doc. no. 4.

10   Barausse 2008, 338, doc. no. 31.

11   Maze 2013, 800n68.

12   Fry [1899] 1995, 12, 18; and Brown and Pizzati 2014, 148–52.

13   Maze 2013, 783–823.

14   Maze 2013, 817–18.

15   Barausse 2008, 330, doc. no. 3. Franceschina was not considered pregnant at the time of the will (Maze 2013, 792n33).

16   Vasari [1550, 1568] 1966–87, 3:441.

17   Franceschina was Nicolò's current wife in his will of April 11, 1424 (Barausse 2008, 330, doc. no. 3), at which time Nicolò had only one legitimate son, that by his former wife, Giovannina (Zanina). No evidence suggests Nicolò was married a third time. Since Nicolò died prior to July 23, 1429 (Maze 2013, 819), we can thus conclude that Franceschina was the mother of Nicolò's other legitimate son, Giovanni Bellini, identified as Nicolò's son in the *divisio* of 1440, a document enacted on behalf of legitimate sons.

18   Barausse 2008, 330, doc. no. 3.

19   Barausse 2008, 330, doc. no. 3.

20   Brown and Pizzati 2014, 152n43, arrived at a similar conclusion about Samaritana; also personal correspondence with Pizzati, April 2015.

21   See Maze 2013, 791n29,

792n33, 794–95, for additional information about Franceschina.

22 Brown and Pizzati 2014, 152: "Ioannem Bellinum . . . qui me semper eque ac matrem et amore et beneficiis prosecutus est." Note that Samaritana's wishes were rendered into legal language by the notary. In October 1427 Filelfo described plague-ridden Venice as nearly deserted of patricians (Robin 1991, 12–13, 22). Also see Maze 2013, 794–95, for additional support for Franceschina's death during or soon after Giovanni's birth. Note also that Samaritana drew up her will on January 19, 1509, suggesting she was at least in her early to mid-nineties at the time. This was probably not that unusual, as demographic analyses of a later period of Renaissance Venice indicate the presence of a significant elderly population above age ninety (D. Beltrami 1954, especially 92; my thanks to Alexandra Bamji for this and other demographic references). We can perhaps imagine a twelve- or fourteen-year-old Samaritana regularly visiting a two-year-old Giovanni.

23 Maze 2013, 819.

24 The signature on the dispersed Gattamelata altarpiece was recorded in 1590 by Fra Valerio Polidoro (Callegari 1997, 30); Barausse 2008, 354, doc. no. 105: "Iohannes frater meus carissimus."

25 In February 1530, Sanudo 1879–1903, 54:292, reported that "Nicolò Belin," age eighty, was made caretaker of the castle at Soave; this may be Jacopo Bellini's son.

26 Barausse 2008, 332–33, doc.

no. 11: "ex debito tam karitatis quam affinitatis."

27 See the studies of the class by Zannini 1993; Bellavitis 2001.

28 Bellavitis 2001, 67.

29 For an overview of the Scuole Grandi, see Pullan 1971; and Pullan 1990.

30 P. Brown 1988, especially 31–50.

31 Barausse 2008, 331–32, doc. nos. 6, 10.

32 P. Brown 1988, 266–68; Ridolfi [1648] 1914–24, 1:53; and Hammond 2016.

33 P. Brown 1988, 268.

34 Ridolfi [1648] 1914–24, 1:35–36, describes Giovanni and Gentile assisting Jacopo on the San Giovanni Evangelista narratives.

35 Christiansen 2006, 19–52; and De Marchi, in Fabriano 2006, 62–63, 94–95, 124–27, 180–81, 220–21, 244–47, 296–97.

36 Apparently Jacopo was Gentile's assistant by January 1412: Lametti 2001, 428, 440.

37 Joost-Gaugier 1974, 21–38; Eisler 1989, 183–211; and P. Brown 1992, 65–84.

38 Pincus 2008, 89–119; and P. Brown 2015, 245–66.

39 Degenhart and Schmitt 1990, 5: 59–94.

40 Godla and Allen 2015, 132–53, though with some caveats noted in my forthcoming review in *Studies in Iconography* 38 (2017).

41 The two major studies of Jacopo's drawings are Eisler 1989; and Degenhart and Schmitt 1990.

42 For early influences, see, e.g., Robertson 1968, 1–28; and Goffen 1989, 1–19. For Netherlandish influences, see Lucco 2004, 75–94.

43 Christiansen 2004c, 54; Robertson 1968, 16.

44 Lightbown 1986, 15–29; and Shaw and Boccia 2016,

317–24.

45 Barausse 2008, 334, doc. no. 14.

46 For example, Bellosi 2008, 103.

47 For example, Longhi 1949; Christiansen 2004c; and Bellosi 2008.

48 Huse 1972, 14.

49 Trevisan 2008, 176.

50 Barausse 2008, 334, doc. no. 16. Giovanni signed the document on January 30, 1459, and not on April 2, 1459, as is sometimes indicated.

51 Goffen 1989, 9.

52 Goffen and Scirè 2000, 26–35, 122–26.

53 Gibbons 1962, 127; Tempestini 2004, 259–60; and Blass-Simmen 2015, 77–92. Also see Davide Gasparotto's essay in this volume.

54 Humfrey 1985, 41–46; Humfrey 1988, 401–23; Goffen 1985, 2:277–96; and Zucchetta 2008, 31–51.

55 Barausse 2008, 341, doc. no. 42: this document of July 30, 1485, is the earliest to report Giovanni married.

56 Barausse 2008, 335, doc. no. 21: this document of July 6, 1466, lists Scuola Grande di San Marco members Francesco and Alvise Bocheta (the very rare surname does not appear in da Mosto), who may be identified, respectively, as Ginevra's brother and, perhaps, her father or at least another close relative.

57 Maze 2013, 798n64.

58 Neff 1985, 36ff, 370; and Barausse 2008, 344, doc. no. 57.

59 Barausse 2008, 338, doc. no. 31.

60 Barausse 2008, 337–38, doc. no. 30.

61 Meyer zur Capellen 1985, 121, doc. no. 80: "Ma'l gran

Giovanni e'l buon Gentil Belino."

62 Barausse 2008, 338, doc. no. 32.

63 Baxandall 1971, 1–120.

64 Zovenzonii 1950, 78: "Ioanni Bello Bellino Pictori Clarissimo. / Qui facis ora tuis spirantia, Belle, tabellis / dignus Alexandro principe pictor eras"; Fletcher 1991b, 153–57.

65 Agosti 2009, 20, 63–64n35: "In Ioannem Bellinum venetum pictorem egregium."

66 Humfrey 1993b, 184–93, 343–44; Lucco 2008, 190–201.

67 Lucco 2008, 28–30.

68 Wilson 1976, 378–90, 463–64; Gibbons 1977, 179; and Blum 2015, 200–201.

69 Poldi and Villa 2011, 28–36. For the use of oil possibly as a binder in Giovanni's works as early as the 1450s, see Dorigato 1993, 46, 48, 219; and Dunkerton 2004, 195–225.

70 Vasari [1550, 1568] 1966–87, 3:306–10; and Ridolfi [1648] 1914–24, 1:65. Note that Giovanni continued to use both tempera and oil paints (Rutherglen and Hale 2015, 196n7).

71 Borchert 2006, 27–41.

72 Lucco 2004, 75–94.

73 Humfrey 2011, 48–63.

74 Perkins 2015, 127–41.

75 Goffen 1989, 219–21. *Portrait of a Humanist* (Milan, 1480s), attributed to Bellini by some scholars, engages the viewer.

76 Vasari [1550, 1568] 1966–87, 3:438–39.

77 Greer 2008, 108–9, cat. no. 15.

78 Lucco 2006, 226–31; and Humfrey 1993b, 184–217.

79 On the relative ages of Giovanni and Gentile, the sources conflict: Francesco Negro, a contemporary

Venetian, referred to Gentile as "maior natu," or born first; Jacopo Filippo Foresti (1434–1520) in his regularly updated *Supplementum chronicarum* described Gentile in 1503 as the younger brother ("Gentilis minimus frater"); and in 1550 Giorgio Vasari also described Gentile as younger than Giovanni (Vasari [1550, 1568] 1966–87, 3:435). For a discussion and further references, see Maze 2013, 801–4; and Worthen 2015, 39–59.

80 Goffen 1989, 293n2.

81 Lorenzi 1868, 86, doc. no. 189: "instauratio et reparatio." Gentile replaced the decayed frescoes with narrative paintings on canvas. For the *sansaria* income, see Lorenzi 1868, 219, doc. no. 462; and Hope 1980, 301–5.

82 P. Brown 1988, 269–70.

83 Meyer zur Capellan 1980, 105.

84 Barausse 2008, 339, 342–43, doc. nos. 37, 51.

85 Barausse 2008, 340, doc. no. 39; and Hope 1980, 301–5.

86 Barausse 2008, 342–43, doc. no. 51.

87 Sanudo 2004, 2:209: "sì che in ditta salla è quadri di tutti do, ma quelli di Zuane è più belli"; Vasari [1550, 1568] 1966–87, 3:433: "veramente bellissime."

88 Heinemann 1962–91, 1:87–214; 3:33–101; and Tempestini 2004, 256–71.

89 Barausse 2008, 340, doc. no. 39: "exemptus factus fuit ab omnibus officiis et beneficiis scolle seu fratalee pictorum."

90 Barausse 2008, 340, doc. no. 39; Favaro 1975, 55–66, 79–92; Fletcher 2004, 19–21.

91 Heinemann 1962–91, 2:218–34; and Goffen 1989, 23.

92 Barausse 2008, 341, doc. no. 44; and Fletcher 2004, 35–36.

93 Delaney 1977, 331–35; Fleming 1982; Gentili 2004, 173–76; Lavin 2007, 231–56; and Dalhoff 2002, 22–23.

94 Barausse 2008, 340, 342, 353, doc. nos. 40, 50, 102.

95 Barausse 2008, 341, 344, doc. nos. 45, 57.

96 Cf. Meyer zur Capellen 1980, 108n31.

97 Cf. Kristeva 1980, 237–70; Kristeva would disagree with what I have written.

98 Dürer 1913, 6, trans. Fry with minor adjustments; Rupprich 1956–69, 1:44: "Aber Sambelling der hett mich vor vill czentillomen fast ser globt. Er . . . jst selber zw mir kumen vnd hat mich gepetten, jch solt jm etwas machen, er wols wol czalen. Vnd sagen mir dÿ lewt alle, wy es so ein frumer man seÿ, daz jch jm gleich günstig pin." See also Fara 1997, 93, for a letter dated February 15, 1506, written by frate Jacopo describing Bellini's kindness to Dürer.

99 Vasari [1550, 1568] 1966–87, 3:440; 6:158–59: "nella maniera de' panni è un certo che di tagliente, secondo la maniera tedesca, ma non è gran fatto, perché imitò una tavola d'Alberto Duro fiammingo"; Fletcher 1998, 143.

100 Brown and Lorenzoni 1982, 149–71; and Brown and Lorenzoni 2006, especially 284.

101 Braghirolli 1877, 377: "va al paragone di quel opera de M. Andrea . . . in questa istoria non pole fare chosa che stia bene"; Campbell 2004, 169–90.

102 Fletcher 1971, 711, 713; and Braghirolli 1877, 380–81.

103 Gaye 1840, 2:80: "la inventiva poetica."

104 Gaye 1840, 2:71: "La invenzione, che mi scrive V. S. che io truovi al disegno, bisognerà che l'accomodi alla fantasia di lui chel ha a fare, il quale ha piacere che molto signati termini non si diano al suo stile, uso, come dice, di sempre vagare a sua voglia nelle pitture, che quanto in lui possano soddisfare a chi le mira."

105 Venturi 1884, 604n3; and Eisler 1989, 531.

106 Braghirolli 1877, 376–77.

107 Pino, 1548, 16v: "n'ancho disegnare le tavole con tanta istrema diligenza . . . come usava Giovan Bellino, perch'è fatica gettata, havendosi à coprire il tutto con li colori."

108 Wilson 2004, 95–121; Dunkerton 2004, 220–25; and Villa 2009, especially 114–23.

109 Rowley 2008, 849. The della Robbia workshop, producing glazed terracotta sculptures, perhaps functioned similarly.

110 Rancière 2005, 22.

111 Longhi 1927, 134, first proposed the attribution; Gilbert 1956, 296–97, instead suggests Lotto; for other attributions, see Villa 2008, 320–22.

112 Rowley 2008, 848.

113 Longhi 1956: "[L]a prima opera della pittura moderna."

114 Sanudo 2004, 23:256: "Zuan Belin optimo pytor . . . la cui fama è nota per il mondo."

115 Anderson 2006, 156–59; Meyer zur Capellan 1985, 131–32; and Wilson 2004, 121.

116 Botti 1992, 60–66.

117 Sanudo 2004, 23:256.

118 This is metaphoric: the *Belliniani* presumably completed Bellini's various unfinished paintings.

119 [Michiel] 1888, 108. Recent studies considering Gentile's (almost certain) gift of the Paris sketchbook to Sultan Mehmet II include Fournier 2006, and Sizonenko 2013.

120 For Bellini's *fortuna critica* in various countries and periods, see Toscano 2004, 197–249; Tempestini 2013, 49–54; and Humfrey 2015.

121 Ruskin 1877, 38.

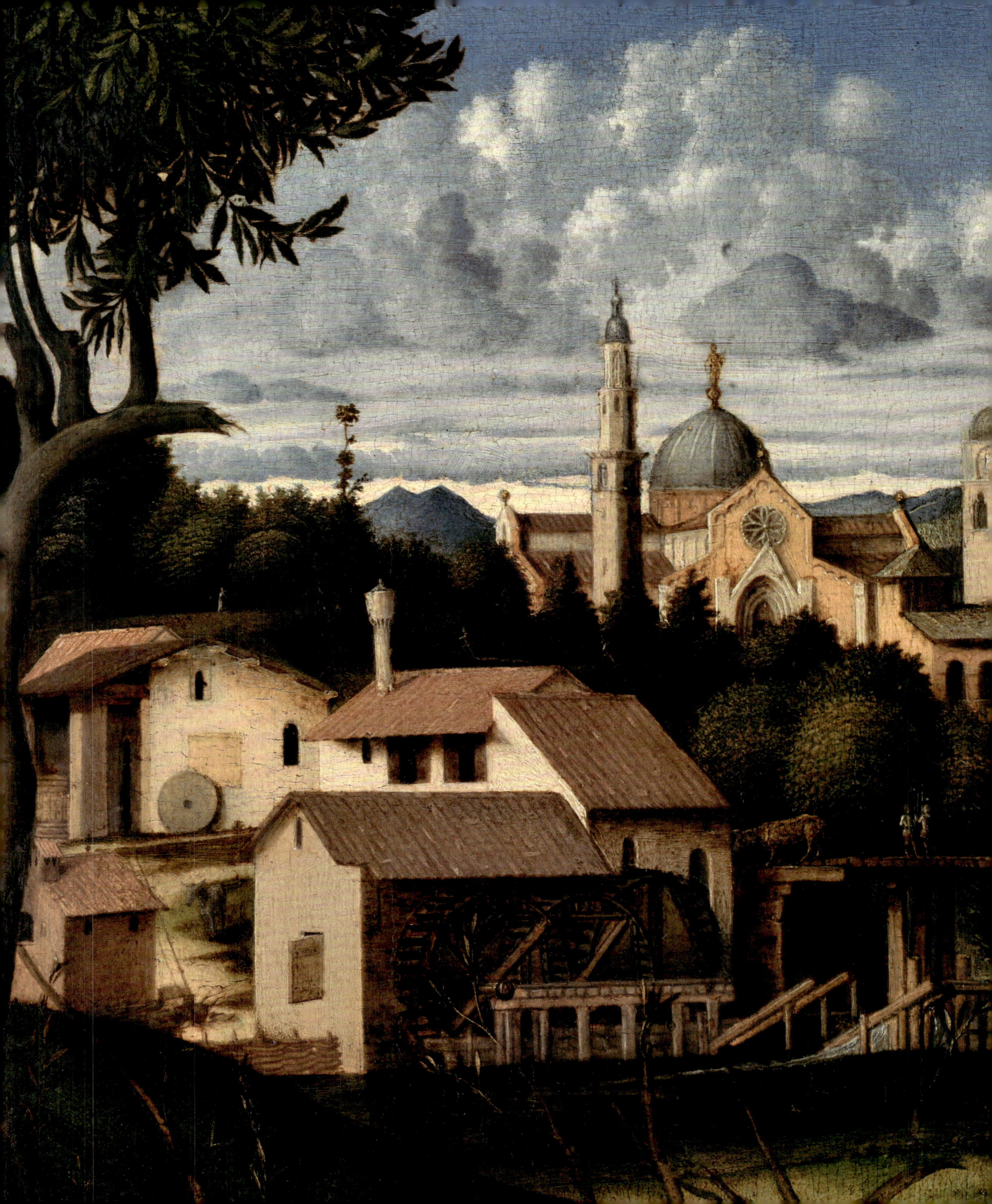

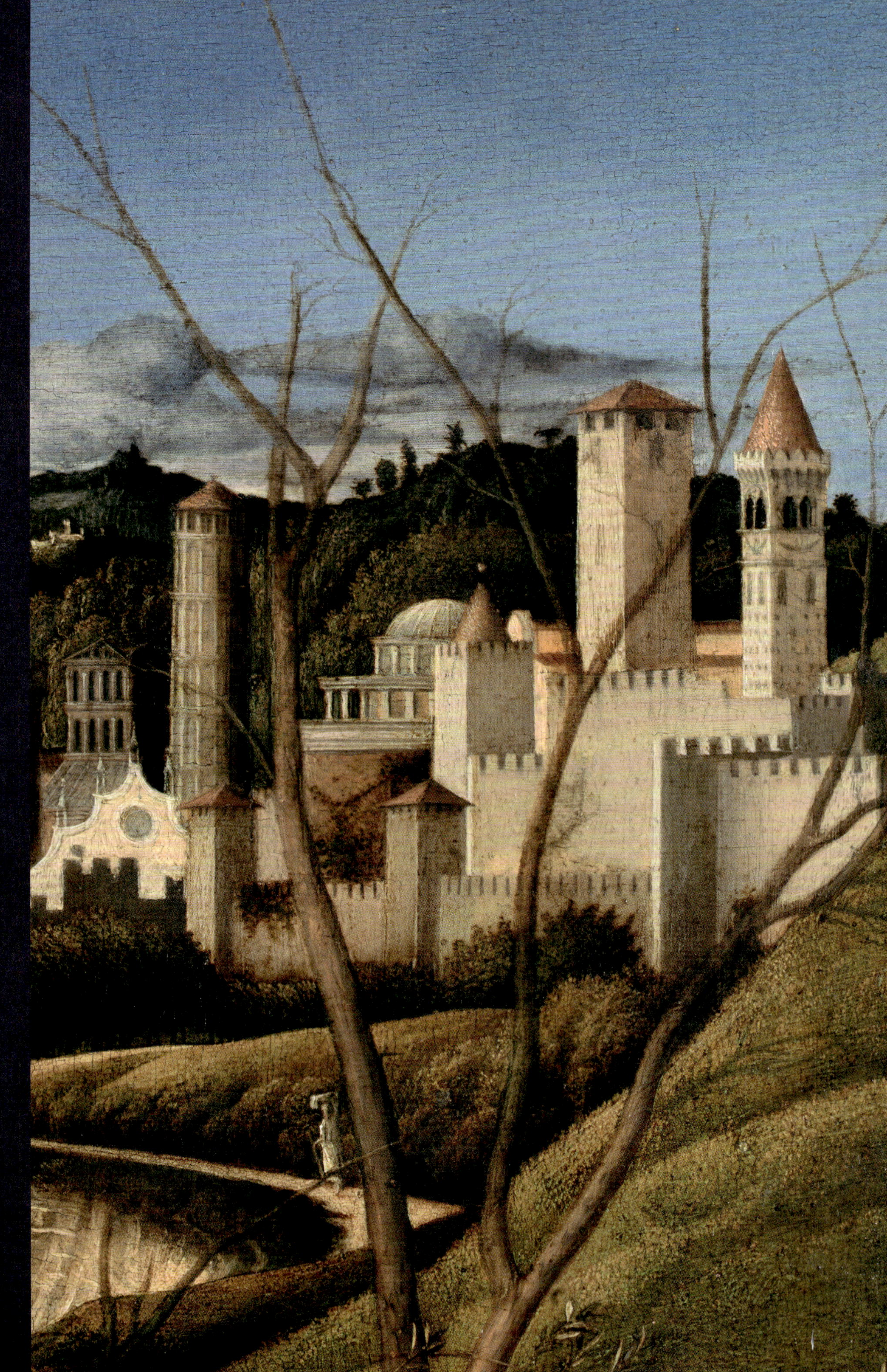

ALOGUE

1 | SAINT JEROME IN THE WILDERNESS

In the late Middle Ages, the great hagiographic collections by thirteenth-century treatise writers, such as the *Speculum historiale* by Vincent of Beauvais and the *Legenda aurea* by Jacopo da Varagine, codified the image and essential features of the life of Saint Jerome (ca. 347–420). Over the course of the fourteenth century, two texts closely associated with the Dominican culture, *Legendae de sanctis* by the Dominican friar Pietro Calò da Chioggia and *Hieronymianus* by Giovanni Andrea da Bologna, contributed to the propagation of the saint's cult, especially in northern Italy.[1] The life of Saint Jerome, one of the four doctors of the Latin Church and the author of the Vulgate, the translation of the Bible into Latin, lent itself to the emblematic representation of every aspect of Christian spirituality, from conversion following a dissolute life to ascetic meditation, from the study of sacred scriptures to apostolic and antiheterodox activity. Throughout the quattrocento and into the earliest years of the cinquecento, the image of the penitent Saint Jerome was extraordinarily widespread in the painting of the Veneto and the Po region, in particular on small panels made for private devotion. The success of the subject was certainly related to the publication, in Italian as well as Latin, of hagiographic texts and little treatises narrating his life, but it can also be tied to the inclinations of the humanists, who perceived the saint as a model of philological research into the texts of the classical authors, combined with the highest degree of Christian religiousness. The renowned humanist Guarino Veronese, for example, owned a painting on the subject by Pisanello that is now lost, but Pisanello's work was celebrated both by Guarino in verse and by Bartolomeo Facio in his brief biography of the painter.[2] The humanist Angelo Decembrio in his *De Politia Litteraria* (1462), a dialogue dedicated to the cultivated Marquess of Ferrara Leonello d'Este, argued for the great utility of "some pleasant pictures of Saint Jerome at his writing in the wilderness, by which we direct the mind to the privacy and quiet of the library and the application necessary to study and literary composition."[3] Thus paintings like the lost Pisanello and those by Bono da Ferrara (ca. 1440, London,

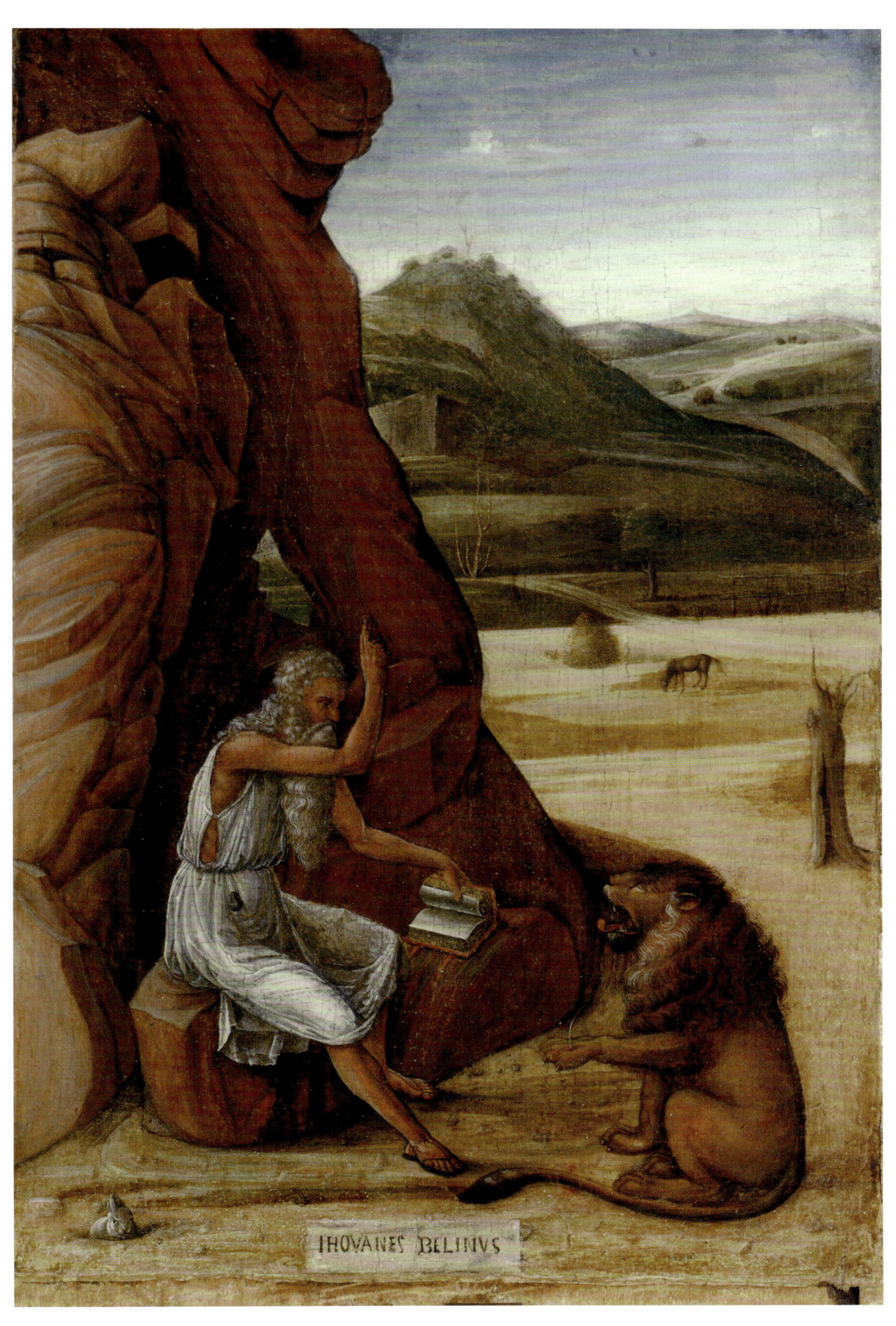

IHOVANES BELINVS

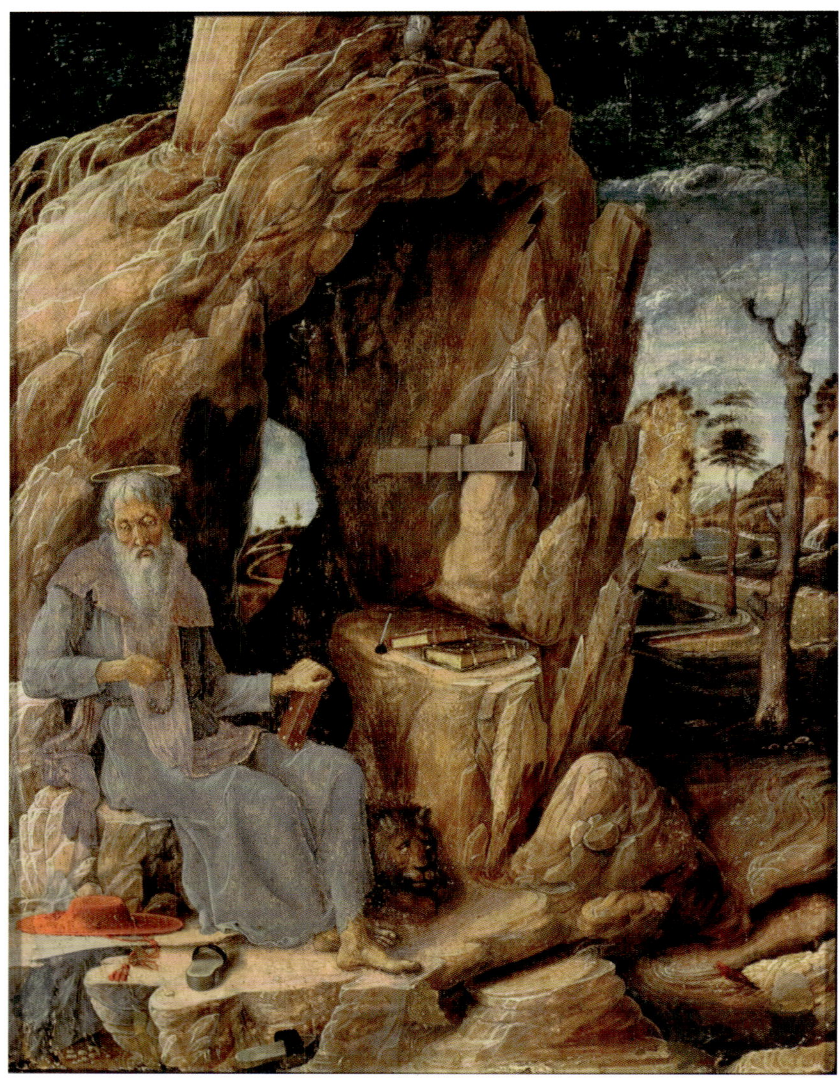

Figure 18
ANDREA MANTEGNA
(Italian, ca. 1431–1506), *Saint
Jerome in the Wilderness*,
ca. 1448–50. Panel, 48 × 36
cm (18⅞ × 14¼ in.). Museu
de Arte de São Paulo Assis
Chateaubriand, Gift Câmara
Municipal de São Paulo, 1952

National Gallery), Andrea Mantegna (ca. 1448–50,
São Paulo, Museu de Arte; fig. 18), Jacopo Bellini
(ca. 1450, Verona, Museo di Castelvecchio), and
Marco Zoppo (ca. 1450–55, Madrid, Thyssen-
Bornemisza Collection) provide a context for
understanding this important youthful effort by
Giovanni Bellini.

Bellini presents the saint as a hermit in the
Syrian desert, dressed only in a thin, white tunic
and seated on a rock in front of his cave; with his
raised right hand he blesses the lion before him,
which, roaring in pain, raises its left paw to show
a large thorn implanted in the middle. The most
significant feature of Bellini's painting lies in the
confluence within a single image of various ways
of figuring Saint Jerome: the saint as hermit and
the saint as scholar and exegete of the Bible. The
penitent described in the *Legenda aurea*—his limbs
rubbed raw by the sackcloth of his robe, his flesh
lacerated by self-mortifications and dark from
long hours exposed to the sun's rays—is effec-
tively evoked in the saint's skeletal figure, while
his devotion to the study of the sacred scriptures is
suggested by the book (its pages still blank) and the
eyeglass case hanging from his belt. The lion with
the thorn in its paw refers to another episode from
Jerome's life: after the wounded animal caused panic
among the monks of the monastery in Bethlehem
to which the saint had retired, Jerome, recogniz-
ing it as a divine messenger, took it in and healed
it, after which the lion became the saint's faithful
companion.[4] Beyond the rocky outcropping and the
cave that together dominate the painting's left foreground, a broad, deep landscape opens out; rather
than the Syrian desert, it recalls the gentle slopes of
the foothills of the Veneto that would feature prom-
inently in so many of Bellini's subsequent paintings.
Certain elements of this view could be interpreted

as other traditional symbols of the hermit's life: the dying tree in the background could represent the saint's solitary meditation and the fact that his writings would revive the sere plant of the scriptures; the donkey is a symbol of a life of solitude, penitence, and poverty; the dry, hollow tree near the protagonist would instead stand for the danger of his temptations, while the rabbit in the foreground could be a metaphor for the hermit's life in a cave.[5]

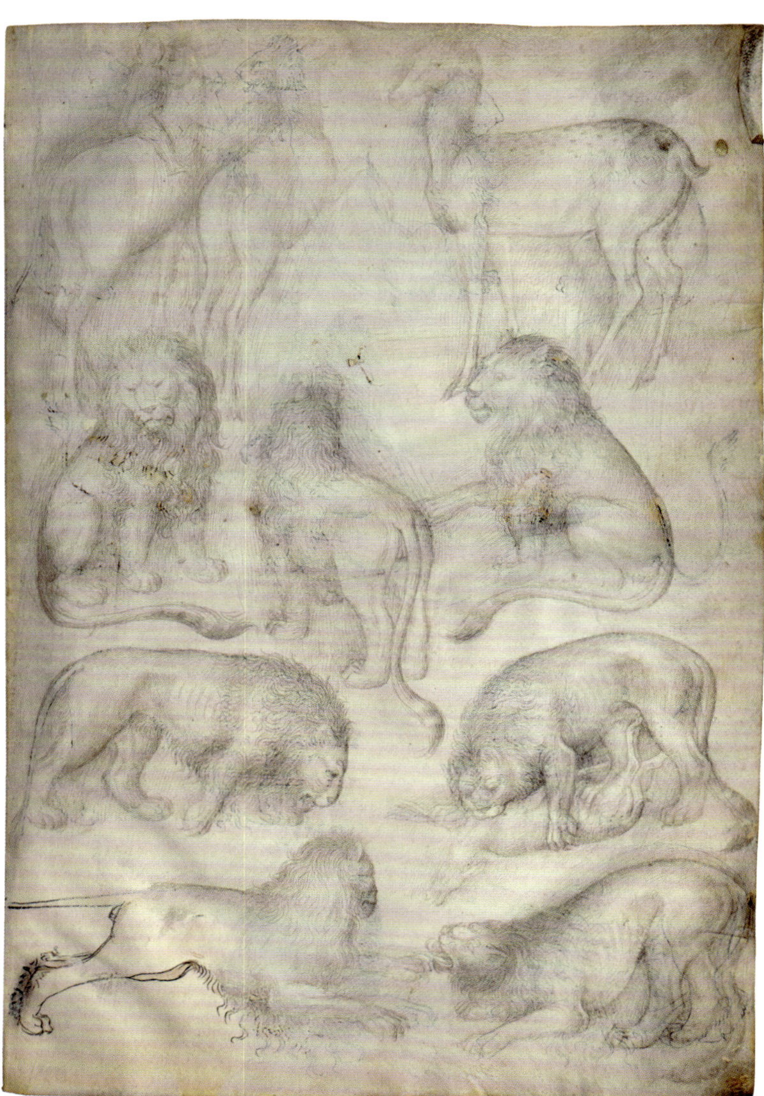

But even in this very early work by the Venetian painter, the ultimate significance of the landscape, beyond any recondite symbolic meanings, is the restoration of the profound harmony between humankind and nature. Bellini evokes the breath of the divine presence in every detail of the visible world, depicted with a naturalness and a capacity for poetic transfiguration unparalleled in the painting of the time.

Since its rediscovery in the nineteenth century, this work has generally been considered one of Bellini's very first efforts. Particularly telling in this regard is the observation by Giovanni Battista Cavalcaselle, to whom we owe the earliest description of the painting, written in 1856: "Without the name I would have suspected it to be by Jacopo himself; if it is by Giovanni it is certainly after a drawing by his father and when he was young."[6] And indeed, as has been aptly noted more than once, the point of departure for Bellini's composition appears to be his father's work, in particular the sketchbooks of drawings today in the Louvre and the British Museum:[7] Two sheets in the sketchbook in the Louvre are especially relevant: one with several drawings of lions (fol. 72v; fig. 19), one of which seems to have been borrowed directly by Giovanni for his depiction of the animal, and the other an ambitious drawing in a horizontal format, a *Saint Jerome in the Wilderness* (fol. 18v; see fig. 2). Jacopo's desert looks like an island surrounded by a sea (a city and boats can be seen in the distance beyond the inlet), densely populated by monsters and wild animals, and littered with the remains of a shipwreck on the shore. The saint, seated on a rock, is absorbed in his reading, apparently utterly undisturbed by the wild beasts. An ancient pedestal in ruins and a broken column clearly allude to the end of paganism. These same elements will

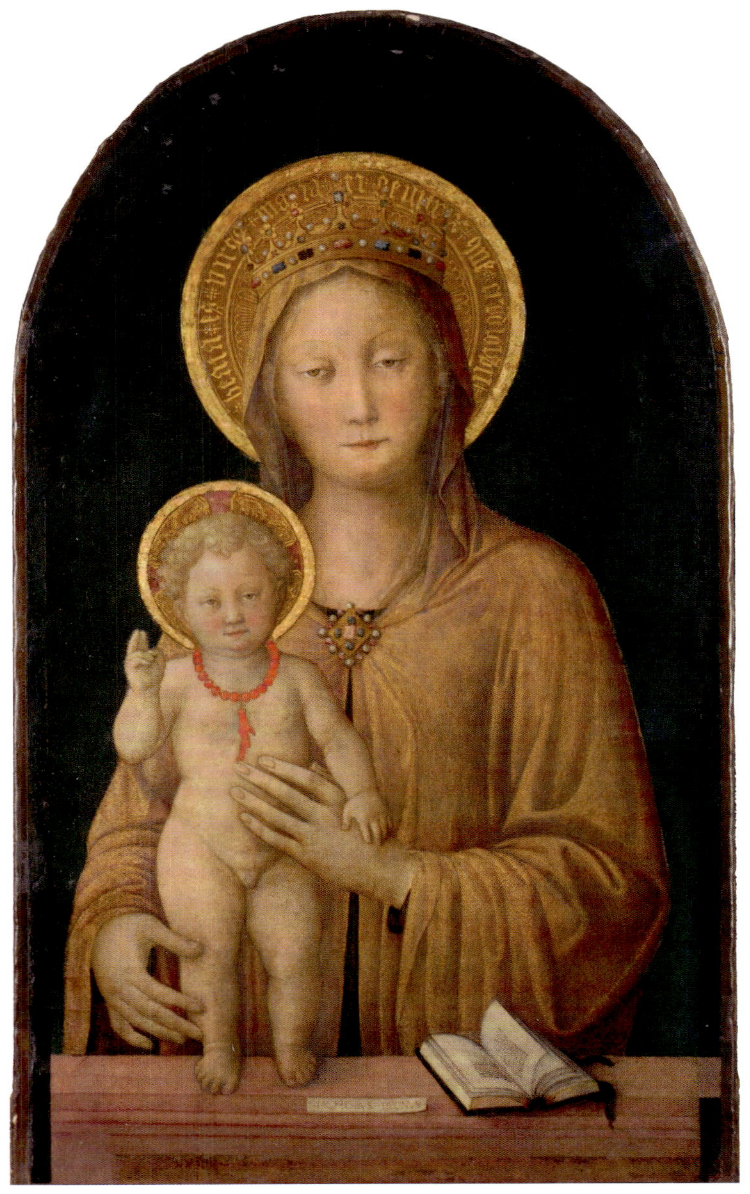

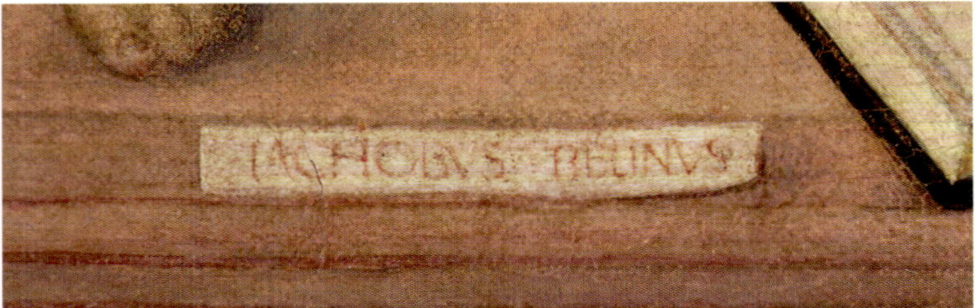

recur later in Jacopo's painting of the same subject, today in the Museo di Castelvecchio, Verona.[8] Compared with his father's compositions, crowded with details, Giovanni's vision seems decidedly more economical, with the principal figures—the saint and the lion—in the foreground and the hilly landscape extending into the distance, bathed in a soft, golden light. The underdrawing, however, recently revealed by reflectographic analysis, shows Giovanni's ongoing debt to his father: the figure of the saint displays thick contour lines, drawn directly freehand with the brush and then built up with short, precise hatchmarks that outline the passages that would later be modeled in chiaroscuro, such as the musculature of the raised arm and the folds of the robe.[9] The second important point of reference for Giovanni lay in the works of Mantegna: the composition of the Birmingham painting in fact recalls Mantegna's fresco with the *Calling of Saints James and John* in the upper register of the Ovetari Chapel in the church of the Eremitani, Padua (ca. 1450) and also the superb *Saint Jerome in the Wilderness* in the Museu de Arte, São Paulo (ca. 1448–50; see fig. 18).[10] Clearly, Giovanni drew on these two sources for his idea of the powerful rock formation that dominates the left side of the composition, while, on the right, the luminous landscape stretches into the background.

Figure 20
JACOPO BELLINI
(Italian, ca. 1390–95–
ca. 1470/71), *Madonna and
Child* (*Tadini Madonna*),
ca. 1450. Canvas, 98 × 58 cm
(38⅝ × 22⅞ in.). Lovere,
Galleria dell'Accademia
Tadini, P 27. The detail below
shows Jacopo's signature.

All the scholars who have studied this work agree that it is probably Giovanni Bellini's earliest, but opinions on the date of its execution vary considerably, ranging from 1445 to about 1460.[11] The differences in the dates proposed depend largely on what birth date is put forward for the artist, one of the most vexed questions in the entire history of Italian Renaissance art.[12] I am convinced that Giovanni was born around 1435, that he was somewhat younger than his brother-in-law, Andrea Mantegna, and that he began painting independently toward the mid-1450s. In my view, the Birmingham *Saint Jerome* should be dated about 1455, the first in a series of masterpieces that would include, in the second half of the 1450s and the early 1460s, works characterized by an increasingly intense dialogue with Mantegna, such as the *Imago Pietatis* in the Museo Poldi Pezzoli, Milan, and the *Transfiguration* in the Museo Correr, Venice, and culminate in the climax of this exchange with the great Paduan painter represented by the *Agony in the Garden* in the National Gallery, London (see fig. 1). It should be noted that this exchange in no way negates Giovanni's notable independence of mind: even when he appears to be copying Mantegna almost literally, he always introduces a vision that is subtly antithetical to his brother-in-law's and absolutely personal.

The letters of the signature on the *cartellino* in the foreground, accepted as autograph by nearly all scholars,[13] are in Roman capitals that are still rather "primitive," compared with the more sophisticated *litterae antiquae* that appear later in the artist's paintings (for example, in the only slightly later *Pietà* in the Accademia Carrara, Bergamo). What is entirely unusual is the spelling of his given name (IHOVANES, instead of the more customary IOHANNES), while the single *L* in the last name—also written in a similarly styled capital —also appears in the signature of Jacopo Bellini's *Madonna and Child* in the Accademia Tadini, Lovere (ca. 1450; fig. 20).[14]

D.G.

<hr>

1 See Lattanzi 1983, 55–59.

2 The writings by Guarino and Bartolomeo Facio on Pisanello's lost *Saint Jerome* are in Cordellier 1995, doc. nos. 10 and 75.

3 "Ideoque saepenumero cernere est quibusdam iucundissimam imaginem esse Hieronymi describentis in eremo, per quam in bibliothecis solitudinem et silentium, et studendi scribendique sedulitatem opportunam advertimus": see Baxandall 1965, 196.

4 For this episode's iconographic tradition, see Ring 1945.

5 Gentili 2004, 167–68.

6 Cf. D. Levi 1988, 66, 94n174.

7 Degenhart and Schmitt 1990.

8 See, most recently, Marini, in Marini et al. 2010, 115–17, cat. no. 72.

9 Villa 2009, 18–19.

10 Humfrey, in Edinburgh 2004, 60, cat. no. 2; on the Ovetari frescoes, cf. Lightbown 1986, 394–96; for the São Paulo *Saint Jerome*, see Christiansen, in London 1992a, 114–16, cat. no. 3.

11 For a summary of the various opinions expressed by scholars on the painting's chronology, see Lucco, in Rome 2008, 136–38, cat. no. 2.

12 See the essay by Daniel Wallace Maze in this volume.

13 Debra Pincus believes this to be a later addition; Pincus 2008, 114n17.

14 Eisler 1989, 53–56

ca. 1458–59, panel, 53.3 × 29.5 cm (21 × 11⅝ in.)

Venice, Museo Correr, inv. cl. I, 28

2 | CRUCIFIXION WITH THE VIRGIN AND SAINT JOHN THE EVANGELIST

INSCRIPTIONS
ΙΗΣΟΣ ΒΑΣΙΛΕΥΣ ΤΩΝ ΟΜΟ
ΛΟΓΟΥΜΕΝΩΝ (Jesus, King
of the Confessors) (on the
titulus on the cross); IC XC
(Jesus Christ) (on the arms of
the cross)

PROVENANCE
Teodoro Correr, bequeathed
to the museum in 1830

RESTORATIONS
1946 (Mauro Pellicioli); 1991–92
(Sabina Vedovello, CBC—
Conservazione Beni Culturali)

EXHIBITIONS
Venice 1949, cat. no. 40; Venice
1999, cat. no. 12; Venice 2000,
cat. no. 24; Rome 2008, cat.
no. 15

The panel's small size and the extremely meticulous approach to its execution indicate that this is a painting intended for private devotion. In the center, the crucified Christ is set off against an intensely blue sky, on which is painted, with delicate gold highlights, a crowd of cherubim, while below, at the foot of the cross and in the foreground, are the grieving figures of the Virgin and Saint John the Evangelist. The foreground and middle ground are clearly distinct from one another: The cross is planted into a rocky shelf that forms almost a natural stage on which the actors in the sacred performance are arranged, while beyond it a luxuriant rural landscape opens out, populated with soldiers, horses, and other figures that sometimes interact with one another, entirely unaware of what is taking place in the foreground. Our gaze is thus lost in the distance, wandering over the delicate contours of the verdant hills, along the road leading to a rustic bridge across a river that winds its meandering way back, until it vanishes in the azure distance of the far off mountains in the background.

It has been convincingly demonstrated, on the basis of epigraphic and X-ray analyses, that the Greek inscription on the *titulus* on the cross (which may be translated as "Jesus, King of the Confessors) is a later, probably sixteenth-century addition.[1] And indeed the Greek letters are unlike the elegant characters employed in the trilingual inscription—in Latin, Greek, and Hebrew—of the *titulus* in the Niccolini *Crucifixion* (see cat. no. 8).

It has been observed that the composition's structure, with Christ on the cross flanked by the two mourners and watched by choirs of cherubim above him, goes back to a drawing by Giovanni's father, Jacopo, in his album of drawings in the Louvre (fol. 55r; fig. 21).[2] However, while this was undoubtedly Giovanni's starting point, the sculptural power and muscular configuration of Christ's body, like the calligraphic quality of the draperies of the Virgin and Saint John, testify to the contact between Bellini and Mantegna that had occurred by this date—a contact that proved especially important for Bellini, as evidenced by the painting's foreground. It has been noted that the rocky

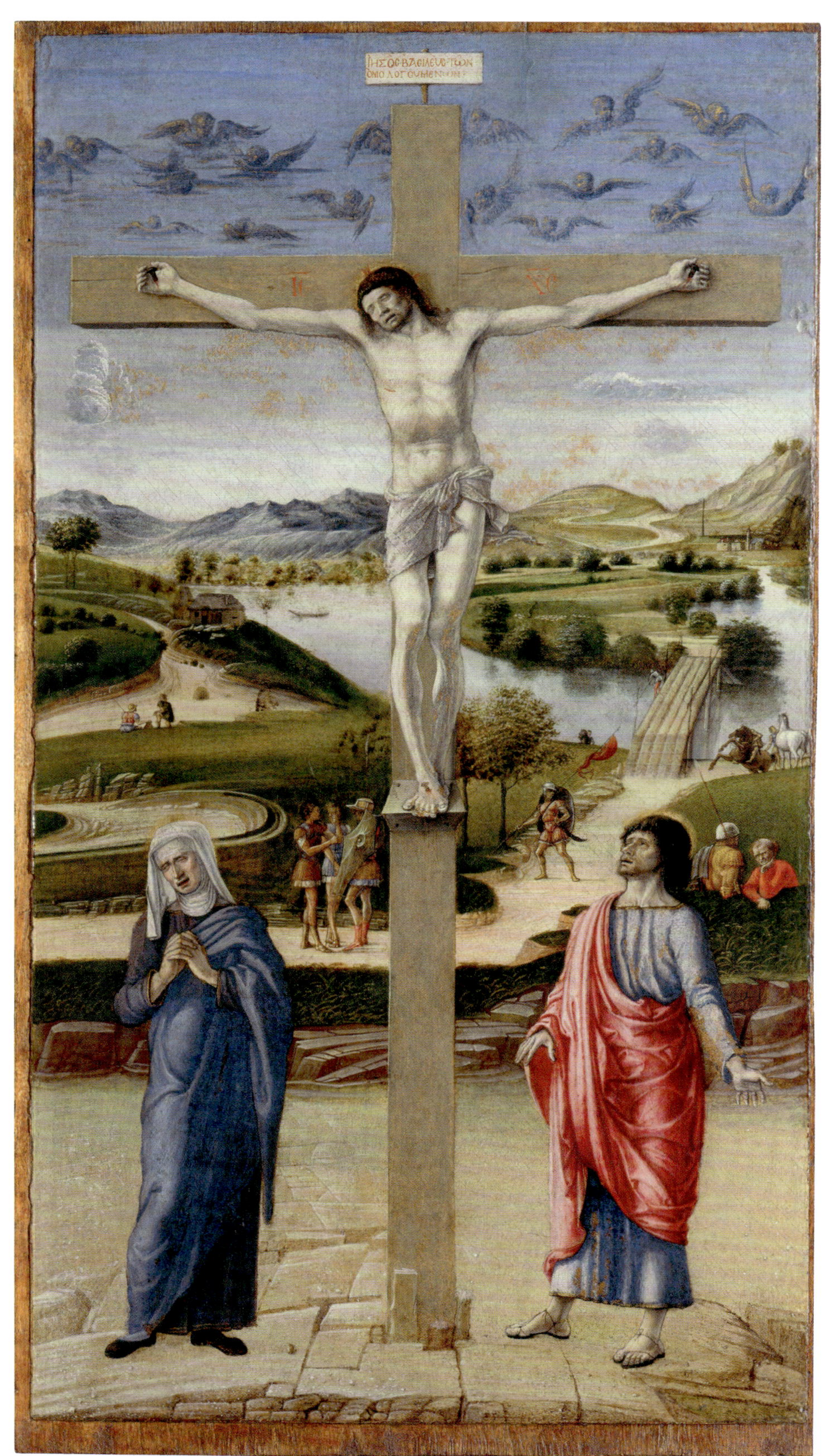
ΙΗΣΟϹ ΒΑϹΙΛΕΥϹ ΤΩΝ
ΟΜΟΛΟΓΟΥΜΕΝΩΝ

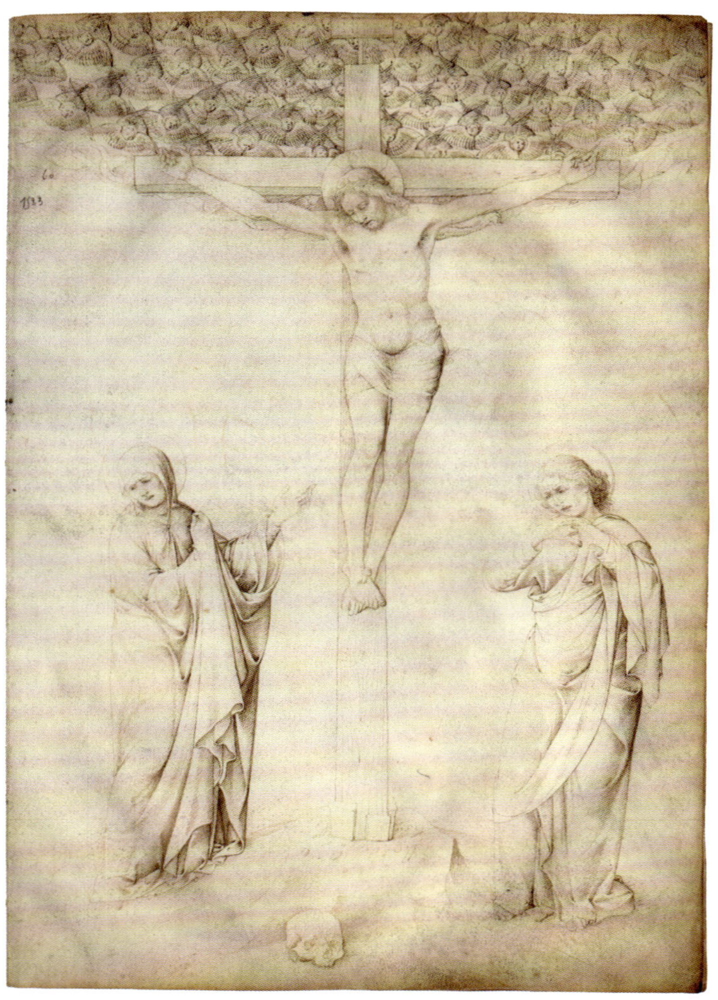

platform on which the figures stand—and even the way in which the cross is literally stuck into the stone—would be inconceivable without the precedent of Mantegna's *Crucifixion*, today in the Louvre, but once the central element of the predella of the Saint Zeno altarpiece in Verona, which the Paduan painter executed between 1457 and 1459 (fig. 22).[3] We can imagine that Bellini had immediate access to the latter work while Mantegna was painting it in Padua (we should recall that in 1453 Andrea had married Giovanni's sister, Nicolosia, and that relations between the two families were very close). The specific pattern of the rocks that can be seen just behind the cross appears in another of Bellini's works as well, the *Transfiguration* (ca. 1457–58) in the Museo Correr, Venice, and it also recurs in a drawing by Mantegna, *Christ's Descent into Limbo* (ca. 1465, Paris, École des Beaux-Arts),[4] suggesting a likely exchange of models between the two workshops. Similar rock formations, as well as the landscape visible in the distance (and even the shape of the trees), appear in the *Imago Pietatis* in the Museo Poldi Pezzoli, Milan, which has convincingly been assigned a date of about 1457.[5] Further proof of Bellini's intense dialogue with Mantegna in the late 1450s, and of the profound impression made upon him by the *Crucifixion* in the predella of the Saint Zeno altarpiece, lies in a beautiful drawing in the British Museum with a *Crucifixion* (see fig. 28), generally attributed to a follower of Mantegna, but which several scholars have persuasively ascribed to the hand of the young Bellini.[6]

The wonderful landscape that opens out behind the foreground figures is unquestionably the painting's most innovative and impressive feature, as well as Bellini's most important landscape before the *Agony in the Garden* in the National Gallery, London (see fig. 1). Here, too, there is evidence of the

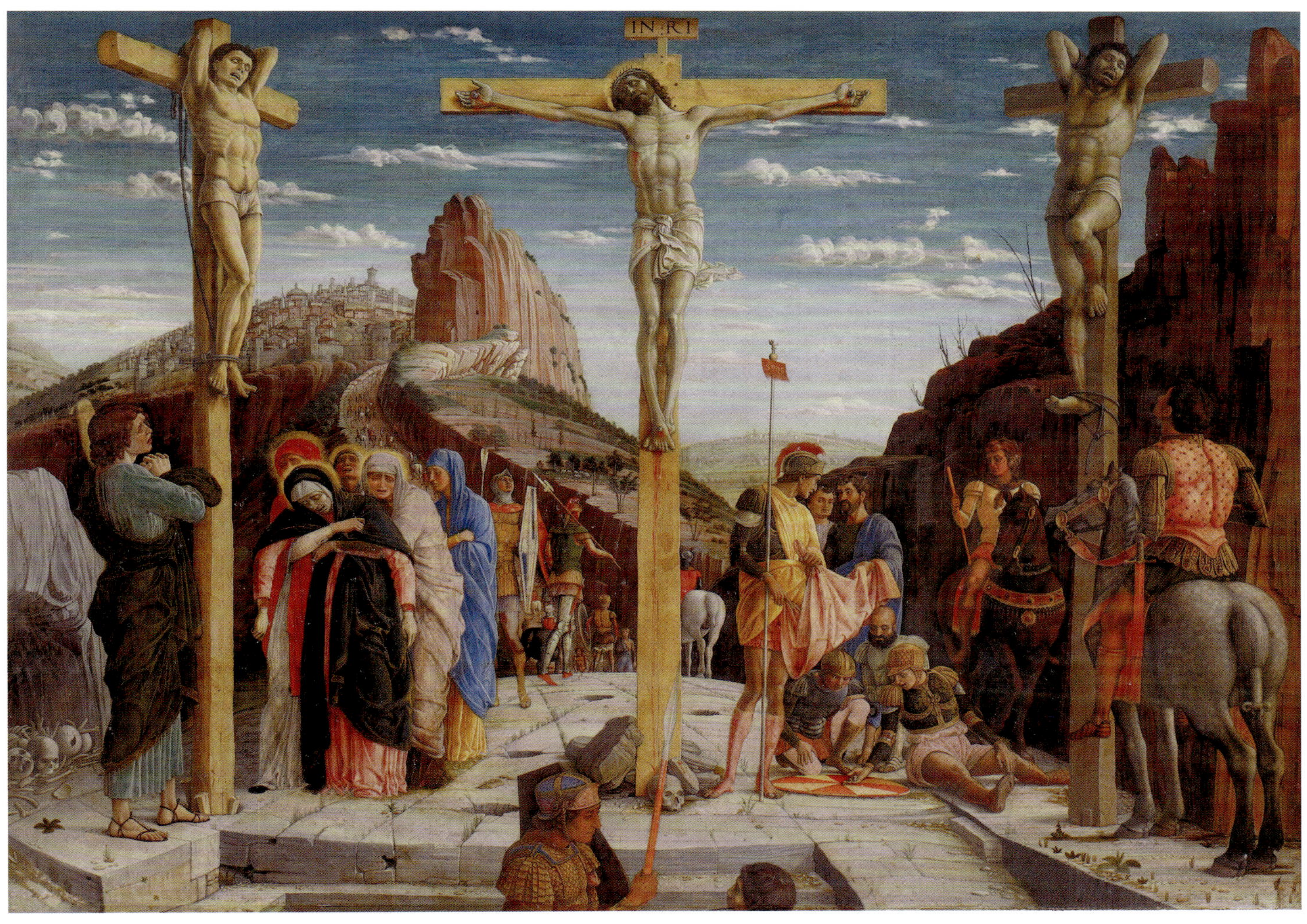

Figure 22
ANDREA MANTEGNA
(Italian, ca. 1431–1506),
Crucifixion, ca. 1457–59. Panel,
76 × 96 cm (29⅞ × 37¾ in.).
Paris, Musée du Louvre, 368

dialogue with Andrea Mantegna: in the only slightly earlier *Adoration of the Shepherds* (ca. 1455–56, New York, Metropolitan Museum of Art), his analytical description of the rock formations, the river meandering toward the horizon, and the excavated paths peopled with small figures offer one of the earliest examples in quattrocento Italian painting of a landscape in the Flemish style.[7]

Indeed, the topography of Giovanni's landscape seems to descend directly from northern European models that were certainly known in Venice at the time. One significant example is a *Crucifixion* (after 1430, Venice, Cà d'Oro) attributable to a Flemish follower of Jan van Eyck (ca. 1390–1441), who must certainly have been in the Veneto at an early date, since an exact replica of the work (unfinished) is known, probably executed by a Paduan painter about 1450 (Padua, Museo Civico).[8] The aspects that must have struck the imagination of Italian artists would have been, on the one hand, the extraordinarily meticulous execution of the details and the fantastic cityscape in the background, and,

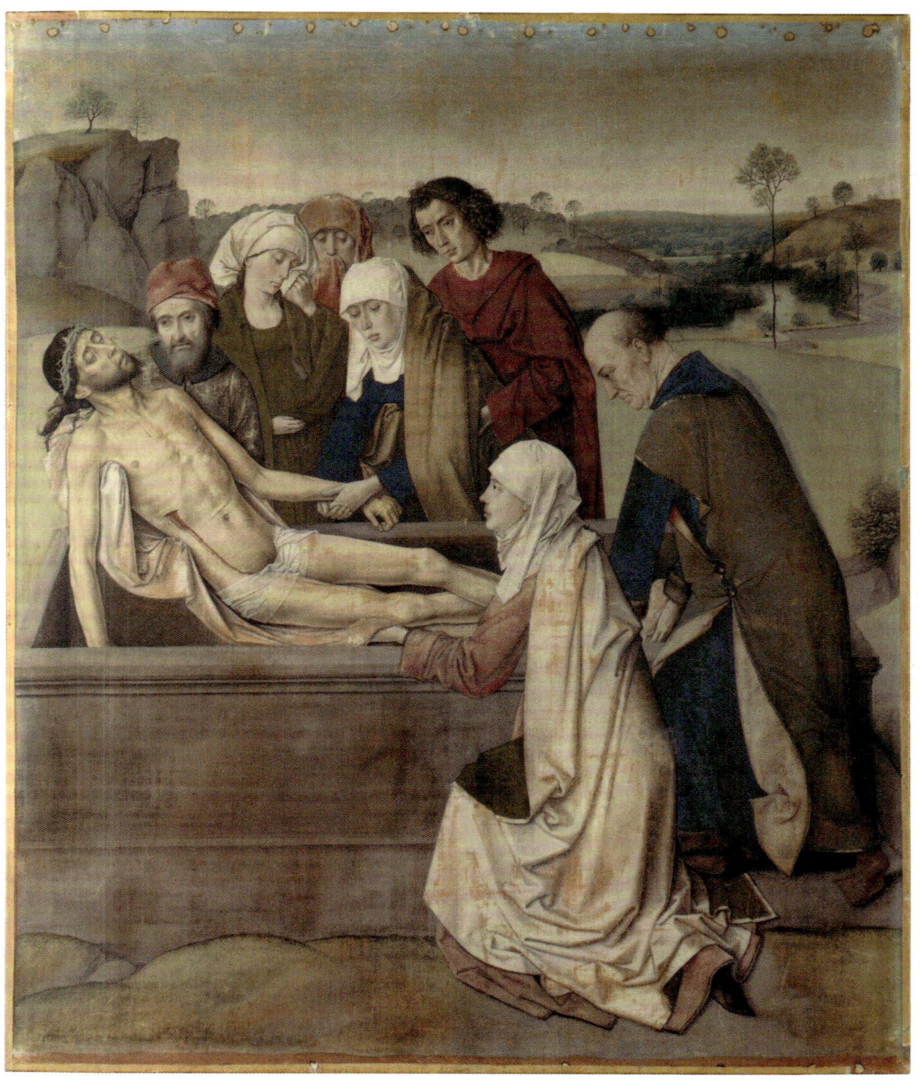

on the other, the contrast between the crucified Christ and the mourning figures in the foreground and, behind them, opening out as far as the eye can see, a vast landscape in which other figures act, completely indifferent to the drama taking place in the foreground. Another model that might have directly influenced the composition of Giovanni's landscape in the Museo Correr's small panel is a series of paintings on canvas by Dieric Bouts the Elder, today dispersed among several collections, but which at one time probably made up the various compartments of a polyptych that was likely displayed in a Venetian church as early as the 1450s.[9] It is possible that the central element of this polyptych was the badly damaged *Crucifixion* today in Brussels (Musées Royaux des Beaux-Arts), which displays a broad vista with a river at the center that winds into the background amid a hilly landscape enlivened by copses and views of buildings. Bellini must also have carefully studied the landscape in the background of another painting of this group, the London *Entombment* (fig. 23), which depicts a sheet of water surrounded by clusters of little trees and a view that extends to the far horizon.[10]

As with many others of Bellini's youthful works, there is a great diversity of opinion about the precise date of this painting, and a very wide range, from 1453 to 1471.[11] In my view, a date of the late 1450s is the most compatible with its stylistic features. Keith Christiansen has insightfully pointed out that in this work, more than in any other, Bellini demonstrates a meticulous attention to the details, "which are painted with the exquisite touch of a miniaturist."[12] Especially telling to me is the comparison with the miniatures in Guarino Veronese's translation of Strabo's *Geography* (Albi, Bibliothèque Municipale), executed between 1458 and 1459 for the Venetian nobleman Jacopo Antonio Marcello and convincingly attributed to Bellini by Luciano Bellosi.[13] The type of the figures in the miniatures, with their prominent chin and jaw and the particular shape of the palm of the hand and of the fingers, is very close to that in the Venice *Crucifixion*, while the palette of sharp colors and the analytical taste for detail displayed in the two sheets have much in common with our *Crucifixion*.

In this youthful work, Bellini already reveals his extraordinary capacity for combining devotional feeling with a faithfulness to nature that would make him the most important religious painter in the second half of the quattrocento. No one was able to evoke better than he the intangible substance of air by means of delicate light and color, to suggest the perfect integration of the figures with their surroundings, or to emphasize the dramatic contrast between the sorrow that suffuses the foreground and the indifference of human beings and things in the distance. Christ's sacrifice is placed dramatically before our eyes, while in the background the world presents itself in all the blazing beauty of a radiant spring day.

D.G.

---

1   Lucco and Pontani 1997, 111–20.

2   See, for example, Robertson 1968, 31–32.

3   See, for example, Aikema, in Venice 1999, 206–7, cat. no. 12; Christiansen 2004a, 54–56.

4   This was observed by Antonio Mazzotta (quoted in Servi, in Paris 2008, 200–201, cat. no. 68) and Lucco, in Rome 2008, 148–51, cat. no. 6.

5   Di Lorenzo, in Milan 2012, 56–59, cat. no. 4.

6   See Bellosi, in Paris 2008, 168–69, cat. no. 56.

7   See De Marchi, in Paris 2008, 160–61, cat. no. 50.

8   Aikema 2003, 39–43.

9   For Bouts's polyptych, see L. Campbell 1998, 38–45; Wolfthal and Metzger 2014, 46–87.

10 Lucco 2004, 82, and Christiansen 2004a, 56, have correctly emphasized how important the model of Bouts's canvases was to Bellini.

11 A specific survey of these different opinions was recently published by Lucco, in Rome 2008, 182–85, cat. no. 15.

12 Christiansen 2004a, 54.

13 Bellosi, in Paris 2008, 122–23, cat. nos. 32, 33; for the comparison between the figures in the *Crucifixion* and those in the Albi miniatures, see Christiansen 2004a, 57–58.

GIOVANNI BELLINI (Venice, ca. 1435–1516)

ca. 1465, panel, 71.2 × 62.4 cm (28 × 25¼ in.)

Paris, Musée du Louvre, R.F. 1970-39

3 | CRUCIFIXION WITH THE VIRGIN AND SAINT JOHN THE EVANGELIST

INSCRIPTION
I[esus] N[azarenus] R[ex]
I[udaeorum] (Jesus of
Nazareth, King of the Jews) (in
Latin, on the arms of the cross)

PROVENANCE
Venice, Santa Maria della
Carità, by about 1807 (?); Hill
Top, Midhurst, Sussex, Richard
Fisher — Richard Chester
Fisher, documented in 1865 and
1887; London, Agnew; Paris,
Rudolf Kann, documented
in 1900 and 1907; New York,
Joseph Duveen, documented
in 1907; Florence, Elia Volpi,
1907–13; Florence–London,
Charles Fairfax Murray,
documented in 1913; Florence,
Alessandro Contini Bonacossi
and his heirs until 1970

RESTORATION
1996–97 (Musée du Louvre)

EXHIBITIONS
London 1865, cat. no. 69;
Venice 1949, cat. no. 42; Rome
2008, cat. no. 8; Milan 2014,
cat. no. 22

The painting's critical fortunes in modern art historical scholarship began with Giovanni Battista Cavalcaselle's memorable stylistic analysis.[1] In 1865 the Italian art historian saw this *Crucifixion with the Virgin and Saint John the Evangelist* exhibited at the British Institution, London, as a work by Andrea Mantegna and attributed it to Giovanni Bellini, an opinion endorsed by all subsequent commentators. At the time, the panel belonged to a connoisseur of Italian prints, Richard Fisher, and it was still in his collection in 1887, when Jean-Paul Richter saw it and wrote about it with equal insight to Giovanni Morelli on September 1, 1887, observing that the work was "in excellent condition."[2] Today, however, there are abrasions on the Virgin's mantle; the background is in particularly poor condition, dotted with mountains that have all but faded away and with trees and bushes whose greenery has deteriorated. In addition, scoring has surfaced at the level of the rightmost tower, evidence that the paint has worn away. Richter, who visited the Fisher collection at Hill Top, in Midhurst, Sussex, between August 20 and 22, noted in his diary, "he

has a Crucifixion by Bellini" and recorded that he had made a sketch of the painting.[3]

We next find Giovanni Bellini's *Crucifixion* in Rudolf Kann's collection in Paris, where it was recorded by Wilhelm Bode and Émile Michel in 1900, and then in 1907, when it was perceptively discussed by the anonymous author of the catalogue of the Kann collection.[4] We also know that the painting was in the possession of the Florentine dealer Elia Volpi and that eventually (and regrettably), through the agency of Alessandro Contini Bonacossi, it left Italy to be acquired by the Louvre in 1970.[5] A letter of September 24, 1913, sent from Charles Fairfax Murray in Florence to Richard Fisher, allows us to add new details to what had been known about the collection history of the *Crucifixion* during the eighteenth and nineteenth centuries.[6] From this document we learn that the work's passage from the Fisher collection to Kann's was brokered by the London antiques dealer Agnew, and that it was passed from Kann to Volpi through the influential Anglo-American art dealer Joseph Duveen. Duveen had enlisted Bode, the first director

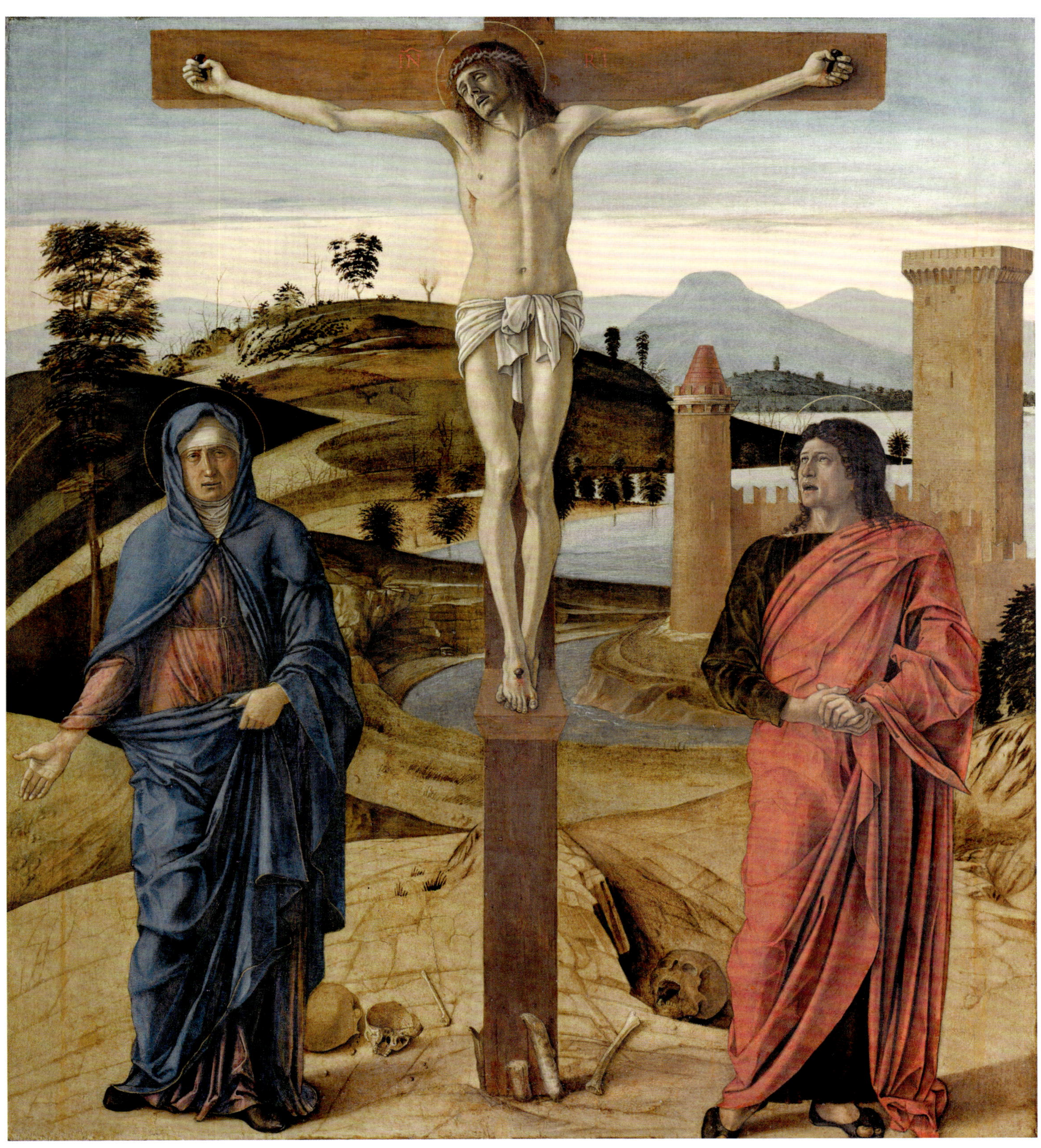

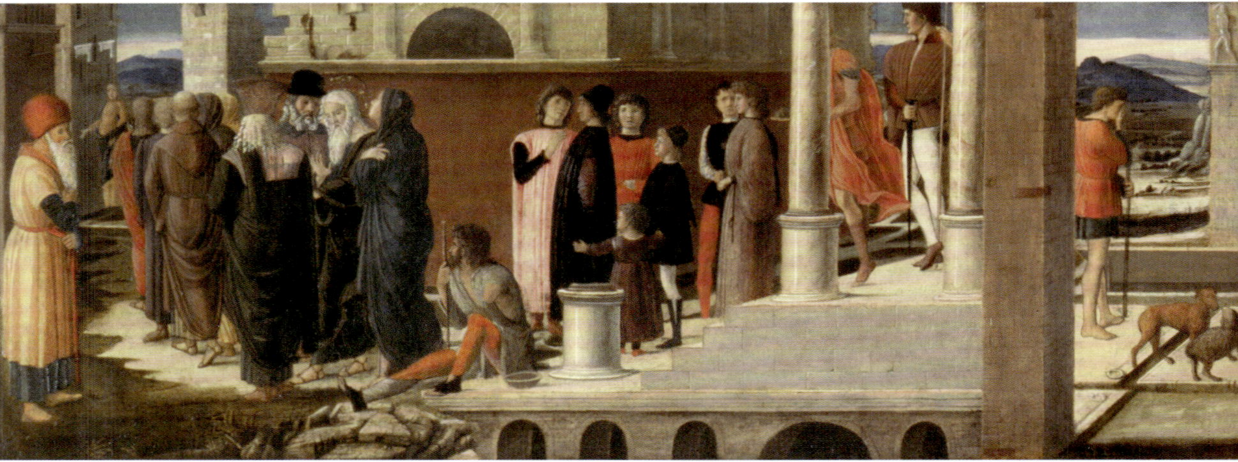

of Berlin's Kaiser-Friedrich-Museum, to help in selling the Kann collection. Curiously, though, Duveen had been unable to interest him in Bellini's *Crucifixion*, a painting that Bode had long been aware of, since he had compiled the catalogue of the collection in 1900. It is here where Charles Fairfax Murray enters our story with his 1913 letter. Besides recounting the episodes summarized above, Murray informed Fisher, the painting's former owner, that he had bought it from Volpi, who had been compelled to sell the picture, having brought in less than he had hoped from selling his collection.[7]

With regard to the work's original location, Mauro Lucco recently revived a suggestion by Alessandro Conti—also posited by Giles Robertson in 1968, who, however, attributed the painting not to Giovanni Bellini but to Lauro Padovano. According to this hypothesis, the Louvre *Crucifixion* was the apex of an altarpiece installed in the chapel of Saint John the Evangelist, on the Epistle side of the high altar of the church of Santa Maria della Carità in Venice.[8] The altarpiece was recorded in situ in Marcantonio Michiel's *Notizia*, Antonio Maria Zanetti's guides to the city, and Vittorio Malamani's index.[9]

We owe the earliest and most detailed description of the work to Marco Boschini: "In the chapel of Saint John, on the left side of the high altar, there is a panel with many buildings and numbers of figures; it is said to concern the life of Saint John the Baptist: as at the bottom, too, there is another, smaller compartment, with many figures, and above on top Our Lord on the Cross; a work entirely by Vittore Carpaccio."[10]

The poor state of conservation bemoaned by Zanetti must have affected chiefly the middle panel, which is considered lost, whereas the third part of the decorative complex, as remarked upon in a letter of April 20, 1902, from Gustav Ludwig to Georg Gronau, is identified with the predella with *Stories of Saint John the Evangelist and Drusiana*, now in Schloss Berchtesgaden, Munich, but then in Berlin in the Richard von Kaufmann collection (fig. 24).[11] An eighteenth-century inscription recently discovered on the back of this panel reads: "N. 22 / Chiesa della Carità."[12] This definitively resolves the inconsistency in the hypothesis of Ulrike Bauer Eberhardt, who rejected the identification of the Berchtesgaden panel as the predella from the chapel

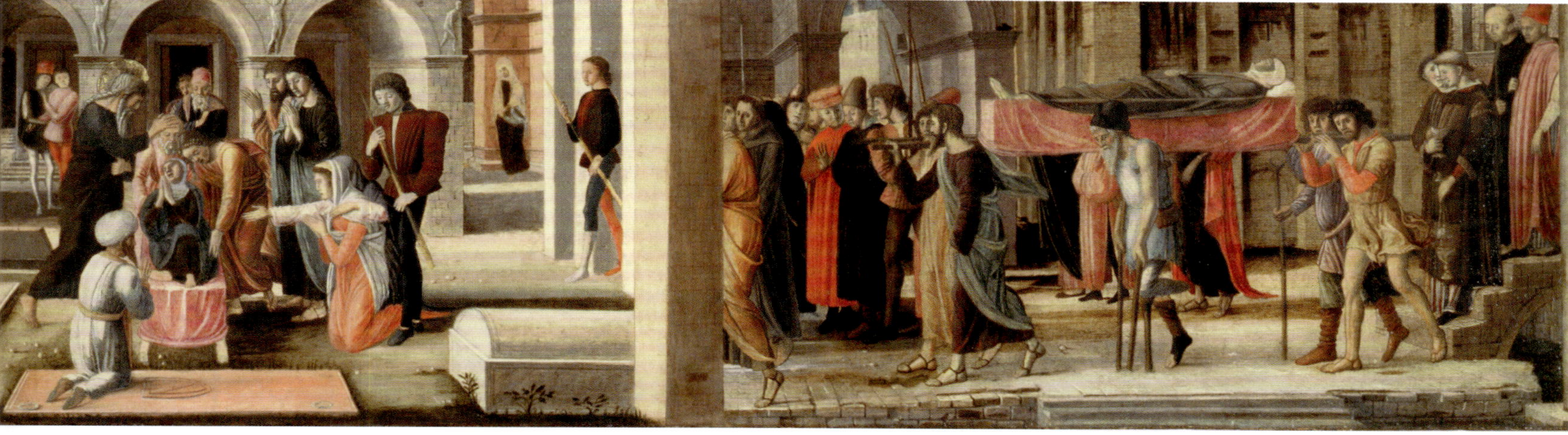

of Saint John the Evangelist in Santa Maria della Carità.[13] As Andrea De Marchi pointed out to me, a further indication of the predella's provenance from Santa Maria della Carità is the narrative sequence of the episodes from right to left, that is, toward the high altar, a seemingly eccentric choice but perfectly appropriate for the altar's placement on the Epistle side. What remains unclear, however, is the subject of the main panel. Even Boschini was unsure, cautiously prefacing his description of the subject with "it is said." We can, however, suppose with some certainty that it showed Saint John the Evangelist, given that on the opposite side of the church there was a chapel dedicated to Saint John the Baptist, adorned with Benedetto Diana's *Baptism of Christ with Angels and Saints Paul, James, Augustine, and Jerome* (Vercelli, Museo Borgogna).[14]

On the back of the Berchtesgaden panel, a sketch of the loincloth and legs of the crucified Christ, hidden by brown paint and revealed by infrared reflectography (fig. 25),[15] confirms the hypothesis and helps to date the predella to a period close to that of the San Zanipolo polyptych (ca. 1465), which, famously, displays a great many

sketches, especially caricatures, on the back of the panels.[16] The reconstruction proposed by Lucco, following the model of the square altarpieces painted by Marco Zoppo and Giovanni Bellini for Pesaro, is also supported by the similar proportion of *cimasa* to predella—1:3. Even though neither the Louvre *Crucifixion* nor the Berchtesgaden predella has come down to us with its original dimensions—the former was, in fact, cut down and cradled—it seems likely that they were reduced only slightly. It should also be noted that the *Crucifixion*'s ratio of height to width is smaller in its vertical dimensions than the ratios of the Crucifixions made for private devotion and now in Venice (cat. no. 2), Florence (cat. no. 6), and Prato (cat. no. 8).

On the question of the shape of the altarpiece, guided by the observations of Boschini and Zanetti, it appears unlikely that the lost central panel consisted of a single field.[17] It might instead have been a hagiographic panel, given the "quantities of figures" and the "many buildings" mentioned by Boschini. I have argued elsewhere that this may have been organized along similar lines to Antonio Vivarini's now fragmentary *Stories of Saint Peter*

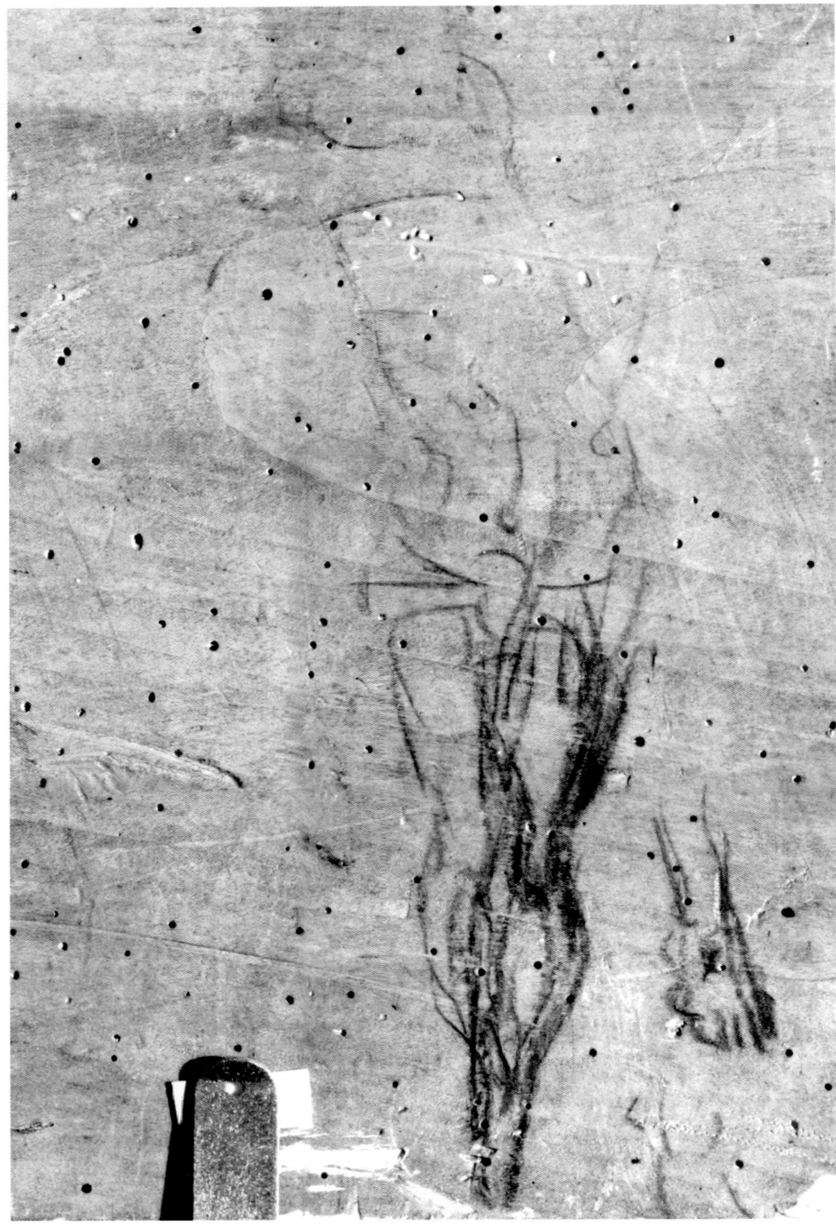

Martyr and the *Saint Apollonia* and *Saint Augustine* executed in collaboration with Giovanni d'Alemagna.[18] Alternatively—and I now believe this to be the most likely hypothesis, given the predella's structure—it took the form of a polyptych and was only slightly earlier in date to the one in San Zanipolo, which also displays many compartments and many figures. This altarpiece for Venice's Dominican church also resembled the painting in the Carità with its *cimasa* that rose above the main register, but whose subject was *God the Father*.[19] This structural innovation would be developed definitively by Giovanni Bellini himself and by Marco Zoppo in their single-field altarpieces for Pesaro's two Franciscan churches.

This structural typology that informed the development of the altarpiece in the 1460s makes it difficult to date the Berchtesgaden predella to 1453–55, as Luciano Bellosi has proposed.[20] Another argument against an early date is the fact that Antonio Vivarini, a painter of the older generation, was paid for the high altarpiece on July 25, 1456, and that the three Bellinis—Jacopo, Gentile, and Giovanni—began to receive commissions for the Carità only after 1460, when they produced four triptychs for the rood screen (1462–64).[21]

It seems equally difficult to maintain a date of around 1470 for the *Crucifixion*,[22] an argument based on the endowment provided by the procurator Domenico Marin in 1469 for the celebration of masses and the consecration of the church's altars in 1471 by the bishop of Modena.[23] We know that the endowment of a chapel did not necessarily imply the commission of an altarpiece; therefore these dates represent only *termini ante quem*.

As noted by Cavalcaselle and Richter, the first to write about the Louvre *Crucifixion*, there is a significant gap between this work and the Museo

Correr's *Transfiguration* and the *Crucifixion with the Virgin and Saint John the Evangelist* (cat. no. 2), which is distinguished by a more tormented expressiveness, in the manner of Mantegna.[24] Nevertheless, the Louvre *Crucifixion* and the Berchtesgaden predella also display traces of the works of Giovanni Bellini's brother-in-law, such as the quotation from the figure of Saint John the Baptist in Mantegna's San Zeno altarpiece (Verona) for the depiction of Saint John the Evangelist: in both cases, the figure's right foot extends slightly beyond level ground, hovering over a lip at the forefront of the picture plane. The Louvre's *Crucifixion* retains a livelier trace of Mantegna's influence than the San Zanipolo triptych, although the study of light has become more refined, and Giovanni's unmistakable naturalistic sensibility profoundly pervades the figures in the foreground and the landscape in equal measure. The highlights that carve the bodies and faces are recalled in the dramatic *Pietà with the Virgin and Saint John the Evangelist* in the Ducal Palace, Venice, of about 1465. On a different front, as Roberto Longhi and, more recently, Andrea De Marchi have maintained, there are obvious ties between the perspectival constructions of the predella with *Stories of Saint Vincent Ferrer* in the San Zanipolo triptych and the slightly earlier predella with *Stories of Saint John the Evangelist and Drusiana* in Berchtesgaden, which represent the profound ongoing dialogue with the work of Mantegna, even though this painter had left the Veneto several years earlier.[25]

M.V.

1. Graves 1913–15, 2:745; Crowe and Cavalcaselle 1871, 142.
2. Richter 1960, 513.
3. "Er hat Bellini Kreuzigung"; New York, Metropolitan Museum of Art, Onassis Library, Jean-Paul Richter Diaries, 1887.
4. Bode 1900, note 78; Michel 1901, 496–97; *Catalogue* 1907, I: xix–xx; 2:25, pl. 118.
5. Agosti 2009, 174–75, note 31.
6. London, Richard Ford, http://www.richardfordmanuscripts.co.uk/catalogue/14605. Personal communication with Davide Gasparotto.
7. *Catalogue* 1910, 42, cat. no. 370, pl. 1.
8. Mauro Lucco, in Rome 2008, 156–59, cat. no. 8; Conti 1993, 288; Robertson 1968, 49.
9. [Michiel] 1884, 231; Zanetti 1733, 342; Zanetti 1771, 39; Malamani 1888, 368.
10. Boschini 1664, 358–59: "Nella cappella di San Giovanni, dalla parte sinistra dell'altare maggiore, vi è una tavola con molti casamenti, e quantità di figure; si dice concernenti la vita di San Giovanni Battista: come anco a basso, vi è un altro comparto in picciolo, con molte figure, e di sopra nella cima Nostro Signore in Croce; opera tutta di Vittore Carpaccio."
11. Zanetti 1733, 342: "poorly conserved" ("mal conservata"); Zanetti 1771, 39: "time has almost destroyed it" ("il tempo l'ha quasi ridotta all'ultimo fine"); Gronau 1921, 103.
12. Lucco, in Rome 2008, 156–59, cat. no. 8.
13. Bauer Eberhardt 1989.
14. Humfrey 1977, 36–39; Humfrey 1979, 253.
15. Lucco, in Rome 2008, 158; Villa 2009, 49, fig. 2.
16. Fogolari 1932.
17. Lucco, in Rome 2008, 28.
18. Pallucchini 1962, 97–98, cat. nos. 18–22; Vinco, in Milan 2014, 169–70, cat. no. 22.
19. Sponza, in Venice 2000, 145–49, cat. no. 27.
20. Bellosi, in Paris 2008, 124–25, cat. no. 33.
21. Fogolari 1924, 80, 82–84.
22. Pallucchini 1959, 48; Tempestini 1997, 60, 199, cat. no. 19; Aikema 2003, 40; Lucco, in Rome 2008, 156, cat. no. 8; Villa 2009, 44; Agosti 2009, 117–19.
23. Fogolari 1924, 78–79, 86.
24. Crowe and Cavalcaselle 1871, 142; Richter 1960, 513.
25. Longhi [1925–26] 1995, 378–79; De Marchi 2009, 21n14.

GIOVANNI BELLINI (Venice, ca. 1435–1516)

ca. 1470, pen and brown ink, slightly washed with brush, on paper;
both upper corners cut, 20.1 × 21.5 cm (7^{15}⁄$_{16}$ × 8^{7}⁄$_{16}$ in.)
London, The Samuel Courtauld Trust, The Courtauld Gallery,
inv. no. D.1978.PG.79

4 | NATIVITY

In the immediate foreground, on the right, the newborn Jesus is laid on his mother's extended legs. Mary—the only figure with a halo—sits on the ground like a Madonna of Humility and adores her son, her hands clasped in prayer.[1] She keeps his nude body comfortable with her broad mantle folded on her knees and he faces her, his head resting on a cushion positioned on her feet. Next to them, the ox and the ass kneel in worship, warming the child with their breath as a sort of rudimentary incubator. This intimate scene is watched over by old Saint Joseph, who stands meekly on the right, one hand grasping his stick, the other his mantle. Behind him is a beautifully built wooden hut, as if it was the result of his famous mastery as a carpenter. This sacred space is *conclusus* (enclosed) by a wattle fence with an elegant gate formed by two pilasters topped by two octahedrons. Two figures, probably the first shepherds to arrive to adore the Child, are about to invade this space, and one of them is bringing a basket with gifts, perhaps food for the exhausted mother. Their sheepdog is already inside and busy sniffing the

rear ends of the ox and the ass. Behind the wattle fence, two other shepherds, surrounded by their flocks, contemplate the landscape from a rocky hill. At the center of the composition, added at a later stage, is a tall tree whose bare branches reach for the sky. The ornate skyline of a wealthy civilized town can be seen in the distance, and beyond it, barely visible on the right, are two mountains.

This marvelous drawing was in the seventeenth-century part of the great collection of the Dutch-born artist Peter Lely, who lived most of his life in England.[2] His ownership is confirmed by his collector's mark, which appears twice on the drawing. Lely's drawing collection was sold at auction in London on two occasions, the first in April 1688 and the second in November 1694, but no catalogues of the sales exist.

The drawing appeared in public for the first time when it was auctioned at Sotheby's, London, in 1955. The auction catalogue, where the drawing is reproduced on the frontispiece, stated that, together with an important group of drawings offered for sale, it was the "Property of the Misses

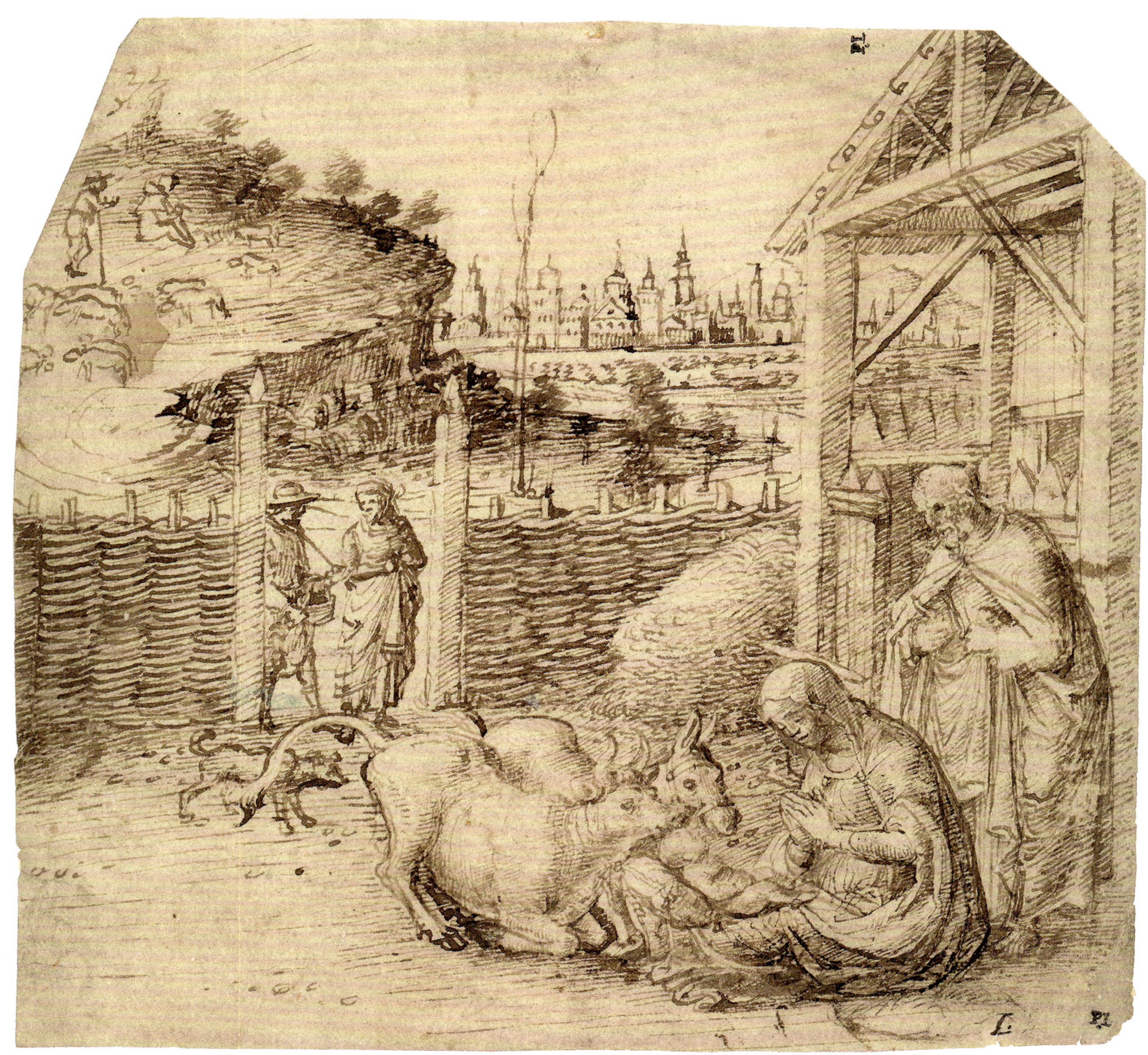

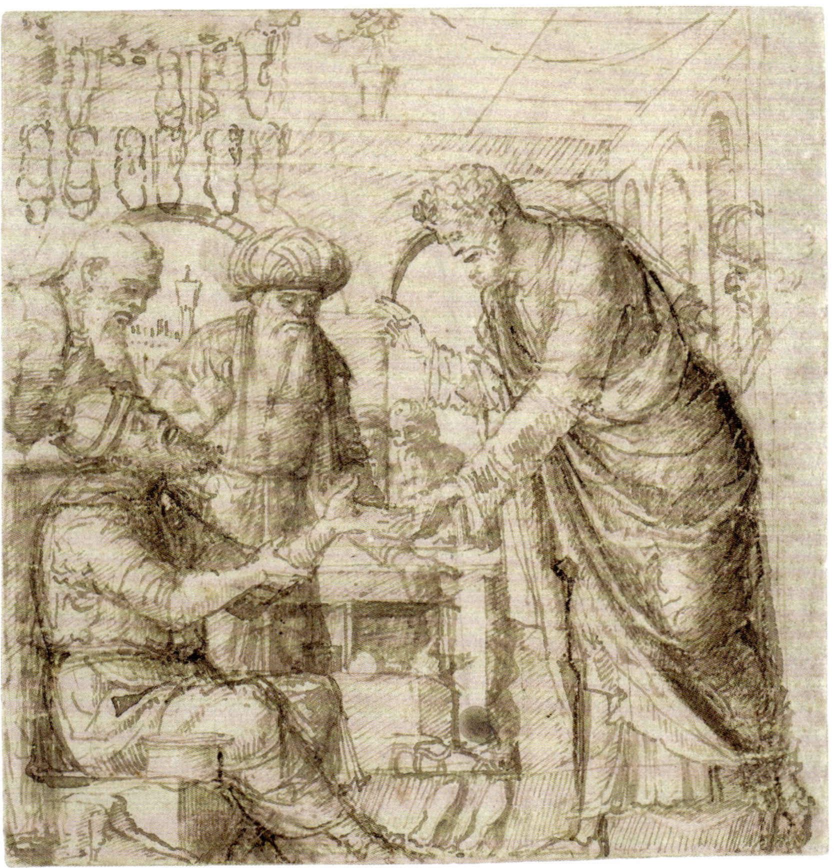

Healing Anianus (fig. 26), and with Bellini's altarpiece with the *Coronation of the Virgin* in Pesaro (see fig. 13), which has a predella panel with the *Nativity* (fig. 27).

The Colnaghi gallery bought the drawing at the 1955 auction on behalf of Count Antoine Seilern for £4,000 (which is comparable to about $127,000 today — an extremely good price for a drawing of this quality, rarity, and importance).[5] The 1959 catalogue of the Seilern collection confirmed the attribution of the sheet to Bellini, but cited a "group of drawings [by Bellini] to which this is clearly related," and for the author of the entry "the closest similarity . . . is with two beautiful drawings": the *Entombment* (Brescia, Pinacoteca Tosio Martinengo, Sezione Disegni e Stampe, inv. no. 147) and *Two Holy Women* (London, British Museum, Department of Prints and Drawings, inv. no. 1909.4.6.3v).[6] Those two drawings, which today are commonly ascribed to Andrea Mantegna, were then considered to be by Bellini.[7]

The arrival in the Seilern collection of the *Studies for a Christ at the Column* (London, The Samuel Courtauld Trust, Courtauld Institute Galleries, inv. no. D.1978.PG.345), which today is also widely accepted as by Mantegna, led Johannes Wilde, in his 1969 catalogue entry for that drawing, to make an "appeal" that was "not for a simple transfer of the drawings from Bellini to Mantegna, but for an attempt to sift them."[8] In Wilde's opinion, the *Nativity* could be used "with some confidence" as an example of Bellini's graphic style of the 1470s. The other examples of this style provided by Wilde were the *Anianus* (see fig. 26) and a *Pietà* in Paris (Musée du Louvre, Département des Arts Graphiques, inv. no. R.F. 436).[9]

In 1968 Giles Robertson proposed another comparison that would eventually feature in most of

M. H., L. E. and M. D. Le Hunte, (dec'd)," and that it had been in the family's collection for more than one hundred years. The sale catalogue also states that on the drawing's mount, which no longer exists, there were numbers that referred to a manuscript list of the Le Hunte collection, which had been compiled in 1842 by "George Le Hunte of Artramont, Co. Wexford."[3]

In the catalogue not only was the attribution to Giovanni Bellini proposed; the best possible comparisons were also made.[4] We shall see shortly that those arguments and comparisons are still valid for this drawing. It was compared with a drawing that was already then attributed to Bellini, *Saint Mark*

the literature on the *Nativity*, that is, the drawing
Vulcan Building a Fence around the Mount of Venus
(New York, The Metropolitan Museum of Art,
The Robert Lehman Collection, inv. no. 1975.1.320),
which is today considered to belong to the circle
of Giovanni Bellini.[10] According to Robertson,
"we may particularly compare the drawing of the
head of the bull in the sky in the Lehman drawing
with that of the ox in the Nativity and the drawing of the wattle fence in both. In each case the

comparisons . . . reveal the superior sensibility of
the drawing in Count Seilern's sheet."[11] I agree
with Robertson's statement that "the Lehman
drawing would be broadly classed as Squarcion-
esque," although it seems to date rather late in the
fifteenth century.

In recent literature the *Nativity* has often been
used as one of the few unquestionable examples
of Bellini's graphic style.[12] However, Caroline
Campbell recently stated that "one of the central

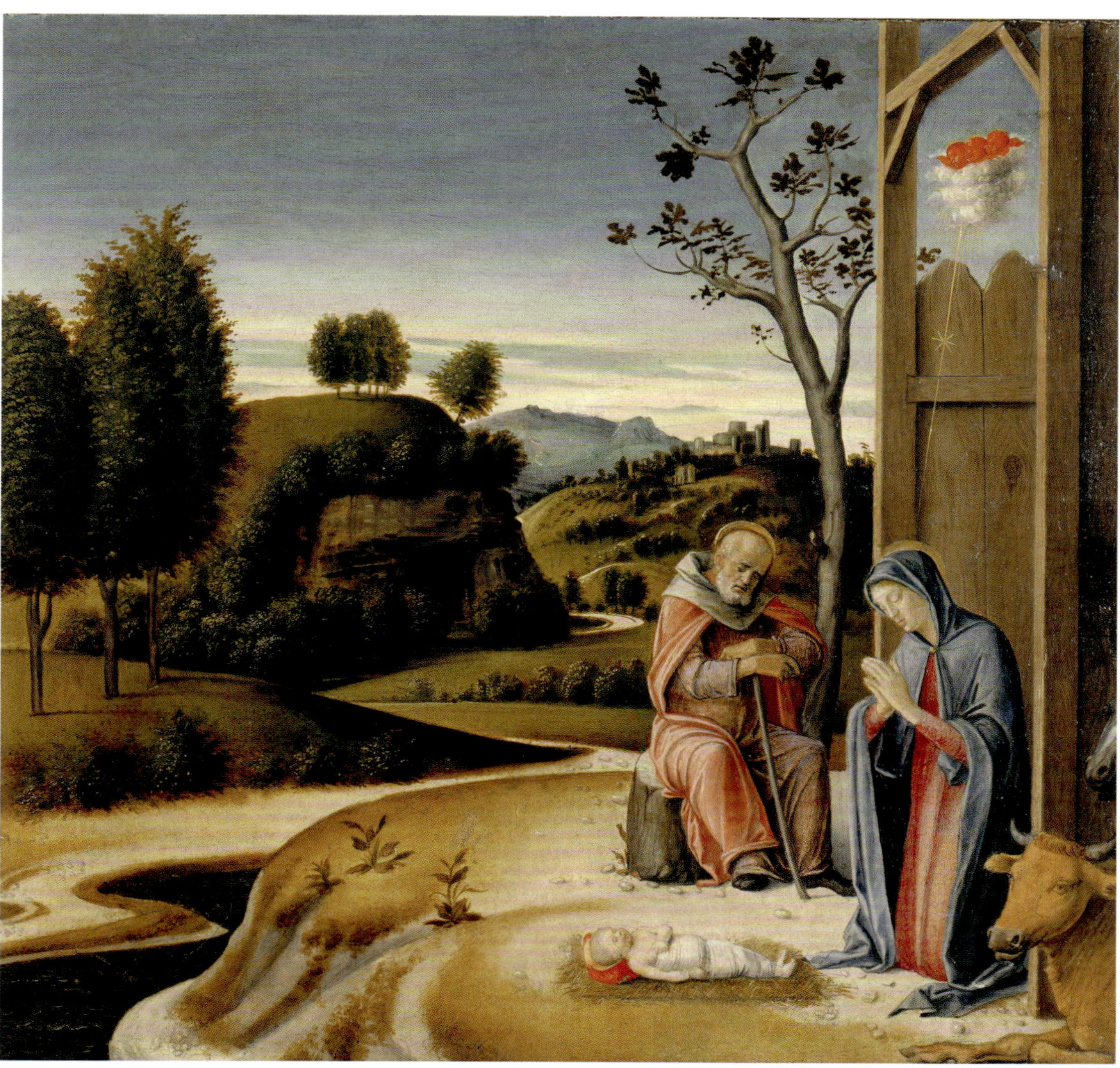

Figure 27
GIOVANNI BELLINI
Nativity (predella panel,
Pesaro altarpiece), ca. 1472–
75. Panel, 40 × 42 cm
(15¾ × 16½ in.). Pesaro,
Museo Civico

problems with ascribing the Courtauld drawing to Giovanni Bellini is that its spatial organization contrasts with that found in many of his securely attributable paintings"; it shows a "disjunction between the foreground and background"; and its "peculiarly crooked lines" would make us "seek its author in Ferrara or the Marches rather than necessarily in Venice."[13]

It would be wise to instead agree, once again, with Wilde's words: "The use of the constantly broken, vibrating lines is Bellini's own invention; the color and light effect produced by this method are startling."[14] In the *Nativity*, the spatial planes are not disjunct but part of a perspectival system comparable to the wings of a theater stage, functioning as chapters of our visual experience and guiding our eyes from the very near to the far distance, never losing the fluidity of viewing and the focus. It seems miraculous that this harmony is rendered just with the use of pen and ink, which does not allow pentimenti and radical changes. This way of structuring space can be found in the work of Bellini throughout his career and is comparable, for example, to the sense of space in the *Saint Jerome Reading in the Wilderness* (cat. no. 7).

The comparison of the Pesaro predella panel (see fig. 27), part of an altarpiece that is datable to circa 1472–75, with the *Nativity* is still valid, as the basic compositional scheme is similar. However, the painting is more simplified, as if it were an abstract of the drawing, leading us to think that the latter was executed first. In both the drawing and the painting, the trees on the hill are in soft and transparent contrast against the sky, with an effect that is not too different from that in the nearly contemporary drawing *View of the Valdarno* by Leonardo, dated 1473 (Florence, Galleria degli Uffizi).[15] Another *terminus ante quem* might be the

Nativity by Bartolomeo Vivarini, dated 1475 (the central piece of the Conversano polyptych, Venice, Gallerie dell'Accademia, inv. no. 581), where the structure of the wooden hut seems strongly inspired by Bellini's. The Berlin *Anianus*, which is the drawing always associated with the *Nativity*, could find its *terminus ante quem* in the 1479 polychromed relief of the same subject in the lunette of the gate of the Scuola dei Calegheri, the confraternity of shoemakers, in Campo San Tomà, Venice.[16]

The Nativity is not a common subject in Bellini's oeuvre. Relatively early in his career, in about 1465, he painted a Nativity as a central panel for one of the Carità triptychs (the Nativity triptych), which today are in Gallerie dell'Accademia, Venice, and toward the end of his career he was asked to paint a *presepio* (see cat. no. 11). In planning the Courtauld drawing, which a few frames later would have become an *Adoration of the Shepherds*, as the shepherds are about to arrive, Bellini almost surely had access to the *Meditations on the Life of Christ*, the fourteenth-century Franciscan text that describes in detail the worshipping of the ox and the ass (which Bellini transforms into a proper Adoration of the Animals), as well as the carpentry of the wattle fence and the stable alluding to Saint Joseph's skills.[17] This Franciscan link is even more interesting in light of the original destination of the Pesaro altarpiece—the high altar of San Francesco—and since its *Nativity* predella panel (see fig. 27) is so closely related to the present drawing.

This drawing should become the core of a group that is stylistically consistent: the Berlin *Anianus* (see fig. 26), the Louvre *Pietà*, as well as the *Pietà* in Rennes (Musée des Beaux-Arts, inv. no. 794.1.2503) and the one at the British Museum (inv. no. 1895.9.791), which has on the verso studies for a Christ child that seem compatible with the one drawn in the *Nativity*.[18]

The Courtauld *Nativity* must be considered, in Wilde's words, "one of the few surviving composition studies by Giovanni Bellini," and "it may be the preparation for a picture of private devotion, or a *modello* to be shown to a patron."[19] Another drawing that is perhaps attributable to Bellini and that might have had the same function (even if executed in a slightly different technique) is the earlier and still highly Mantegnesque *Crucifixion* (see fig. 28).[20]

A.M.

---

1   On the Madonna of Humility, see Meiss 1936.

2   On his prints and drawings collection, which consisted of some ten thousand pieces, see Dethloff 2003. The inscription "BAC n° 19" on the back of the drawing probably refers to Roger North's numbering of the portfolios after Lely's death (on which see Dethloff 1996, 20–21).

3   *Catalogue* 1955, 10, cat. no. 43. The whereabouts of the manuscript inventory of the Le Hunte collection are unknown.

4   It is possible that attribution and comparisons were made by Philip Pouncey, as he was responsible for another important attribution (as stated in Lehman, in New York 1965, 23–24, cat. no. 10) for the Le Hunte sale: the *Design for a Wall Monument* by Francesco di Giorgio Martini (New York, Metropolitan Museum of Art, Robert Lehman Collection, inv. no. 1975.1.376).

5   A copy of Colnaghi's receipt is kept in the dossier of the drawing at the Courtauld Institute.

6   Seilern 1959, 21–22, cat. no. 79. In Seilern 1971, cat. no. 79, it is reported that James Byam Shaw "independently from the editor of Sotheby's sale catalogue…had suggested that Giovanni Bellini was the author of the Nativity."

7   For a summary of their critical history and the arguments in favor of the attribution to Mantegna, see Mazzotta, in Paris 2008, 143–44, 166–67, cat. nos. 43, 54, 55. For the persistence of the attribution of the British Museum drawing to Bellini, see Goldner 2004, 227–31; Valagussa, in Rome 2010, 38, cat. no. 5.

8   Wilde, in Seilern 1969, 40–41, cat. no. 345.

9   For the Paris *Pietà* and its attribution to Bellini, see Mazzotta, in Paris 2008, 148–49, cat. no. 47. The attribution to Mantegna was recently reproposed in Lucco 2009, 96n13; Lucco 2013, 128, 132, 134 (who refuses to attribute any existing drawing to Bellini himself).

10   Robertson 1968, 72–73. In the Lehman drawing the wattle fence has a very similar gate with two pilasters topped by two octahedrons, as in the *Nativity*.

11   The wattle fence was interpreted as a reference to Borso d'Este's heraldic device (*impresa*) of the *paraduro* for the *Adoration of the Shepherds* by Mantegna (New York, Metropolitan Museum, inv. no. 32.130.2) by Christiansen, in Milan 1991, 307–12, cat. no. 78.

12   See, for example, Goldner 2004, 238, 242–43, fig. 82; Chapman 2010, 18, fig. 2.

13   Campbell, in London 2012, 52–55, cat. no. 5.

14   Wilde 1974, 26, 28, fig. 25.

15   Chapman, in London 2010, 202–3, cat. no. 49.

16   It is attributed to Antonio Rizzo in Schulz 1983, 66, 181–82.

17   As pointed out in London 1991, cat. no. 7. For the English translation of the text, once attributed to Saint Bonaventure, see *Meditations* 1961. This text is today attributed to Giovanni de' Cauli (see Arosio 2001). The worshipping animals in the *Nativity* might also be a reminiscence of Donatello's *Miracle of the Ass* for the Altare del Santo in the basilica of Sant'Antonio, Padua.

18   For the two *Pietàs* by Bellini, see Mazzotta, in Paris 2008, 145–48, cat. nos. 45, 46; Vinco, in Milan 2014, 166, cat. nos. 16, 17. They are attributed to Mantegna in Lucco 2013, 128, 133–34.

19   Wilde 1974, 28.

20   Bellosi, in Paris 2008, 168–69, cat. no. 56.

ca. 1475, both oil on canvas, transferred from panel and laid down
on a plywood support and cradled
Left panel: 79.4 × 29.3 cm (31¼ × 11⁹⁄₁₆ in.); painted surface:
77.6 × 27.4 cm (30⁹⁄₁₆ × 10¹³⁄₁₆ in.); right panel: 79.1 × 29.4 cm
(31⅜ × 11⁹⁄₁₆ in.); painted surface: 77.2 × 27.2 cm (30⅜ × 10¹¹⁄₁₆ in.)
Newark, Delaware, The Alana Collection, inv. no. 2003.03ab

5 | THE GOOD AND BAD THIEVES, DISMAS AND GESTAS

PROVENANCE
Possibly Vienna, Baron Carl
von Krauss; possibly Vienna,
Josef Weinberger; possibly
England, private collection;
Sotheby's, London, November
20, 1957, lot 77; Christie's, New
York, January 24, 2003, lot 76

RESTORATION
2011 (Nicola Ann MacGregor)

Virtually all of Bellini's surviving paintings of the
Crucifixion show the crucified Christ extracted
from the Gospel narratives and their account of soldiers and bystanders hurling abuses, Christ charging
Saint John with the care of his mother, and two
criminals crucified, "one on his right and the other
on his left" (Mt 27:38; Mk 15:27; Lk 23:32–33; Jn 19:18).
Only the *Crucifixion* in the Museo Correr (cat.
no. 2), which includes diminutive figures of soldiers milling around in the landscape, alludes to a
broader narrative, and that work is keenly indebted
to the example of Giovanni's great brother-in-law,
Andrea Mantegna, whose great strength was in dramatically or emotionally pitched narratives. These
two panels—of high quality despite their compro-
mised condition—are thus of unique interest. They
are from a triptych—most likely stationary rather
than folding—depicting the Gospel account.[1] Presumably, the center panel showed Christ on the
cross, his mother, and the apostle John, as well as
Roman soldiers and Pharisees. As noted by Mauro
Minardi, who has provided the most exhaustive
discussion of the two pictures,[2] pertinent analogies

for this narrative treatment can be found in a drawing by Bellini's father, Jacopo, from the celebrated
sketchbook in the Louvre, and in a canvas by Dieric
Bouts the Elder in Brussels (Musées Royaux des
Beaux-Arts) that formed part of an altarpiece destined for Venice and known to Bellini (see Gasparotto essay, p. 17, and cat. no. 2).[3] Yet, whereas the
compositions of Jacopo and Bouts, with their unified picture fields, have as their focus the crucified
Christ and his mother, collapsed in grief at the foot
of the cross and comforted by attendants, Bellini
took advantage of the unusual triptych format to
give each panel a meditative focus. In the left-hand
panel the thief who showed remorse for his sins
(apocryphal sources give his name as Dismas),
gazes toward Christ, his hands spread pleadingly.
It is the moment when, rebuking the taunts of his
fellow criminal, Gestas, he addresses Jesus, "remem-
ber me when thou comest into thy kingdom," and
Jesus responds, "Today shalt thou be with me in
paradise" (Lk 23:42–43). A soldier with a lance stares
up at him, while the gaze of a companion soldier
holding a mace seems directed, instead, toward

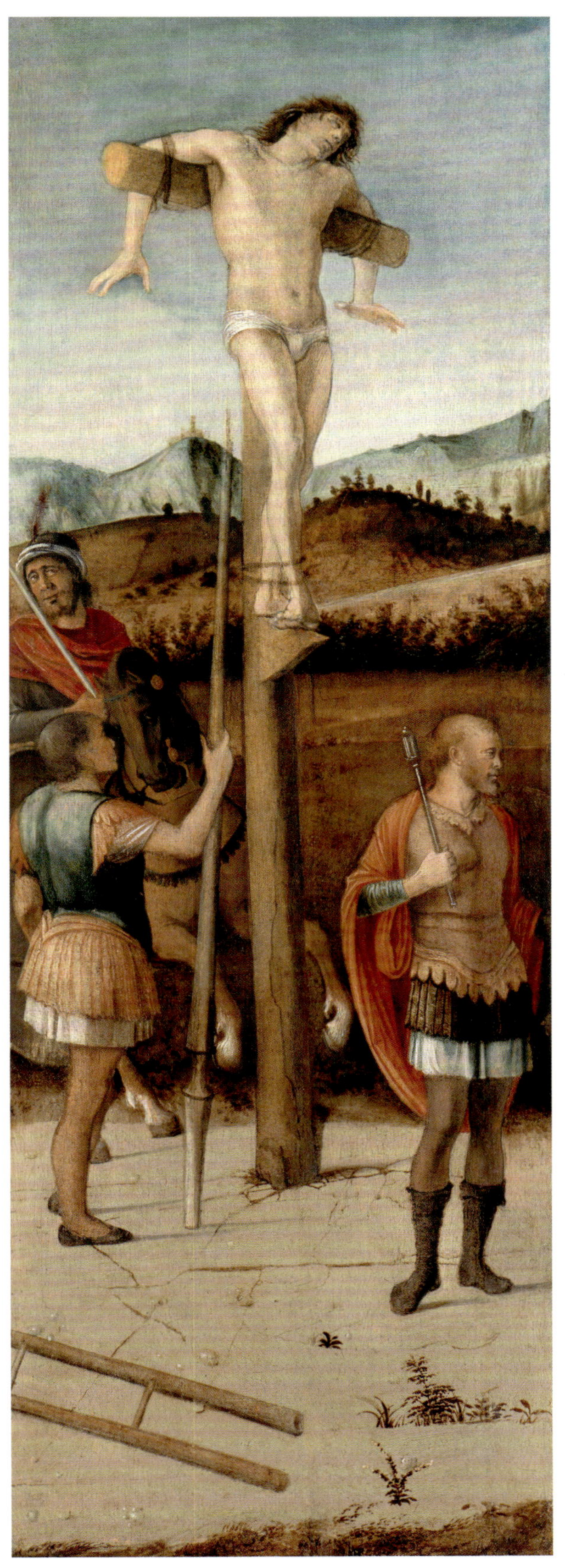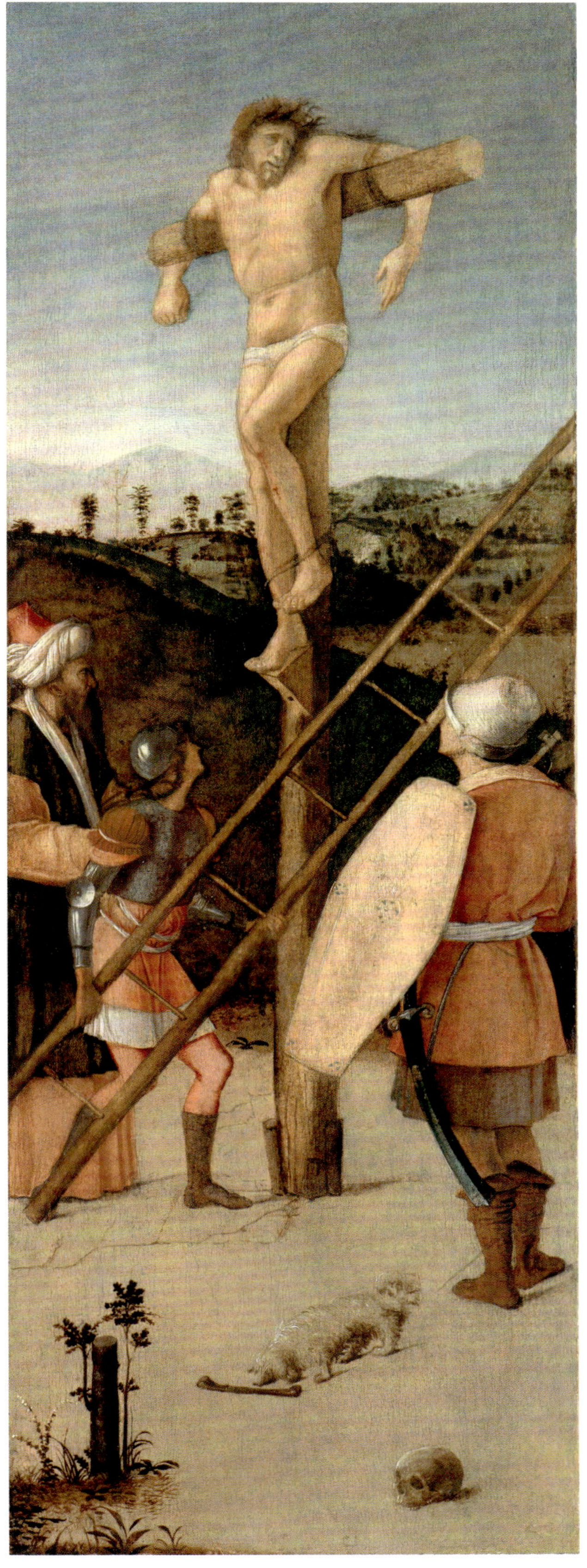

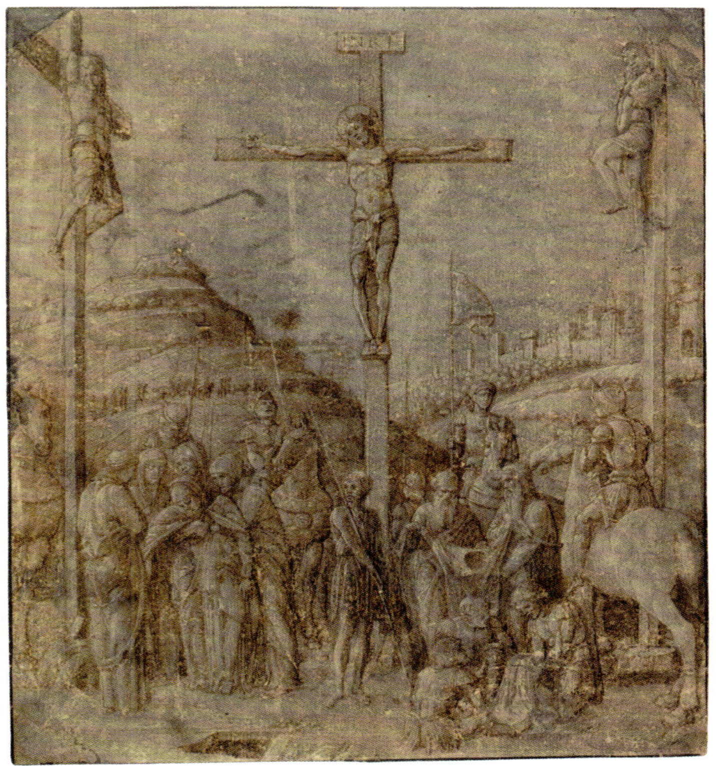

Figure 28
FOLLOWER OF
ANDREA MANTEGNA
Crucifixion, ca. 1460. Pen
and brown ink on paper,
24 × 21.5 cm (9⁷⁄₁₆ × 8½ in.).
London, British Museum,
Pp, 1.22

the figures in the lost center panel—probably the mourning Virgin and her companions, but perhaps also soldiers throwing dice for Christ's robe, as in a Mantegnesque drawing in the British Museum (fig. 28). By contrast, in the right-hand panel, the attention of the two soldiers and the turbaned Pharisee is focused entirely on the tormented figure of the unrepentant Gestas, his head turned away from Christ, his hair in symbolic disarray, and his arms hanging limp. As in Mantegna's predella for the San Zeno altarpiece (Paris, Musée du Louvre; fig. 22), his shins bleed, for his legs have been broken to precipitate his death, "that the bodies should not remain upon the cross on the Sabbath day" (Jn 19:31). The ladder is being removed following this grisly task. The contrast between the two panels is thus developed in terms of Bellini's

persistent interest in creating sites for meditation. Other details serve as prompts: the oak stump that has sent forth new shoots (a visual metaphor for the Resurrection), the dog sniffing the bone (a reference to Christ's tormentors: Ps 22:16), and the skull designating the site of Golgotha as "the place of the skull."[4]

Behind the figures is an expansive landscape of remarkable depth and richness that unified all three panels and that has led to comparisons with the Corsini and Niccolini *Crucifixions* (cat. nos. 6, 8), neither of which, however, are candidates for the lost center panel and, indeed, have an altogether different emotional tenor.[5] In the 1490s Perugino painted for Bartolommeo Bartoli, the bishop of Cagli, a triptych with the Crucifixion on the center panel and a continuous landscape (Washington, DC, National Gallery of Art). Its lateral panels show Saints Jerome and Mary Magdalene, but they are close in scale to Bellini's, thus suggesting the probable width of the lost center panel as perhaps around 50 to 55 centimeters and the overall width of the altarpiece as 100 to 150 centimeters. Bartoli bequeathed Perugino's triptych to the convent of San Domenico in San Gimignano, where it adorned an altar, reminding us of the interchangeability of works painted for private devotion and those for public use. Nonetheless, Bellini's modest-scaled triptych seems more likely to have been conceived for private use. Who the patron was remains an open question. It first came to notice in 1957, and there is no information on the possible provenance prior to the late nineteenth century. Might it have had a non-Venetian destination, possibly a city along the Adriatic coast?[6] The primary reason for suggesting this is the close relationship in style—universally recognized—that the two panels bear with the

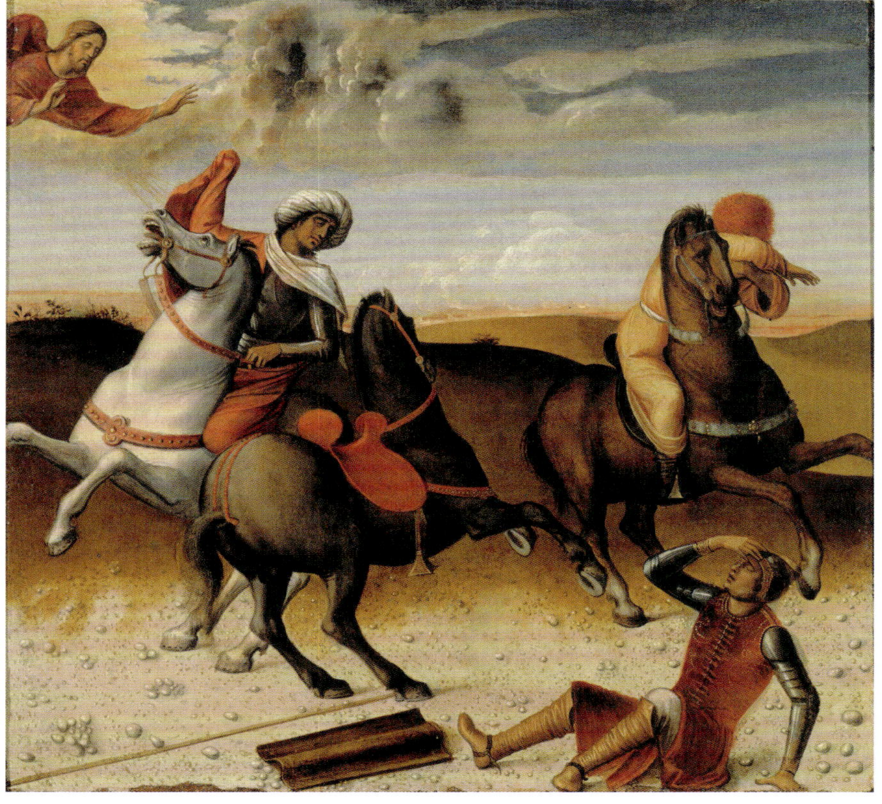

The Crucifixion was a subject particularly favored by Franciscans, who enjoyed the support of the rulers of the various Marchigian states, whether Montefeltro, Malatesta, Sforza, or Della Rovere. During a trip to the Netherlands in 1458, Alessandro Sforza, ruler of Pesaro, commissioned a portable triptych of the Crucifixion from the workshop of Rogier van der Weyden (Brussels, Musées Royaux des Beaux-Arts); it included in a lateral panel Saint Francis with his hands raised to receive the stigmata. Both Alessandro and his son Costanzo have sometimes been put forward as the possible patron of Bellini's *Coronation of the Virgin* altarpiece, and while all of this remains entirely conjectural, it does suggest the kind of patron and circumstances that may lie behind these survivors of a unique work.

K.C.

Figure 29
GIOVANNI BELLINI
Conversion of Saint Paul
(predella panel, Pesaro altarpiece), ca. 1472–75. Panel,
40 × 42 cm (15¾ × 16½ in.).
Pesaro, Museo Civico

predella scenes of Bellini's great *Coronation of the Virgin* altarpiece for the church of San Francesco in Pesaro (see fig. 13). There are the somewhat awkward proportions of some of the figures and their genial but mannequin-like poses, notable, for example, in the shield-bearing soldier in the right-hand panel. The soldier on a rearing horse seems almost interchangeable with similar figures in the *Conversion of Saint Paul* (fig. 29). Because of abrasion, the effects of light, which are such a singular achievement in the Pesaro altarpiece, can no longer be fully appreciated, but the panoramic landscape, with its succession of verdant hills and planted plains extending to distant mountains, one crowned by a castle, belongs to the same stage in Bellini's development.

1   Minardi, in *Alana Collection* 2014, 3:127–33, gives a detailed account of their condition. Examination with George Bisacca of the Metropolitan Museum of Art, New York, confirms that: (1) the white gesso surrounds are not original and in places have created a false raised edge that might be mistaken for a barb; (2) nonetheless, the painted edge along the right side of the left panel is original (there is a vertical score there as well as on the bottom); (3) vertical cracks, easily visible in the 2003 sale catalogue, run through the left-hand panel.

2   See Minardi, in *Alana Collection* 2014, 3:127–33.

3   Humfrey 1993, 159–60.

4   As Marrow 1979, 36–43, has shown, the dog is a commonplace of late medieval Passion literature in the north of Europe.

5   See Minardi, in *Alana Collection* 2014, 130; and Villa, in Rome 2008, 214, 218.

6   Heinemann 1959, 1:48, cat. no. 155 bis, gave its first two owners as Josef Weinberger (1855–1928) and "Consul Krauss," possibly Baron Carl von Kraus, the Austro-Hungarian consul general in Venice in 1891 and a known collector: see the sale catalogue, Christie's 2003, lot 76. Baron Kraus is recorded as general consul to Venice in *Hof- und Staats-Handbuch* [1891], 271, and is noted, in passing, in Frimmel 1899, 480.

6 | CRUCIFIXION

INSCRIPTIONS
INRI (on the cross); 80
(bottom left)

PROVENANCE
Rome, Colonna Collection,
1714–16; documented in the
Corsini Collection from 1886

RESTORATION
2005–6 (Muriel Vervat)

EXHIBITIONS
Venice 1949, cat. no. 84; Rimini
2001, cat. no. 173; Rome 2006,
cat. no. 57; Rome 2008, cat.
no. 22

The *Crucifixion* is first mentioned in the inventory drawn up between 1714 and 1716 following the death of Philip II Colonna (1663–1714), probably by Giuseppe Bartolomeo Chiari, a pupil of Carlo Maratta. At this time it was correctly attributed to Giovanni Bellini.[1] Entry number 865 lists "a painting on panel of a similar size to the aforementioned representing a Christ on the Cross, an original by Giovanni Bellini with its black frame, and its own carved gilded shutters as above."[2] The work's presence in the Colonna family collection is attested not only by the coat of arms on the panel, at the lower right, and by the inventory number "80," in the same place on the left, but also by the inscription "Property of Princess Anna Corsini Barberini: from Palazzo Colonna,"[3] quoted in the entry of the 1886 catalogue of the Galleria Corsini, compiled by its curator, Ulderigo Medici.[4] In the same entry Medici recalled that the panel had been "enlarged in modern times, rendering it arched in the upper part." The *Crucifixion* must have come into the Florentine collection precisely in those years, since it does not appear in the preceding catalogue (1880). Finally, it

is mentioned in the inventory drawn up in 1911 after the death of Princess Anna Barberini, wife of Tommaso Corsini.[5]

The correct attribution to Bellini that appears in the Colonna inventory was lost when the painting entered the Florentine collection. First Medici, then Édouard Gerspach, director of the Manufacture des Gobelins, Paris, in a posthumous article in the periodical *Les Arts*, attributed the work to Antonello da Messina. Gerspach further — and forcefully — proposed a date of 1477, probably on the basis of recent archival discoveries concerning the documented sojourn of Antonello in northern Italy.[6] If we compare the painting's present state of conservation with that evidenced in the 1906 photograph published by Gerspach, we see that there has been no change since then. Giovanni Bellini's masterpiece, still perfectly legible in every part, must have undergone a drastic cleaning that abraded the painted surface before 1906. We cannot determine the painting's color values correctly because of the deterioration of the verdigris, which gives the color harmonies a dimness that the work certainly never

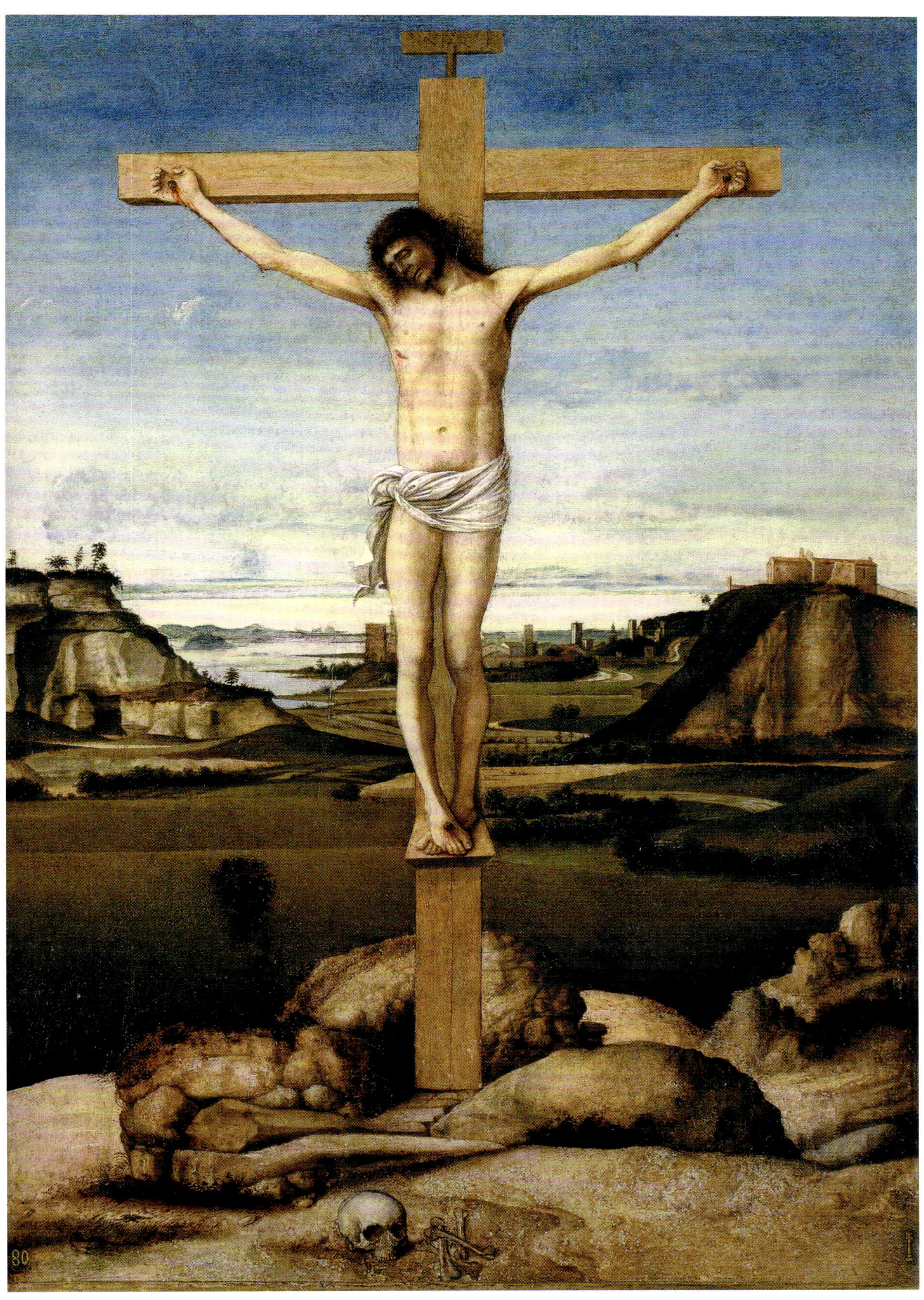

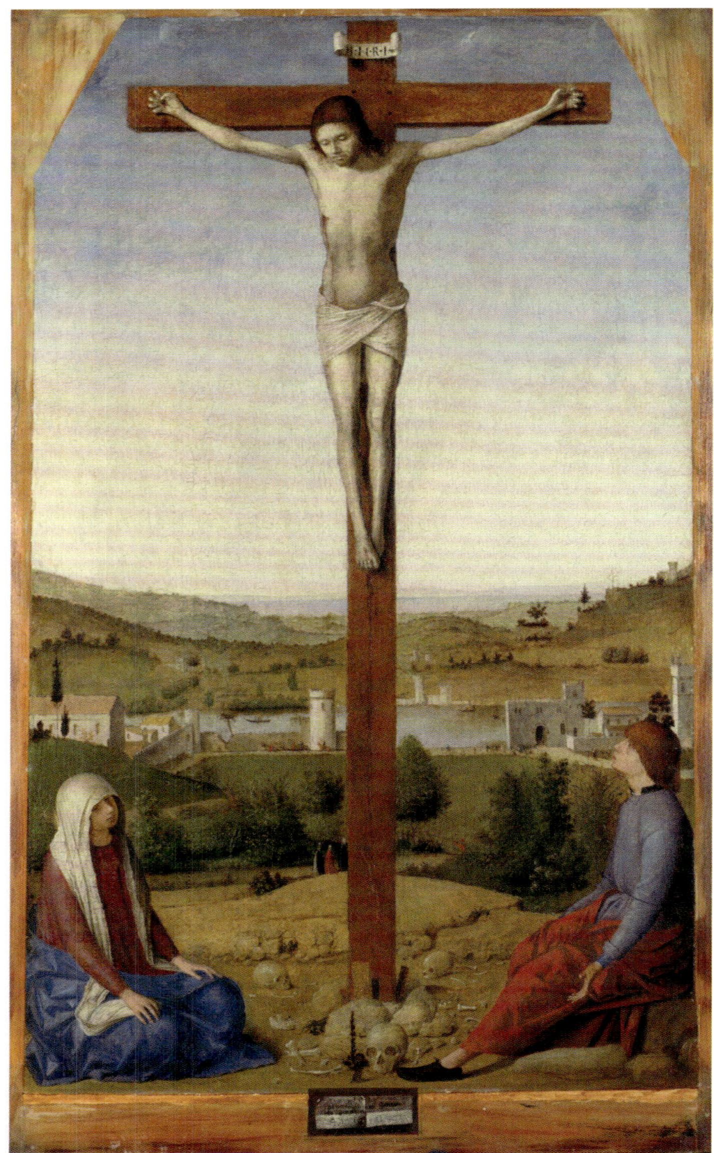

Figure 30
ANTONELLO DA MESSINA
(Antonello di Giovanni
d'Antonio) (Italian,
ca. 1430–1479), *Crucifixion
with the Virgin and Saint John
the Evangelist*, ca. 1475. Panel,
41.9 × 25.4 cm (16½ × 10 in.).
London, National Gallery,
NG1166

had in its original state. In fact, details such as the microscopic analysis of the pebbles and rocks in the foreground, the skillful ripples on the waterway, and the neat unfurling of the paths through the fields to the water and sky in the background allow us to piece together in the mind's eye the naturalistic wonder that Bellini devised to serve as the backdrop for this solitary Christ on the cross.

As already argued by Keith Christiansen, Bellini's religious works intended for private devotion should be interpreted while keeping in mind the comments of the Venetian historians Francesco Sansovino and Carlo Ridolfi, who repeatedly emphasized their "devotional" qualities.[7] Ridolfi, in particular, carefully observed the figures in the San Giobbe altarpiece (Venice, Gallerie dell'Accademia): "In truth, these figures were depicted as natural, well-considered figures, into which Giovanni sought to infuse that piety required of images of the saints: ignoring those foreshortenings and poses that were practiced later by painters who came after; one cannot fully describe the grace and the beauty of three little angels who sit at the feet of that Virgin playing the viola, the lute, & the violin: with delicate airs, and such sweet movements, they enrapt souls, the way that figures do when they awaken the greatest devotion in the minds of the faithful."[8]

The powerful emotional effect that Bellini sought to arouse with his works is stated explicitly in the inscription on the *Pietà* in the Pinacoteca di Brera (see fig. 12): "If these tear-swollen eyes were to break out weeping, then Bellini's work itself would weep"[9] ("HAEC FERE QVVM GEMITVS TVRGENTIA LVMINA PROMANT / BELLINI POTERAT FLERE IOANNIS OPVS"), words that, as Giles Roberston first observed, echo Propertius's elegiac distich: "Soldier, who hastens to escape your comrade's doom, flying wounded from the Etruscan ramparts, and turns

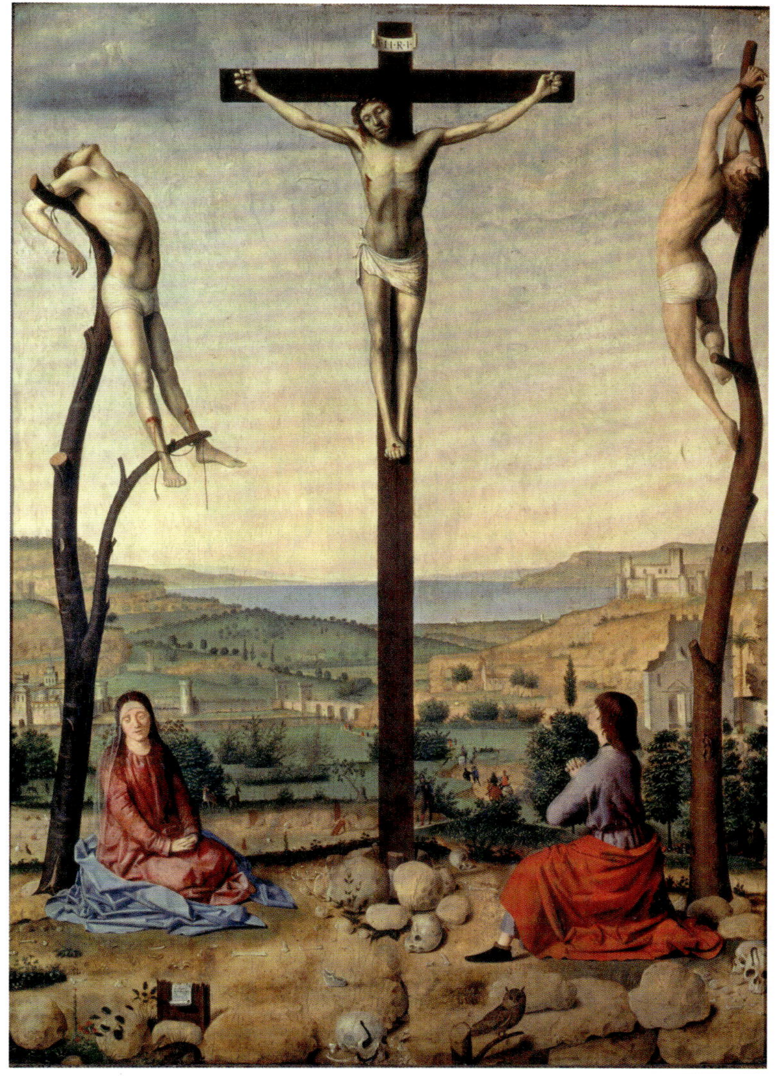

Figure 31

ANTONELLO DA MESSINA
(Antonello di Giovanni
d'Antonio) (Italian, ca. 1430–
1479), *Crucifixion with the Virgin
and Saint John the Evangelist,*
1475. Panel, 52.5 × 42.5 cm
(16½ × 16¾ in.). Antwerp,
Koninklijk Museum voor
Schone Kunsten, 4

your swollen eyes at the sound of my moaning, I am one of your nearest comrades in arms."[10] This poetic mode of expression, as demonstrated by Hans Belting, derives directly from the principles set out in Leon Battista Alberti's *De Pictura* (1435), in particular the notion that paintings should "move the soul" and "emphatically" engage the spectator.[11]

In this lofty rhetorical exercise, the landscape plays a fundamental role in multiple and even opposing semantic modalities. Bellini's attentive depiction of the time of day can be observed in the leaden dawn of the *Imago Pietatis* (Milan, Museo Poldi Pezzoli) and the summer afternoon of the *Pietà with Two Angels* (Venice, Museo Correr). But most striking is how he infuses his landscapes with symbolic value and rhetorical function so as to arouse "the greatest devotion in the minds of the faithful."[12] In the Mantegnesque *Crucifixion* (cat. no. 2) and *Pietà with Two Angels* (both Venice, Museo Correr), the background is populated with figures who are indifferent to the drama taking place in the foreground.[13] By contrast, in the Corsini *Crucifixion*, the solitary Christ is in a natural setting without narrative elements, which, in its silence, amplifies a sorrow that no sign of earthly life can interrupt. In other words, what is employed here is the rhetorical mechanism of the *Andachtsbild*. While in the Poldi Pezzoli *Imago Pietatis* and in the Brera *Pietà* the drama of Christ's death is amplified by means of the compositional device of the "dramatic close-up," whose tight cropping compels participation in the action depicted,[14] in the Corsini *Crucifixion* an opposite principle is at work. The rhetorical device that Bellini has employed to intensify the event of Christ's death depends upon both the powerful visual effect *di sotto in su*, which emphasizes the impression of monumentality in the figure of Christ, and a low horizon line, never before so radically deployed by the artist, which extends the landscape as far as the eye can see.

Giovanni Bellini's familiarity with the Flemish paintings in Venice may have played a part in his choice to articulate the landscape in this manner, but his principal source of inspiration is undoubtedly to be found in Antonello da Messina's *Crucifixions* in London and in Antwerp (figs. 30, 31). As Robertson has pointed out, the Corsini *Crucifixion* and Antonello's London painting share the relationship of "the vertical cross to the horizontal rhythm of the landscape."[15] But while the landscape in the Antwerp *Crucifixion* is even closer, Christiansen has rightly observed that "in both the tragic event from sacred history is set against a serenely panoramic landscape of fifteenth-century Italy, creating an effect of isolation and tragedy. There is, of course, the difference that Antonello describes a narrative while Bellini's picture does not. Both [the Antwerp and Corsini *Crucifixions*] are meditations, but Bellini's alone falls into the category of an *Andachtsbild*."[16]

As we have seen, when modern scholars have assigned the Corsini *Crucifixion* to someone other than Bellini it is to Antonello da Messina. This "intelligent" mistake can be used to support a date in the mid-1470s, a time when the two great artists were engaged in an intense dialogue in terms of both iconography (the Crucifixions and Pietàs) and composition (Antonello's altarpiece for San Cassiano, Bellini's lost Saint Catherine and Saint Job altarpieces). Georg Gronau was the first modern scholar to assign the Corsini *Crucifixion* to Giovanni Bellini, an attribution that all subsequent commentators have endorsed unanimously.[17] Gronau was probably inspired by the perceptive stylistic reading of Adolfo Venturi, who assigned the work to a "follower of Antonello," pointing out, however, that in the *Crucifixion* "Giambellino's shapes overpower those that imitate the Messinese; and Antonello's model is visible only in the arc formed by the profile of the rocks on either side and in the long, straight lines of the planes extending toward the horizon."[18]

The proposed date of the mid-1470s for the *Crucifixion*, like the attribution to Bellini, has been generally considered sound by commentators. Robertson in particular brought the discussion back to the close relationship between Antonello da Messina and Bellini, at its most intense during 1475 and 1476.[19] Antonello had arrived in Venice by August 1475, as we know from an exchange of letters between Galeazzo Maria Sforza and the nobleman Pietro Bono, who commissioned the San Cassiano altarpiece. On March 9, 1476, Galeazzo Maria Sforza, upon the death of his court painter

Zanetto Bugatto, wrote from Vigevano to his ambassador in Venice, Leonardo Botta, that he should persuade Antonello "with whatever words will seem expedient to you that he may desire to come to us with all his things."[20] The messenger was Aloysio Cagnola, "a merchant and Milanese citizen of ours who knows and is very well informed about this painter."[21] This correspondence reveals the growing fame of Antonello, who shortly thereafter would become famous throughout northern Italy. Galeazzo Maria was familiar with Antonello's art through his younger brother Sforza Maria Sforza, who had brought him "a picture from life, by a Sicilian painter who lived in that city, with which he was very pleased."[22] But Antonello was already much admired in Venice, where since August 1475 he had been working on the San Cassiano altarpiece. Its patron's response to the duke's request conveys the master's considerable reputation among a well-versed clientele. Bono explained to Galeazzo Maria on March 16, 1476, that "sparing no expense from this past month of August, I ordered this work [the San Cassiano altarpiece], which from this day is believed to be in such condition, that in 20 days it will be perfect and finished: this work, my most illustrious lord, will be among the most excellent works of the brush to be found in Italy or outside Italy."[23]

The Corsini *Crucifixion* thus represents an immediate response to Antonello's presence in Venice, one that offered Giovanni Bellini the opportunity to revisit the *Andachtsbild* type in a novel way. The "greatest devotion," however, is attained here not by means of a "dramatic close-up" but by transforming the landscape into an instrument that amplifies the melancholy of Christ's death.

M.V.

1 Safarik 1996, 302, no. 865. I thank Davide Gasparotto for bringing this to my attention.

2 Safarik 1996, 302, no. 865: "un quadro in tavola dj misura simile à d[ett]o rapp[resentan]te un Cristo in Croce, originale dj Gio[vanni] Bellino con sua cornice nera, e battentj intagliatj doratj spett[ant]e come sopra."

3 "Proprietà della Principessa Anna Corsini Barberini: proviene da Casa Colonna."

4 Medici 1886, 117, no. 416. I thank Antonio Mazzotta for bringing this to my attention.

5 Villa, in Rome 2008, 212.

6 Gerspach 1906, 14, 17; and L. Beltrami 1894, 56–57.

7 Christiansen 2004c, 132–33; and Christiansen 2004b, 22–25.

8 Sansovino 1564; Ridolfi 1648, 50: "In vero naturali considerate figure, nelle quali Giovanni cercò di imprimere quella pietà che si richiede alle imagini de' Santi: non badando a scorci, o ad atteggiamenti, che furono poscia praticati da seguenti pittori: ne si può descrivere a pieno la gratia, e la bellezza di tre angeletti, che siedono a pie di quella Vergine, chi di loro tocca la viola, il liuto, & il viuolino: d'arie così gentili, e di movimenti così soavi, che rapiscono gli animi, qual maniere di figure destano somma divotione nelle menti de fedeli."

9 "Se questi occhi gonfi di lacrime prorompessero per così dire in pianto, allora la stessa opera di Bellini potrebbe piangere."

10 Roberston 1968, 54–55.

11 Belting 1996, 33–36.

12 For this argument, see also Gentili 1991, 41.

13 Christiansen 2013, 12.

14 Ringbom 1965; Nova 2008; De Marchi 2012; De Marchi 2014.

15 Robertson 1968, 75.

16 Christiansen 2013, 12.

17 Gronau 1930, 200, no. 26: "Die echt bellineske Landschaft gibt den wirklichen Autor sicher zu erkennen." Most recently, Villa, in Rome 2008, 212–14.

18 Venturi 1915, 89 and fig. 48.

19 Robertson 1960, 58–59.

20 Rugolo 2006, 361, doc. xxx: "con tucte quelle parole ve pareranno expediente che voglia venire da noi con tucte sue cose."

21 Rugolo 2006, 361, doc. xxx: "mercadante et cittadino nostro milanese che cognosce ed è informatissimo del dicto pictore."

22 Rugolo 2006, 361, doc. xxx: "una figura cavata al naturale per uno pictore ciciliano quale stanzia in quella città quale molto ne è piaciuto."

23 Rugolo 2006, 361–62, doc. xxxi: "non sparagnando denar alchuno dal mese d'avosto prossimamente passato, detti tal opera [la pala di San Cassiano] la quale sin questo dì creduta in chotal termine, che in zorni 20 sarebe perfeta e finita: la quale opera ilustrissimo mio singor sera de le più eczelenti opere de penelo che habia Italia e fuor d'Italia."

ca. 1485, panel, 47 × 33.7 cm (18½ × 13¼ in.)
London, National Gallery, NG281

7 | SAINT JEROME READING IN THE WILDERNESS

Saint Jerome, dressed in blue, sits in a rather uncomfortable position on a stone softened by a layer of grass. In order to keep his balance, he grabs his natural chair with his right hand while his left keeps his large book open as he reads with deep concentration. On the right, at the bottom of a rocky cliff, the lion—his only company—seems to be suffering from the heat. Another cliff surrounded by a river closes the canyon at the left, and it is uselessly linked by a rudimentary bridge to the top of a natural tower. In between are fields and gardens, and in the distance, a hill with a town at the bottom and a castle at the top, the two linked by towered walls. Above, mountains, sky, and clouds seem to be fused together. This heavenly view at the top is invaded only by the capillary twigs of a dry tree. A white dove roosted on its lower branch contemplates the landscape with us.

Our knowledge of this painting starts in 1855 in Venice. Under Charles Lock Eastlake's directorship, the National Gallery traveling agent Otto Mündler went on October 20, 1855, accompanied by "Professor Lorenzi," to visit "Sr. Marcovich, who possesses a charming little picture, S. Jerome in the Wilderness, evidently by M. Baxaiti, proved by one of the pictures in the Accademia." Professor Lorenzi was the painter and restorer Giuseppe Gallo Lorenzi, who was a professor at the Accademia in Venice, whereas Sr. Marcovich was probably the Dalmatian artist and engraver Bartolomeo Marcovich.[1] The Accademia painting that was brought as a comparison for the attribution was Marco Basaiti's *Saint Jerome* (inv. no. 107). On October 22, Mündler had another "appointment with Sr. de Lorenzi at S. Marcovich," and "re examined the little picture by M. Baxaiti, found it well worth having." On November 12 he "met Sr. Marcovich, went with him and offered 50 Nap. for the little M. Baxaiti. Della Rovere says it is engraved in the collection Salvator Rossetti." The latter information was provided by the "erudito antiquario" Federico Della Rovere, who mistook the London *Saint Jerome* for another *Saint Jerome*, by Giovanni Mansueti, that was indeed engraved when it was in Salvatore Orsetti's collection and that is today in Bergamo (Accademia Carrara, inv. no. 58 AC 00026).[2]

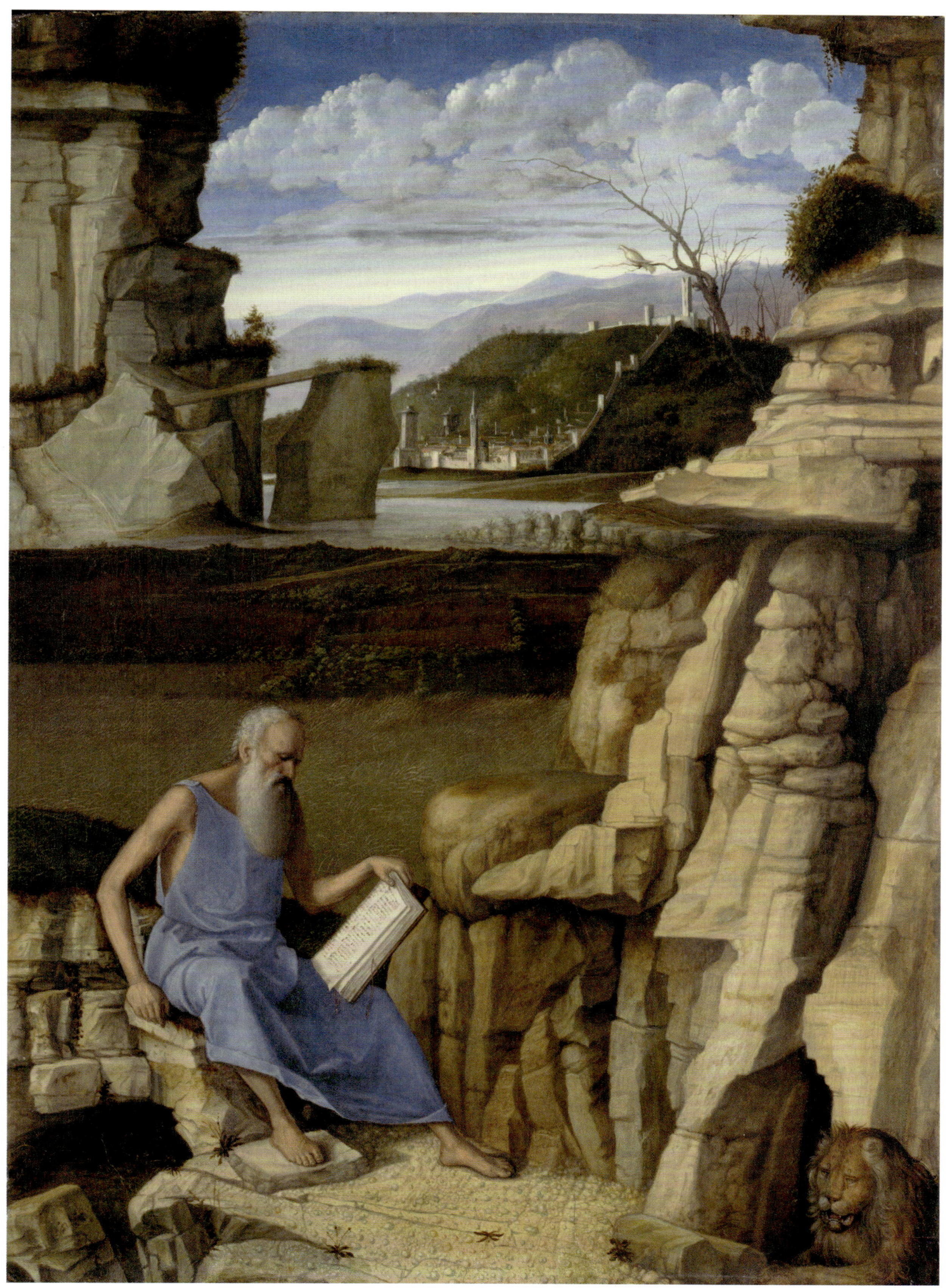

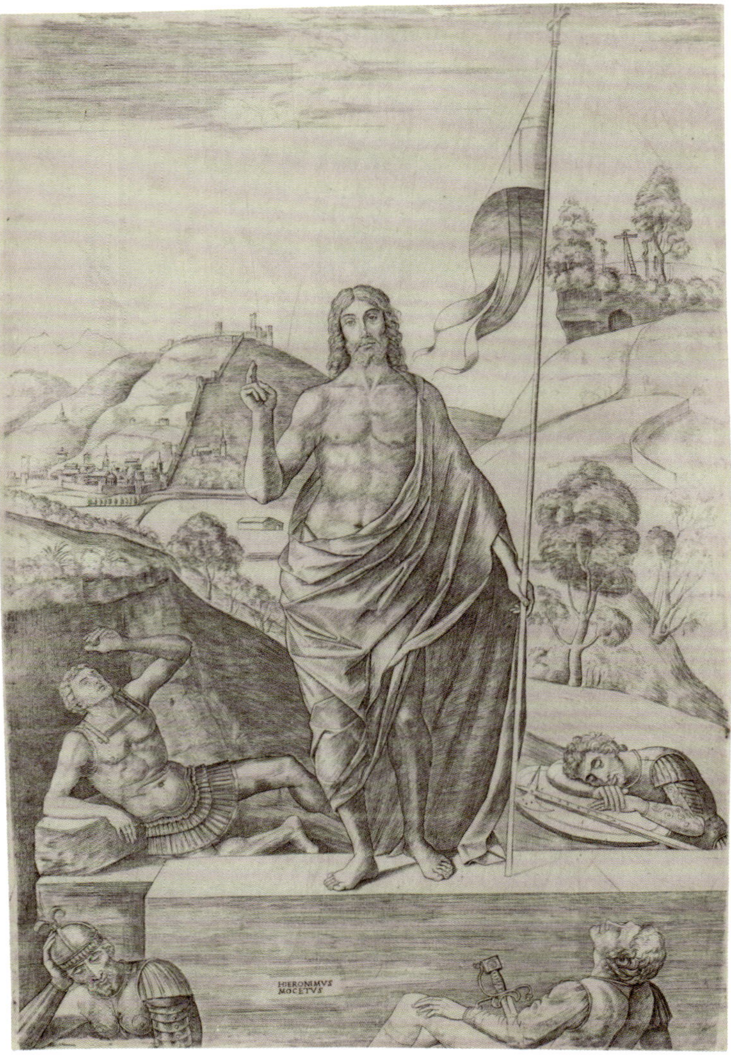

The deal was closed on November 14: "Purchased the little picture, M. Basaiti, from Sr. Marcovich for 50 Napol. and 4 Napol. for Prof. Lorenzi." In spring 1856 the *Saint Jerome* was shipped to London, and by the summer it was glazed and put on display as Basaiti at the National Gallery. In 1857 Gustav Friedrich Waagen confirmed the attribution to Basaiti, but admitted that "in delicacy and solidity of execution, this picture strikingly recalls the smaller works of Antonello da Messina, nay even shows an affinity to Van Eyck. . . . the preservation leaves nothing to be desired."[3] However, already by 1859 it had been restored twice, the second time by Raffaele Pinti (1826–1881).[4]

In 1865 Giovanni Battista Cavalcaselle visited the National Gallery and sketched the painting, taking interesting notes such as "sparing use of color," "aerial perspective," "Bellinesque mountains," "head in the noble style of Bellini," and, more interestingly, "see Papafava [version in] Padua."[5] This last note referred to another *Saint Jerome* (see fig. 7), where the figure of the saint is nearly identical but painted on a panel that is much larger in size (151 × 113 cm), then in the Papafava collection in Padua and today in Florence (Galleria degli Uffizi, inv. Contini Bonacossi no. 25). As we shall see shortly, this is a key comparison for our understanding of the painting under examination. A few years later Cavalcaselle and Joseph Archer Crowe expressed in print their thoughts on both paintings, which they attributed to Basaiti, but although they considered the National Gallery version a "more Bellinesque treatment" and "finished with Flemish minuteness," and said of it "originally we believe in San Giorgio Maggiore at Venice."[6] This provenance hypothesis was based on the fact that a small Saint Jerome was recorded there by Marco Boschini in 1664 and also in an 1806 inventory (as Basaiti), but this painting from San Giorgio Maggiore is today proven to be Cima da Conegliano's *Saint Jerome* (Milan, Pinacoteca di Brera, inv. no. Reg. Cron. 324).[7]

The London *Saint Jerome* was praised in Ernst Zimmermann's pioneering book on early Venetian landscape painting.[8] However, the attribution to Basaiti remained unquestioned even by modern connoisseurs such as Bernard Berenson, who also listed

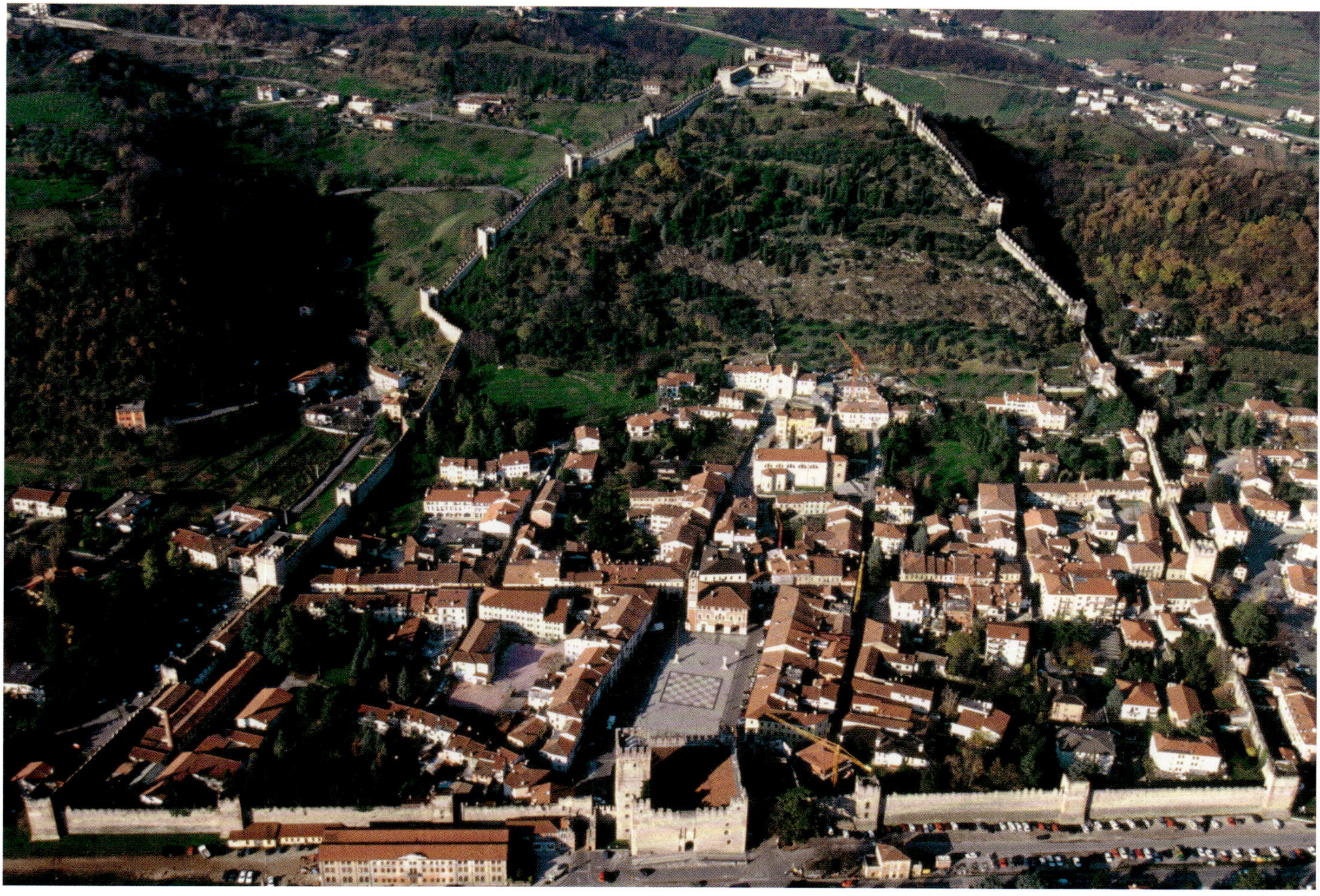

under Basaiti other paintings that are now unanimously attributed to the mature Bellini, including, for example, the Washington *Saint Jerome* exhibited here (cat. 12) and the *Madonna of the Meadow* in the National Gallery, London (see fig. 38).[9]

It is only because of Georg Gronau, who radically reconstructed Bellini's late career and demolished the overblown catalogue of Basaiti (and of the phantom Pseudo-Basaiti), that in 1930 the attribution to Bellini finally was proposed, and since then it has been only rarely questioned.[10] Gronau reproduced this *Saint Jerome* alongside the Contini

Bonacossi one, which he considered to be earlier. He also was the first to link this larger version with a lost altarpiece representing Saint Jerome in the Wilderness that was mentioned as early as 1581, in the Venetian church of Santa Maria dei Miracoli.[11] This lost work, which was sometimes wrongly identified with the London version, was most probably executed while the church was under construction (1480–89).[12] Martin Davies, in his fully informed entry, still considered the *Saint Jerome* to be by a "follower of Giovanni Bellini" and provided a list of versions of this composition, including "a variant of the same general scheme" at the Ashmolean Museum, Oxford (inv. no. WA1899.CDEF.P1).[13]

In 1950 James Byam Shaw, in reviewing Hind's volumes on early Italian engravings, noticed the close similarity between the walled town in the distance and the walled town that appears in the background of Girolamo Mocetto's *Resurrection* (fig. 32), a print that dates to about 1500.[14] It has been rightly noted that this view evokes towns in the Veneto such as Marostica (fig. 33), but without necessarily referring to a particular one.[15] The fact that it reappears in Mocetto's print tells us that in this painting Bellini employed a series of studies on paper (which evidently remained in his workshop for decades) and fused them together, as he did on many other occasions in his career. They were not cartoons, since the figure of Saint Jerome, for example, is depicted in a very different scale in the two versions, whose rocks on the right are also similar. Bellini learned this method in his youth from the example of his father, and from Jacopo's sketchbooks and compositional repertoires, but also when he was in close contact with his brother-in-law, Mantegna.[16] Despite employing motifs that originate from a pattern book, Bellini is able to magically and harmoniously create a natural landscape where the human figure is unified by the use of a warm light that melts the elements together. The painting is characterized by a series of visual echoes: the blue of the mantle and of the sky, the hair of the saint and the tufts of grass behind him, the walls on the hill and the naked tree, which, mirroring each other, form a reversed *C*. Moreover, this harmony and humanization of nature are sensitively reinforced by some anthropomorphic rocks on the right.[17] Bellini had demonstrated his ability to depict a coherent perspectival landscape early in his career (see cat. no. 1), but a decisive development in terms of harmonizing light, color, and spatial planes happened around the time of the Pesaro altarpiece (ca. 1472–75), as shown by his *Nativity* drawing exhibited here (cat. no. 4).

In terms of dating, it has been noted that the landscape of the *Saint Jerome* is very close to that of the Paliotto Barbarigo of 1488 (Murano, San Pietro Martire).[18] This is a very convincing comparison, also in light of the closeness in shape, and the soft transition of the light and shade, of Saint Jerome's beard and that of Doge Agostino Barbarigo.[19] A date in the mid-1480s therefore seems plausible for the little *Saint Jerome*.

The subject of Saint Jerome, which was much in demand in humanists circles, was continually experimented with in Bellini's career (cat. nos. 1, 12), and—together with his Madonnas and his Pietàs—one of the most representative of his poetry.[20] Guarino Veronese—a humanist whose work Bellini knew, because in 1459 he illuminated a copy of Guarino's translation of Strabo's *Geography*—gave a description of a painting of Saint Jerome that Pisanello presented him which is highly evocative of the spiritual and visual values of Bellini's interpretations of the theme: "the noble whiteness of his beard, the stern brow of his saintly countenance—simply to behold these is to have one's mind drawn to higher things. He is present with us and yet seems also absent, he is both here and somewhere else."[21]

A.M.

1   Togneri Dowd 1985, 74–75, 80–81. On Giuseppe Gallo Lorenzi (who restored, among many paintings, Bellini's *Baptism* in Santa Corona, Vicenza): Avagnina 2007, 58–59; and Manieri Elia 2014, 36. On Marcovich, see Donati 1931; and Avery-Quash 2011, 2:63.

2   The description by Della Rovere is given in Levi 1900, 1: CXXXIII. Federico Della Rovere had been an agent for British collectors, for example, in 1849 for William Bankes at Kingston Lacy; see Bradley 2004. The engraving of Mansueti's *Saint Jerome* was executed when the painting was in the Orsetti collection for Giovanni Maria Sasso's *Venezia pittrice* (on which, see Borea 1994). That this provenance is wrong is confirmed by the fact that the painting does not appear in the 1803 catalogue of the Orsetti collection (Accademia Carrara, Archivio Commisarìa, fald. B.35, fasc. 512).

3   Waagen 1857, 59.

4   National Gallery Conservation Record, vol. 1, no. 281. On Pinti working for the National Gallery (and for London collectors), see Anderson 1996; Brambilla Ranise 2007, 18–19; http://www.npg.org.uk/research/programmes/directory-of-british-picture-restorers.php.

5   "parsimonia di colore," "prospettiva aerea," "montagne alla Bellini," "testa tipo nobile belliniano," "vedi Papafava Padova." Venice, Biblioteca Marciana, Fondo Cavalcaselle, It. IV. 2033 (=12274), fasc. XIX, fol. 26r.

6   Crowe and Cavalcaselle 1871, 1:268n3.

7   Boschini 1664, 564; Cicogna 1834, 388.

8   Zimmermann 1893, 65–66.

9   Berenson 1894, 82.

10 Gronau 1930, 206, fig. 83.

11 Sansovino 1581, 63.

12 Heinemann 1962/1991, 1:66, no. 224. On the lost altarpiece, the correct information can be found in Humfrey 1991; Rearick 2003.

13 Davies 1951, 71–72, cat. no. 281. The Oxford *Saint Jerome* is of high quality, although only partially autograph. Pallucchini 1951, 196, reestablished the attribution of the National Gallery *Saint Jerome* to Bellini.

14 Byam Shaw 1950, 60.

15 Gamba 1937, 107.

16 Jacopo's two sketchbooks are in Paris (Musée du Louvre, Département des Arts Graphiques, inv. no. R.F. 1489) and London (British Museum, Department of Prints and Drawings, inv. no. 1855.8.11.1/98). A strip of rocks appears in Bellini's early *Transfiguration* (Venice, Museo Correr, inv. no. cl. I, n. 27) and the identical rocks appear on a strip of paper attached to the bottom of Mantegna's *Descent into Limbo* (Paris, École des Beaux-Arts, inv. no. 189), as pointed out by the present writer (see Servi, in Paris 2008, 200–201, cat. no. 68; and Lucco, in Rome 2008, 148–51, cat. no. 6. The same rocks were used decades later at the bottom of the *Apostle* (?) (Florence, Galleria degli Uffizi, inv. no. 1890/9939), usually ascribed to Bellini's pupil Vittore Belliniano.

17 Berra 1999; Agosti 2009, 144. Infrared photography reveals even more "faces" in the rocks on the right (see National Gallery Conservation Record, vol. 1, no. 281).

18 Humfrey, in Rome 2008, 242–45, cat. no. 32.

19 On the Paliotto Barbarigo, see Humfrey, in Rome 2008, 258–61, cat. no. 38.

20 On Bellini and the humanists, see Fletcher 2004, 32–41.

21 The translation is taken from Baxandall 1971, 92; Guarino's passage has been related to Bellini's *Saint Jerome* by Alexander-Skipnes 2003, 290–91. On Bellini's 1459 illuminations for Guarino's book, which are part of a manuscript kept in Albi, Bibliotheque municipale (inv. no. ms. 77), see Bellosi, in Paris 2008, 122–23, cat. nos. 31–32.

ca. 1495–1500, panel, 81 × 49 cm (32 × 19¼ in.)
Collection of Banca Popolare di Vicenza, inv. no. 112

8 | CRUCIFIXION

The first mention of this painting with a correct attribution to Giovanni Bellini was by Jean-Paul Richter, who, on May 5, 1891, made the following annotation in his notebook: "Later I met Marquess Niccolini. He has a splendid *Crucifixion* by Bellini."[1] The painting was not brought to wider attention, however, until 1937, when Carlo Gamba saw it in the same collection and also attributed it to Bellini.[2]

The extensive research conducted by Anchise Tempestini in 2003, on the occasion of the exhibition *Bellini e Vicenza*, unfortunately provided no new evidence on the provenance of this work. However, he made the interesting suggestion that the painting could have been acquired by Filippo Niccolini, 3rd Marquess of Ponsacco and Camugliano (1655–1738). According to Luigi Passerini, Niccolini was "a passionate art lover," whose collection was admired in 1698 by the Maurine Benedictine monk Bernard de Montfaucon during his visit to Italy.[3]

Bellini's documented regular visits to Vicenza and the inclusion of the city's most famous structures in the background of the Niccolini *Crucifixion* have understandably led commentators to believe that the painting was originally owned by a local patron.[4] Regarding the relationship between Bellini and Vicenza, we know that the second chapel in the cathedral was dedicated to the "Transfiguration of the Savior" and that "a very beautiful painting by Giovanni Bellino"—replaced in 1613—"could be seen there" (see fig. 6).[5] Between 1501 and 1503 Bellini also painted the *Baptism of Christ* for the altar founded by Giovanni Battista Graziani, known as Garzadori, in the Dominican church of Santa Corona (see fig. 38). A third work by Bellini for Vicenza is documented—either lost or perhaps never executed—commissioned by Gaspare Trissino, the father of the great humanist Giangiorgio. In his will, dated June 30, 1483, Gaspare asked that there be spent "two hundred ducats thus, one hundred for the altarpiece with its altar with the Resurrection of our Lord Jesus Christ in the way I have ordered from Zuan Bellin, the other hundred to be spent in that chapel on all the episodes of the Passion of Christ."[6]

Several buildings from Vicenza appear in the backgrounds of a number of paintings by Giovanni

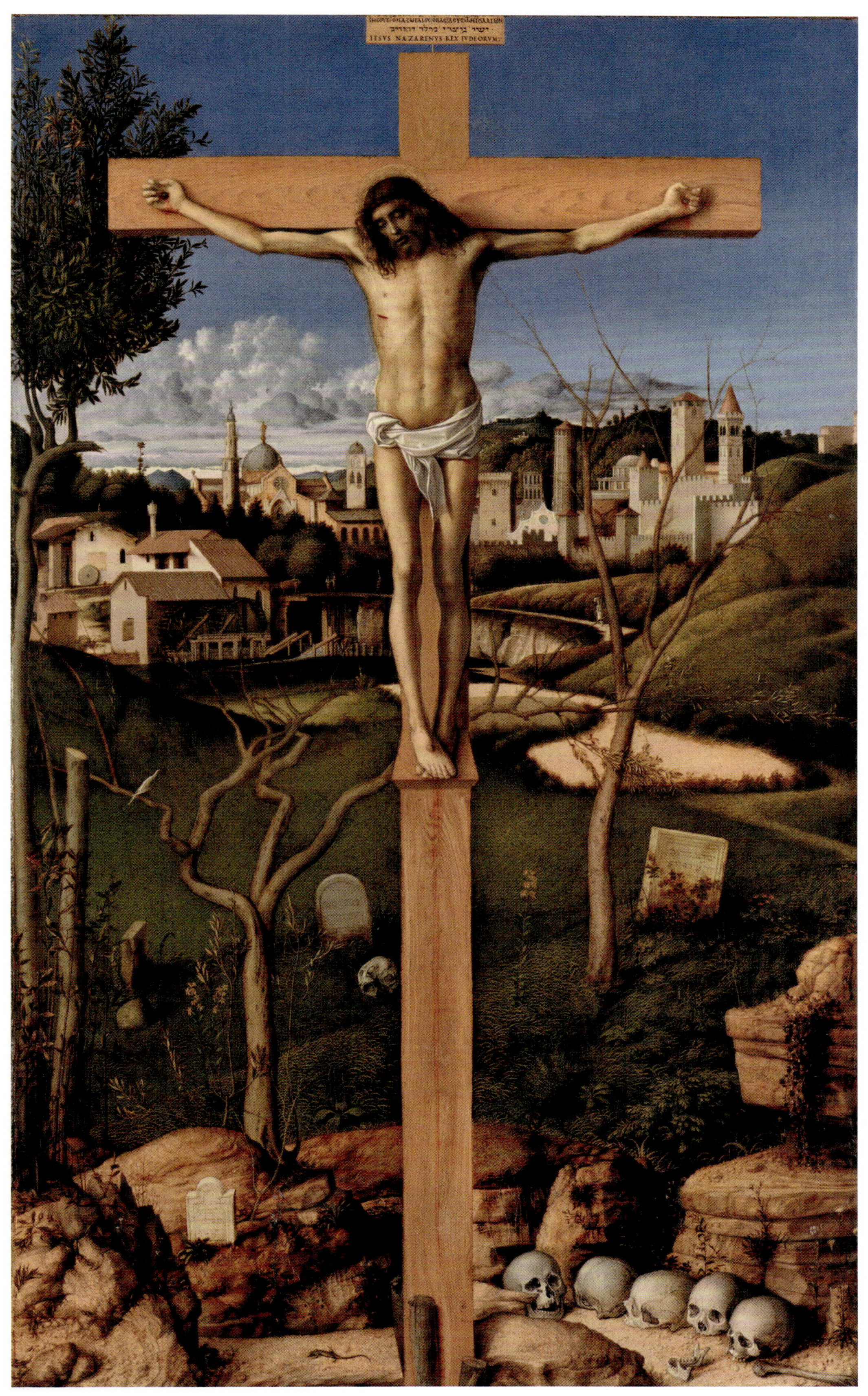

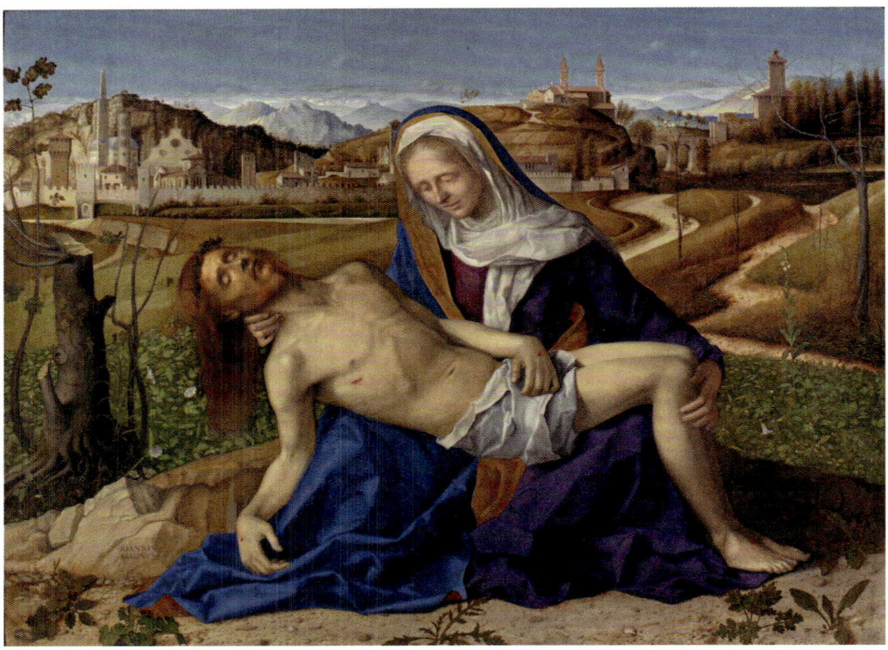

Figure 34
GIOVANNI BELLINI
Pietà (Donà delle Rose),
ca. 1495–1500. Panel,
65 × 87 cm (25⅝ × 34¼ in.).
Venice, Gallerie dell'Accademia, 883

Bellini. The silhouette of the Torre di Piazza is clearly visible in the Contarini *Virgin and Child* in Venice (Gallerie dell'Accademia), and in the *Virgin and Child* in Stuttgart (Staatsgalerie). The latter work in particular exhibits a collection of celebrated buildings in Vicenza (Torre di Piazza, Palazzo della Ragione, the cathedral), which, as attested by the engraving adorning Giambattista Dragonzino da Fano's *Nobility of Vicenza* (1521), would become a recognizable emblem of the city's institutions.[7] The same group of buildings from Vicenza recurs in the *Pietà (Donà delle Rose)* (fig. 34), enhanced by a campanile that scholars have attempted to identify as that of Caorle, Tessera, or Sant'Apollinare in Classe, Ravenna. The other recognizable structures are all located in Vicenza: the section of the city walls called Pallamaio; the Porta Castello; the side of the Dominican church of Santa Corona in its thirteenth-century appearance; the oratory of Santa Chiara; what may be the cathedral's Romanesque

tower, or the campanile of Sant'Agostino; and possibly the tower of the bishop's palace.

Recognizable in the Niccolini *Crucifixion* are the facade of the cathedral of San Ciriaco, Ancona, and the campanile of the Venetian church of Santa Fosca, as well as echoes of many buildings in Vicenza: the fifteenth-century tower of the bishop's palace, the Romanesque towers of the Tormento, the Castello del Territorio, the fourteenth-century campanile of San Vincenzo, and the tower of the basilica of San Felice.[8] Bellini portrays Vicenza's skyline almost as it would be later immortalized by Dragonzino da Fano, but with a significant variation: the cathedral is on the opposite side, and in its place is the cathedral of San Ciriaco, Ancona.

In his search for a connection between a high-ranking citizen of Vicenza and the city of Ancona, Enrico Maria Dal Pozzolo recalled the curious episode in which the bishop of Vicenza, Battista Zeno, in that office from 1471 to 1501, "coming from Rome to Ancona hid twenty-six thousand gold ducats in a wall of the church."[9] If the event seems rather random, it should be mentioned that the bishop was very attached to the city of Vicenza, so much so that at his death, which occurred in Padua on May 8, 1501, he left five thousand ducats to "build the principal chapel of the Vicenza cathedral."[10] In any case, the presence of Ancona's cathedral in the painting establishes a timeframe within the first years of the cinquecento, since during this time the iconographic fortunes of the Adriatic city reached their height in the Veneto. We know from a letter of Vittore Carpaccio, dated August 15, 1511, that when he offered *View of Jerusalem* to Francesco Gonzaga, Marquess of Mantua, he reminded him that he was that "painter brought by their excellencies the Council of Ten to paint in the large hall [the Great Council Hall in the Ducal Palace in Venice] our work,

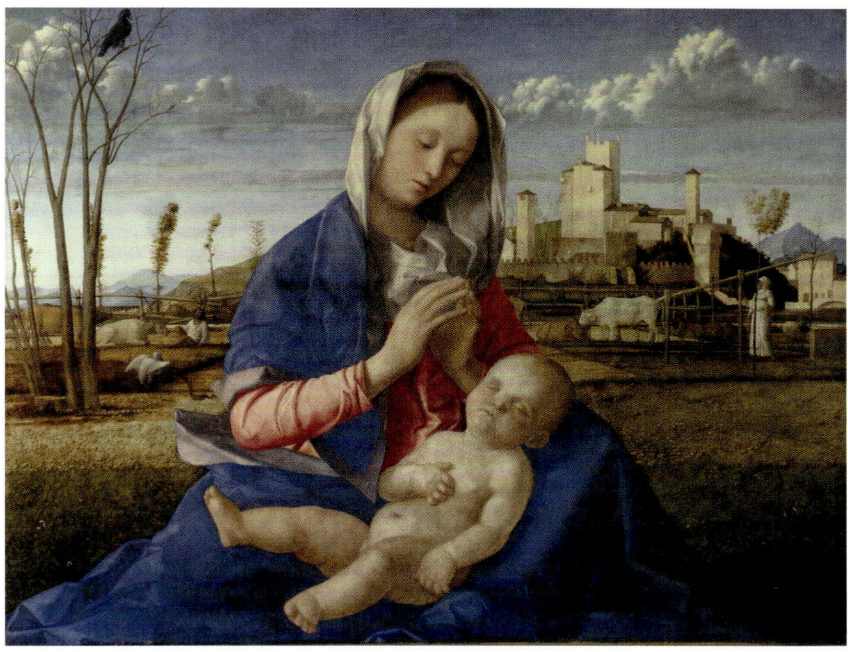

which is the history of Ancona. And my name is said Victor Carpathio."[11] Unfortunately, we have no other information establishing when Carpaccio received this commission. Works by him, that can be dated to the first decade of the sixteenth century, however, suggest that the painter spent time in Ancona during those years, deriving material for the backgrounds of his own paintings, as attested by a sheet from life in the British Museum, London (inv. 1897, 0410.1).

In addition to the depiction of Ancona's cathedral, an indication of a date in the early cinquecento is offered by the allusion to the *Titulus Crucis,* said to be a fragment of the inscription from Christ's cross, which was found in Rome in 1492. The discovery generated considerable excitement, and reference to the *Titulus* is also made in two canvases by Luca Signorelli and a triptych by Francesco Granacci executed around the same date.[12] However, the notion that the Hebrew inscriptions on the tombstones can be used to date the Niccolini *Crucifixion* must be discounted.

According to insights kindly communicated to me by Malachi Beit-Ariè and Menahem Schmelzer, it is impossible to confirm the reading of the dates 1501 and 1502–3, as previously suggested by Elio Toaff and Giuliano Tamani.[13]

Vicenza's aggressive policies against Jews may, however, explain the many references to Judaism that appear in both the Capodimonte *Transfiguration* (see fig. 6) and the Niccolini *Crucifixion.* Hatred of Jews exploded in 1485 following the death of the Blessed Lorenzino Sossio da Valrovina in Marostica, and subsided only with their expulsion in 1486. Even before these events Jews had suffered persecutions in Vicenza and nearby cities by local officials of the Church for many years. The canon Alessandro Nievo's *Consilia contra Iudaeos foenerantes* (Actions against Jews lending money at interest) was published in 1474 (reprinted in 1477). In 1477 Pietro Bruto, Bishop Zeno's regent, published an *Epistula contra Iudaeos* (Letter against the Jews), which demanded justice for the death in 1475 of the Blessed Simon of Trent, the first and most famous case of heinous ritual sacrifice reported to have taken place in those years.[14] This episode is relevant to our investigations, since among the humanists enlisted in this battle against the Jews by the prince-bishop of Trent, Johannes Hinderbach, were Raffaele Zovenzoni and Felice Feliciano, who were some of the earliest admirers of Bellini's art.[15]

As has been pointed out on several occasions, the cemetery strewn with skulls and bones represents the world of death, above which rises Christ, who leads humanity to salvation in the heavenly Jerusalem. As Augusto Gentili suggested, Bellini was inclined to introduce into his landscapes certain elements apparently unrelated to the principal narrative that in fact led the devotee to penetrate the subtleties of the painting's message.[16] In the Niccolini *Crucifixion* in particular, Keith Christiansen has pointed out that the landscape resembles a "poetic fantasy" or, rather, a "devotional poesia." He cites a passage from Saint Bernard: "he began to wander, a foolish boy, among the mountains of pride, the valleys of curiosity, the fields of licentiousness, the woods of lechery, the swamps of carnal desires, and the waters of worldly cares."[17] Christiansen then suggests pursuing a similar journey in order to assimilate the complexity of the work, along the paths that lead from the earthly Vicenza — the human city in the background — to the heavenly Jerusalem through the suffering of the crucified Christ, placed in the foreground and isolated from his surroundings. The devotee will encounter the skulls, the worn tombstones with their Hebrew inscriptions, the withered tree, the budding tree with a dove, the luxuriant tree farther back, and the silent village with its mill, where daily activities are taking place.[18] The painting, besides being in a

remarkable state of preservation, retains its original dimensions, allowing us to marvel at the profound emotive impact of Bellini's choices in imagining this work. Here, unlike what he conceived in his other *Crucifixions* (cat. nos. 2, 3, 6), Bellini set the cross directly on the edge of the frame, so that the body of Christ is on the threshold between the viewer's space and the fictive space of the landscape.

The date of the Niccolini *Crucifixion* has been the object of much scholarly debate owing to the worn condition of the tombstones (supposedly bearing the date 1501–2) and the composition of the landscape, which in certain ways recalls that of the *Saint Francis in the Desert* (see fig. 8), unanimously dated to about 1480.[19] But as Carlo Gamba, Giles Robertson, Bernard Aikema and Neville Rowley, among others, have pointed out, the similarities are less substantial than they appear.[20] In the Niccolini *Crucifixion* there is none of the sharp angularity of Saint Francis's face and body, nor is the landscape investigated with the clarity of summer morning light as in the Frick picture. Everything seems instead softened and immersed in a hazy atmosphere, which suggests the dialogue between the elderly Bellini and the young Giorgione at the dawn of the *maniera moderna*.

Giorgione's early efforts in painting such as the *Homage to a Poet* (see fig. 42), the *Trial of Moses* (Florence, Galleria degli Uffizi), and the Benson *Holy Family* (Washington, DC, National Gallery of Art) share the same mood as late masterpieces by Bellini such as the *Pietà (Donà delle Rose)* (see fig. 34) and the *Madonna of the Meadow* in London (fig. 35), which have been evoked as stylistic points of comparison for the Niccolini *Crucifixion*. In these late works the colors are rendered vibrant with pearly, nearly transparent tints, with landscapes that are ever more atmospheric. The new relationship between figure and landscape recalls Giorgione's *Virgin and Child in a Landscape* (Saint Petersburg, State Hermitage Museum), or at least its sources.[21] The Niccolini *Crucifixion* should be situated precisely in this context, slightly earlier than the *Baptism of Christ* in Santa Corona (see fig. 38), which can be dated with some confidence after 1502. In December of that year, the documents make reference only to building works relating to the construction of the chapel, with no mention of a commission for an altarpiece. Based on what we know of the typical sequence of such projects, the altarpiece was probably delivered the following year.[22]

M.V.

1 "dann bei Marchese Niccolini. Diese [marchese] hat her[rlichen] Bellini (?) Christus am Kreuk"; Metropolitan Museum of Art, New York, Onassis Library, Jean-Paul Richter, Diaries, 1891.

2 Gamba 1937, 146–47, fig. 158.

3 Tempestini 2003, 61.

4 For a summary, see Dal Pozzolo 2003.

5 Barbarano 1649–1762, 5:29. These events took place in 1613, as indicated by the inscription placed there for the new dedication of the chapel reported by Barbarano. Edoardo Arslan (Arslan 1956, 28) connected the altarpiece to the terms of the 1467 will of the archpriest Alberto Fioccardo and identified with the *Transfiguration* in The Museo Nazionale di Capodimonte, Naples (inv. Q 56), which, however, bears the much later date of 1478–79, given in Hebrew characters (for a summary, see Dal Pozzolo 2003, 15–18).

6 Barausse 2008, 340, doc. no. 40:"ducati duecento in questo modo, cento in la palla con lo altar in qual sia depenta la Ressuretion del nostro signore Gesù Christo nel modo ho ordinato Zuan Bellin, li altri cento sia da depenzer detta capella a capituli di tutta la Passion di Christo."

7 Rigon 2003.

8 Rigon 2003.

9 Barbarano 1649–1762, 4: 68; Riccardi 1786, 182; Dal Pozzolo 2003, 28.

10 "la fabbrica della cappella maggior del duomo di Vicenza"; Barbarano 1649–1762, 4:71; Riccardi 1786, 182; Dal Pozzolo 2003, 28.

11 "pictor dallo excello Consiglio de i Diece conducto per dipinger in salla grande [sala del Maggior Consiglio in Palazzo Ducale a Venezia] l'opra nostra che è la historia de Ancona. Et il nome mio è dicto Victor Carpathio."The Carpaccio-Ancona file was compiled systematically in Zampetti 1997.

12 Francesco Granacci's triptych, ca. 1510, New York, Metropolitan Museum of Art, 2006.409. We should recall at least the two-sided standard, with a documented date of 1494, that Luca Signorelli painted for Urbino's confraternity of the Holy Spirit (Urbino, Galleria Nazionale delle Marche, inv. 1990 D 60, 61) and his *Crucifixion with Mary Magdalene* (Florence, Galleria degli Uffizi, inv. 1890, no. 8368), from the convent of San Vincenzo di Annalena, Florence, datable to the turn of the sixteenth century. For these works, see Ronen 1992.

13 Dal Pozzolo 2003, 29n42, with a summary of the various proposed readings. Giuliano Tamani essentially confirmed Elio Toaff's reading, identifying the date 1501 or 1502 on the right tombstone. Ida Zatelli, on the other hand (see Marchini 1981, 18), had read the dates as 1441–42 and 1462–63. Malachi Beit-Ariè and Menahem Schmelzer, who studied the inscriptions using a high-resolution image, kindly informed me that they "could not read any clear dates, and the fragmented texts imply that they were not dating indications but rather incoherent imitation of Jewish gravestones." I am very grateful to Evelyn Cohen for helping me in this research.

14 Dal Pozzolo 2003, 24–28. On the Blessed Simon of Trent episode and other cases of anti-Judaism in the Triveneto in these years, see Callegari 1998, 88–90.

15 On the relations between Giovanni Bellini and the humanists, see Agosti 2009, 7–22; Vinco 2014, 97.

16 Gentili 1991, 41–56; Gentili 2004.

17 Christiansen 2004b, 57 no. 55.

18 Christiansen 2004b, 49–51; Christiansen 2013, 12. For a different iconographic reading of the painting, in which the upper section is identified with the *salvatio* of the heavenly Jerusalem/ Vicenza, in contrast to the earthly, mortal lower zone, see Aikema, in Venice 1999, 210, cat. 14.

19 A date around 1480 is favored by Heinemann 1962, 1:47; Lucco 1990, 2:451; Lucco 1994, 24; and, most recently, by Tempestini, in Vicenza 2003, 61–63; Tempestini, in Paolucci 2004, 53–57, cat. no. 3; Villa, in Rome 2008, 216–18, cat. no. 23.

20 Gamba 1937, 146–47; Robertson 1968, 115; Aikema, in Venice 1999, 210, cat. 14; Rowley 2008, 849.

21 On Giorgione's first phase, see Ballarin 1978, 228–29; on the relationship between Giovanni Bellini and Giorgione, see Mazzotta 2009, 14–17.

22 Garzadori's request to use "the empty space near the altar of the Madonna, toward the choir" [lo spazio vuoto presso l'altare della Madonna, dalla banda del Coro] (Bortolan 1889, 264) of the church of Santa Corona was recorded on November 2, 1500. Initial work on the chapel began, however, only in December 1502, when the patron "had placed in that chapel all the columns carved in stone with a frame and a frieze above the altar [fece mettere alla detta capela tutte quelle colone intagliate di preda con la cornice et friso di sopra dal altare] (Bortolan 1889, 265).

ca. 1500, panel, 59 × 47 cm (23¼ × 18½ in.)

Fort Worth, Kimbell Art Museum, inv. AP 1967.07

9 | CHRIST BLESSING

Christ is depicted after having risen from the tomb (not shown in the painting) in a strictly frontal image. The waist-height figure's right hand is raised in blessing, while the left holds the staff of the banner of the Resurrection. A cloth of various shades of lilac descends from his left shoulder in broad folds onto his arm, and he wears a white loincloth round his waist (a whiter area of flesh around the navel reveals there had been prudish covering up at a later date, but this repainting was removed during the 1958 restoration). Christ gazes straight out at the viewer, as if lost in thought. Parted in the middle of the forehead of his perfectly oval face, his slightly wavy hair falls over his shoulders. His classical athletic torso is modeled with anatomical accuracy and extremely delicate chiaroscuro transitions (see, for example, the beautiful shadow cast by the blessing arm onto his ribs). The landscape is a perfect counterpoint to the rarefied spirituality and, as Antonio Morassi has rightly observed, "it may be included among those [landscapes] most deeply felt and permeated with poetic mystery ever created by the brush of Giovanni Bellini."[1] The sun is about to rise behind the hills and the already bright sky is tinged with tones ranging from orange to yellow and blue. The same colors are found in the long, thin clouds, streaked on the horizon, which become denser and almost solid higher up. The Earth is still shrouded in semidarkness. On the right, the small cloaked figures of the three Marys hurry toward the tomb, whereas in the background, a bell tower — one can almost hear the bells tolling — stands out against the sky. On the left, under a large wizened tree with a bird on its dead branches, a shepherd drives his flock into a fold, while in the foreground two small rabbits linger and dally (a little later they also appear in the Washington *Saint Jerome,* cat. no. 12). As always in Bellini's works, the symbolic level is wonderfully merged with a feeling of absolute naturalness. When faced with images like this, some lines of verse by Andrea Michiel, called Squarzòla, a Venetian poet and contemporary of Bellini, acquire even greater poignancy. In one of his sonnets Squarzòla puts some words into the mouth of a Christ painted by an unknown artist called Ombrone: Christ complains that he has

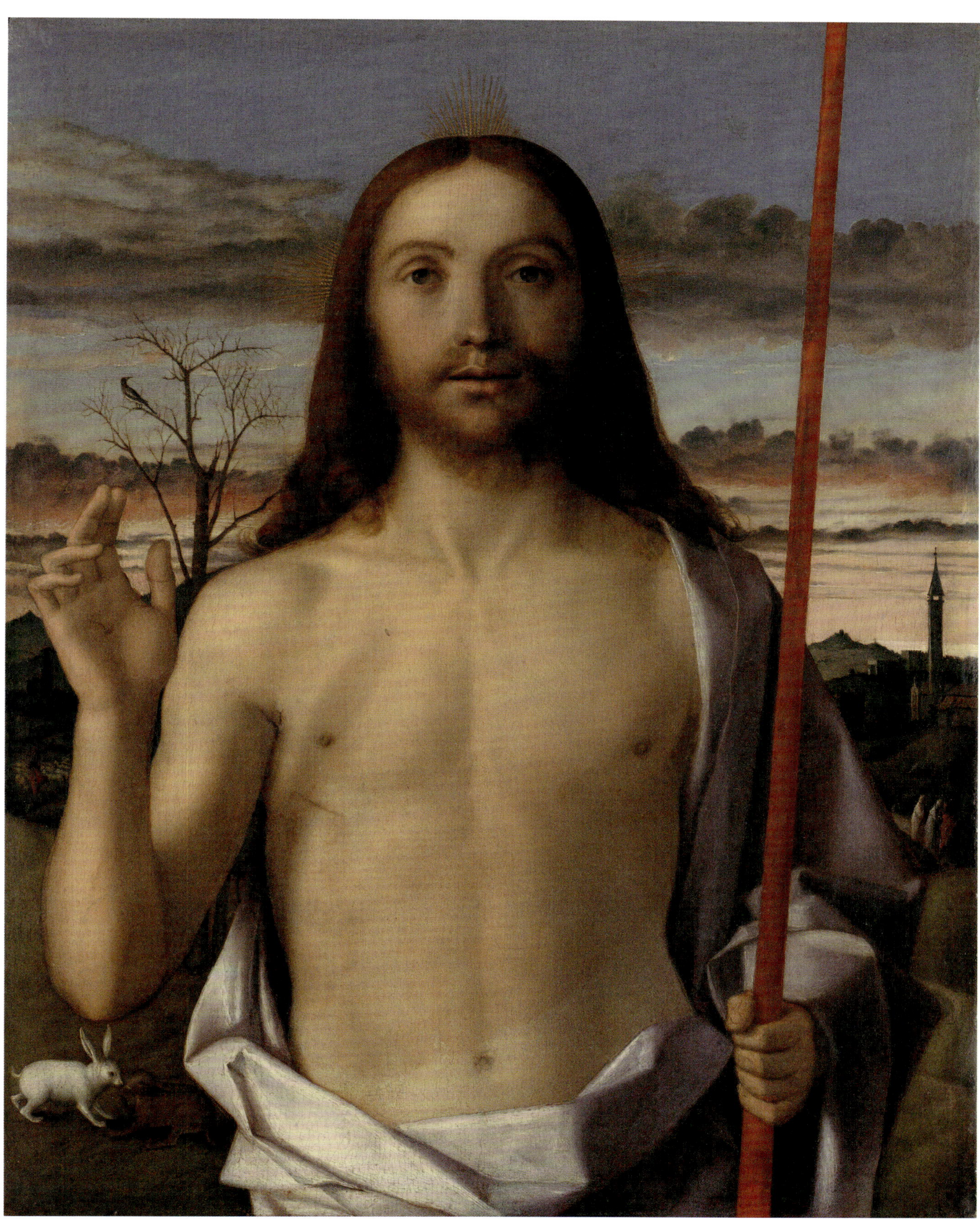

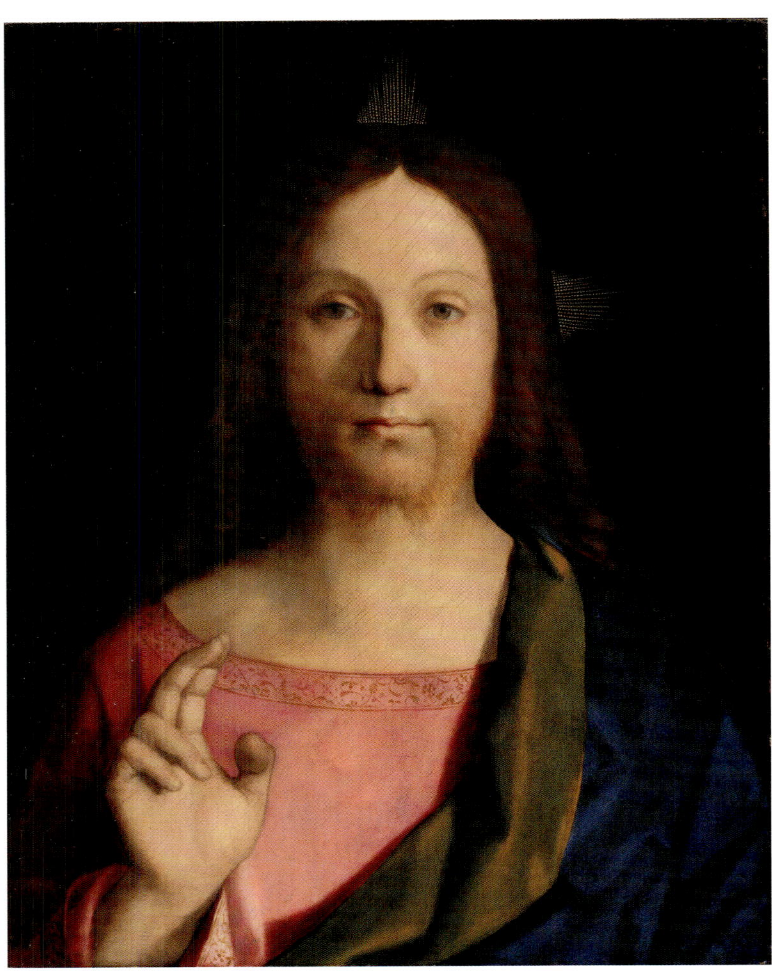

been painted so clumsily that he is totally unable to arouse any feelings of devotion in the faithful, whereas if he had been painted by Bellini he would have been "much more human and more divine."[2]

The size of the panel and the close-up image suggest that this painting was for individual devotion. The iconography is an innovative blend of imagery of the resurrected Christ, risen from the tomb with the banner (usually depicted full-length and also with the tomb) and the kind of close-up *Christ Blessing* set against a neutral background, which Bellini had already tried out on several occasions, such as the now unfortunately greatly damaged work in Ottawa (fig. 36) or the *Christ Blessing* in Galerie Hans, Hamburg. Both borrow the invention of the celebrated prototypes by Antonello da Messina (1475, London, National Gallery) and Hans Memling (1478, Pasadena, Norton Simon Museum).[3] The hieratic frontal view of the figure of Christ and the presence of the landscape are reminiscent, as Mauro Lucco has perceptively pointed out,[4] of the *Resurrection* by Dieric Bouts the Elder, now in the Norton Simon Museum (see fig. 3). The Netherlandish artist's painting on canvas must have been part of a polyptych that could originally have been seen in a church in Venice and that was certainly known to Bellini from the time in the mid-1470s when he was engaged in painting the *Resurrection* now in Berlin (see fig. 4).[5] In the eyes of Bellini's contemporaries, the immobile frontal image would have recalled the ancient sacred aura of Byzantine icons, at that time still a part of Venetians' everyday religious experience. The refined palette and a complete mastery of the sophisticated oil medium enabled Bellini to create an atmosphere of rarefied suspension that, with its perfect fusion of figure and landscape, ushered in a new season of Venetian painting in the early

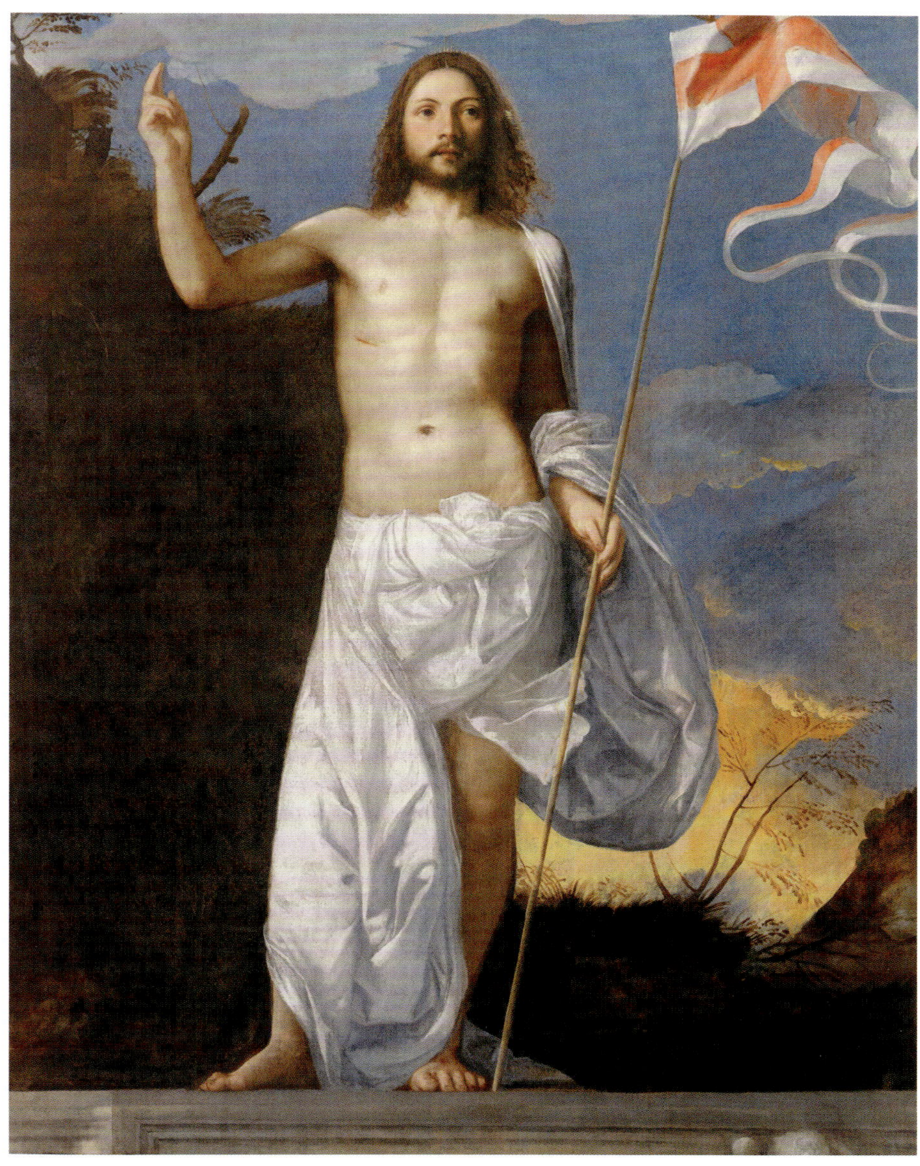

sixteenth century, dominated by Giorgione and the young Titian. There can be no doubt that a few years later, when Titian painted a full-length *Risen Christ* (fig. 37),[6] a recently rediscovered youthful masterpiece, he had closely studied this great work by Bellini. For, in the words of another young artist, Albrecht Dürer, on a visit to Venice in 1506, Bellini was still "the best in painting," despite his venerable age.[7]

The style of the *Christ Blessing* suggests a late date in Bellini's career, and this opinion is shared by nearly all scholars who have considered the work. There are, however, some significant variations in attempts at a more precise date, ranging from

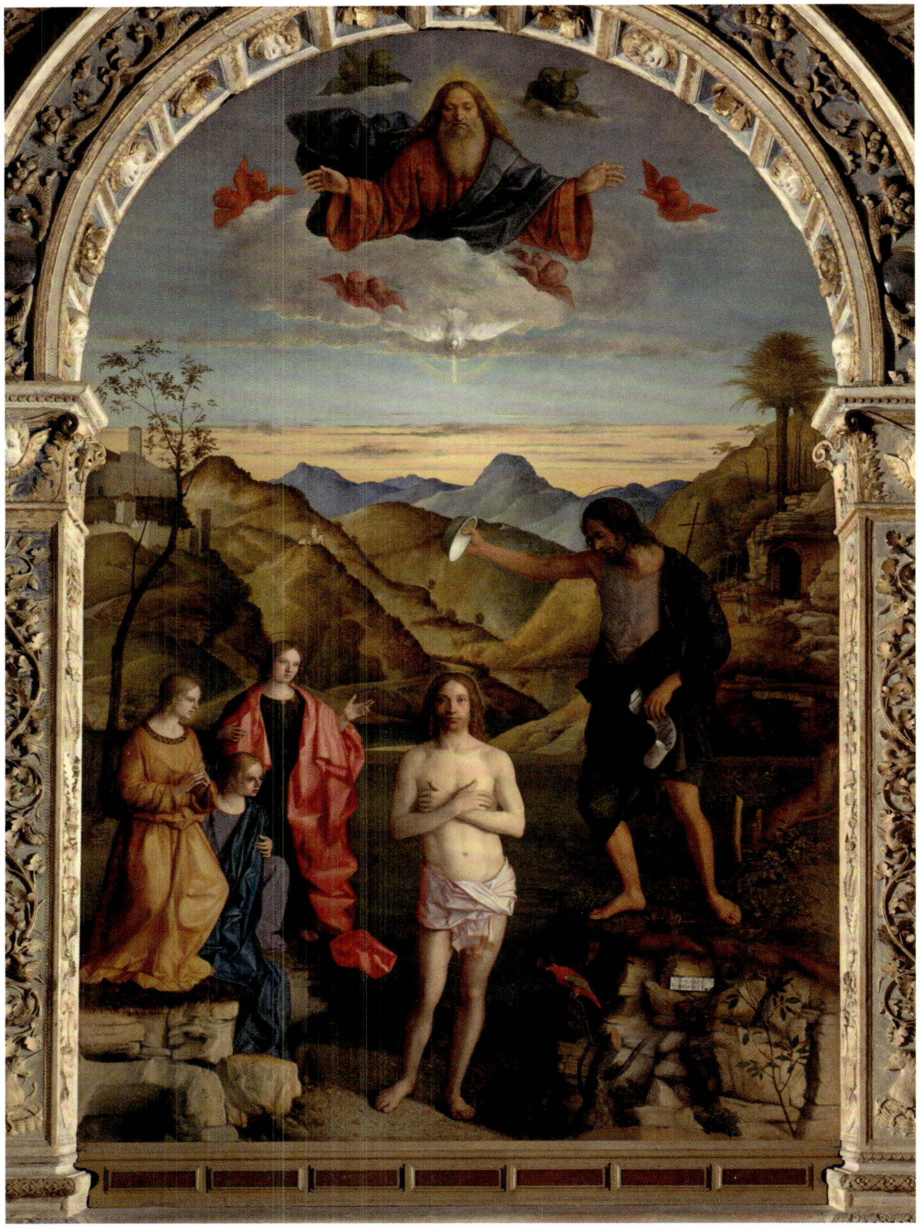

1490 to 1495, proposed by Antonio Morassi, to after 1507, suggested by Anchise Tempestini.[8] I think a date of around the year 1500 is most compatible with the elements and the style, as suggested by comparisons with some of Bellini's more firmly dated works: the Christ in this work is almost a twin of both the full-length figure dominating the *Baptism* in the church of Santa Corona, Vicenza (fig. 38),[9] a work painted between 1501 and 1503, and the wonderful Saint Dominic, now in a private collection in Denver (see fig. 40), which has been convincingly identified as the "half-length figure of Saint Dominic . . . very beautiful," completed in August 1501 for the Duke of Ferrara, Alfonso I d'Este.[10] As in the *Saint Dominic* or the Giovanelli *Sacra Conversazione* (cat. no. 10), the field of the painting is almost entirely occupied by the figure, who seems to lean forward toward the space of the viewer, whereas the landscape with various details in the background endows the image with an intensely poetic character. Bellini in fact referred to this kind of background detail when in a letter to Isabella d'Este of 1502, having refused to paint a profane allegory, he promised to send her a painting on a sacred subject enhanced with "some distant views and other fantasies," that is, a landscape with imaginary details.[11] By then these words summed up what was evidently a kind of trademark for the elderly Venetian painter.

There is no certain information about the provenance of the work until it surfaced in England with an attribution to Cima da Conegliano at the auction of the famous collection of William Coningham in 1849.[12] The painting was then exhibited at the British Institution in 1865, again attributed to Cima, by the new owner, Richard Fisher, an artist and collector who had also lent to the same exhibition Bellini's *Crucifixion*, now in the Louvre (cat. no. 3), at the time attributed to Mantegna. In Tancred Borenius's notes to Joseph Archer Crowe and Giovanni Battista Cavalcaselle's *History of Painting in North Italy*, the painting was mentioned as a work by Marco Basaiti,[13] and this attribution endured until a Sotheby's auction of 1958, just before Antonio Morassi's publication with the correct attribution to Bellini.[14] In presenting the painting, Morassi suggested it should be identified with a work described by Carlo Ridolfi (1648)—"an effigy of the Savior in the act of blessing, extremely rare for the devotion and diligence employed therein, including every last hair and fully expressing the particular feeling of the face"—that Bellini gave to the Augustinian monks in the monastery of Santo Stefano in Venice.[15] Recently Antonio Mazzotta has tried to corroborate this suggestion by arguing that the painting mentioned by Ridolfi is the same work recorded in the will of Giuliano Zancaruol, dated February 1515 (or 1516). The "painting of the figure of Christ" by Giovanni Bellini was thought to have cost fifty ducats and the testator wished to leave it to the church of Santo Stefano, where his tomb was to have been built by Tullio or Antonio Lombardo.[16] Unfortunately, the idea that this painting may be the work now in the Kimbell Museum has been disproved in a recent analytical investigation conducted by Sara Menato: she convincingly demonstrates that the *Christ Blessing* by Bellini still in the Venetian monastery of Santo Stefano in the mid-nineteenth century, before going on the antiquarian market, is very likely the painting now in Galerie Hans, Hamburg.[17]

D.G.

---

1   Morassi 1958, 49.
2   On Bellini and Squarzòla's poems, see, most recently, Wilson 2015, 9.
3   For the Ottawa *Christ Blessing*, see Villa, in Rome 2008, 290–91, cat. no. 49; for the Hamburg painting, see Tempestini 2000, 171.
4   Lucco 1997.
5   There is an excellent discussion of this dismembered polyptych in L. Campbell 1998, 38–45; see also Wolfthal and Metzger 2014, 46–87.
6   Rosenauer 2013.
7   Dürer 1956, 1:43–44.
8   For a date around 1490–95, see Morassi 1958; Pallucchini 1959, 88, 148; Heinemann 1962/1991, 1:57; Bottari 1963, 25; Robertson 1968, 113, 155; and Robb 1972, 30–32. Mazzotta 2009, 14–15, suggests 1498–99. Those who propose a date around 1500 include Pignatti 1969, 103; Clifton 1997, 94; and Lucco 1997. Tempestini 2000, 183, on the other hand, argues for a date later than the Dolfin *Sacra Conversazione* (1507) in San Francesco della Vigna, Venice.
9   Villa, in Rome 2008, 284–87, cat. no. 47.
10 "Una meza figura de San Domenicho . . . asai bela." See Barausse 2008, 345–46, no. 66, for the document; on the painting, see, most recently, Mazzotta 2009, 15; Mazzotta 2015, 192–93.
11 See Barausse 2008, Michele Vianello to Isabella d'Este, November 3, 1502, 347–48, doc. 77: "qualche lontani et altra fantaxia"; on this subject, see my essay in this volume for further details.
12 Haskell 1991, especially 681, no. 37.
13 Crowe and Cavalcaselle 1912, 1:275n2, no. 3.
14 Morassi 1958.
15 Ridolfi [1648] 1914–24, 71n6: "Effigie del Salvatore in atto di benedire, rarissimo per la divotione e per la diligenza usatavi, annoverandovisi ogni minuto pelo, ed esprimendovi ogni particolare sentimento del volto." Cf. Morassi 1958, 50.
16 Mazzotta 2009, 8; for Giovanni Zancaruol's will, see Barausse 2008, 357–58, doc. no. 122: "el chadro de la figura di Christo."
17 Menato 2012.

ca. 1501, panel, 54 × 76 cm (21¼ × 29¹⁵⁄₁₆ in.)
Venice, Gallerie dell'Accademia, inv. no. 881 (Moschini Marconi)

10 | VIRGIN AND CHILD WITH SAINT JOHN THE BAPTIST AND A FEMALE SAINT IN A LANDSCAPE

SIGNATURE
IOANNES BELLINVS (at
bottom center, on parapet)

PROVENANCE
Venice, Giovanelli collection,
from before 1706 until
1925; Venice, Gallerie
dell'Accademia, since 1925

RESTORATION
Before 1925; 1997–98 (Alfeo
Michieletto)

EXHIBITIONS
Rome 1932, cat. no. Sala I,
4; Paris 1935, cat. no. 38; San
Francisco 1939, cat. no. 21;
Rome 1945, cat. no. 21; Venice
1946, cat. no. 140; Venice 1949,
cat. no. 113; Venice 2000, cat.
no. 19; Rome 2008, cat. no. 46

Behind a narrow red marble parapet that bears the signature of the artist, under a summer afternoon light coming from the left, the Virgin Mary sits on an invisible throne at the center and holds the Child Jesus on her knees, keeping him in balance with an extremely soft touch of both hands. The child seems to have just awakened, and while he stares at the viewer he grabs his soft belly with his right hand. On the left stands Saint John the Baptist in a meditative pose, his head and body in a luminous shade. On the right, a female saint without identifying attributes also stands; she crosses her hands on her chest and absently gazes toward an indefinite point in the viewer's space. The three figures seem to be positioned on a rocky pier. On the left, behind a body of water, is a walled town set with its harbor on a steep coast so densely built up that Luciano Bellosi compared it to a Moroccan Casbah.[1] On the right are hills with churches, towers, shepherds, and flocks. Far in the distance is a vast panoramic view of the Alps, topped by a yellow-striped sky.

In an inventory drawn up in 1706 of the Giovanelli family's Venetian palace, this painting is described as "a painting on panel, with gilded frame, with the top carved and gilded, Virgin, Saint John, and another female Saint by Giovanni Bellini," along with measurements nearly identical to this one.[2] In about 1851–52, when the painting was still in the Giovanelli collection, Giovanni Battista Cavalcaselle saw it and made a sketch filled out with many notes,[3] drawing a comparison with an altarpiece by Andrea Previtali in the church of San Giobbe, where the figure of Saint John is nearly identical to the Saint John in the Giovanelli picture, a similarity that led Joseph Archer Crowe and Cavalcaselle to publish the work as by Previtali, despite the signature.[4] In 1854 the soon-to-be first director of London's National Gallery, Charles Lock Eastlake, saw it and believed it to be (incredibly) "an early Bellini," and in 1856 his travel agent Otto Mündler described it as "a very amiable picture, in excellent state."[5] In 1880 Giovanni Morelli rejected the attribution to Previtali, opting for another Bellinesque painter, Vincenzo Catena, an idea that was later accepted by his admirer Bernard Berenson.[6] A few years later, in 1910, Giorgio Bernardini associated

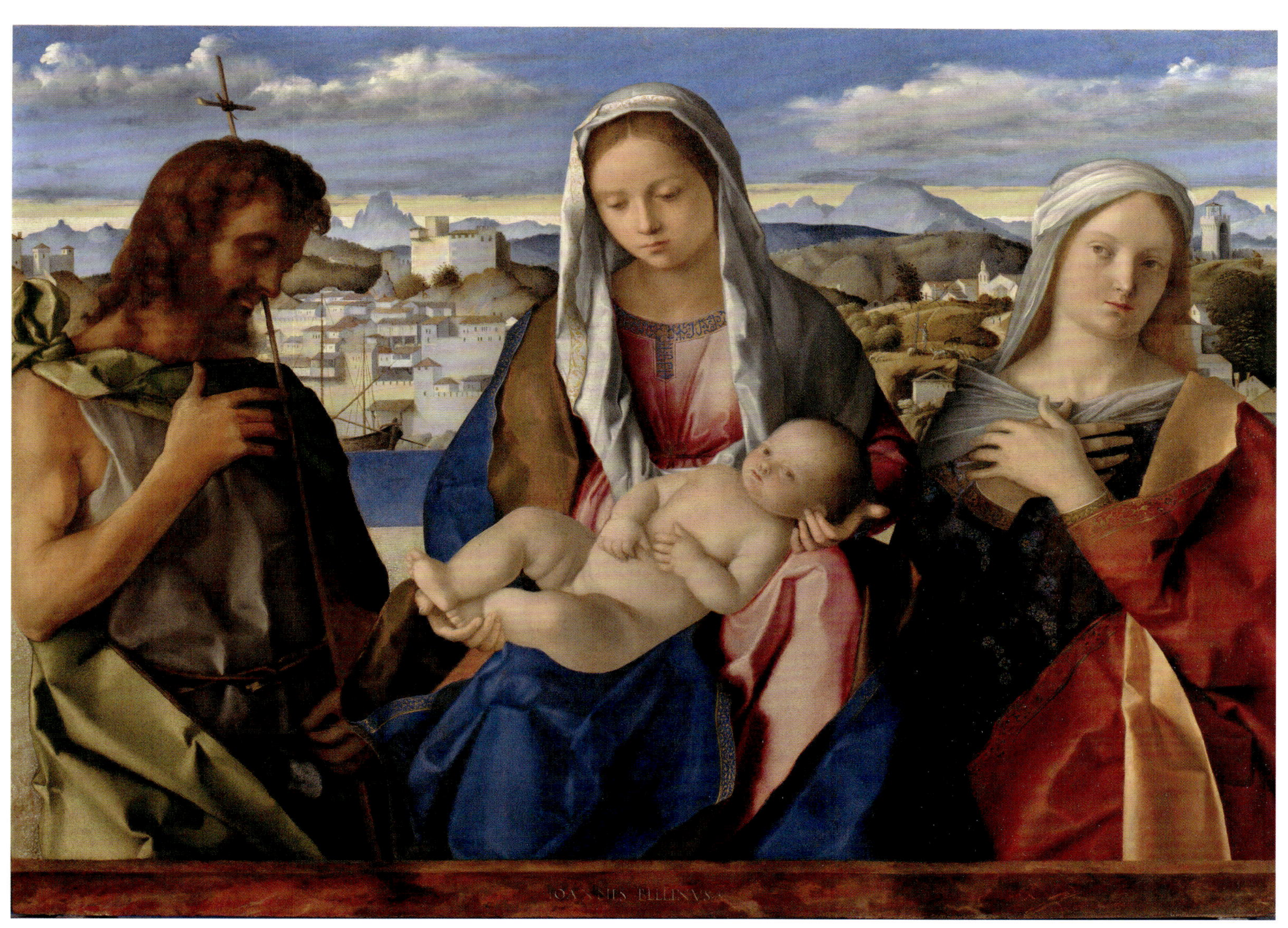

IOANNES BELLINVS

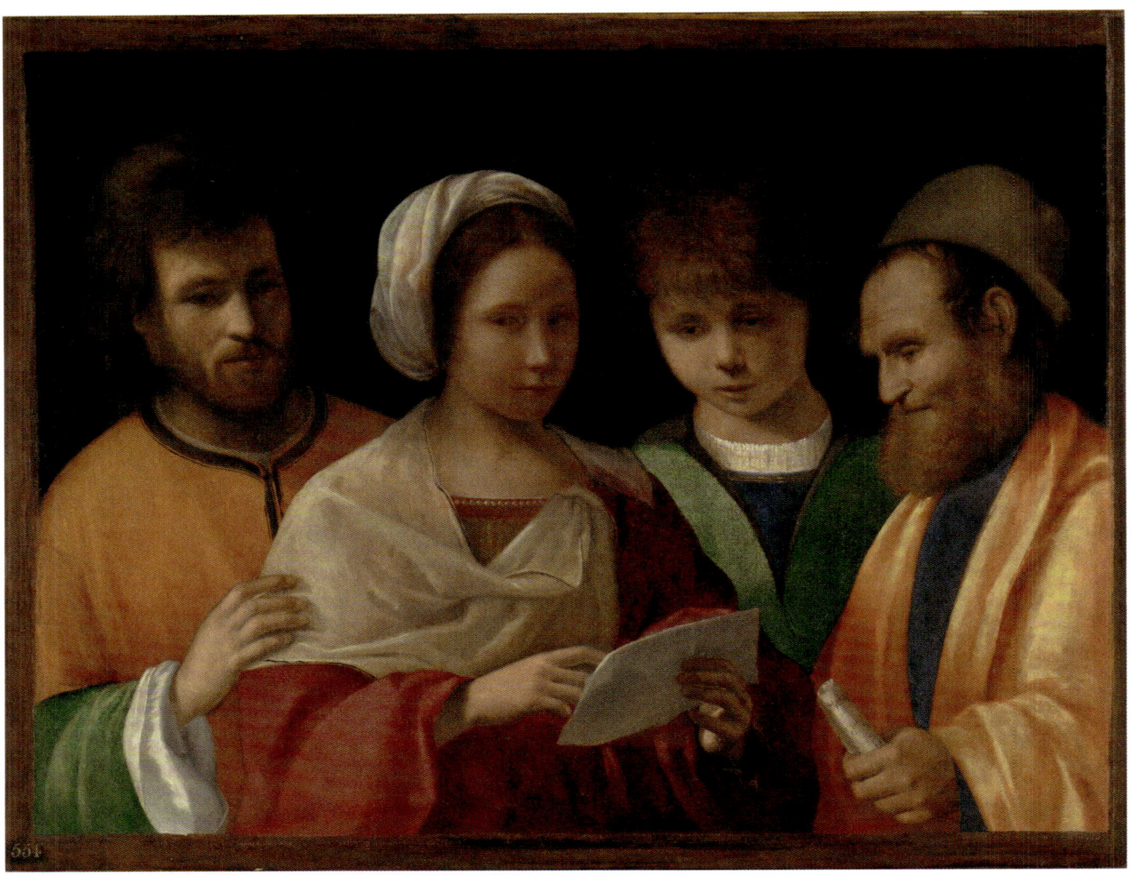

Figure 39
Here attributed to
GIORGIONE
(Italian, ca. 1477/78–1510),
Concert, ca. 1500. Canvas,
77.8 × 99.8 cm (30⅝ ×
39¼ in.). Windsor, Royal
Collection, RCIN 400025c

the Giovanelli *Sacra Conversazione* with a *Madonna and Child* (Rome, Galleria Borghese, inv. no. 176), but attributed both to Catena.[7] Giorgio Bernardini added as a comparison another painting in the Giovanelli collection then (and now) attributed to Catena, the *Virgin and Child between Saint John the Baptist and Saint Peter*, today in the New Orleans Museum of Art (inv. no. K1904). The following year Georg Gronau, while accepting the close similarity between the Borghese *Madonna* and the Giovanelli *Sacra Conversazione* (but not of the other Giovanelli painting), attributed them to the Pseudo-Basaiti, a stylistic designation that in those years contained several paintings that today are commonly

considered to belong to Bellini's late career.[8] As we shall see, the extreme similarity between the Borghese and the Giovanelli paintings must be sustained.[9] In 1914 Giulio Cantalamessa finally attributed the Borghese *Madonna* to Giovanni Bellini himself, but considered the Giovanelli *Sacra Conversazione* of very inferior quality, and therefore the work of an anonymous follower of Bellini.[10] Despite this painting's early twentieth-century misfortune, in 1922 the artist Filippo De Pisis considered it "something to die for."[11]

In 1925 Prince Alberto Giovanelli donated the painting to the Gallerie dell'Accademia in Venice; the controversial dynamic of this bequest is recounted in an editorial in *Dedalo* of 1925 by the Accademia's director, Ugo Ojetti.[12] Prince Giovanelli bequeathed his *Sacra Conversazione* to the Italian state in lieu of paying export taxes on *Portrait of a Man*, then attributed to Titian which he sold to the influential Anglo-American dealer Joseph Duveen.[13] In Ojetti's opinion, this was a big loss for the nation, especially since the *Sacra Conversazione* was still considered to be by a follower of Bellini. Soon after, Roberto Longhi finally recognized the "splendid" *Sacra Conversazione* as an autograph work of Giovanni Bellini. The "Titian" *Portrait*, today in New York (Metropolitan Museum of Art, Jules Bache Collection, inv. no. 49.7.14), is now rightly attributed to Lambert Sustris.[14] In the same moment, Georg Gronau reconstructed Bellini's late career and considered the *Sacra Conversazione* to be one of the milestones of that period.[15] Gronau also linked it with Previtali's *Virgin and Child with Saint John the Baptist and Saint Catherine of Alexandria* (London, National Gallery, inv. no. NG1409), a version of the painting at San Giobbe but in this case bearing the date 1504, which implies that this date must be considered a *terminus ante quem* for the chronology of Bellini's painting.[16] The painting became famous, as evidenced by its inclusion in the propaganda exhibitions of Italian art in Rome (1932), Paris (1935), and San Francisco (1938), and since then its attribution has been only rarely questioned.[17]

The Giovanelli *Sacra Conversazione* is not only a painting by Giovanni Bellini; it is one that represents a turning point in his career and that became a model for painters of later generations. As we pointed out, Previtali based at least two of his works on it, but also Palma il Vecchio, in his *Virgin and Child between Saint John the Baptist and Saint Mary Magdalene* (Genoa, Palazzo Rosso, inv. no. P.B. 283), of about fifteen years later, took great

inspiration from Bellini's model, as did Titian in a drawing in Copenhagen (Statens Museum for Kunst, Den Kongelige Kobberstiksamling, inv. no. 1960-908).[18] It has been argued that the "cold and translucent tones" of the Giovanelli *Sacra Conversazione* can also be found in the early works of Lorenzo Lotto.[19] Bellini was probably able to still be of great inspiration for *maniera moderna* painters because at this stage he updated his style with the innovations of one of his great pupils.

Giles Robertson wrote in 1968 that the "soft modeling" and "chromatic brilliance" of the Giovanelli *Sacra Conversazione* should be interpreted "as a direct reaction to the work of Giorgione as we see it in the Castelfranco Madonna."[20] Giorgione gave much importance to landscape, and it is not a coincidence that this is the first composition by Bellini with the Madonna and two saints in half or three-quarter length that shows a proper landscape behind the figures (previously there had been only black background or sky). Less evident, yet also important, is the Giorgionesque way Bellini uses light, with luminous shadows and sharp cuts on the draperies and figures—for example, on the top of the Madonna's thumb, which catches a spot of light. The same use of light is in Giorgione's *Concert* (fig. 39), where a similar glint catches the left hand of the female figure, and she also directs her eyes toward our space in an ambiguous way, very similar to the gaze of the female saint in Bellini's painting.[21] The gesture of the hands, as well, expresses in both paintings exactly what Walter Pater defined in his essay "The School of Giorgione" as "exquisite pauses in time"—suspended moments of apparent non-action, combined with deep thoughts.[22] The concentrated and thoughtful expressions in Bellini's painting are what make us define this genre

as the *sacra conversazione*: it is as if the holy figures
are in telepathic communication one with the
other. Giorgione employs the same focused yet
absent poses for profane subjects, which is one of
his great innovations. He experimented with the
same skills in a painting of similar format to that
of the Giovanelli *sacra conversazione*, but very dif-
ferently interpreted: the *Virgin and Child with Saint
John the Baptist and Saint Catherine of Alexandria* in
the Gallerie dell'Accademia, Venice (inv. no. 70).

In Bellini's *Sacra Conversazione* there are symbolic references to the Passion—for instance,
Christ's feet are crossed one on top of the other, as
in the Crucifixion.[23] Christ's left leg covers his geni-
tals, but only partially, allowing a glimpse.[24] This is
an elegant allusion to Christ's sexuality, following
Saint Augustine's statement in his *Civitas Dei* (22.18):
Christ was "made up of all the members." The religious symbolism of some details of the landscape
is less evident.[25] Here Bellini displays his peculiar
skill for creating spatial echoes (also emphasized in
cat. no. 7); far in the distance, towers and dolomitic
peaks seem to compete.

In terms of dating, the closeness to the *Baptism of Christ* (see fig. 36), which is documented
between 1501 and 1503, already seems to pinpoint
a date for the *Sacra Conversazione*. But there is a
twin painting, a *Saint Dominic* (fig. 40), which with
all probability is the same "small picture with a
rather lovely half-length figure of Saint Dominic"
that Bellini had just finished on August 3, 1501, and
that was painted for Alfonso d'Este.[26] This would
imply that the *Sacra Conversazione*, which is stylistically very close in all features (figures, landscape)
to the *Saint Dominic*, was painted in 1501 as well.
In the summer of 1501 Bellini spent some time at
his villa, and one could imagine that his sojourns

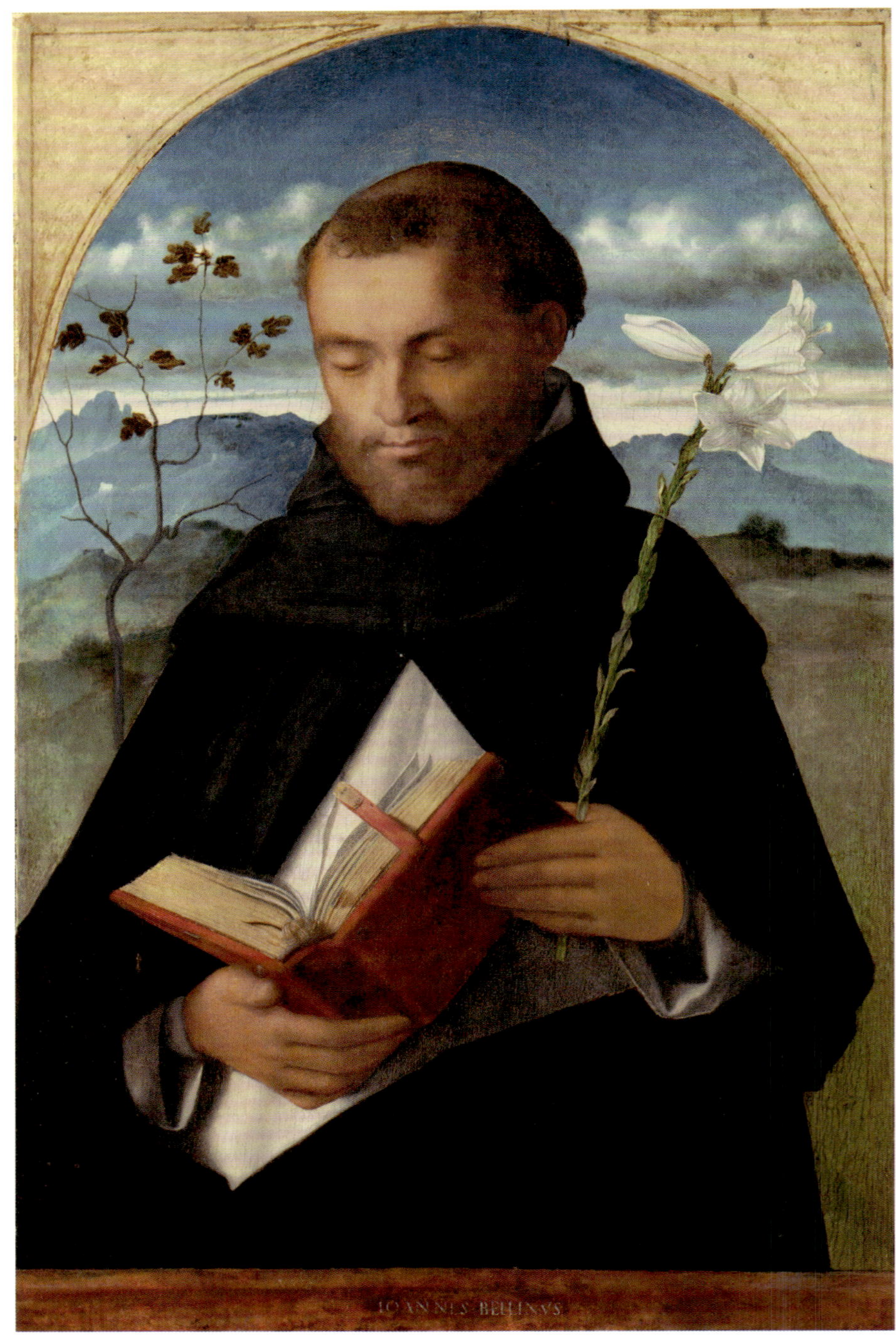

Figure 40 (opposite)
GIOVANNI BELLINI
Saint Dominic, 1501. Panel,
43 × 28 cm (17 × 11 in.).
Denver, private collection

INSCRIPTION
IOANNES BELLINVS
(on the parapet)

PROVENANCE
Ferrara, Alfonso d'Este, later
Duke Alfonso I, by August 1501;
London and Llandaff House,
Weybridge (Surrey), Arthur L.
Nicholson, by 1926 and until
October 14, 1948; New York,
Sotheby's, October 14, 1948;
New York, Mr. and Mrs.
Charles V. Hickox, from before
1955 until after 1969; Denver,
Frederick and Jan Mayer, from
before 1989

RESTORATIONS
After 1928 and before 1968

EXHIBITIONS
Denver 2016, cat. no. 28

in the Veneto countryside inspired the wonderful
views with the Alps behind the hills that are shown
in those two paintings in particular.[27]

To this pair of paintings, then, which were
most probably both executed in 1501, should be
added the previously discussed Borghese *Madonna*
and the little-known and unfortunately badly pre-
served *Madonna and Child with a Donor* in Poznań
(Muzeum Narodowe, inv. no. MO.2).[28]

A.M.

1   Luciano Bellosi, in his
    "Grandezza e precocità
    di Giovanni Bellini," a
    memorable lecture given
    three times (Siena, May 4,
    2009; Venice, July 15, 2010;
    Bergamo, April 13, 2011),
    which will soon be pub-
    lished.

2   "Un quadro in tavola,
    con soazza d'oro, e Cima
    d'intaglio d'oro, Madonna,
    S. Giovanni et altra Santa
    di Giovanni Bellini alto
    quarte 3 crescenti largho
    quarte 4." As reported in
    Barbantini 1908, 187, note
    1. The inventories are not
    available in public archives
    and are probably still in
    the private archive of the
    Giovanelli heirs. On the
    Giovanelli, who were of
    Bergamasque origin and
    were ennobled only in
    1668, and their collection,
    see Haskell 1963, 262n6;
    and Lauber 2009.

3   Venice, Biblioteca Marci-
    ana, Fondo Cavalcaselle, It.
    IV. 2037 (=12278), Taccuino
    IV, fols. 18v–19r. There is
    another sketch, but with
    Joseph Archer Crowe's
    notes in English, in Lon-
    don, National Art Library,
    Special Collections, no.
    86.ZZ.33, box 10, Italian
    Galleries.

4   Crowe and Cavalcaselle
    1871, 1:273–74. For the
    San Giobbe painting, see
    Penny 2004, 278, fig. 2.

5   Avery-Quash 2011, 1:217 (he
    saw it again in 1864: Avery-
    Quash 2011, 1:665); and
    Dowd 1985, 138, 215.

6   Morelli 1880, 208–9n1;
    Berenson 1894, 97. Morelli
    saw the Giovanelli painting
    in 1872: Anderson 1999,
    144–45, doc. no. 3.

7   Bernardini 1910, 142.

8   Gronau 1911. The Pseudo-
    Basaiti stylistic group was
    invented by Ludwig and
    Bode 1903, 141.

9   Today this similarity is
    unfortunately not sus-
    tained anymore, as the two
    works are considered to be
    about ten years apart; see,
    for instance, Villa, in Rome
    2008, 280–83, 314–17, cat.
    nos. 46 and 60.

10 Cantalamessa 1914.

11 "roba da morire"; see
    Agosti 2009, 150–51,
    191nn95–97.

12 [Ojetti] 1925–26.

13 Secrest 2004, 305, 307, 493.

14 Longhi [1927] 1967, 182.
    The attribution to Sustris
    of the portrait was first
    made, hesitantly, by Wilde
    1934, 172n27; and then
    definitively by Ballarin
    1962, 73, 77, fig. 89.

15 Gronau 1928, 18–19, pl. xv;
    Gronau 1930, 152, 214. Fol-
    lowed by Moschini Mar-
    coni 1955, 76–77, cat. no.
    77 (this entry provides the
    information that the paint-
    ing was restored before
    it entered the Accademia
    collection).

16 Previtali's paintings were
    reproduced together
    already by Crowe and
    Cavalcaselle 1912, 1:280.

17 Berenson 1932, 74, finally
    accepted the attribution
    to Bellini and considered
    it to be "L" (late). On the
    San Francisco propaganda
    exhibition, see Carletti
    and Giometti 2011. The
    attribution was more
    recently questioned only
    by Goffen 1989, 58–62
    ("Giovanni Bellini with
    probable assistance").
    Infrared reflectography
    revealed several pentimenti
    in the Madonna and in
    the head of the Baptist
    (Spezzani 1992, 53, figs.
    a–b), and they were con-
    firmed by conservation
    treatment and radiography
    (Michieletto, in Venice
    2000, 86–87, fig. 1).

18 On the Titian drawing, see
    Weston-Lewis 2002.

19 Longhi [1946], 1978, 11:
    "toni freddi e traslucidi."

20 Robertson 1968, 115. The
    Castelfranco altarpiece
    should be dated 1500, as
    demonstrated by Cortesi
    Bosco 2005; and Cortesi
    Bosco 2009.

21 This painting, despite its
    extremely high quality, is
    today attributed to Vittore
    Belliniano, most probably
    due to its mediocre state
    of conservation: Lucy
    Whitaker, in London 2007,
    182–84, cat. no. 57. For the
    attribution to Giorgione
    and its Bellinesque links,
    also with the Giovanelli

Sacra Conversazione: see
    Mazzotta 2009, 6, 12, 15,
    figs. 8, 10, 16, 24n21; Maz-
    zotta 2015, 191–94, figs. 8
    and 13, 201n23, 375, 378,
    plates 50, 53.

22 Pater 1893, 157.

23 Gentili 1991, 45–46, fig. 16.

24 Steinberg 1983, 15–16.

25 As proposed by Battisti
    1980.

26 Barausse 2008, 345–46,
    doc. no. 66: "meza figura
    de San Domenicho ch'è
    asai bela su un quadreto
    picolo." It is discussed and
    first reproduced in color
    in Mazzotta 2009, 7, fig. 9,
    15–16, 24n71 (see also Maz-
    zotta 2015, 192–93, fig. 12,
    197, 377, plate 52).

27 Bellini's being at his "villa"
    is mentioned in a letter
    from Michele Vianello to
    Isabella d'Este, June 25,
    1501: Barausse 2008, 345,
    doc. no. 64. It is worth
    noting that in November
    1502, at the time of the
    difficult deal with Isabella
    d'Este for a *presepio* (see
    cat. no. 11), Bellini offered
    to paint instead a Madonna
    and Child with Saint John
    the Baptist in a landscape;
    see Barausse 2008, 348,
    doc. no. 78.

28 For the Borghese and
    Poznań paintings in
    relation to the Giovanelli
    Sacra Conversazione, see
    Mazzotta 2012, 39, 44, 46,
    48–49, figs. 22–23, 78–80,
    fig. 51.

ca. 1500–1504, panel, 73 × 119 cm (28¾ × 46⅞ in.)

Florence, Galleria degli Uffizi, inv. 1890 no. 903

11 | SACRED ALLEGORY

The setting for this scene is a raised terrace, which is enclosed except on the viewer's side, by a white stone balustrade and paved with finely laid geometric slabs of colored marbles (antique green, red marble from Verona, and white and black marbles). The spectator's point of view is pushed slightly toward the right, stationing the florid tree in a planter in the exact middle of a cross of marble slabs on the terrace, which seems slightly off center. This space is populated by a number of figures of every age, the most prominent being a woman, on the left, sitting on an elevated throne with an elegantly designed baldachin. She and four other figures — two young females (one kneeling) and two elderly males (one of whom stands next to a young man, whose hands are tied) — are shown in an attitude of contemplation, with the hands joined in prayer, while another figure stands behind the barrier with his sword raised and seems to be shouting toward a turbaned figure leaving the painted space at the left. Three children — two nude and one dressed and seated on a cushion — play with apples that have just fallen from the tree shaken by another child, who is also nude and slightly older than the others. Behind the terrace, beyond a narrow strip of grass with bare trees (in contrast to the tree inside the terrace), is a lake, whose motionless waters reflect the shores and the figures who populate them. On the closest shore, at far right, an elderly monk is descending stairs from a natural terrace surmounted by a cross, keeping his balance with the help of a wooden handrail. He is not aware of a centaur hiding in the shadows ready to ambush him. On the same shore, farther to the left, a male figure surrounded by sheep and goats sits in a melancholic pose inside a partly artificial cavern, his red robe reflected in the waters of the lake. Deeper into the distance, on the lake cove, is a rural town with a few figures, two dressed in white absorbed in discussion, the other two herding a donkey. On a farther plane are wooded hills, with a castle at the center and an imposing cliff on the left. A cloudy and slightly agitated sky contrasts with the placid lake below.

The first record of this painting appears in the inventory of the collection of the Venetian

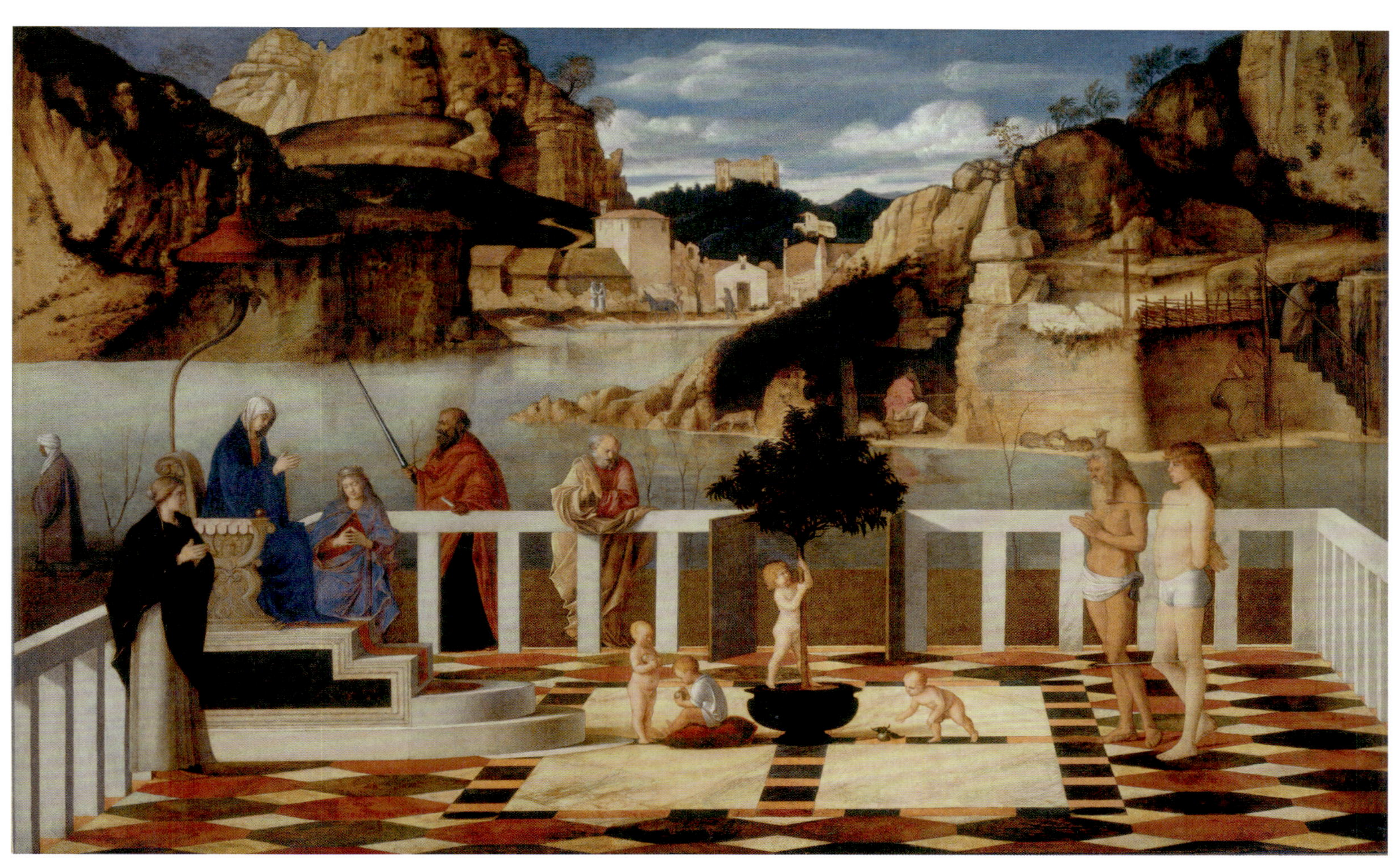

merchant Bartolomeo della Nave, drawn up sometime after his death and certainly before January 12
or 22, 1638: "126. A Garden—which is the garden of
the Holy Church—with various figures, numbering
13. Very beautiful. *6 palmi* in length, 4.5 in height,
by Gio Bellino."[1] The number 126 is still visible in
white chalk on the back of the panel. In March 1638
Viscount Basil Feilding, the English ambassador to
Venice, concluded the deal on behalf of his brother-
in-law James Hamilton, a Scottish-born favorite
of Charles I, for the acquisition of the della Nave
collection. During the same year, shortly after its
acquisition, the painting appeared in the inventory
of Hamilton's collection: "8. An excellent piece of a
nativity wherein is 7 figures, and a rare landscape of
John Belline."[2] A few years later, in 1642, probably
owing to the outbreak of the English Civil War, the
Hamilton collection was placed in cases, and this
painting was listed in the twenty-second case as
"a pece where in is four boyes one of which holds
a tree," thereby losing the name of the painter.[3]
Hamilton was executed on March 9, 1649, and
almost immediately Archduke Leopold Wilhelm of
Austria, governor of the Spanish Low Countries,
bought a large part of the Hamilton collection and
drew up an inventory in French, which included
this work under "Jean Beline": "161. Our Lord in
the Garden with many Saints."[4] Leopold Wilhelm
brought the paintings to Brussels soon after, as
evidenced by the famous views of his galleries by
David Teniers the Younger (although this painting
cannot be seen).[5] A decade or so later, Leopold
Wilhelm brought his collection to the Stallburg in
Vienna. Its inventory, written in German in July
1659, provides the first extended iconographic interpretation of this painting, identifying the Virgin on
the throne, and also Saints Peter and Paul, but lists
it as by an unknown master (adding, interestingly,

that it still had an old gilt frame, a different one
from today).[6] The measurements reported in this
inventory (ca. 91.5 × 133 cm), even though they
might include the frame, seem to indicate that the
panel was later reduced in height, a hypothesis that
apparently finds confirmation in the missing top of
the cliff and in a later catalogue with more accurate
measurements.[7] In 1735 it appeared in Frans von
Stampart and Anton Joseph von Prenner's *Prodromus*, a volume with views of fictive walls of the
imperial collection; in 1783 Christian von Mechel
included it as the work of "Giacomo Bellino dem
ältern" [Jacopo Bellini] in his catalogue of the galleries that had just been reinstalled in the Obern
Belvedere in Vienna.[8]

A few years later, in 1792–93, because of
Habsburg-Lorraine family relations there was a
large exchange of paintings between the imperial
gallery in Vienna and the grand duke's gallery in
Florence. On the Florentine side, this project was
devised by Giuseppe Pelli Bencivenni and Luigi
Lanzi and completed by Tommaso Puccini. On February 29, 1793, this painting is listed among works
that had just arrived in Florence from Vienna: "Gio.
Bellino—Saint Sebastian with Saint Onuphrius,
and other small figures."[9] The painting stayed at
the Medici Villa del Poggio Imperiale for a couple
of years, and in 1795 it finally entered—as a work
by Giovanni Bellini—the Galleria degli Uffizi.[10]
The attribution was soon changed: in the 1817 catalogue of the Uffizi (written in French), the painting
is attributed to Giorgione owing to its apparent
association with the *Judgment of Solomon*, which
is still attributed to him (Florence, Galleria degli
Uffizi, inv. 1890 no. 947).[11] The catalogue described
it as: "The vision of a saint, subject nearly unintel-
ligible."[12] In the 1825 inventory of the Uffizi it also
appeared as the work of Giorgione, still associated

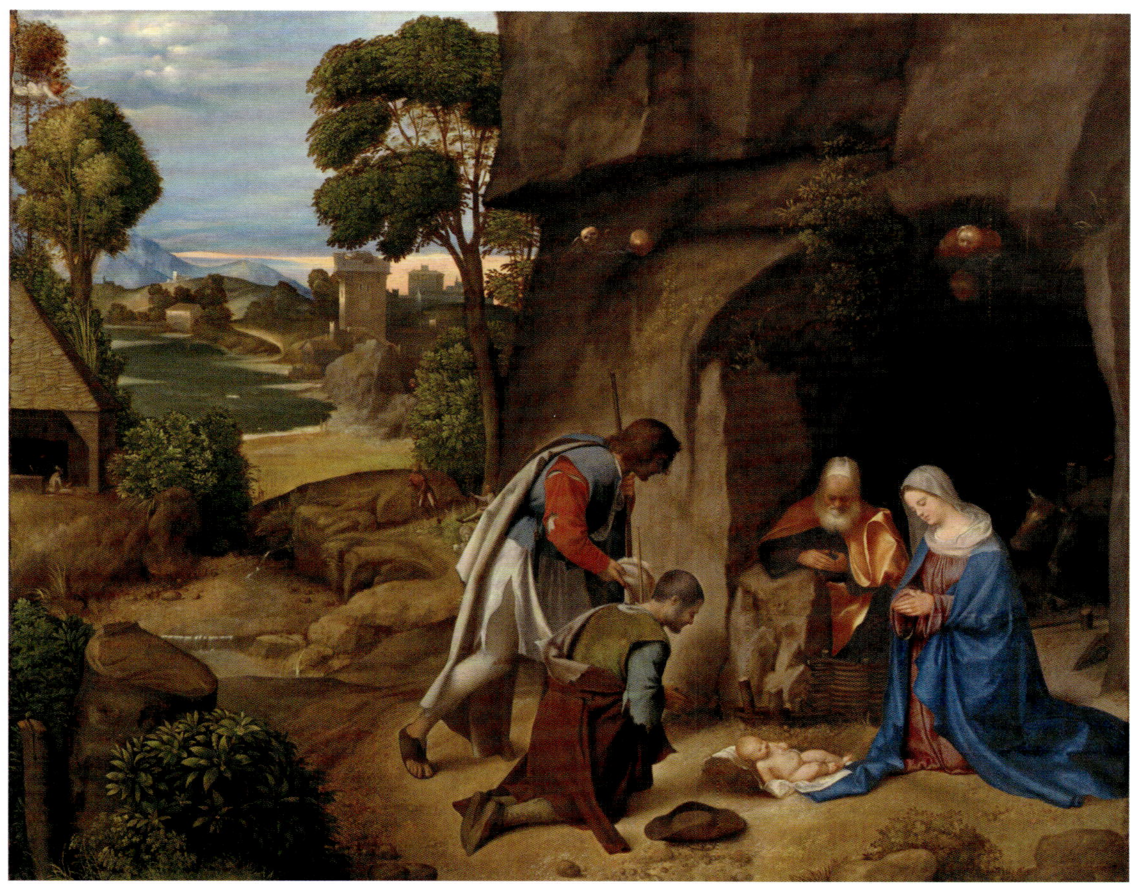

with the *Judgment of Solomon,* and this time also with the latter's true pendant, the *Trial of Moses* (Florence, Galleria degli Uffizi, inv. 1890 no. 945).[13] In the mid-nineteenth-century printed catalogues of the Uffizi paintings, it started to be called an "allégorie" and to be defined as "a holy group" ("une Sainte Société"), still listed as by Giorgione and as a pendant of the *Judgment of Solomon.*[14] This is the moment when, in about 1858–59, Edgar Degas copied it, probably thinking he was copying a Giorgione.[15] In the 1864 catalogue the two true Giorgiones were finally labeled as pendants, and this picture appeared for the first time with today's conventional title — *Sacred Allegory* ("allégorie religieuse") and as questionably by Giorgione.[16] Joseph Archer Crowe and Giovanni Battista Cavalcaselle in 1871 discussed the three "Giorgione" "Cabinet Pictures" at the Uffizi, but considered this allegory to be by Bellini and the other two to be by Giorgione, and compared all of them with another "Cabinet Picture": the Allendale *Adoration of the Shepherds* (fig. 41).[17] In the 1870s Karl Eduard von Liphart attributed the *Sacred Allegory* to Marco Basaiti, Liphart's authority having been given weight by his attribution of the *Annunciation* (Florence, Galleria degli Uffizi, inv. 1890 no. 1618) to Leonardo da Vinci; it had arrived at the Uffizi in 1867 as a Ghirlandaio.[18] The "Allegoria Sacra" was

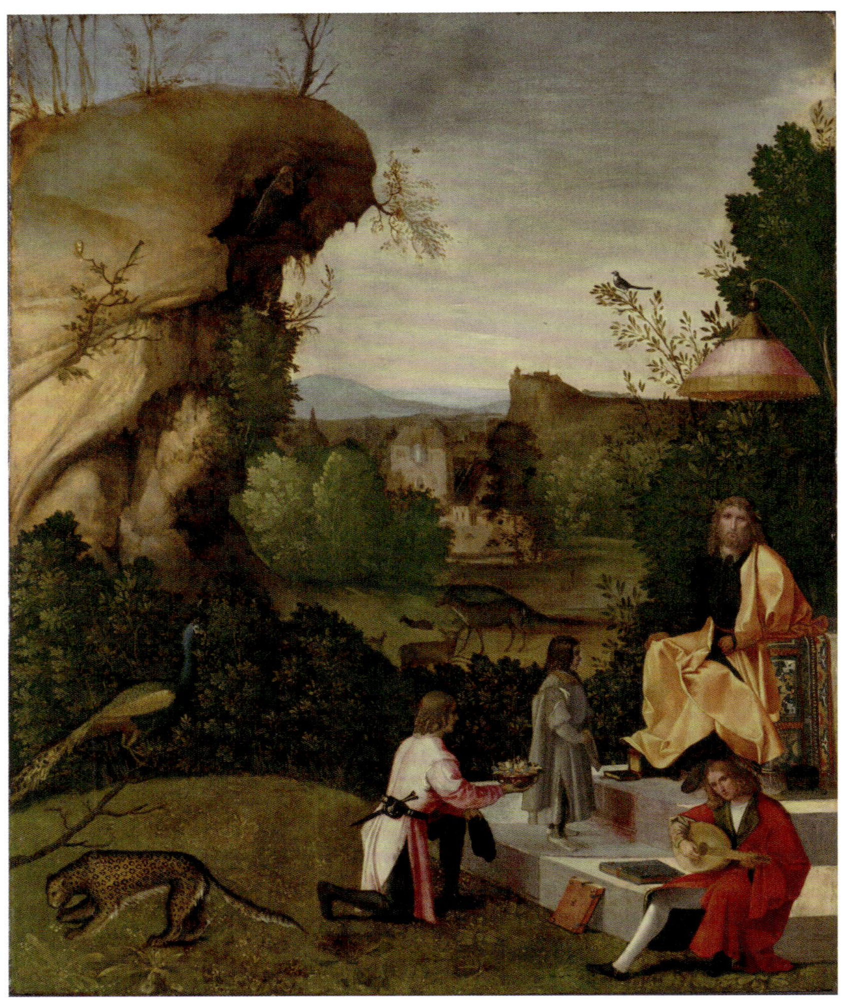

recorded as a Basaiti in the 1880–82 and 1890 inventories, an attribution accepted by Wilhelm Bode.[19] By then, Basaiti's oeuvre was inflated and included many of the late masterpieces today accepted as by Bellini (see cat. nos. 7, 10, 12). Finally, first Giovanni Morelli in 1890 and then Bernard Berenson in 1894 restored the painting definitively to Giovanni Bellini's oeuvre.[20] Morelli rather interestingly compared the predominance of landscape in the *Sacred Allegory* to that in the *Adoration of the Kings,* at that time in the Layard collection in Venice (today

London, National Gallery, inv. no. NG3098), which he considered to be by Gentile Bellini; Berenson called it *Allegory of the Tree of Life* and designated it an "L" (late). Since then, it has been considered one of the most representative of Bellini's works, and especially at the beginning of the twentieth century it was held in particular esteem by artists and intellectuals.[21] Still much debated, and far from resolved, are the chronology and the interpretation of the subject; scholars therefore still use the conventional title, *Sacred Allegory.*

In terms of chronology, in the last century there have been many different interpretations, ranging from a date in the late 1470s to one in the first decade of the sixteenth century.[22] In my opinion, the deeply Giorgionesque component of this painting, so strongly perceived in the first half of the nineteenth century, should be interpreted as Bellini's reaction to the work of the younger artist (on Giorgione and Bellini, see also cat. no. 10). In fact, Bellini's treatment of landscape in the *Sacred Allegory* is very different from that in the works of the 1480s (for example, cat. no. 7) and much closer, in the impressionistic quality of the rocks and atmosphere, to works such as the *Baptism of Christ* in Santa Corona, Vicenza, executed in about 1501–3, arguably one of Bellini's most Giorgionesque works.[23] Even though the *Baptism* is very different in size, scale, and function from the *Sacred Allegory*, one can find in both the same mirrorlike surface of the water and pastoral tranquility — for example, the elderly man who descends from his hermitage in the *Baptism* is similar in character and painterly effects to the figure descending the stairs in the *Sacred Allegory*.

The *Homage to a Poet* (fig. 42), arguably Giorgione's earliest surviving work, is also a painting whose subject is indecipherable.[24] Giorgione's and Bellini's two paintings also have in common the compositional scheme of an enthroned figure and baldachin on one side, and we have the sense that in adapting this motif, Bellini took inspiration from his pupil — and not the other way around. A similar compositional scheme, with a lateral view of the throne and set outdoors, was used by Giorgione in the Uffizi *Solomon* and *Moses* panels, two other early works that were closely associated with and displayed alongside Bellini's *Sacred Allegory* in the nineteenth century.[25]

Another Giorgionesque feature in the *Sacred Allegory* is the luminous orange-yellow drapery of the elderly figure in the middle. It seems lit from within, and similar characteristics of light were used by Giorgione in one of his early masterpieces, the Allendale *Adoration of the Shepherds* (see fig. 41). In Giorgione's work, Saint Joseph's drapery, with its metallic yellow folds and strong highlights, appears to be a painterly model for Bellini's elderly figure.

The *Sacred Allegory* is Giorgionesque not only in its stylistic and painterly qualities but also in its enigmatic subject and in the way human figures coexist with the vast and fused landscape; compare, for instance, Giorgione's *Tramonto* (London, National Gallery, inv. no. NG6307) and *Tempesta* (Venice, Gallerie dell'Accademia, inv. no. 915). Bellini had never painted a work with such proportions: horizontal in format, it is similar to but not as large as his *Transfiguration* (see fig. 6), but the *Sacred Allegory*'s main figures are much smaller and confined to the lower half of the painted space, leaving the top half for an expansive landscape. A few years later Bellini would again experiment with this idea of turning over half of the painted space to pure landscape in his *Assassination of Saint Peter Martyr* (London, National Gallery, inv. no. NG812). It would also be a feature of the first large Venetian landscapes, such as Titian's *Flight into Egypt* (Saint Petersburg, State Hermitage Museum, inv. no. GE245).[26]

As for the subject and real meaning of the *Sacred Allegory*, our point of departure should be John Pope-Hennessy's assertion: "No one looking at the picture can doubt that it has a programmatic source which has not been identified."[27]

Gustav Ludwig's 1902 article was the first and only real attempt to interpret the *Sacred Allegory* through a precise source: Guillaume de

Deguileville's *Pèlerinage de l'âme*, a fourteenth-century allegorical poem. Ludwig interpreted the painting as an allegorical view of Purgatory, with the Garden of Paradise in the foreground, where the purified souls (represented by the playing children) await judgment before entering Eternal Glory. This interpretation was influential for nearly half a century, until it was first dismissed by Niccolò Rasmo, who preferred to identify the work as a *sacra conversazione*.[28]

In the absence of a precise source that explains the painting's entire meaning, one should first identify the main figures with some degree of certainty.[29] For Keith Christiansen, "the picture was clearly done for an individual rather than for the open market, and its components are mnemonic and intended to provide meditational themes as the worshipper's eyes wander from motif to motif."[30]

The enthroned figure is the Virgin Mary, a fact confirmed by infrared reflectography that reveals that she initially had a halo, which the painter himself later suppressed.[31] She is in an attitude of prayer toward the child seated on a cushion on the marble floor; he probably represents the Christ child. The two female figures on either side of the throne are not securely identifiable (one is crowned and kneeling on the steps of the throne), but they seem to be saints.[32] The two figures leaning against the balustrade are Saint Paul on the left, with his typical sword, and Saint Peter on the right (without his attribute, the keys). The former seems to be banishing an Asian figure; the latter has a paternal and protective attitude toward the children, an attitude that, together with the colors of his clothes, has led some scholars to identify him as Saint Joseph. However, a red robe with a yellow mantle is sometimes worn by Saint Peter as well, as, for instance, in the *Saint Peter* by Bellini

and his workshop in Venice (Gallerie dell'Accademia, inv. no. 734). Both Saint Paul and Saint Peter therefore appear as guardians and protectors of the sacred space of the terrace. The potted tree, often interpreted as the Tree of Life, is positioned at the center of a cross of marble slabs.[33] The other children playing with the apples are probably wingless angels, but the child who plays with the tree, who is somewhat taller and has longer hair—two elements that seem to indicate that he is slightly older—might be identified with the young Saint John the Baptist.[34] The two seminude saints standing on the right are Saint Sebastian and possibly—as often stated—Saint Job, the two joint protectors from the plague who are often depicted together, as they were years before by Bellini himself in the Saint Job altarpiece (Venice, Gallerie dell'Accademia, inv. no. 38). This sacred vision happily matches the identification of the subject as "the garden of the Holy Church" in Bartolomeo della Nave's inventory, the earliest description of the painting. The word *giardino* (garden) brings to mind the *Zardino de oratione* (Garden of prayer), an anonymous Franciscan text written in the Veneto in 1454 and first published in Venice in 1493.[35] This text advises that prayer should consist of mentally composed scenarios, such as "gardens," in which the lives of the saints and the characters and events of the life and Passion of Christ are played out.

The elderly monk on the other side of the lake is, as has been stated many times, Saint Anthony Abbot, and the centaur symbolizes his temptations, as described in the *Vita Pauli primi eremitae* (*Life of Paulus, the First Hermit*) by Saint Jerome.[36] I believe the figure in the grotto in a melancholic pose is simply a Giorgionesque shepherd. A visual element that is often overlooked comes from the monochromatic frieze at the base of the throne.[37] It was recently

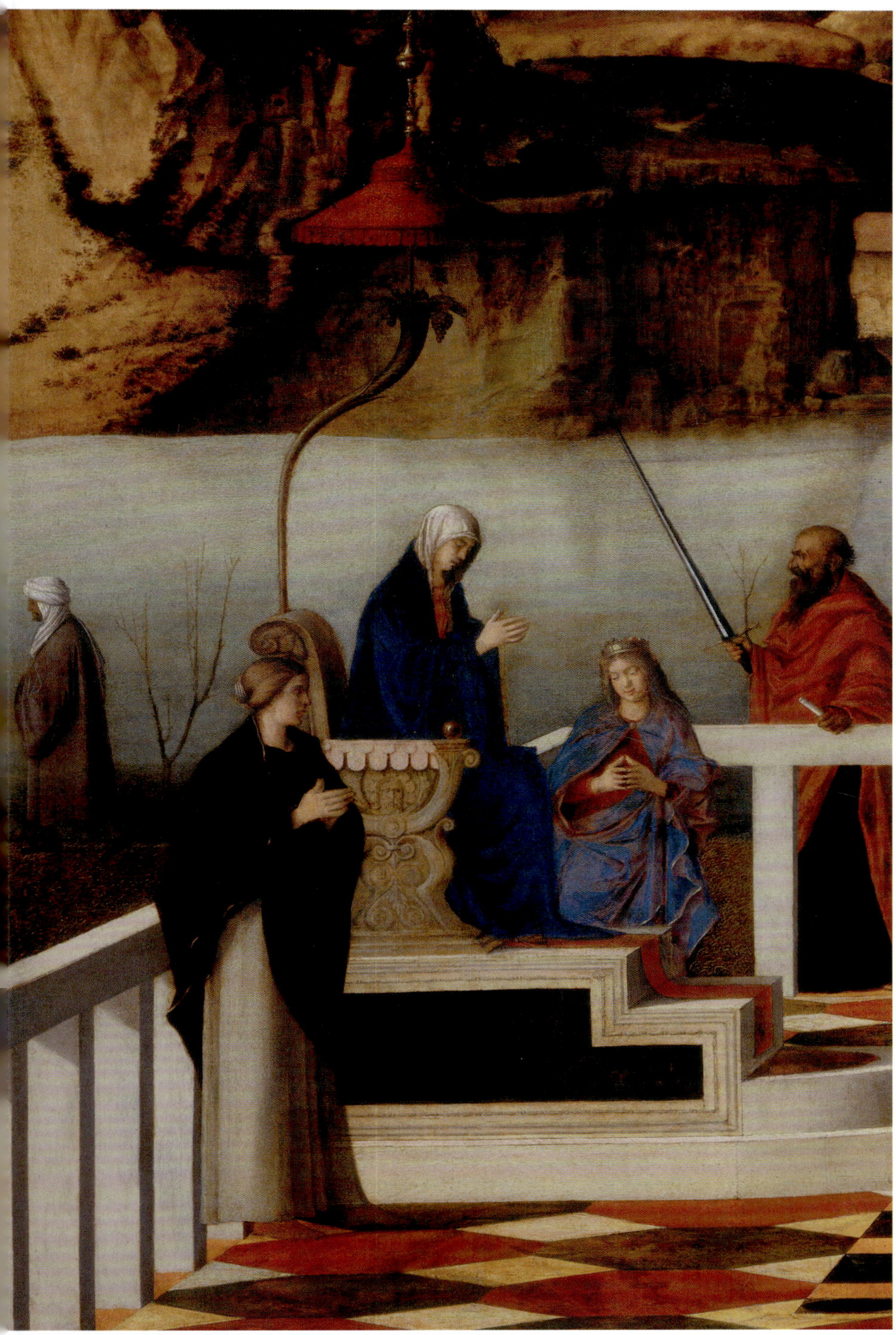

Detail of cat. no. 11

suggested that the frieze represents the flaying of Marsyas.[38] Close inspection seems to exclude this. Instead, it probably represents a satyresque scene: on the left a satyr pours wine from a flask into a jar; at the center is a tree with a syrinx hanging from it; and on the right another satyr-like figure points toward the first satyr. On the far bottom right there seems to be a third, perhaps female, figure reclining on the ground.

It is not known who commissioned the *Sacred Allegory*, but since it is arguably the most iconographically complex painting that Bellini ever executed, he or she must have been very important. One extremely fascinating idea — with no evidence to refute it and only more attractive in light of the proposed chronology of the work — was first pursued by Niccolò Rasmo in 1946. He argued that this might be the painting that Isabella d'Este commissioned from Bellini and that was executed and finally delivered in 1504 after a draining negotiation that lasted nearly ten years, delayed in part because Bellini was busy with the Ducal Palace decorations.[39] In the correspondence, the first mention of a "camerino" painting that Bellini was supposed to execute appears in 1496.

The scarce visual information provided in the ensuing correspondence does not clash with the appearance of the *Sacred Allegory*. In 1501 Isabella wanted Bellini to paint an "ancient story or fable of his invention"[40] and she advanced the painter 25 ducats, but later, on August 31, 1502, one of the agents, Lorenzo da Pavia, wrote to her that Bellini had not yet started the painting and that he probably would never do so, as he was not "a man adept at painting histories."[41] But Bellini insisted that he could, so on September 10, Lorenzo da Pavia reported that the artist "will execute a painting using his own imagination."[42] Later in September

Isabella replied that she no longer wanted a "camerino" picture, but just a "presepio" with the Madonna and Child, Saint Joseph, Saint John the Baptist, and the ox and the ass (and she therefore cut to 50 ducats the price of 100 ducats she had initially offered). Bellini seems to have agreed, but with reservations about including Saint John the Baptist in a Nativity. He therefore offered to paint a Madonna and Child with Saint John the Baptist. We can imagine that Bellini had in mind a composition very similar to the Giovanelli *Sacra Conversazione* (cat. no. 10), which was probably painted during the same period. On November 12 Isabella wrote that she also wanted a Saint Jerome in the composition. Shortly after, on November 22, she wrote that he could instead paint a "presepio" with a Madonna and saints but without the Baptist, as previously requested. Correspondence dated October 6 and 8, 1503, reported that Bellini was finally working on the composition, that he needed a month and a half or so, but that nobody could see the work in progress, as Bellini "never shows anyone his works that are not yet finished."[43] On April 10, 1504, a furious Isabella proclaimed in a letter that she did not want the painting anymore and she wanted her money back. On July 2 Bellini wrote his only surviving letter, apologizing for the delay. On July 6 Lorenzo da Pavia declared that the painting was finished and that it was more beautiful than he had anticipated, but that in "invencione" did not reach the level of Andrea Mantegna, and a few days later he added that he thought that the figures were too small and that the panel support was of bad quality. On October 18, 1505, Isabella wrote to Bellini that she very much appreciated the "presepio" that he had just painted for her and that she wanted another painting from him, this time a "historia," which was to be produced through the mediation of Pietro Bembo.

If the *Sacred Allegory* was indeed the *presepio* painted for Isabella, Bellini, possibly inspired by a written source, found the best way to please his patron's many requests — for instance, with a Saint Peter who acts as a Saint Joseph and with one of the children possibly as the young John the Baptist — yet also found his own personal way to depict the sacred scene. It was exactly this highly individual approach to painting that Bembo described to Isabella in his famous letter: "The invention, for which Your Excellency wrote me to find a design, will need to be adjusted according to the imagination of the man executing it [Bellini], who is pleased when many stipulations do not limit his style, it being accustomed, as he says, always to wander at will in paintings, so that to the best of his ability they may satisfy whoever admires them."[44]

A.M.

1   "Un Giardino con diverse figure, figurine al numero di 13 che è il Giardino di S[an]ta Chiesa, bellissimo lungo palmi 6 alto 4½ di Gio. Bellino." Lauber 2008, 283. The inventory in Italian (surely the first version of it) was only recently rediscovered; previously only a later English version of it was known (the painting here discussed is in Waterhouse 1952, 18, no. 115). On Bartolomeo della Nave's collection, see Lauber 2007.

2   Garas 1967, 64, no. 8.

3   Garas 1967, 72.

4   "Notre Seigneur dans le Jardin avec beaucoup des Saincts." Garas 1967, 79, no. 161.

5   See London 2006.

6   Berger 1883, CII, no. 266; and also Garas 1968, 219, no. 266.

7   The painting apparently does not appear in either of the Stallburg illustrated inventories by Ferdinand Storffer (1720–1733), on which see *Die Galerie* 2010.

8   Stampart and Prenner 1735, pl. 10; Mechel 1783, 6, cat. no. 11, but with an error in the measurements; see the French edition, Mechel 1784, 6, cat. no. 11, for the precise measurements, equal to about 81 × 118.5 cm. Since the width is identical to that of the panel today, this seems evidence that the panel was reduced by about 8 cm in height after 1784, possibly to adapt it to a new frame when it arrived in Florence. Paolucci, in *Gli Uffizi* 1979, 161, cat. no. P194, stated that the current frame is datable to about 1800, but there are no clues

to support this dating.

9 Spalletti 2008, 133, doc. no. XIX: "Gio. Bellino — San Sebastiano con Sant'Onofrio, et altre figure piccolo."

10 This information is given in later inventories of the Uffizi.

11 *Galerie* 1817, 150.

12 *Galerie* 1817, 150: "la Vision d'une Sainte, sujet presqu'inintelegible."

13 Florence, Biblioteca degli Uffizi, *Inventario generale dei dipinti posseduti dalla R. Galleria*, 1825, no. 568.

14 *Galerie* 1844, 172; *Galerie* 1850, 167–68.

15 Many years later Bernard Berenson brought Degas's copy to the Uffizi to compare it with the original. The anecdote is recounted in Gamba 1937, 121; and Mariano 1969, 142. On the copy, now lost, see Lemoisne 1946–49, vol. 2, cat. no. 67; and Minervino 1970, 88–89, cat. no. 50. For Degas's copies after other paintings in the Uffizi, see Rome 1984, 72–75, cat. nos. 17–18; 80, cat. no. 21.

16 *Catalogue* 1864, 62.

17 Crowe and Cavalcaselle 1871, 2:124–25. Cavalcaselle's sketches and notes on the painting are in Venice (Biblioteca Marciana, Cavalcaselle, lt IV, 2030 (-12271), facs. XVI/1, fol. 18v) and Crowe's copy with notes in English is in London (National Art Library, Special Collections, inv. no. 86.zz.33, box 1, *Italian Galleries*).

18 Liphart's attribution to Basaiti is reported in a typescript entry in the painting's dossier (Florence, Archivi della Soprintendenza, *Allegoria sacra*, inv. 1890 no. 903).

19 Florence, Archivio Storico degli Uffizi, *Inventario generale dei dipinti posseduti dalla R. Galleria*, 1880–82, vol. 2 (1881), no. 620; Florence, Archivio Storico degli Uffizi, *Inventario generale dei dipinti posseduti dalla R. Galleria*, 1890, no. 903. See Bode's opinion in his edition of *Der Cicerone* (Burckhardt 1884, 641).

20 [Morelli] 1890, 341; Berenson 1894, 86.

21 See Agosti 2009, 145–47, 189–90nn81–89. As proven by his notes and by visual evidence, Le Corbusier was inspired by the terrace of the *Sacred Allegory* in designing in 1912 the "chambre d'été" of his family villa (Villa Janneret-Perret) at Le Chaux-de-Fonds, in Switzerland (Schubert 2006, 77–81, figs. 104, 106).

22 Summarized by Humfrey, in Rome 2008, 236–39, cat. no. 30.

23 As noted as early as 1676 by Boschini 2000, 168.

24 All the attempts to identify the subject, including, more recently, Joannides 2011, are unconvincing.

25 The innovative setting of the *Sacred Allegory* is discussed in Settis 1978, 121.

26 On the development of landscape painting in sacred subjects in early sixteenth-century Venice, see Mazzotta 2012.

27 Pope-Hennessy [1990] 1994, 127; see also Agosti 2009, 146. On the other hand, Coltellacci and Lattanzi 1979, 59–79; and Gentili 2004, 173–76, think that there are multiple sources for it.

28 Rasmo 1946, 229–40.

29 For a summary of the identifications, see Humfrey, in Rome 2008, 236–39, cat. no. 30.

30 Christiansen 2004b, 49.

31 Signorini 2006, 83, fig. 3. No scientific analysis has been undertaken on the trees on the hills in the background. They look very odd for Bellini, and Roberto Longhi was likely right in suggesting that they were probably added in the seventeenth century (Longhi 1973, 9–11).

32 They were identified as Allegories of Charity and Justice in Verdier 1952–53, 97–116.

33 Gentili 2004, 173.

34 As asserted by Huse 1972, 82–86.

35 On the *Zardino de oratione*, see Campagnola 1971.

36 Coltellacci and Lattanzi 1981, 63–64.

37 Bellini had a predilection for such motifs, as demonstrated by his early *Blood of the Redeemer* in the National Gallery, London (inv. no. NG1233).

38 After an inspection with infrared reflectography, see Signorini 2006, 83, fig. 4.

39 Rasmo 1946, 240. On Isabella's commission, see also Fletcher 1971. All the letters were recently retranscribed; see Barausse 2008, 343–51, doc. nos. 52, 58–80, 82–84, 87–92. A list of positive responses to Rasmo's hypothesis is provided by Agosti 2005, 248–49n72.

40 Barausse 2008, 345, doc. no. 65: "Historia o Fabula antiqua aut de sua inventione."

41 Barausse 2008, 346, doc. no. 72: "omo per fare istorie."

42 Barausse 2008, 347, doc. no. 73: "farà el quadro e farà una fantasia a modo suo."

43 Barausse 2008, 348, doc. no. 80: "non mostra mai ad alchuno alchuna chosa sua che non sia finita."

44 "la inventione, che mi scrive vostra signoria che io truovi al dissegno, bisognerà che s'accomodi alla fantasia di lui che l'ha fare, il quale ha piacere che molto signati termini non si diano al suo stile, uso, come dice, di sempre vagare a sua voglia nelle pitture che, quanto è in lui, possano sodisfare chi le mira." (Pietro Bembo to Isabella d'Este, January 11, 1506): Barausse 2008, 352, doc. no. 99.

GIOVANNI BELLINI (Venice, ca. 1435–1516)

1505, panel, 48.9 × 39.5 cm (19¼ × 15⁹⁄₁₆ in.); painted surface:
47 × 37.5 cm (18½ × 14¾ in.)
Washington, DC, National Gallery of Art, Samuel H. Kress
Collection, 1939.1.217

SIGNATURE AND
INSCRIPTIONS
[Johannes Bellinu]s MCCCCCV
(on a mortised stone in the
lower left corner)

PROVENANCE
Frederick John Monson,
5th Baron Monson, Gatton
Park, near Reigate, Surrey,
before 1841; by inheritance to
his cousin, William John
Monson, 6th Baron Monson,
Gatton Park and Burton Hall,
Lincolnshire, until 1862; by
inheritance to his son, William
John Monson, Viscount Oxen-
bridge and 7th Baron Monson,
Burton Hall, Lincolnshire;
Monson sale, Christie, Manson
& Woods, London, May 12, 1888,
no. 12; purchased by Murray
[probably Charles Fairfax Murray,
London and Florence]; Charles
Butler, London and Warren
Wood, Hatfield, Hertford; pur-
chased 1891 by Robert Henry and
Evelyn Holford Benson, London
and Buckhurst Park, Sussex;
sold in 1927 to Duveen Brothers,
Inc., London and New York;
sold October 1, 1928, to Clarence
H. Mackay, Roslyn, New York;
sold May 1936 through Duveen
Brothers to the Samuel H. Kress
Foundation, New York; gift 1939
to the National Gallery of Art

RESTORATIONS
ca. 1936 and 2005

EXHIBITIONS
London 1894, cat. no. 169; London 1909, cat. no. 78; London
1912, cat. no. 35; Manchester 1927,
cat. no. 35; London 1930, cat. no.
292; New York 1938, cat. no. 2;
Venice 1999, cat. no. 121; Washington 2006, cat. no. 22

12 | SAINT JEROME READING IN THE WILDERNESS

Bellini's *Saint Jerome Reading* of 1505 attests to the importance of the desert hermit as a subject for small-scale Venetian paintings in the domestic sphere, long after this theme had graduated to the field of monumental altarpieces. Securely dated by the inscription on the masonry block at lower left,[1] the panel falls between the artist's two pictures of Jerome in the wilderness for the churches of Santa Maria dei Miracoli and San Giovanni Crisostomo, and in the same year as his lost version for San Cristoforo della Pace.[2] As in these larger works, Bellini presents the saint tranquilly reading in a remote natural habitat that evokes his retreat in the steppelands of Syria. This variant of Jerome's iconography marries traditional images of the church doctor at work in his study with scenes of his deprivation and self-mortification in the desert, as described in contemporary printed editions of his biography and letters. The holy man's contem-plative and penitential selves are reconciled, their unity manifest in the subdued harmonies of the pastoral landscape. Previously explored by Pisanello in Ferrara and Jacopo Bellini in Venice, the type offered spectators an occasion for solitary medita-tion analogous to that undertaken by the saint in his austere seclusion.[3] Devotional images of Jerome were prized by such illustrious figures as Cardinal Domenico Grimani, whose will of 1523 recorded a picture of the subject by Giovanni that has been tentatively associated with the Washington panel (whose secure provenance begins, however, only in the early nineteenth century).[4]

In contrast to Bellini's earlier, more centralized portrayals of Jerome, the National Gallery of Art's painting relegates the figure to the lower right corner of the composition. The aged recluse sits before a cave behind a natural arch (or, according to some authors, inside a grotto viewed from within), an unusual vantage point that may have inspired Albrecht Dürer's 1512 woodcut of the subject (fig. 43).[5] Though rough and rocky, Jerome's her-mitage hosts a range of vegetation, including a fig tree and climbing ivy, and is watered by a cistern of hewn stones secured by metal ties. Plants hang in silhouette against the opening of the arch, which frames the view of a grassy bank and hill before

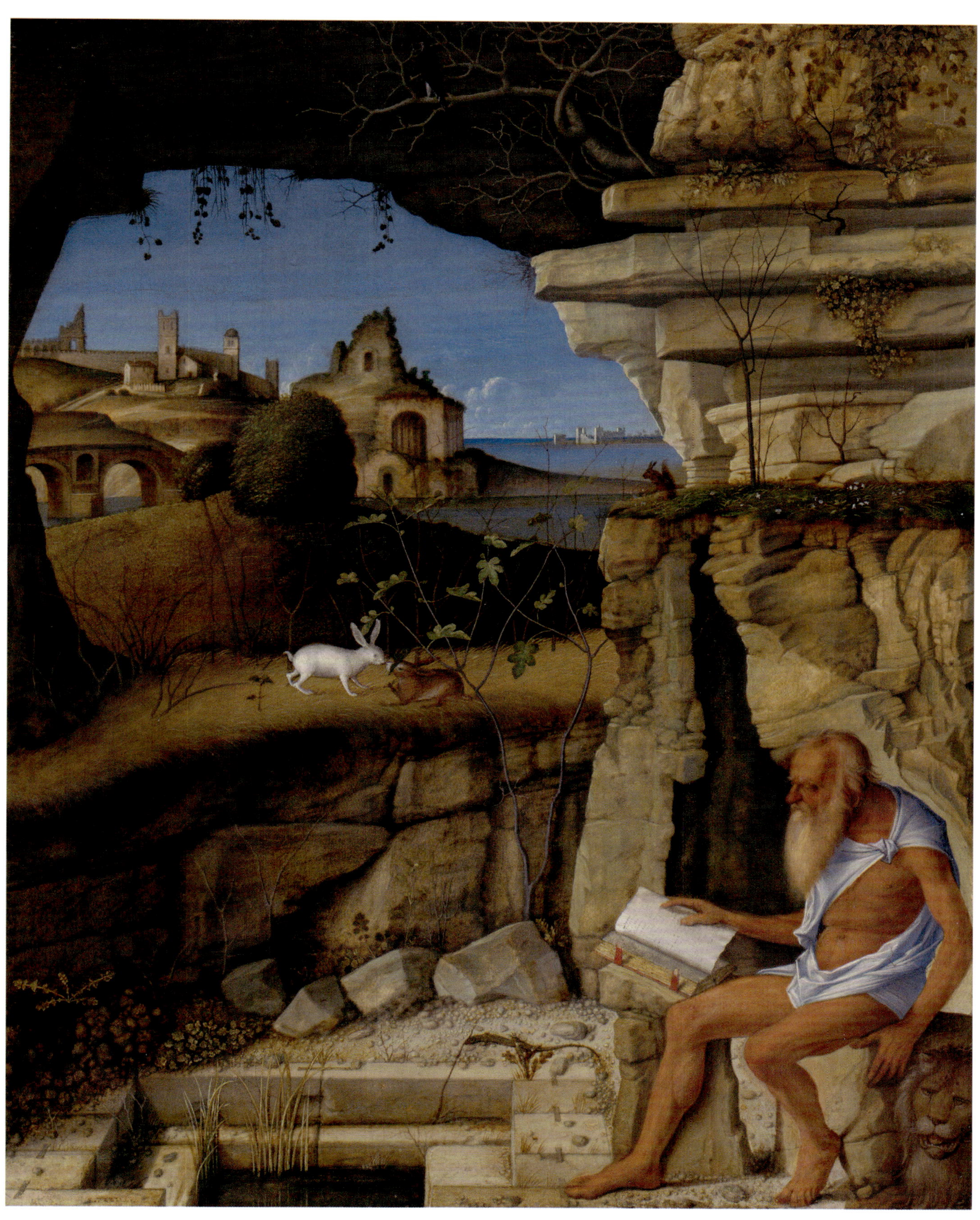

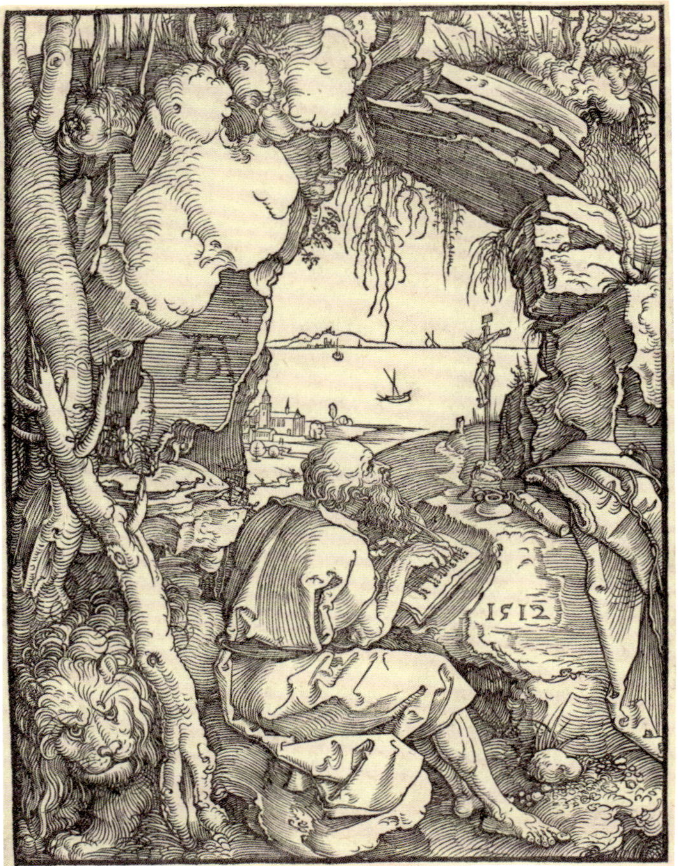

Figure 43
ALBRECHT DÜRER
(German, 1471–1528), *Saint
Jerome in a Cave*, 1512.
Woodcut on laid paper,
17.2 × 12.9 cm (6¾ × 5¹⁄₁₆ in.).
Washington, DC, National
Gallery of Art, Robert A.
McNeil Fund, 1992.43.1

an island or peninsula of crumbling walls, colonnade, and towers. These structures give way to a panorama of distant fortifications against brilliant blue water and sky. The marine vista links Jerome's desert retreat to the lagoon surroundings of Venice, while the intervening landscape of ruins conjures the antiquarian milieu of the north Italian mainland and also suggests the saint's conflicted regard for classical civilization. The broken bridge, however, serves to separate organized society from the eremitical experience of the individual and reveals the impermanence of human constructions within the eternal cycles of nature. The watery setting may have been inspired by a composition of circa

1445 from Jacopo's Louvre sketchbook (see fig. 2), although the environment of his drawing is harsher and more overtly moralizing than Giovanni's peacefully glimmering oasis.[6]

The scholar and anchorite of the Washington painting has neither halo, as in Bellini's Birmingham *Saint Jerome in the Wilderness* (cat. no. 1), nor devotional cross, as in his Contini Bonacossi *Saint Jerome in the Wilderness* (see fig. 7). His ecclesiastical garb, worn by the saint in the artist's San Zaccaria altarpiece of the same year, is absent; instead, the ascetic's blue-tinged tunic is knotted to expose his hunched but robust form, roughened skin, and bare torso. This detail alludes subtly to his self-mortification, as images of the penitent Jerome, including a predella panel of the Pesaro altarpiece (ca. 1472–75; see fig. 13), invariably reveal his chest. Bellini's idiosyncratic portrayal of the elderly hermit may reflect his own meditations on old age, as the *Saint Jerome Reading* dates to later in his lifetime. The figure also shows affinities with the posture and dress of the saint in Vittore Carpaccio's *Meditation on the Passion* (ca. 1490; fig. 44). Where Carpaccio's Jerome assertively regards the viewer, however, Bellini's figure bespeaks absorption and quietude. As the humanist Guarino Veronese wrote of a painting of the holy man by Pisanello, "he is present with us and yet seems also absent, he is both here and somewhere else: the grotto may hold his body, but his soul has the freedom of Heaven."[7]

The use of atmospheric perspective to create a sweeping, unified natural prospect, already observed in the artist's early Birmingham *Saint Jerome*, is less evident in this picture, whose limpid light clarifies forms both near and far. The painting's abundance of finely rendered detail is unusual for a late work by Bellini—in which one might expect to find a more generalized, brushy, and integrated style—and has prompted occasional debates over its attribution and period of execution.[8] Rather than adopting a Giorgionesque technique of blended contours, the artist has developed a harmony of rich, pure tonal rapports that invites comparison with the Niccolini di Camugliano *Crucifixon* (cat. no. 8).[9] The crystalline landscape reflects the influence of northern European painting, and the rock formations framing the distant view at right, in particular, may have been inspired by those in a small work by Jan van Eyck, *Saint Francis of Assisi Receiving the Stigmata*, which was in Venice in 1471 (see fig. 5).[10] The Washington picture's wealth of particularized animal and botanical motifs, also evocative of Netherlandish art, has

encouraged contradictory symbolic readings relating to Jerome's trials in the desert. The lizard near his feet has been identified with the serpent of the Garden of Eden as well as with the concept of Resurrection; the pair of facing rabbits, with Christian meekness and reserve as well as with sinful lust; the squirrel on the high bank, with intellectual pride and resistance to adversity; the fig tree, with temptation and the cross of Christ; the water in the cistern, with demonic polymorphism and the rite of baptism.[11]

While there can be no doubt that Bellini embeds richly significant narrative and symbolic vignettes in the natural surroundings of his sacred figures, recent studies have emphasized the formal and expressive

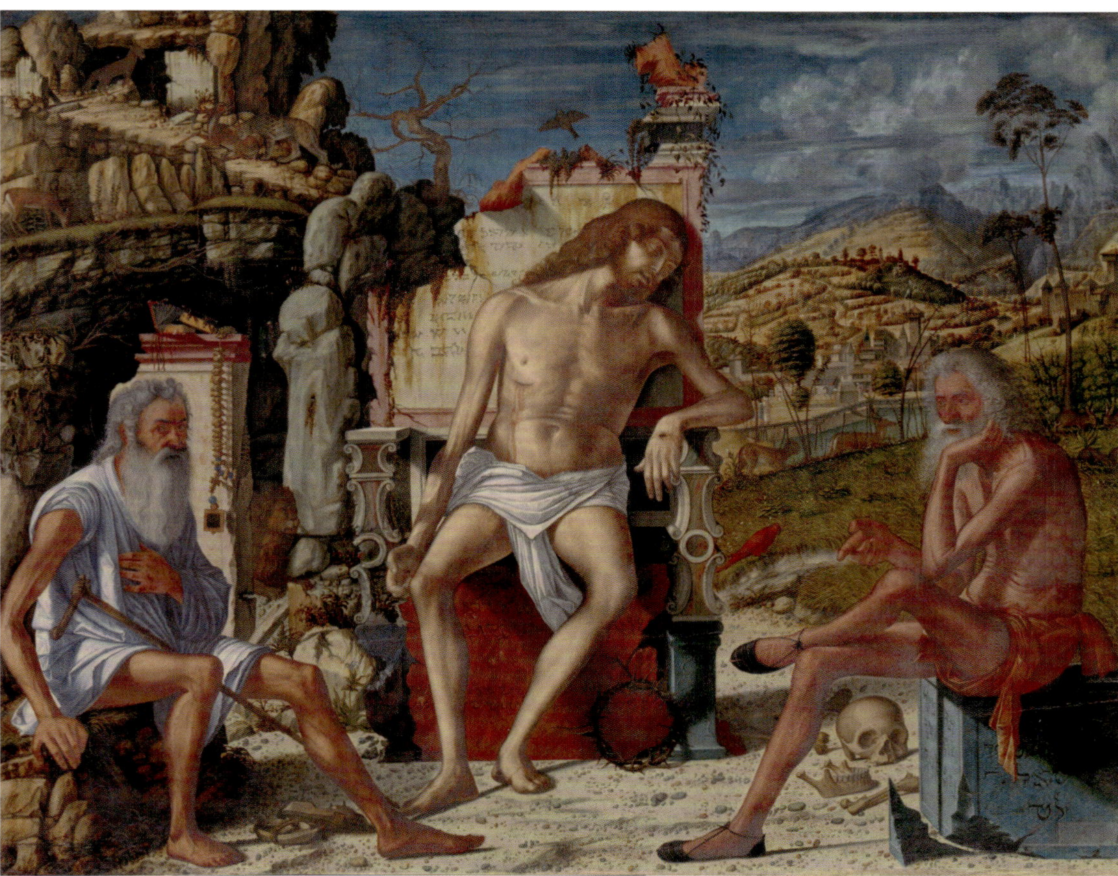

Figure 44
VITTORE CARPACCIO
 (Italian, ca. 1465–1525/26),
Meditation on the Passion,
ca. 1490. Panel, 70.5 × 86.7 cm
(27¾ × 34⅛ in.). New York,
The Metropolitan Museum
of Art, John Stewart Kennedy
Fund, 1911, 11.118

character of such elements over textual explications of their meaning.[12] Thus the wild animals cluster around the central axis of this scene, while Jerome and his tamed lion appear at far right, suggesting that the fauna collectively signify the saint's withdrawal to a world in which human life is marginal. The bird of prey perched on the tracery of bare branches overhead has been associated with magnanimity and mystical contemplation; in visual terms, though, he looms forebodingly over the idyllic sanctuary as an obvious emblem of death, the impending reward of earthly sinfulness, and the consequent urgency of Jerome's penitence.[13] In this guise, he replaces the skull that often appears as a harbinger of death in paintings of the saint. Similarly, the lizard with its darting movements might allude to the aged scholar's still vigorous intellect.[14]

Many of the painting's individual details of plant and animal life recur across diverse compositions by Bellini and other Venetian artists, further indicating that their significance is not fixed. The pair of rabbits facing each other on the high bank can be traced back to the model drawings of Pisanello and reappears in works of Carpaccio and Bellini, while the bird of prey on a barren branch also originates with a design by Pisanello and is repeated in numerous Venetian and Paduan pictures of the fifteenth century.[15] Such connections reveal that Bellini's landscapes neither enunciated strict symbolic programs nor straightforwardly transcribed the natural world, but, rather, creatively responded to preexisting artistic conventions and motifs. Like the saint's own letters from the desert, *Saint Jerome Reading in the Wilderness* is a poetic invention that articulates the contrast between social life and retreat in sacred solitude.[16]

S.R.

---

1 The complete original inscription probably read "Johannes Bellinus MCCCCCV," of which only the last letter of the artist's name and the date remain visible; see Boskovits and Brown 2003, 70, 73n1.

2 Humfrey 1991, 109–17.

3 Baxandall 1965, 196–97. Jacopo Bellini completed a painting (ca. 1450–55; Verona, Museo di Castelvecchio) and five drawings of Jerome in the Wilderness (Louvre and British Museum sketchbooks). Three of the drawings depict the traditional penitent or praying saint in a desert landscape, but two show the innovative form of the saint reading. See Degenhart and Schmitt 1990, 6:327–28, 337, 458–60, 504, 530; 7: pls. 18, 25; 8: pls. 151–52, 244, 292. The early painting of Jerome with books in the desert by Andrea Mantegna (see fig. 18 in the present volume) may also have influenced Bellini; see De Marchi 2014, 74.

4 The painting, then in the Palazzo Venezia in Rome, was bequeathed by Grimani to Stafileo, bishop of Sibenic; see Dengel 1913, 36; Paschini 1943, 151; and Fletcher 1991a.

5 Kalina 2012, 352, 354–56.

6 Degenhart and Schmitt 1990, 6:327–28; 7: pl. 18; Lynn-Davis 1998, 205.

7 Baxandall 1965, 196.

8 Robertson 1968, 78; Gofen 1989, 288–90; Brown, in Venice 1999, 454. The work is now universally accepted as an autograph Bellini completed in 1505.

9 Venturi 1924, 61–62.

10 Christiansen 2004c, 141–42; Christiansen 2004b, 40–41.

11 See, for example, Lattanzi and Mercalli 1983, 90–93; Gentili 1985, 164–66; Friedmann 1980.

12 Echols 1994, 47–69; Lynn-Davis 1998, 215–16; Lucco, in Washington 2006, 132.

13 Echols 1994, 61.

14 Oettinger 2012, 117.

15 Blass-Simmen 2006, 82–83; Echols 1994, 58.

16 Belting 2014. See also Belting's essay in this volume.

REFERENCES

Exhibitions and Catalogues

Budapest 2009
Botticelli to Titian: Two Centuries of Italian Masterpieces. Exh. cat. edited by Dóra Sallay, Vilmos Tátrai, and Axel Vécsey. Budapest, Szépművészeti Múzeum, October 28, 2009–February 14, 2010. Budapest: Szépművészeti Múzeum.

Castelfranco Veneto 2009
Giorgione. Exh. cat. edited by Enrico Maria Dal Pozzolo and Lionello Puppi. Castelfranco Veneto, Casa di Giorgione, December 12, 2009–April 11, 2010. Milan: Skira.

Cologne 1977
Meisterwerke venezianischer Malerei im Wallraf-Richartz-Museum. Exh. cat. edited by Homan Potterton and Gerhard Bott. Cologne, Wallraf-Richartz-Museum/ Museum Ludwig, April 19–June 5, 1977. Cologne: Greven & Bechtold.

Denver 2016
Glory of Venice: Masterworks of the Renaissance. Exh. cat. edited by Angelica Daneo and Giovanna Damiani. Denver Art Museum, October 2, 2016–February 12, 2017; Raleigh, North Carolina Museum of Art, March 4–June 18, 2017. Denver: Denver Art Museum.

Edinburgh 2004
The Age of Titian: Venetian Renaissance Art from Scottish Collections. Exh. cat. edited by Peter Humfrey, Timothy Clifford, Aidan Weston-Lewis, and Michael Bury. National Galleries of Scotland, August 5–December 5, 2004. Edinburgh: National Galleries of Scotland.

Fabriano 2006
Gentile da Fabriano and the Other Renaissance. Exh. cat. edited by Laura Laureati and Lorenza Mochi Onori. Fabriano, Spedale di Santa Maria del Buon Gesù, April 21–July 23, 2006. Milan: Electa.

Forlì 2005
Marco Palmezzano e il Rinascimento nelle Romagne. Exh. cat. edited by Antonio Paolucci, Luciana Prati, and Stefano Tumidei. Forlì, Musei di San Domenico, December 4, 2005–April 30, 2006. Cinisello Balsamo: Silvana.

Houston 1997
The Body of Christ in the Art of Europe and New Spain 1150–1800. Exh. cat. edited by James Clifton. Museum of Fine Arts, Houston, December 21, 1997–April 12, 1998. Munich: Prestel.

London 1894
Exhibition of Venetian Art. Exh. cat. by L. C. Lindsay. London, New Gallery, 1894–95. London: New Gallery.

London 1909
A Catalogue of the Pictures and Drawings in the National Loan Exhibition: In Aid of the National Gallery Funds Held in the Grafton Galleries. London, Grafton Galleries, 1909–10. London: Ballantyne.

London 1912
Catalogue of a Collection of Pictures of the Early Venetian School and Other Works of Art. London, Burlington Fine Arts Club, 1912. London: Burlington Fine Arts Club.

London 1930
Exhibition of Italian Art, 1200–1900. London, Royal Academy of Arts, Burlington House, January 1–March, 20, 1930. London: Royal Academy of Arts.

London 1981
The Princes Gate Collection: Selection A. Exh. cat. London, Courtauld Institute Galleries, July 17, 1981–January 26, 1982. London: Courtauld Institute Galleries.

London 1983
Mantegna to Cézanne: Master Drawings from the Courtauld; A Fiftieth Anniversary Exhibition. Exh. cat. edited by William Bradford and Helen Braham. London, British Museum, February 24–June 19, 1983. London: British Museum Publications.

London 1987
100 Masterpieces from the Courtauld Collections: Bernardo Daddi to Ben Nicholson: European Paintings and Drawings from the 14th to the 20th Century. Catalogue edited by Dennis Farr. London, Courtauld Institute Galleries. London: Courtauld Institute of Art Fund.

London 1991
Master Drawings from the Courtauld Collections. Exh. cat. edited by William Bradford and Helen Braham. London, Courtauld Institute Galleries, October 16, 1991–January 19, 1992. London: Courtauld Institute Galleries.

London 1992a
Andrea Mantegna. Exh. cat. edited by Jane Martineau. London, Royal Academy of Arts, January 17–April 5, 1992; New York, Metropolitan Museum of Art, April 28–July 12, 1992. London: Thames & Hudson.

London 1992b
Themes and Variations: Saint Jerome. Exh. cat. London, National Gallery, September 30–December 13, 1992. London: National Gallery.

London 1997
Dürer: St. Jerome. London, National Gallery, March 14–June 8, 1997 (no catalogue).

London 2006
David Teniers and the Theatre of Painting. Exh. cat. edited by Ernst Vegelin van Claerbergen et al. London, Courtauld Institute of Art, October 19, 2006–January 21, 2007. London: Paul Holberton.

London 2007
The Art of Italy in the Royal Collection: Renaissance and Baroque. Exh. cat. edited by Lucy Whitaker and Martin Clayton. London, Queen's Gallery, May 29, 2007–January 19, 2008. London: Royal Collection Publications.

London 2008
Renaissance Faces: Van Eyck to Titian. Exh. cat. edited by Lorne Campbell et al. London, National Gallery, October 15, 2008–January 18, 2009. London: National Gallery Company.

London 2010
Fra Angelico to Leonardo: Italian Renaissance Drawings. Exh. cat. edited by Hugo Chapman and Marzia Faietti. London, British Museum, April 22–July 25, 2010; Florence, Galleria degli Uffizi, February 1–April 30, 2011. London: British Museum Press.

London 2012
Mantegna to Matisse: Master Drawings from The Courtauld Gallery. London, Courtauld Gallery, June 14–September 9, 2012; New York, Frick Collection, October 2, 2012–January 27, 2013. (*Master Drawings from the Courtauld Gallery* accompanied the exhibition.) London: Paul Holberton.

Los Angeles 1979
The Golden Century of Venetian Painting. Exh. cat. edited by Terisio Pignatti with the collaboration of Kenneth Donahue. Los Angeles County Museum of Art, October 30, 1979–January 27, 1980. Los Angeles: Los Angeles County Museum of Art.

Manchester 1927
Loan Exhibition of the Benson Collection of Old Italian Masters. Exh. cat. edited by Lawrence Haward. Manchester, City Art Gallery, April 27–July 30, 1927. Manchester: City Art Gallery.

Milan 1991
Le muse e il principe: Arte di corte nel Rinascimento padano. Exh. cat. edited by Andrea Di Lorenzo, 2 vols., Milan, Museo Poldi Pezzoli, September 20–December 1, 1991. Modena: Panini.

Milan 2012
Giovanni Bellini: Dall'icona alla storia. Exh. cat. edited by Andrea De Marchi, Andrea Di Lorenzo, and Lavinia Galli Michero. Milan, Museo Poldi Pezzoli, November 9, 2012–February 25, 2013. Turin: Allemandi.

Milan 2014
Giovanni Bellini: La nascita della pittura devozionale umanistica; Gli studi. Exh. cat. edited by Sandrina Bandera Bistoletti and Emanuela Daffra. Milan, Pinacoteca di Brera, April 9–July 13, 2014. Milan: Skira.

New York 1938
Venetian Paintings of the 15th and 16th Centuries: Loan Exhibition. New York, M. Knoedler & Co., April 11–30, 1938. New York: Spiral Press.

New York 1965
The Italian Renaissance: Drawings from New York Collections. Exh. cat. edited by Jacob Bean and Felice Stampfle. New York, Metropolitan Museum of Art, November 8, 1965–January 9, 1966. Greenwich, CT: New York Graphic Society.

New York 1998
From Van Eyck to Bruegel: Early Netherlandish Painting in the Metropolitan Museum of Art. Exh. cat. edited by Maryan Ainsworth and Keith Christiansen. New York, Metropolitan Museum of Art, September 22, 1998–January 3, 1999. New York: Metropolitan Museum of Art.

New York 2011
The Renaissance Portrait from Donatello to Bellini. Exh. cat. edited by Keith Christiansen and Stefan Weppelmann. New York, Metropolitan Museum of Art, December 21, 2011–March 18, 2012. New York: Metropolitan Museum of Art.

Padua 2013
Pietro Bembo e l'invenzione del Rinascimento. Exh. cat. edited by Guido Beltramini, Davide Gasparotto, and Adolfo Tura. Padua, Palazzo del Monte di Pietà, February 2–May, 19, 2013. Venice: Marsilio.

Paris 1935
Exposition de l'art italien de Cimabue à Tiepolo. Exh. cat. edited by Ugo Ojetti and Paul Jamot. Paris, Musée du Petit Palais, May 10–July 10, 1935. Argenteuil: R. Coulouma.

Paris 2008
Mantegna 1431–1506. Exh. cat. edited by Giovanni Agosti and Dominique Thiébaut, with the assistance of Arturo Galansino and Jacopo Stoppa. Paris, Musée du Louvre, September 26, 2008–January 5, 2009. Paris and Milan: Officina Libraria.

Rimini 2001
Il potere, le arti, la guerra: Lo splendore dei Malatesta. Exh. cat. edited by A. Donati and A. Emiliani. Rimini, Castel Sismondo, March 3–June 15, 2001. Milan: Electa.

Rome 1932
Mostra d'arte antica. Exh. cat. Rome, Galleria Nazionale a Valle Giulia, April–June 1932. Rome: Istituto Poligrafico dello Stato.

Rome 1945
Mostra d'arte italiana a Palazzo Venezia. Exh. cat. Rome, Museo Nazionale di Palazzo Venezia, 1945. Rome: R. Danesi.

Rome 1983
Il San Girolamo di Lorenzo Lotto a Castel Sant'Angelo. Exh. cat. edited by Bruno Contardi. Rome, Museo Nazionale di Castel Sant'Angelo, January 15–May 15, 1983. Rome: Romana Società Editrice.

Rome 1984
Degas e l'Italia. Exh. cat. edited by Henri Loyrette and Jean Leymarie. Rome, Académie de France, December 1, 1984–February 10, 1985. Rome: Palombi.

Rome 2006
Antonello da Messina: L'opera completa. Exh. cat. edited by Mauro Lucco and Giovanni Carlo Federico Villa. Rome, Scuderie del Quirinale, March 18–June 25, 2006. Cinisello Balsamo: Silvana.

Rome 2008
Giovanni Bellini. Exh. cat. edited by Mauro Lucco and Giovanni Carlo Federico Villa. Rome, Scuderie del Quirinale, September 30, 2008–January 11, 2009. Cinisello Balsamo: Silvana.

Rome 2010
I grandi veneti: Da Pisanello a Tiziano, da Tintoretto a Tiepolo; Capolavori dall'Accademia Carrara di Bergamo. Exh. cat. edited by Giovanni Valagussa and Giovanni Carlo Federico Villa. Rome, Chiostro del Bramante, October 14, 2010–January 30, 2011. Cinisello Balsamo: Silvana.

San Francisco 1939
Masterworks of Five Centuries. Exh. cat. San Francisco, Golden Gate International Exposition, 1939. San Francisco: Golden Gate International Exposition.

Stockholm 1962
Konstens Venedig. Exh. cat. edited by Grate Pontus. Stockholm, Nationalmuseum, October 20, 1962–February 10, 1963. Stockholm: Nationalmuseum.

Tokyo 1976
Masterpieces of World Art from American Museums from Ancient Egyptian to Contemporary Art. Exh. cat. Tokyo, National Museum of Western Art, September 11–October 17, 1976; Kyoto, National Museum, November 2–December 5, 1976. Tokyo: National Museum of Western Art.

Tours 2009
Mantegna: La prédelle de San Zeno de Vérone, 1457–1459. Exh. cat. edited by Philippe Le Leyzour, Andrea De Marchi, Annie Gilet. Tours, Musée des Beaux-Arts, April 4–June 22, 2009. Cinisello Balsamo: Silvana.

Venice 1946
I capolavori dei musei veneti. Exh. cat. edited by Rodolfo Pallucchini. Venice, Procuratie Nuove, 1946. Venice: Arte Veneta.

Venice 1949

Mostra di Giovanni Bellini. Exh. cat. edited by Rodolfo Pallucchini. Venice, Palazzo Ducale, June 12–October 5, 1949. Venice: Alfieri.

Venice 1978

Giorgione a Venezia. Exh. cat. edited by Adriana Augusti Ruggeri and Pier Luigi Fantelli. Introduction by Terisio Pignatti and Rodolfo Pallucchini. Venice, Gallerie dell'Accademia, September–November 1978. Milan: Electa.

Venice 1993

Carpaccio, Bellini, Tura, Antonello e altri restauri quattrocenteschi della Pinacoteca del Museo Correr. Exh. cat. edited by Attilia Dorigato. Venice, Museo Correr, March 26–May 24, 1993. Milan: Electa.

Venice 1999

Renaissance Venice and the North: Crosscurrents in the Time of Bellini, Dürer and Titian. Exh. cat. edited by Bernard Aikema and Beverly Louise Brown. Venice, Palazzo Grassi, September 5, 1999–January 9, 2000. Milan: Bompiani.

Venice 2000

Il colore ritrovato: Bellini a Venezia. Exh. cat. edited by Rona Goffen and Giovanna Nepi Scirè. Venice, Gallerie dell'Accademia, September 30, 2000–January 28, 2001. Milan: Electa.

Venice 2012

Tiziano: La Fuga in Egitto e la pittura di paesaggio. Exh. cat. edited by Irina Artemieva and Giuseppe Pavanello. Venice, Gallerie dell'Accademia, August 29–December 2, 2012. Venice: Marsilio.

Vicenza 2003

Bellini e Vicenza: Capolavori che ritornano. Exh. cat. edited by Fernando Rigon. Vicenza, Palazzo Thiene Bonin Longare, December 5, 2003–January 25, 2004. Citadella: Biblos.

Washington 2006

Bellini, Giorgione, Titian, and the Renaissance of Venetian Painting. Exh. cat. edited by David A. Brown and Sylvia Ferino-Pagden. National Gallery of Art, Washington, DC, June 18–September 17, 2006; Vienna, Kunsthistorisches Museum, October 17, 2006–January 7, 2007. New Haven: Yale University Press.

Books and Articles

Agosti 2005

Agosti, Giovanni. *Su Mantegna. I: La storia dell'arte libera la testa.* Milan: Feltrinelli.

Agosti 2009

Agosti, Giovanni. *Un amore di Giovanni Bellini.* Milan: Officina Libraria.

Aikema 2000

Aikema, Bernard. *De Heilige Hieronymus in het studeervertrek.* Nijmegen: Nijmegen University Press, 2000.

Aikema 2003

Aikema, Bernard. "I Crocifissi di Giovanni Bellini: Genesi e significato di un tema pittorico nel Quattrocento, fra Nord e Sud." In Vicenza 2003, 39–43.

Alana Collection 2014

The Alana Collection: Italian Paintings from the 14th to 16th Century. Edited by Sonia Chiodo and Serena Padovani. Florence: Mandragora.

Alexander-Skipnes 2003

Alexander-Skipnes, Ingrid. "St. Jerome in the Wilderness: Paintings in Venice by Piero della Francesca, Giovanni Bellini and Hieronimus Bosch." In *Jérôme Bosch et son entourage et autres études,* edited by Hélène Verougstraete and Roger Van Schoute, 286–97. Leuven: Uitgeverij Peeters.

Anderson 1996

Anderson, Jaynie. "Sir Charles Eastlake e i suoi restauratori italiani: Giuseppe Molteni e Raffaele Pinti." *Bollettino d'arte,* suppl. 98:57–62.

Anderson 1999

Anderson, Jaynie. *Collecting Connoisseurship and the Art Market in Risorgimento Italy: Giovanni Morelli's Letters to Giovanni Melli and Pietro Zavaritt (1866–1872).* Venice: Istituto Veneto di Scienze, Lettere ed Arti 1999.

Anderson 2006

Anderson, Jaynie. "Allegories and Mythologies." In Washington 2006, 147–87.

Arosio 2001

Arosio, Marco. "Giovanni de' Cauli." In *Dizionario biografico degli italiani,* 55:768–74. Rome: Treccani.

Arslan 1956

Arslan, Edoardo. *Catalogo delle cose d'arte e di antichità d'Italia: Vicenza: Le chiese.* Rome: La Libreria dello Stato.

Avagnina 2007

Avagnina, Maria Elisa. "La pala del Battesimo di Cristo attraverso i secoli: Storia di una contrastata conservazione." In *Bellini a Vicenza* 2007, 57–63.

Avery-Quash 2011

Avery-Quash, Susanna. "The Travel Notebooks of Sir Charles Eastlake." *Walpole Society* 73, no. 1:1–674; no. 2:1–314.

Ballarin 1962

Ballarin, Alessandro. "Profilo di Lamberto d'Amsterdam (Lamberto Sustris)." *Arte veneta* 16:1–81.

Ballarin 1979

Ballarin, Alessandro. "Una nuova prospettiva su Giorgione: La ritrattistica degli anni 1500–1503." In *Giorgione: Atti del convegno internazionale di studio per il 5° centenario della nascita,* 227–52. Castelfranco Veneto: Banca Popolare di Asolo e Montebelluna.

Barausse 2008

Barausse, Manuela. "Giovanni Bellini: I documenti." In Rome 2008, 327–59.

Barbantini 1908

Barbantini, Nino. "La quadreria Giovanelli." *Emporium* 27:183–205.

Barbarano 1649–1762

Barbarano, F. *Historia ecclesiastica della città, territorio e diocesi di Vicenza.* 6 vols. Vicenza. Vol. 1, 1649; vol. 2, 1652; vol. 3, 1653; vol. 4, 1760; vol. 5, 1761; vol. 6, 1762.

Barocchi 1960

Barocchi, Paola, ed. *Trattati d'arte del Cinquecento fra Manierismo e Controriforma.* Vol. 1. Bari: Laterza.

Bätschmann 2008

Bätschmann, Oskar. *Giovanni Bellini.* Munich: Beck.

Battisti 1991

Battisti, Eugenio. "Le origini religiose del paesaggio veneto." In *Venezia Cinquecento* 1, no. 2:9–25.

Bauer-Eberhardt 1989

Bauer-Eberhardt, Ulrike. "Lauro Padovano und Leonardo Bellini als Maler, Miniaturen und Zeichner." *Pantheon* 47:49–82.

Baxandall 1965

Baxandall, Michael. "Guarino, Pisanello and Manuel Chrysoloras." *Journal of the Warburg and Courtauld Institutes* 28:183–204.

Baxandall 1971
Baxandall, Michael. *Giotto and the Orators: Humanist Observers of Painting in Italy and the Discovery of Pictorial Composition, 1350–1450*. Oxford: Clarendon.

Bellavitis 2001
Bellavitis, Anna. *Identité, mariage, mobilité sociale. Citoyennes et citoyens à Venise au XVIᵉ siècle*. Rome: École Français de Rome.

Bellini a Vicenza 2007
Bellini a Vicenza: Il Battestimo di Cristo in Santa Corona. Edited by Maria Elisa Avagnina and Giovanni Carlo Federico Villa. Cittadella: Biblos.

Bellosi 2008
Bellosi, Luciano. "Giovanni Bellini e Andrea Mantegna." In Paris 2008, 103–49.

Belting 1996
Belting, Hans. *Giovanni Bellini: La Pietà*. Modena: Franco Cosimo Panini.

Belting 2014
Belting, Hans. "St. Jerome in Venice: Giovanni Bellini and the Dream of Solitary Life." *I Tatti Studies in the Italian Renaissance* 17, no. 1 (Spring):5–33.

D. Beltrami 1954
Beltrami, Daniele. *Storia della popolazione di Venezia dalla fine del secolo XVI alla caduta della Repubblica*. Padua: C.E.D.A.M.

L. Beltrami 1894
Beltrami, Luca. "Antonello da Messina chiamato alla corte di Galeazzo Maria Sforza." *Archivio storico dell'arte* 7, no. 1:56–57.

Bembo 1525
Bembo, Pietro. *Prose della volgar lingua*. Venice: Tacuino.

Bembo 1987
Bembo, Pietro. *Lettere*. Edited by E. Travi. Vol. 1. Bologna: Commissione per i Testi di Lingua.

Berenson 1894
Berenson, Bernard. *The Venetian Painters of the Renaissance, with an Index to Their Works*. New York: Putnam's.

Berenson 1932
Berenson, Bernard. *Italian Pictures of the Renaissance: A List of the Principal Artists and Their Works with an Index of Places*. Oxford: Clarendon Press.

Berger 1883
Berger, Adolf. "Inventar der Kunstsammlung des Erzherzogs Leopold Wilhelm von Österreich." *Jahrbuch der Kunsthistorische Sammlungen des Allerhöchsten Kaiserhauses* I:LXXIX–CLXXVII.

Bernardini 1910
Bernardini, Giorgio. "Alcuni dipinti della Galleria Borghese." *Rassegna d'arte* 10:142–44.

Berra 1999
Berra, Giacomo. "Immagini casuali, figure nascoste e natura antropomorfa nell'immaginario artistico rinascimentale." *Mitteilungen des Kunsthistorischen Institutes in Florenz* 43:358–419.

Blass-Simmen 2006
Blass-Simmen, Brigit. "Studi dal vivo e dal non più vivo: Carpaccio's Passion Paintings with Saint Job." *Metropolitan Museum Journal* 41:75–90.

Blass-Simmen 2015
Blass-Simmen, Brigit. "'Qualche lontani': Distance and Transcendence in the Art of Giovanni Bellini." In Wilson 2015, 77–92.

Blum 2015
Blum, Gerd. *Fenestra prospectiva: Architektonisch inszenierte Ausblicke: Alberti, Palladio, Agucchi*. Berlin: De Gruyter.

Bode 1900
Bode, Wilhelm, ed. *Gemälde-Sammlung des Herrn Rudolf Kann in Paris*. Vienna: Gesellschaft für vervielfältigende Kunst.

Bomford et al. 1986
Bomford, David, Ashok Roy, and Alistair Smith. "The Techniques of Dieric Bouts: Two Paintings Contrasted." *National Gallery Technical Bulletin* 10:39–57.

Borchert 2006
Borchert, Till-Holger. "Antonello da Messina e la pittura fiamminga." In *Antonello da Messina, l'opera completa*, edited by Mauro Lucco, 27–41. Cinisello Balsamo: Silvana.

Borea 1994
Borea, Evelina. "Per la fortuna dei primitivi: La Istoria Pratica di Stefano Mulinari e la Venezia Pittrice di Gian Maria Sasso." In *Hommage à Michel Laclotte: Études sur la peinture du Moyen Age et de la Renaissance*, edited by Pierre Rosenberg et al., 503–21. Milan: Electa.

Bortolan 1889
Bortolan, Domenico. *Santa Corona: Chiesa e convento dei Domenicani in Vicenza. Memorie storiche*. Vicenza: San Giuseppe.

Boschini 1660
Boschini, Marco. *La carta del navegar pitoresco*. Venice: Baba.

Boschini 1664
Boschini, Marco. *Le minere della pittura*. Venice: Nicolini.

Boschini [1676] 2000
Boschini, Marco. *I gioielli pittoreschi: Virtuoso ornamento della città di Vicenza* (1676), edited by Deborah Marchioro. Rome: Lithos.

Boskovits and Brown 2003
Boskovits, Miklós, and David Alan Brown, eds. *Italian Paintings of the Fifteenth Century: The Collections of the National Gallery of Art. Systematic Catalogue*. New York and Oxford: Oxford University Press.

Bottari 1963
Bottari, Stefano. *Tutta la pittura di Giovanni Bellini*. 2 vols. Milan: Rizzoli.

Botti 1992
Botti, Isabella. "Tra Venezia e Alessandria. I teleri belliniani per la Scuola Grande di San Marco." *Venezia Cinquecento* 2, no. 3:33–73.

Bradley 2004
Bradley, Amanda. "Ancient Exempla at Kingston Lacy." *Apollo* 160, no. 513:82–86.

Braghirolli 1877
Braghirolli, Willelmo. "Carteggio di Isabella d'Este Gonzaga intorno ad un quadro di Giambellino." *Archivio veneto* 7, no. 8:370–83.

Brambilla Ranise 2007
Brambilla Ranise, Giovanna. *La raccolta dimezzata: Storia della dispersione della pinacoteca di Guglielmo Lochis (1789–1859)*. Bergamo: Lubrina.

B. Brown 2015
Brown, Beverly Louise. "Poetry in Motion: Bellini, Titian, and the *all'antica* Relief." In Wilson 2015, 245–66.

P. Brown 1988
Brown, Patricia Fortini. *Venetian Narrative Painting in the Age of Carpaccio*. New Haven: Yale University Press.

P. Brown 1992
Brown, Patricia Fortini. "The Antiquarianism of Jacopo Bellini." *Artibus et Historiae* 13, no. 26:65–84.

Brown and Lorenzoni 1982
Brown, Clifford M., and Anna Maria Lorenzoni. *Isabella d'Este and Lorenzo Da Pavia: Documents for the History of Art and Culture in Renaissance Mantua.* Geneva: Droz.

Brown and Lorenzoni 2004
Brown, Clifford M., and Anna Maria Lorenzoni. "Digest of the Correspondence Concerning the Paintings Commissioned for the *Studiolo* in the Castello (1496–1515)." In S. Campbell 2004, 280–301.

Brown and Pizzati 2014
Brown, David Alan, and Anna Pizzati. "'Meum amantissimum nepotem': A New Document Concerning Giovanni Bellini." *Burlington Magazine* 156, no. 1332 (March):148–52.

Burckhardt 1884
Burckhardt, Jacob. *Der Cicerone: Eine Anleitung zum Genuss der Kunstwerke Italiens*, edited by Wilhelm Bode. Vol. 2. Leipzig: Seemann.

Byam Shaw 1950
Byam Shaw, James. "Early Italian Engraving by A. M. Hind.' *Connoisseur*, March, 58–60.

Callegari 1997
Callegari, Raimondo. "Su due polittici di Giorgio Schiavone." *Arte veneta* 50:24–37.

Callegari 1998
Callegari, Raimondo. "Il 'Beato' Simonino da Trento: Un riconoscimento al Museo civico di Padova." *Bollettino dei Museo Civico di Padova* 81 (1992): 99–127, reprinted in Raimondo Callegari, *Scritti sull'arte padovana dei Rinascimento*, 87–108. Udine: Forum.

Campagnola 1971
Campagnola, Stanislao da. "Il Giardino d'orazione e altri scritti di un anonimo del Quattrocento." *Collectanea franciscana* 41:5–59.

Campana 1970
Campana, Agusto. "Epitafi." In *Enciclopedia Dantesca*, 2:710–13. Rome: Istituto dell'Enciclopedia Italiana.

L. Campbell 1981
Campbell, Lorne. "Notes on Netherlandish Pictures in the Veneto in the Fifteenth and Sixteenth Centuries." *Burlington Magazine* 123:467–73.

L. Campbell 1998
Campbell, Lorne. *National Gallery Catalogues: The Fifteenth Century Netherlandish Schools.* London: National Gallery.

S. Campbell 2004
Campbell, Stephen. *The Cabinet of Eros: Renaissance Mythological Painting and the Studiolo of Isabella d'Este.* New Haven: Yale University Press, 2004.

Cantalamessa 1914
Cantalamessa, Giulio. "La Madonna di Giovanni Bellini nella Galleria Borghese." In *Bollettino d'arte* 8:105–14.

Carletti and Giometti 2011
Carletti, Lorenzo, and Cristiano Giometti. "'San Francisco Will See Old Masters: La fiera delle vanità del regime nel 1939." *Studi storici* 52:465–89.

Castiglione 1560
Castiglione, Sabba. *Ricordi overo ammaestramenti.* Venice: Paolo Gerardo.

Catalogue 1864
Catalogue de la R. Galerie de Florence. Florence: Murate.

Catalogue 1907
Catalogue of the Rodolphe Kann Collection. 2 vols. Paris: Rahir.

Catalogue 1910
Catalogue de la vente des objets d'art ancien composant les collections Elie Volpi. Rome: Jandolo e Tavazzi.

Catalogue 1955
Catalogue of Important Old Master Drawings. Auction cat. Sotheby's, London, June 9.

Chapman 2010
Chapman, Hugo. "Introduction." In London 2010, 15–75.

Christie's 2003
Important Old Master Paintings. Sale catalogue. Christie's, London, January 24.

Christiansen 1998
Christiansen, Keith. "The View from Italy." In New York 1998, 39–61.

Christiansen 2004a
Christiansen, Keith. "Bellini and Mantegna." In Humfrey 2004, 48–74.

Christiansen 2004b
Christiansen, Keith. "Giovanni Bellini and the Practice of the Devotional Painting." In Kasl 2004, 7–57.

Christiansen 2004c
Christiansen, Keith. "Giovanni Bellini e la maniera divota." In *Da Bellini a Veronese: Temi di arte veneta*, edited by Gennaro Toscano and Francesco Valcanover, 123–53. Venice: Istituto Veneto di Scienze, Lettere ed Arti.

Christiansen 2006
Christiansen, Keith. "The Art of Gentile da Fabriano." In Fabriano 2006, 19–52.

Christiansen 2013
Christiansen, Keith. "Bellini and the Meditational 'Poesia.'" *Artibus et Historiae* 34, no. 679:9–20.

Cicogna 1834
Cicogna, Emanuele Antonio. *Delle iscrizioni veneziane.* Vol. 4. Venice: Giuseppe Picotti, 1834.

Clark 1949
Clark, Kenneth. *Landscape into Art.* London: Murray.

Coltellacci and Lattanzi 1981
Coltellacci, Stefano, and Marco Lattanzi. "Studi belliniani: Proposte iconologiche per la Sacra allegoria degli Uffizi." In *Giorgione e la cultura veneta tra '400 e '500: Mito, allegoria, analisi iconologica*, edited by A. Gentili and C. Ceri Via, 59–79. Rome: De Luca.

Conti 1987
Conti, Alessandro. "Giovanni Bellini fra Marco Zoppo ed Antonello da Messina." In *Antonello da Messina: Atti del convegno di studi*, 275–303. Messina: Università degli Studi.

Cordellier 1995
Cordellier, Dominique. "Documenti e fonti su Pisanello." Special issue, *Verona illustrata* 8.

Cortesi Bosco 2005
Cortesi Bosco, Francesca. "Per la data della pala di Castelfranco di Giorgione." *La rivista di Bergamo*, n.s., 42:54–56.

Cortesi Bosco 2009
Cortesi Bosco, Francesca. "Matteo Costanzo nella guerra del Casentino: Considerazioni sull'esecuzione della tavola di Giorgione a Castelfranco." In Castelfranco Veneto 2009, 113–22.

Crowe and Cavalcaselle 1871
Crowe, Joseph Archer, and Giovanni Battista Cavalcaselle. *A History of Painting in North Italy, Venice, Padua, Vicenza, Verona, Ferrara, Milan, Friuli, Brescia, from the Fourteenth to the Sixteenth Century.* 2 vols. London: John Murray.

Crowe and Cavalcaselle 1912
Crowe, Joseph Archer, and Giovanni Battista Caval-
caselle. *A History of Painting in North Italy, Venice,
Padua, Vicenza, Verona, Ferrara, Milan, Friuli, Brescia,
from the Fourteenth to the Sixteenth Century*, edited by
Tancred Borenius. 3 vols. London: John Murray.

Dalhoff 1997
Dalhoff, Meinolf. *Giovanni Bellini: Die Verklärung
Christi. Retorik, Erinnerung, Historie*. Münster: LIT.

Dalhoff 2002
Dalhoff, Meinolf. "Trouble at the Hermitage: A Note
on Giovanni Bellini's Sacred Allegory." *Burlington
Magazine* 144, no. 1186 (Jan.):22–23.

Dal Pozzolo 2003
Dal Pozzolo, E. M. "Giovanni Bellini a Vicenza." In
Vicenza 2003, 13–29.

Da Mosto 1937–40
Da Mosto, Andrea. *L'Archivio di Stato di Venezia: Indice
generale, storico, descrittivo ed analitico*. 2 vols. Rome:
Biblioteca d'Arte Edizioni.

Davies 1951
Davies, Martin. *National Gallery Catalogues: The Earlier
Italian Schools*. London: National Gallery.

Degenhart and Schmitt 1990
Degenhart, Bernhard, and Annegrit Schmitt, with
Hans Joachim Eberhardt. *Corpus der italienischen
Zeichnungen 1300–1450. Teil II: Venedig. Jacopo Bellini*,
vols. 5–8. Berlin: Mann.

De Groër 1987
De Groër, Georgette. "Notes de voyage d'un pèlerin
flamand en Italie au XV siècle." In *Art, objets d'art,
collections. Études sur l'art du Moyen-Age et de la
Renaissance, sur l'histoire du goût, et des collections.
Hommage à Hubert Landais*, 75–83. Paris: Blanchard.

Delaney 1977
Delaney, Susan J. "The Iconography of Giovanni Bellini's Sacred Allegory." *Art Bulletin* 59, no. 3:331–35.

De Marchi 2009
De Marchi, Andrea. "Le triptyque de San Zeno de
Vérone et sa prédelle." In Tours 2009, 16–22.

De Marchi 2012
De Marchi, Andrea. "Im Laufe der Zeit: La 'Pietà' di
Giovanni Bellini." In Milan 2012, 17–31.

De Marchi 2014
De Marchi, Andrea. "Giovanni Bellini, Andrea Mantegna e la tenerezza della madre." In Milan 2014,
73–82.

Demus 1984
Demus, Otto. *The Mosaics of San Marco in Venice*.
2 vols. Chicago: University of Chicago Press.

Dengel 1913
Dengel, Philipp. *Palast und Basilika San Marco in Rom*.
Rome: Loescher.

Dethloff 1996
Dethloff, Diana. "The Executors' Account Book and
the Dispersal of Sir Peter Lely's Collection." *Journal
of the History of Collections* 8, no. 1:15–51.

Dethloff 2003
Dethloff, Diana. "Sir Peter Lely's Collection of Prints
and Drawings." In *Collecting Prints and Drawings in
Europe, c. 1500–1750*, edited by Christopher Baker,
Caroline Elam, and Genevieve Warwick, 123–39.
London: Ashgate.

Die Galerie 2010
*Die Galerie Kaiser Karls VI. in Wien: Solimenas widmung-
bild und Storffers Inventar (1720–1733)*, edited by Sabine
Haag et al. Vienna: Kunsthistorisches Museum.

Dunkerton 2004
Dunkerton, Jill. "Bellini's Technique." In Humfrey
2004, 195–225.

Dürer 1913
Dürer, Albrecht. *Records of Journeys to Venice and the
Low Countries*, edited and translated by Roger Fry.
Boston: Merrymount.

Dürer 1956–69
Dürer, Albrecht. *Schriftlicher Nachlass, I, Autobiograph-
ische Schriften, Briefwechsel, Dichtungen, Beischriften,
Notizen und Gutachten, Zeugnisse zum persönlichen
Leben*, edited by Hans Rupprich. Berlin: Dt. Verein
für Kunstwissenshaft.

Echols 1994
Echols, Robert. "Cima and the Theme of Saint
Jerome in the Wilderness." *Venezia Cinquecento* 4,
no. 8:47–69.

Eisler 1989
Eisler, Colin. *The Genius of Jacopo Bellini: The Complete
Paintings and Drawings*. New York: Abrams.

Eisler 2015
Eisler, Colin. "Giovanni Bellini's *Iris* and *Autopsia's*
Role." In Wilson 2015, 21–38.

"Être dans la solitude" 1987
"Être dans la solitude." Special issue, *Nouvelle revue de
psychoanalyze* 36.

Fara 1977
Fara, Giovanni Maria. "Sul secondo soggiorno di
Albrecht Dürer in Italia e sulla sua amicizia con
Giovanni Bellini." *Prospettiva* 85:91–96.

Favaro 1975
Favaro, Elena. *L'arte dei pittori in Venezia e i suoi statuti*.
Florence: Olschki.

Ferino-Pagden 2006
Ferino-Pagden, Sylvia. "Pictures of Women — Pictures
of Love." In Washington 2006, 89–235.

Finocchi Ghersi 2003
Finocchi Ghersi, Lorenzo. *Il Rinascimento veneziano di
Giovanni Bellini*. Venice: Consorzio Venezia Nuova.

Fiocco 1926
Fiocco, Giuseppe. "Felice Feliciano amico degli
artisti," *Archivio veneto-tridentino* 9:188–201.

Fleming 1982
Fleming, John V. *From Bonaventure to Bellini: An Essay in
Franciscan Exegesis*. Princeton: Princeton University
Press.

Fletcher 1971
Fletcher, Jennifer M. "Isabella d'Este and Giovanni
Bellini's 'Presepio.'" *Burlington Magazine* 113, no. 825
(Dec.):703–13.

Fletcher 1991a
Fletcher, Jennifer M. Review of Rona Goffen, *Giovanni
Bellini*. *Burlington Magazine* 133, no. 1064 (Nov.):
779–80.

Fletcher 1991b
Fletcher, Jennifer M. "The Painter and the Poet:
Giovanni Bellini's Portrait of Raffaele Zovenzoni
Rediscovered." *Apollo* 134:153–57.

Fletcher 1998
Fletcher, Jennifer M. "I Bellini." In *La bottega dell'artista
tra Medioevo e Rinacimento*, edited by Roberto Cas-
sanelli, 131–53. Milan: Jaca Book.

Fletcher 2004
Fletcher, Jennifer M. "Bellini's Social World." In Humfrey 2004, 13–47.

Fletcher and Mueller 2005
Fletcher, Jennifer M., and Reinhold C. Mueller. "Bellini and the Bankers: The Priuli Altarpiece for S. Michele in Isola, Venice." *Burlington Magazine* 147, no. 1222 (Jan.): 5–15.

Fogolari 1924
Fogolari, Gino. *La chiesa di Santa Maria della Carità di Venezia: Ora sede delle Regie Gallerie dell'Accademia. Documenti inediti di Bartolomeo Bon, di Antonio Vivarini, di Ercole del Fiore e di altri artisti.* Venice: R. Deputazione.

Fogolari 1932
Fogolari, Gino. "Disegni per gioco e incunaboli pittorici del Giambellino." *Dedalo* 12, no. 1:360–89.

Folena 1983
Folena, Gianfranco. "La scrittura di Tiziano e la terminologia pittorica rinascimentale." In *Umanesimo e Rinascimento a Firenze e Venezia: Miscellanea di studi in onore di Vittore Branca,* 821–43. Florence: Olschki.

Fournier 2006
Fournier, Mary C. "Drawing as Gift: Jacopo Bellini's Paris Volume in Ottoman Istanbul." PhD diss., University of North Carolina, Chapel Hill.

Friedmann 1980
Friedmann, Herbert. *A Bestiary for Saint Jerome: Animal Symbolism in European Religious Art.* Washington, DC: Smithsonian Institution Press.

Frimmel 1901
Frimmel, Theodor von. *Geschichte der Wiener Gemäldesammlungen.* Leipzig: Meyer.

Fry [1899] 1995
Fry, Roger. *Giovanni Bellini.* Introduction by David Alan Brown and an afterword by Hilton Kramer. London: Ursus.

Galerie 1817
Galerie Impériale et Royale de Florence. Florence: Giuseppe Landi.

Galerie 1844
Galerie Impériale et Royale de Florence. Florence: Giglio.

Galerie 1850
Galerie Royale de Florence. Florence: Soliani.

Gamba 1937
Gamba, Carlo. *Giovanni Bellini.* Milan: Ulrico Hoepli.

Garas 1967
Garas, Klara. "Die Entstehung der Galerie des Erzherzogs Leopold Wilhelm." *Jahrbuch der Kunsthistorischen Sammlungen in Wien* 63:39–80.

Garas 1968
Garas, Klara. "Das Schicksal der Sammlung des Erzherzogs Leopold Wilhelm." *Jahrbuch der Kunsthistorischen Sammlungen in Wien* 64:181–288.

Gaye 1839–40
Gaye, Giovanni. *Carteggio inedito d'artisti dei secoli XIV. XV. XVI: Pubblicato ed illustrato con documenti pure inediti.* 3 vols. Florence: Giuseppe Molini.

Gentili 1985
Gentili, Augusto. "Girolamo nel deserto: L'ideologia, il modello, le varianti." In *I giardini di contemplazione: Lorenzo Lotto, 1503–1512,* edited by Augusto Gentili with Marco Lattanzi and Flavia Polignano, 162–83. Rome: Bulzoni.

Gentili 1991
Gentili, Agusto. "Giovanni Bellini, la bottega, i quadri di devozione." *Venezia Cinquecento* 1, no. 2:27–60.

Gentili 2004
Gentili, Augusto. "Bellini and Landscape." In Humfrey 2004, 167–81.

Gerspach 1906
Gerspach, É. "La Galerie Corsini à Florence." *Les Arts* 52:12–30.

Ghiberti [ca. 1447] 1988
Ghiberti, Lorenzo. *I commentarii,* edited by Lorenzo Bartoli. Florence: Biblioteca Nazionale Centrale di Firenze.

Giannetto 1985
Giannetto, Nella. *Bernardo Bembo umanista e politico veneziano.* Florence: Olschki.

Gibbons 1962
Gibbons, Felton. "Giovanni Bellini and Rocco Marconi." *Art Bulletin* 44, no. 2:127–31.

Gibbons 1977
Gibbons, Felton. "Giovanni Bellini's Topographical Landscapes." In *Studies in Late Medieval and Renaissance Painting in Honor of Millard Meiss,* edited by Irving Lavin and John Plummer, 1:174–84. New York: New York University Press.

Gilbert 1956
Gilbert, Creighton. "Alvise e compagni." In *Scritti di storia dell'arte in onore di Lionello Venturi,* 277–308. Rome: De Luca.

Gli Uffizi 1979
Gli Uffizi: Catalogo generale. Florence: Centro Di.

Godla and Allen 2015
Godla, Joseph, and Denise Allen. "St. Francis in the Desert and the Art of Linear Perspective." In *In a New Light: Giovanni Bellini's "St. Francis in the Desert" at the Frick Collection,* edited by Susannah Rutherglen and Charlotte Hale, 132–53. New York: Frick Collection and D. Giles.

Goffen 1985
Goffen, Rona. "Giovanni Bellini and the Altarpiece of St. Vincent Ferrer." In *Renaissance Studies in Honor of Craig Hugh Smyth,* edited by Andrew Morrough et al., 2:277–96. Florence: Villa I Tatti.

Goffen 1989
Goffen, Rona. *Giovanni Bellini.* New Haven and London: Yale University Press.

Goldner 2004
Goldner, George. "Bellini's Drawings." In Humfrey 2004, 226–55.

Grave 2004
Grave, Johannes. *Landschaften der Meditation: Giovanni Bellinis Assoziationsräume.* Freiburg im Breisgau: Rombach.

Graves 1913–15
Graves, Algernon. *A Century of Loan Exhibitions 1813–1912.* 5 vols. London: A. Graves.

Gronau 1911
Gronau, Georg. "Vincenzo Catena o Vincenzo dalle Destre." *Rassegna d'arte* 11:95–98.

Gronau 1921
Gronau, Georg. "Lauro Padovano, ein Gehilfe des Giovanni Bellini." In *Collectanea variae doctrinae Leoni S. Olschki, bibliopolae florentino sexagenario,* edited by Ludwig Bertalot, 101–12. Munich: Rosenthal.

Gronau 1928
Gronau, Georg. *Spätwerke des Giovanni Bellini.* Strasbourg: Heitz.

Gronau 1930
Gronau, Georg. *Giovanni Bellini: Des Maisters Gemälde
in 207 Abbildungen.* Stuttgart and Berlin: Deutsche
Verlags-Anstalt.

Habert et al. 2007
Habert, Jean, Cécile Scailliérez, Stephane Loire, and
Dominique Thiébaut, eds. *Catalogue des peintures
italiennes du Musée du Louvre.* Paris: Gallimard.

Hammond 2016
Hammond, Joseph. "Five Jacopo Bellinis: The Lives
of Christ and the Virgin at the Scuola Grande di
S. Giovanni Evangelista, Venice." *Burlington Magazine* 158, no. 1361 (Aug.):601–9.

Haskell 1963
Haskell, Francis. *Patrons and Painters: A Study in the
Relations between Italian Art and Society in the Age of
the Baroque.* London: Chatto & Windus.

Haskell 1991
Haskell, Francis. "William Coningham and His Collection of Old Masters." *Burlington Magazine* 13:676–81.

Heinemann 1962/1991
Heinemann, Fritz. *Giovanni Bellini e i belliniani.* Vols.
1–2. Venice: Neri Pozza, 1962; vol. 3. Venice: Neri
Pozza, 1991.

Hof- und Staats-Handbuch [1891]
*Hof- und Staats-Handbuch der Österreichisch-Ungarischen
Monarchie für 1891.* Vienna: K. K. Hof- und Staats-
druckerei.

Hope 1980
Hope, Charles. "Titian's Role as 'Official Painter'
to the Venetian Republic." In *Tiziano e Venezia:
Convegno internazionale di studi, Venezia, 1976,* 301–5.
Venice: Neri Pozza.

Humfrey 1977
Humfrey, Peter. "A Non-Bellini from the Carità in
Venice." *Burlington Magazine* 119, no. 886:36–39.

Humfrey 1979
Humfrey, Peter. "A Non-Bellini from the Carità in
Venice." *Burlington Magazine* 121, no. 913:253.

Humfrey 1985
Humfrey, Peter. "The Life of St Jerome Cycle from the
Scuola di San Girolamo in Cannaregio." *Arte veneta*
39:41–46.

Humfrey 1988
Humfrey, Peter. "Competitive Devotions: The Vene-
tian Scuole Piccole as Donors of Altarpieces in the
Years around 1500." *Art Bulletin* 70, no. 3:401–23.

Humfrey 1991
Humfrey, Peter. "Two Lost St. Jerome Altarpieces
by Giovanni Bellini." *Venezia Cinquecento* 1, no.
2:109–17.

Humfrey 1993
Humfrey, Peter. *The Altarpiece in Renaissance Venice.*
New Haven: Yale University Press.

Humfrey 1996
Humfrey, Peter. "Bellini, Giovanni." In *The Dictionary
of Art,* edited by Jane Turner, 3:657–69. London:
Grove.

Humfrey 2004
Humfrey, Peter, ed. *The Cambridge Companion to
Giovanni Bellini.* Cambridge: Cambridge University
Press.

Humfrey 2011
Humfrey, Peter. "The Portrait in Fifteenth-Century
Venice." In New York 2011, 48–63.

Humfrey 2015
Humfrey, Peter. "The Reception of Giovanni Bellini in
Britain, up to c. 1900." In Wilson 2015, 279–99.

Huse 1972
Huse, Norbert. *Studien zu Giovanni Bellini.* Berlin: De
Gruyter.

Jerome 1933
Jerome. *Select Letters of St. Jerome,* translated by F. A.
Wright. Loeb Classical Library 262. Cambridge,
MA: Harvard University Press.

Jerome 1949–63
Jerome. *Correspondance,* translated and edited by
Jérôme Labourt. 8 vols. Paris: Les Belles Lettres.

Joannides 2001
Joannides, Paul. *Titian to 1518: The Assumption of Genius.*
New Haven: Yale University Press.

Joannides 2011
Joannides, Paul. "Giorgione's 'The Madness of Nebu-
chadnezzar.'" *Paragone* 62, no. 741:3–12.

Joost-Gaugier 1974
Joost-Gaugier, Christiane. "Considerations Regarding
Jacopo Bellini's Place in the Venetian Renaissance."
Arte veneta 28:21–38.

Kalina 2012
Kalina, Pavel. "*Hericiis et leporibus:* Giovanni Bellini's St
Jerome in Washington and the Idea of the Hermit's
Life in Italy and Central Europe in the Early 16th
Century." *Umění Art* 60, no. 5:346–62.

Kasl 2004
Kasl, Ronda, ed. *Giovanni Bellini and the Art of Devotion.*
Indianapolis: Indianapolis Museum of Art.

Kidwell 1993
Kidwell, Carol. *Sannazaro and Arcadia.* London:
Duckworth.

Kidwell 2004
Kidwell, Carol. *Pietro Bembo: Lover, Linguist, Cardinal.*
Montreal: McGill-Queen's University Press.

Kleinbub 2015
Kleinbub, Christian. "Jacopo Bellini and the Drawing
of Idolatry." In *Venetian Painting Matters, 1450–1750,*
edited by Jodi Cranston, 21–34. Turnhout: Brepols.

Koch 1988
Koch, Robert A. "The Getty 'Annunciation' by Dirk
Bouts." *Burlington Magazine* 130:509–22.

Kristeva 1980
Kristeva, Julia. "Motherhood According to Giovanni
Bellini." In *Desire in Language: A Semiotic Approach
to Literature and Art,* edited by Leon S. Roudiez and
translated by Thomas Gora, Alice Jardine, and Leon
S. Roudiez, 237–70. New York: Columbia University
Press.

Lametti 2001
Lametti, Laura. "Il manoscritto intitolato Appunti
sopra la città di Fuligno: Scritti da Lodovico Coltel-
lini accademico fulginio. Parte nona. 1770–1780."
In *Il Palazzo Trinci di Foligno,* edited by Giordana
Benazzi and Francesco Federico Mancini, 427–46.
Perugia: Quatroemme.

La Pala Barbarigo 1983
La Pala Barbarigo di Giovanni Bellini. Venice: Stamperia
di Venezia.

Lattanzi 1981
Lattanzi, Marco. "La pala di S. Giovanni Crisostomo di
Giovanni Bellini." *Artibus et Historiae* 2, no. 4:29–38.

Lattanzi 1983
Lattanzi, Marco. "Il tema del San Girolamo nell'eremo
e Lorenzo Lotto." In Rome 1983, 55–59.

Lattanzi and Mercalli 1983
Lattanzi, Marco, and Marica Mercalli. "Il tema del *San Girolamo nell'eremo* nella cultura veneta tra Quattro e Cinquecento." In Rome 1983, 71–106.

Lauber 2007
Lauber, Rosella. "La collezione di Bartolomeo della Nave." In *Il collezionismo d'arte a Venezia: Il Seicento*, edited by Linda Borean and Stefania Mason, 258–61. Venice: Marsilio.

Lauber 2008
Lauber, Rosella. "Artifices celebratos nominare: Riflessioni sulle opere di Tiziano nel collezionismo veneziano." In *Venezia Cinquecento* 18, no. 36:231–92.

Lauber 2009
Lauber, Rosella. "Giovanelli di San Stin e Giovanelli di Santa Fosca, collezioni." In *Il collezionismo d'arte a Venezia: Il Settecento*, edited by Linda Borean and Stefania Mason, 271–73. Venice: Marsilio.

Lavin 2007
Lavin, Marilyn. "The Joy of St. Francis: Bellini's Panel in the Frick Collection." *Artibus et Historiae* 28, no. 56:231–56.

Lemoisne 1946–49
Lemoisne, Paul-André. *Degas et son oeuvre*. 4 vols. Paris: Arts et Métiers Graphiques.

C. Levi 1900
Levi, Cesare Augusto. *Le collezioni veneziane d'arte e d'antichità dal secolo XIV. ai nostri giorni*. 2 vols. Venice: Ongania Editore.

D. Levi 1988
Levi, Donata. *Cavalcaselle: Il pioniere della conservazione dell'arte italiana*. Turin: Giulio Einaudi.

Lightbown 1986
Lightbown, Ronald. *Mantegna, with a Complete Catalogue of the Paintings, Drawings and Prints*. Berkeley and Los Angeles: University of California Press.

Longhi 1927
Longhi, Roberto. "Un chiaroscuro e un disegno di Giovanni Bellini." *Vita artistica* 2, no. 7:133–38.

Longhi 1949
Longhi, Roberto. "The Giovanni Bellini Exhibition." *Burlington Magazine* 91, no. 559 (Oct.):274–83.

Longhi 1956
Longhi, Roberto. "I primitivi italiani all'Orangerie." *Il Giorno*, May 26.

Longhi [1927] 1967
Longhi, Roberto. "Un chiaroscuro e un disegno di Giovanni Bellini" (1927). In *Saggie Ricerche: 1925–1928*, vol. I, 179–88. Edizione delle opere complete di Roberto Longhi, 2. Florence: Sansoni.

Longhi 1973
Longhi, Roberto. "Problemi di lettura e problemi di conservazione." In *Storia del restauro e della conservazione delle opere d'arte*, edited by Alessandro Conti, 9–30. Milan: Electa.

Longhi [1946] 1978
Longhi, Roberto. *Viatico per cinque secoli di pittura veneziana* (1946). In *Ricerche sulla pittura veneta, 1946–1969*, 3–63. Edizione delle opere complete di Roberto Longhi, 10. Florence: Sansoni.

Longhi [1925–26] 1995
Longhi, Roberto. "Escursioni belliniane, 1925–1926." In *Il palazzo non finito: Saggi inediti, 1910–1926*, 361–33. Milan: Electa.

Lorenzi 1868
Lorenzi, Giambattista. *Monumenti per servire alla storia del Palazzo Ducale di Venezia ovvero serie di atti pubblici dal 1523 al 1797 che cariamente lo riguardano tratti dai veneti archivi e coordinati*. Venice: Visentini.

Lucco 1990
Lucco, Mauro. "Venezia." In *La pittura nel Veneto: Il Quattrocento*, edited by M. Lucco, 2:395–480. Milan: Electa.

Lucco 1994
Lucco, Mauro. "Una nuova opera di Cima da Conegliano." *Venezia Cinquecento* 7:19–24.

Lucco 1997
Lucco, Mauro. "Un'eco fiamminga in Giovanni Bellini." In *Scritti per l'Istituto Germanico di Storia dell'Arte di Firenze*, edited by Cristin Acidini Luchinat et al., 199–204. Florence: Le Lettere.

Lucco 2004
Lucco, Mauro. "Bellini and Flemish Painting." In Humfrey 2004, 75–94.

Lucco 2008
Lucco, Mauro. "La primavera del Mondo tuto, in ato de Pitura." In Rome 2008, 19–38.

Lucco 2009
Lucco, Mauro. "Considerations on Drawing in Renaissance Veneto." In Budapest 2009, 85–97.

Lucco 2013
Lucco, Mauro. *Mantegna*. Milan: 24 Ore Cultura.

Lucco and Pontani 1997
Lucco, Mauro, and Anna Pontani. "Greek Inscriptions on Two Venetian Renaissance Paintings." *Journal of the Warburg and Courtauld Institutes* 60:111–29.

Ludwig 1903
Ludwig, Gustav, and Wilhelm Bode. "Die Altarbilder der Kirche S. Michele di Murano und das Auferstehungsbild des Giovanni Bellini in der Berliner Galerie." *Jahrbuch der Königlich Preussischen Kunstsammlungen* 24, no. 2:131–46.

Lynn-Davis 1998
Lynn-Davis, Barbara. "Landscapes of the Imagination in Renaissance Venice." PhD diss., Princeton University.

Malamani 1888
Malamani, Vittorio. *Memorie del Conte Leopoldo Cicognara*. Venice: Tipografia dell'ancora.

Manieri Elia 2014
Manieri Elia, Giulio. "Le Storie di Sant'Orsola alle Gallerie dell'Accademia (1808–1947): Musealizzazione, restauri, vicende critiche e allestive del ciclo capolavoro di Vittore Carpaccio." In *L'arrivo a Colonia di Vittore Carpaccio: Studio e restauro*, edited by Daila Radeglia, 35–43. Rome: Gangemi.

Marchini 1981
Marchini, Giuseppe. *La Galleria di Palazzo degli Alberti: Opere d'arte della Cassa di Risparmi e Depositi di Prato*, Milan: Electa.

Mariano 1969
Mariano, Nicky. *Quarant'anni con Berenson*. Florence: Sansoni.

Marini et al. 2010
Marini, Paola, Gianni Peretti, and Francesca Rossi, eds. *Museo di Castelvecchio: Catalogo generale dei dipinti e delle miniature delle collezioni civiche Veronesi. I. Dalla fine del X all'inizio del XVI secolo*. Cinisello Balsamo: Silvana.

Marrow 1979
Marrow, James H. *Passion Iconography in Northern European Art of the Late Middle Ages and Early Renaissance: A Study in the Transformation of Sacred Metaphor into Descriptive Narrative*. Kortrijk: Van Ghemmert.

Maze 2013
Maze, Daniel Wallace. "Giovanni Bellini: Birth, Parentage, and Independence." *Renaissance Quarterly* 66, no. 3:783–823.

Mazzotta 2009
Mazzotta, A. "Gabriele Veneto e un ritratto dimenticato di Giovanni Bellini." *Prospettiva* 134–35:2–24.

Mazzotta 2012
Mazzotta, Antonio. *Giovanni Bellini's Dudley Madonna.* London: Paul Holberton.

Mazzotta 2015
Mazzotta, Antonio. *A Portrait of Gabriele Veneto and Some Reflections on Giovanni Bellini's Portraiture around 1500.* In Wilson 2015, 183–201.

McHam 2008
McHam, Sarah Blake. "Reflections of Pliny in Giovanni Bellini's Woman with a Mirror." *Artibus et Historiae* 29, no. 58:157–71.

Mechel 1783
Mechel, Christian von. *Verzeichnis der Gemälde der Kaiserlich Koniglichen Bilder Gallerie in Wien*, Vienna: Gräfer.

Mechel 1784
Mechel, Christian von. *Catalogue des tableaux de la Galerie Impériale et Royale de Vienne.* Basel: the author.

Medici 1886
Medici, Ulderigo. *Catalogo della galleria dei principi Corsini in Firenze.* Florence: Mariani.

Meiss 1936
Meiss, Millard. "The Madonna of Humility." *Art Bulletin* 18:435–64.

Meiss 1964
Meiss, Millard. *Giovanni Bellini's St. Francis in the Frick Collection.* Princeton: Princeton University Press.

Menato 2012
Menato, Sara. "Per la provenienza di un Cristo benedicente di Giovanni Bellini dal complesso agostiniano di Santo Stefano a Venezia." *Arte veneta* 69:128–32.

Meneghin 1962
Meneghin, Vittorino. *San Michele in Isola di Venezia.* Vol. 1. Venice: Stamperia di Venezia.

Meyer zur Capellen 1980
Meyer zur Capellen, Jürg. "Bellini in der Scuola Grande di San Marco." *Zeitschrift für Kunstgeschichte* 43, no. 1:104–8.

Meyer zur Capellen 1985
Meyer zur Capellen, Jürg. *Gentile Bellini.* Stuttgart: Steiner.

Michel 1901
Michel, É. "La galerie de M. Rodolphe Kann (2ᵉ partie)." *Gazette des beaux-arts* 25:493–506.

[Michiel] 1884
[Michiel, Marcantonio]. *Notizia d'opere di disegno, pubblicata e illustrata da D. Iacopo Morelli, seconda edizione riveduta e aumentata per cura di Gustavo Frizzoni.* Bologna: Zanichelli.

[Michiel] 1888
[Michiel, Marcantonio]. *Der Anonimo Morelliano*, edited and translated by Theodor von Frimmel. Vienna: Graeser.

Minervino 1970
Minervino, Fiorella. *L'opera completa di Degas.* Milan: Rizzoli.

Morassi 1958
Morassi, Antonio. "Scoperta di un Cristo benedicente del Giambellino." *Arte veneta* 12:42–52.

[Morelli] 1880
[Morelli, Giovanni]. Ivan Lermolieff. *Die Werke italienischer Meister in den Galerien von München, Dresden und Berlin.* Leipzig: Seemann.

[Morelli] 1890
[Morelli, Giovanni]. Ivan Lermolieff. *Kunstkritische Studien über Italienische Malerei. Die Galerien Borghese und Doria Panfili in Rom.* Leipzig: Brockhaus.

Moschini Marconi 1955
Moschini Marconi, Sandra. *Gallerie dell'Accademia di Venezia: Opere d'arte dei secoli XIV e XV.* Rome: Istituto Poligrafico dello Stato.

Neff 1985
Neff, Mary Frances. "Chancellery Secretaries in Venetian Politics and Society, 1480–1533." PhD diss., University of California, Los Angeles.

Nova 2008
Nova, Alessandro. "Icona, racconto e 'dramatic close-up' nei dipinti devozionali di Giovanni Bellini." In Rome 2008, 105–15.

Oettinger 2012
Oettinger, April. "The Lizard in the Study: Landscape and *Otium* in Lorenzo Lotto's *Portrait of a Young Man* (c. 1530)." *Artibus et Historiae* 33, no. 65:115–25.

[Ojetti] 1925–26
[Ojetti, Ugo]. 1925–1926. "Commenti." *Dedalo* 6:133–36.

Pächt 2003
Pächt, Otto. *Venetian Painting in the Fifteenth Century: Jacopo, Gentile and Giovanni Bellini, and Andrea Mantegna*, edited by Margareta Vyoral-Tschapka and Michael Pächt. London and Turnhout: Brepols.

Pallucchini 1951
Pallucchini, Rodolfo. "Cataloghi." *Arte veneta* 5:194–97.

Pallucchini 1959
Pallucchini, Rodolfo. *Giovanni Bellini.* Milan: Martello.

Pallucchini 1962
Pallucchini. Rodolfo. *I Vivarini (Antonio, Bartolomeo, Alvise).* Venice: Neri Pozza.

Paschini 1943
Paschini, Pio. *Domenico Grimani Cardinale di San Marco.* Rome: Edizioni di Storia e Letteratura.

Pater 1893
Pater, Walter. *The Renaissance: Studies in Art and Poetry.* London: Macmillian.

Penny 2004
Penny, Nicholas. *National Gallery Catalogues: The Sixteenth-Century Italian Paintings.* Vol. 1. *Paintings from Bergamo, Brescia and Cremona.* London: National Gallery.

Perkins 2015
Perkins, Elizabeth. "Giovanni Bellini, Antonello da Messina, and the 'Signs of Men's Character.'" In Wilson 2015, 127–41.

Petrarch [1346–56] 1977
Petrarca, Francesco. *De vita solitaria*, edited by Guido Martellotti. Turin: Giulio Einaudi, 1977.

Pignatti 1969
Pignatti, Terisio. *L'opera completa di Giovanni Bellini detto Giambellino.* Milan: Rizzoli.

Pignatti 1970
Pignatti, Terisio. "Bellini, Giovanni." In *Dizionario biografico degli italiani*, 7:708–12. Rome: Treccani.

Pincus 2008
Pincus, Debra. "Giovanni Bellini's Humanist Signature: Pietro Bembo, Aldus Manutius and Humanism in Early Sixteenth-Century Venice." *Artibus et Historiae* 29, no. 58:89–119.

Pino 1548
Pino, Paolo. *Dialogo di pittura di messer Paolo Pino, nuouamente dato in luce.* In Barocchi 1960, 93–139.

Poldi and Villa 2006
Poldi, Gianluca, and Giovanni C. F. Villa. "Giovanni Bellini e dintorni ovvero appunti veneziani." In *Dalla conservazione alla storia Dell'arte: Riflettografia e analisi non invasive per lo studio dei dipinti,* edited by Gianluca Poldi and Giovanni C. F. Villa, 321–412. Pisa: Edizioni della Normale.

Poldi and Villa 2009
Poldi, Gianluca, and Giovanni Carlo Federico Villa. *Indagando Bellini.* Milan: Skira.

Poldi and Villa 2011
Poldi, Gianluca, and Giovanni Carlo Federico Villa. "A New Examination of Giovanni Bellini's 'Pesaro Altarpiece': Recent Findings and Comparisons with Other Works by Bellini." In *Studying Old Master Paintings: Technology and Practice,* edited by Marika Spring with Helen Howard, 28–36. London: Archetype Publications.

Pope-Hennessy [1990] 1994
Pope-Hennessy, John. "Giovanni Bellini" (1990), in *On Artists and Art Historians: Selected Book Reviews,* edited by Walter Kaiser and Michael Mallon, 119–28. Florence: Olschki.

Pullan 1971
Pullan, Brian. *Rich and Poor in Renaissance Venice: The Social Institutions of a Catholic State.* Cambridge, MA: Harvard University Press.

Pullan 1990
Pullan, Brian. "The Scuole Grandi of Venice: Some Further Thoughts." In *Christianity and the Renaissance,* edited by Timothy Verdon and John Henderson, 272–301. Syracuse: Syracuse University Press.

Puppi 2012
Puppi, Lionello, ed. *Tiziano, L'epistolario.* Afterword by Charles Hope. Florence: Alinari 24 Ore.

Ragusa 1961
Ragusa, Isa, ed. and trans. *Meditations on the Life of Christ: An Illustrated Manuscript of the Fourteenth Century: Paris, Bibliothèque National, Ms. Ital. 115.* Princeton: Princeton University Press.

Rancière 2005
Rancière, Jacques. "From Politics to Aesthetics?" *Paragraph* 28, no. 1:13–25.

Rasmo 1946
Rasmo, Niccolò. "La Sacra Conversazione belliniana degli Uffizi e il problema della sua comprensione." *Carro Minore* 1:229–40.

Rearick 2003
Rearick, William R. "La dispersione dei dipinti già a Santa Maria dei Miracoli." In *Santa Maria dei Miracoli a Venezia: La storia, la fabbrica, i restauri,* edited by Mario Piana and Wolfgang Wolters, 179–92. Venice: Istituto Veneto di Scienze, Lettere ed Arti.

Riccardi 1786
Riccardi, Tommaso. *Storia dei vescovi vicentini.* Vicenza: Mosca.

Rice 1985
Rice, Eugene F., Jr. *Saint Jerome in the Renaissance.* Baltimore: Johns Hopkins University Press.

Richter 1960
Richter, Irma G., ed. *Italienische Malerei der Renaissance im Briefwechsel von Giovanni Morelli und Jean Paul Richter 1876–1891.* Baden-Baden: Grimm.

Ridderbos 1984
Ridderbos, Bernhard. *Saint and Symbol: Images of St. Jerome in Early Italian Art.* Groningen: Bouma's Bookhuis.

Ridolfi [1648] 1914–24
Ridolfi, Carlo. *Le maraviglie dell'arte, ovvero le vite degli illustri pittori veneti e dello Stato,* edited by Detlev von Hadeln. Rome: Soc. Multigrafica.

Rigon 2003
Rigon, Fernando. "L'architettura a Vicenza e Giovanni Bellini." In Vicenza 2003, 31–37.

Ring 1945
Ring, Grete. "St. Jerome Extracting the Thorn from the Lion's Foot." *Art Bulletin* 27:188–94.

Ringbom 1965
Ringbom, Sixten. *Icon to Narrative: The Rise of the Dramatic Close-Up in Fifteenth-Century Devotional Painting.* Turku: Åbo Akademi.

Robb 1972
Robb, David M., Jr., *Kimbell Art Museum: Catalogue of the Collection.* Fort Worth: Kimbell Publication One.

Robertson 1960
Robertson, Giles. "The Earlier Work of Giovanni Bellini." *Journal of the Warburg and Courtauld Institutes* 23:45–59.

Robertson 1968
Robertson, Giles. *Giovanni Bellini.* Oxford: Clarendon Press.

Robin 1991
Robin, Diana. *Filelfo in Milan: Writings 1451–1477.* Princeton: Princeton University Press.

Romano 1978
Romano, Giovanni. *Studi sul paesaggio.* Turin: Giulio Einaudi.

Ronen 1992
Ronen, Avraham. "Iscrizioni ebraiche nell'arte italiana del Quattrocento." In *Studi di storia dell'arte sul Medioevo e il Rinascimento nel centenario della nascita di Mario Salmi,* edited by Maria Grazia Ciardi Duprè Dal Poggetto, 2:601–24. Florence: Polistampa.

Rosenauer 2016
Rosenauer, Arthur. *Titian: The Grimani Risen Christ, an Early Masterpiece.* Munich: Hirmer.

Rowley 2008
Rowley, Neville. "Giovanni Bellini: Rome." *Burlington Magazine* 150, no. 1269 (Dec.):848–49.

Rugolo 2006
Rugolo, C. M. "Antonello da Messina e la sua famiglia: Le fonti scritte." In Rome 2006, 352–67.

Ruskin 1877
Ruskin, John. *St. Mark's Rest: First Supplement. The Shrine of the Slaves, Being a Guide to the Principal Pictures by Victor Carpaccio in Venice.* Sunnyside, Orpington (Kent): George Allen.

Russo 1987
Russo, Daniel. *Saint Jérôme en Italie: Étude d'iconographie et de spiritualité.* Paris: Decouverte.

Rutherglen and Hale 2015
Rutherglen, Susannah, and Charlotte Hale, eds. *In a New Light: Giovanni Bellini's "St. Francis in the Desert."* New York: Frick Collection.

Safarik 1996
Safarik, E. A. *Italian Inventories 2: The Colonna Collection of Paintings. Inventories 1611–1795,* edited by A. Cera Sones. New York: Saur.

Sannazaro [1504] 1926
Sannazaro, Jacopo. *Arcadia,* edited by Enrico Carrara. Turin: Utet.

Sansovino 1564
Sansovino, Francesco. *Dialogo di tutte le cose notabili che sono in Venetia*. Venice: Domenico de' Franceschi.

Sansovino 1581
Sansovino, Francesco. *Venetia città nobilissima et singolare*. Venice: Iacomo Sansovino.

Sanudo 1879–1903
Sanudo, Marin. *I diarii (1496–1533)*, edited by Rinaldo Fulin et al. 58 vols. Venice: F. Visentini.

Sanudo 2004
Sanudo, Marin. *Le vite dei Dogi, 1423–1474. II tomo: 1457–1474*. Introduction and notes by Angela Caracciolo Aricò, transcription by Chiara Frison. Venice: La Malcontenta.

Schiller 1971
Schiller, Gertrud. *Iconography of Christian Art*, translated by Janet Seligman. 2 vols. London: Lund Humphries.

Schubert 2006
Schubert, Leo. *La villa Janneret-Perret di Le Corbusier, 1912: La prima opera autonoma*. Venice: Marsilio.

Schulz 1983
Schulz, Anne Markham. *Antonio Rizzo: Sculptor and Architect*. Princeton: Princeton University Press.

Secrest 2004
Secrest, Meryle. *Duveen: A Life in Art*. New York: Knopf.

Seilern 1959
Seilern, Antoine, ed. *Italian Paintings and Drawings at 56 Princes Gate London SW*. 2 vols. London: Shenval Press.

Seilern 1969
Seilern, Antoine, ed. *Italian Paintings and Drawings at 56 Princes Gate London SW7: Addenda*. London: Shenval Press.

Seilern 1971
Seilern, Antoine, ed. *Corrigenda & Addenda to the Catalogue of Paintings & Drawings at 56 Princes Gate London SW7*. London: Shenval Press.

Settis 1978
Settis, Salvatore. *La Tempesta interpretata: Giorgione, i committenti, il soggetto*. Turin: Giulio Einaudi.

Shaw 1994
Shaw, Keith Vernon. "The Ovetari Chapel: Patronage, Attribution, and Chronology." PhD diss., University of Pennsylvania.

Shaw and Boccia 2016
Shaw, Keith, and Theresa Boccia. "Andrea Mantegna Called Andrea Squarcione." In *Encountering the Renaissance: Celebrating Gary M. Radke and 50 Years of the Syracuse University Graduate Program in Renaissance Art*, edited by Molly Bourne and A. Victor Coonin, 317–24. Ramsey, NJ: Wapaac Organization.

Signorini 2006
Signorini, Mariarita. "Al visibile e all'infrarosso, il gioco delle differenze." In *La terrazza del mistero 2: L'Allegoria sacra di Giovanni Bellini: Analisi storica e interpretazione psicoanalitica con una rilettura dopo il restauro*, 81–92. Florence: Nicomp.

Sizonenko 2013
Sizonenko, Tatiana. "Artists as Agents: Artistic Exchange and Cultural Translation between Venice and Constantinople; The Case of Gentile Bellini, 1479–1481." PhD diss., University of California, San Diego.

Spalletti 2008
Spalletti, Ettore. "Tommaso Puccini e il 'nuovo ordine, e risalto maggiore dato alla Galleria.'" *La Galleria "rinnovata" e "accresciuta": Gli Uffizi nella prima epoca lorenese*, edited by Miriam Fileti Mazza, Ettore Spalletti, and Bruna M. Tomasello, 72–134. Florence: Centro Di.

Speroni 1546
Speroni, Sperone. *Dialoghi*. Venice: Eredi di Aldo Manuzio il Vecchio.

Spezzani 1992
Spezzani, Paolo. *Riflettoscopia e indagini non distruttive: Pittura e grafica*. Milan: Olivetti.

Stampart and Prenner 1735
Stampart, Frans von, and Anton Joseph von Prenner. *Prodromus*. Vienna: Joannis Petri Van Ghelen.

Steinberg 1983
Steinberg, Leo. *The Sexuality of Christ in Renaissance Art and in Modern Oblivion*. New York: Pantheon.

Tempestini 1992
Tempestini, Anchise. *Giovanni Bellini: Catalogo completo dei dipinti*. Florence: Cantini.

Tempestini 1997
Tempestini, Anchise. *Giovanni Bellini*. Milan: Fabbri.

Tempestini 2000
Tempestini, Anchise. *Giovanni Bellini*. Milan: Electa.

Tempestini 2003
Tempestini, Anchise. "Le vicende storiche e critiche." In Vicenza 2003, 61–63.

Tempestini 2004
Tempestini, Anchise. "Bellini and His Collaborators." In Humfrey 2004, 256–71.

Tempestini 2013
Tempestini, Anchise. "Giovanni Bellini nella storia dell'arte del XX secolo." *Artibus et Historiae* 67:49–54.

Theophili 1847
Theophili qui et Rugerus, presbyteri et monachi, libri III. De diversis artibus: Seu, diversarum artium schedula. Translated by Robert Hendrie. London: John Murray.

Togneri Dowd 1985
Togneri Dowd, Carol, ed. "The Travel Diaries of Otto Mündler." *Walpole Society* 51:71–254.

Toscano 2004
Toscano, Gennaro. "Giovanni Bellini et la France (XVIᵉ–XXᵉ siècle): Les aléas d'une reconnaissance." In *Da Bellini a Veronese: Temi di arte veneta*, edited by Gennaro Toscano and Francesco Valcanover, 197–249. Venice: Istituto Veneto di Scienze, Lettere ed Arti.

van Asperen de Boer 1997
van Asperen de Boer, Johan Rudolph Justus, ed. *Jan van Eyck: Two Paintings of St. Francis Receiving the Stigmata*. Philadelphia: Philadelphia Museum of Art.

Varchi [1549] 1960
Varchi, Benedetto. *Lezzione nella quale si disputa della maggioranza delle arti e qual sia più nobile, la scultura o la pittura*. In Barocchi 1960, 3–82.

Vasari [1550, 1568] 1966–87
Vasari, Giorgio. *Le vite de' più eccellenti pittori, scultori e architettori nelle redazioni del 1550 e 1568*, edited by Rosanna Bettarini and Paola Barocchi. 6 vols. Florence: Sansoni e S.P.E.S.

Venturi 1884
Venturi, Adolfo. "I primordi del rinascimento artistico a Ferrara." *Rivista storica italiana* 1:591–631.

Venturi 1915
Venturi, Adolfo. *Storia dell'arte italiana: La pittura del Quattrocento*. Vol. 7.4. Milan: Ulrico Hoepli.

Venturi 1924
Venturi, Adolfo. *L'arte a San Girolamo*. Milan: Fratelli Treves.

Verdier 1952–53
Verdier, Philippe. "L'allegoria della Misericordia e della Giustizia di Giambellino agli Uffizi." *Atti dell'Istituto Veneto di Scienze, Lettere ed Arti*, 111:97–116.

Villa 2009
Villa, Giovanni Carlo Federico. "Indagando Bellini: Quattro ancone in un itinerario." In *Indagando Bellini*, edited by Gianluca Poldi and Giovanni C. F. Villa, 13–127. Milan: Skira.

Vinco 2014
Vinco, Mattia. "L'*Istrias* di Raffaele Zovenzoni e Giovanni Bellini ante 1475." In Milan 2014, 97–101.

Voragine 1850
Jacobus de Voragine. *Legenda Aurea vulgo historia lombardica dicta*, edited by Theodor Graesse. 2nd ed. Leipzig: Librariae Arnoldianae.

Voragine 1993
Jacobus de Voragine. *The Golden Legend: Readings on the Saints*, translated by William Granger Ryan. 2 vols. Princeton: Princeton University Press.

Waagen 1857
Waagen, Gustav Friedrich. *Galleries and Cabinets of Art in Great Britain: Being an Account of More Than Forty Collections of Paintings, Drawings, Sculptures, Mss. &c, Visited in 1854 and 1856, and Now for the First Time Described, Forming a Supplemental Volume to the Treasures of Art in Great Britain*. London: John Murray.

Waterhouse 1952
Waterhouse, Ellis K. *Paintings from Venice for Seventeenth-Century England: Some Records of a Forgotten Transaction*. Italian Studies 7:1–23.

Weston 2009
Weston, Hazel. "Christ's Descent into Limbo at the Bristol City Art Gallery and Museum: A Singular Work of Art." MPhil thesis, University of Birmingham, England.

Weston-Lewis 2002
Weston-Lewis, Aidan. "A Drawing in Copenhagen Attributed to Titian." *Burlington Magazine* 143 (Oct.): 596–600.

Whitehouse 2012
Whitehouse, Fiona Lucy. "The Influence of Netherlandish Paintings on Giovanni Bellini and Cima da Conegliano." PhD diss., Birkbeck College, University of London.

Wiebel 1988
Wiebel, Christiane. *Askese und Endlichkeitsdemut in der italienischen Renaissance*. Weinheim: Acta Humaniora.

Wilde 1934
Wilde, Johannes. "Zwei Tizian-Zuschreibungen des 17. Jahrhunderts." *Jahrbuch der Kunsthistorischen Sammlungen in Wien*, n.s., 8:161–72.

Wilde 1974
Wilde, Johannes. *Venetian Art from Bellini to Titian*, edited by Giles Robertson and Maurice Howard. Oxford: Clarendon Press.

Wilson 1976
Wilson, Carolyn C. "Bellini's Pesaro Altarpiece: A Study in Context and Meaning." PhD diss., New York University.

Wilson 2004
Wilson, Carolyn C. "Giovanni Bellini and the 'Modern Manner.'" In Humfrey 2004. 95–121.

Wilson 2015
Wilson, Carolyn C., ed. *Examining Giovanni Bellini: An Art 'More Human and More Divine.'* Turnhout: Brepols.

Wohl 1999
Wohl, Helmut. "The Subject of Giovanni Bellini's St. Francis in the Frick Collection." In *Mosaics of Friendship: Studies in Art and History for Eve Borsook*, edited by Ornella Francisci Osti, 187–98. Florence: Centro Di.

Wolfthal 1989
Wolfthal, Diane. *The Beginnings of Netherlandish Canvas Painting 1400–1530*. Cambridge: Cambridge University Press.

Wolfthal and Metzger 2014
Wolfthal, Diane, and Cathy Metzger. *Los Angeles Museums*. Vol. 22, *Corpus of Early Netherlandish Painting*. Brussels: Royal Institute for Cultural Heritage.

Worthen 2015
Worthen, Amy. "An Inconvenient Text: The *Supplementum chronicarum* as a Source for Information about Gentile and Giovanni Bellini." In Wilson 2015, 39–59.

Zampetti 1997
Zampetti, P. "Carpaccio, Bellini e Ancona." *Arte documento* 11:76–85.

Zanetti 1733
Zanetti, Anton Maria. *Descrizione di tutte le pubbliche pitture della città di Venezia e isole circonvicine: O sia rinnovazione delle Ricche minere di Marco Boschini, colla aggiunta di tutte le opere, che uscirono dal 1674 fino al presente 1733, con un compendio delle vite e maniere de' principali pittori*. Venice: P. Bassaglia.

Zanetti 1771
Zanetti, Anton Maria. *Della pittura veneziana e delle opere pubbliche de' veneziani maestri*. Venice: Albrizzi.

Zannini 1993
Zannini, Andrea. *Burocrazia e burocrati a Venezia in età moderna: I cittadini originari (sec. XVI–XVIII)*. Venice: Istituto Veneto di Scienze, Lettere ed Arti.

Zeri 1989
Zeri, Federico. *La percezione visiva dell'Italia e degli italiani*. Turin: Giulio Einaudi.

Zimmermann 1893
Zimmermann, Ernst. "Die Landschaft in der venezianischen Malerei bis zum Tode Tizians." *Beiträge zur Kunstgeschichte*, n.s., 20:1–209.

Zovenzonii 1950
Zovenzonii, Raphaelis. "Istrias et Carmina Varia." In *Raffaele Zovenzoni: La vita, i carmi*, edited by Baccio Ziliotto, 67–161. Trieste: Comune di Trieste.

Zucchetta 2008
Zucchetta, Emanuela. "Il polittico di San Vincenzo Ferrer: Chiesa dei Santi Giovanni e Paolo." In *Bellini a Venezia: Sette opere indagate nel loro contesto*, edited by Gianluca Poldi and Giovanni Carlo Federico Villa, 31–51. Cinisello Balsamo: Silvana.

INDEX

All works are by Giovanni Bellini unless otherwise indicated. Institutions and landmarks are indexed by location. Page numbers in *italics* refer to illustrations.

Adorno, Anselmo, 17
Agnew, Thomas, 70
The Agony in the Garden (London, National Gallery; fig. 1), 15, *16*, 44, 63
Alberti, Leon Battista, 89
Albi, Bibliothèque Municipale, 69, 97n21
Alfonso I d'Este, Duke of Ferrara, 108, 114
altarpieces, structural typology of, 73–74
Altinum (ancestor city of Venice), 32
Ancona, San Ciriaco (cathedral), 14, 100–101
Andachtsbild (devotional image), 90, 91
Antonello da Messina: Bellini as influenced by, 15, 48, 90–91, 106; Bellini's work attributed to, 86, 90, 94; *Crucifixion with the Virgin and Saint John the Evangelist* (Antwerp; fig. 31), 89, 90; *Crucifixion with the Virgin and Saint John the Evangelist* (London, National Gallery; fig. 30), 88, 90; *Saint Jerome in His Study* (London, National Gallery; fig. 9), 29, *31*; San Cassiano altarpiece, 48, 90–91
Antwerp, Koninklijk Museum voor Schone Kunsten: *Crucifixion with the Virgin and Saint John the Evangelist* (Antonello; fig. 31), 89, 90

Baptism of Christ (Vicenza, Santa Corona; fig. 38), 18, 97n1, 98, 103, 108, *108*, 114, 121
Barbarigo, Agostino (doge), 34, 51, 96
Barberini Corsini, Anna, Princess, 86
Bartoli, Bartolommeo (bishop), 84
Basaiti, Marco, 28, 92, 94–95, 109, 119–20, 125n18
Basaiti, Pseudo-, 112, 115n8
Bastiani, Lazzaro, 47
Bauer Eberhardt, Ulrike, 72–73
Bellini, Alvise, 47, 51
Bellini, Gentile: death, 41, 53; Ducal Palace commission, 48–50, 55n81; Giovanni's biological relation to, 40–41, 48, 54n79; and Sultan Mehmet II, 49, 53, 55n119; workshop commissions under Jacopo, 17, 54n34, 74; workshop inherited by, 47
Bellini, Giovanni: artistic reputation of, 11–12, 38, 47, 51, 53; birth date and parentage, 39–41, 53n17, 54n22, 54n79, 63; childhood and social class, 41; death, 53, 55n118; early career, overview of, 44–45; final years, overview of, 51–53; and humanist thought, 38, 47, 51; Isabella d'Este's negotiations with, 13–14, 51–52, 108, 115n27, 123–24; marriage and child, 45, 47, 51, 54nn55–56; middle career, overview of, 47–51; oil paints, use of, 17, 38, 43, 48, 53n5, 54nn69–70, 106; as portraitist, 48; and workshop's expansion, 45, 50–51
—INFLUENCES: Antonello, 15, 48, 90–91, 106; Flemish or Netherlandish artists, 15, 17, 48, 52, 53n5, 67–69, 106, 129; Giorgione's dialogue with Bellini, 38, 51, 102–3, 107, 113–14, 121; Jacopo Bellini, 15, 43, 61–62, 96; Mantegna, 15, 17, 39, 45, 62–63, 64–67, 75, 78, 82, 96; Titian's dialogue with Bellini, 34, 38, 107, 113
—LANDSCAPES: animal and plant depictions in, 15, 20, 26–27, 32, 43, 61, 76, 80, 104, 126, 129–30; architectural depictions in, 14–15, 28, 34, 98, 100; artistic evolution of, 12, 15, 17–18; devotional qualities of, 18–22, 37, 88–90, 102; perspective or spatial organization in, 43, 75, 80, 90, 96, 114, 128; terminology used for, 13–14. *See also specific works*
Bellini, Giovannina, 40, 53n17
Bellini, Jacopo: Carità triptychs, 17, 45, 74; *Crucifixion with the Virgin and Saint John the Evangelist* (Paris, Louvre; fig. 21), 64, 66; death, 47; Ferrara commission, 52; and Gentile da Fabriano, 43, 54n36; Giovanni as influenced by, 15, 43, 61–62, 96; Giovanni's biological relation to, 39–41; *Madonna and Child* (Lovere, Accademia Tadini; fig. 20), 62, *63*; marriage and children, 39, 41, 54n25; *Saint Jerome in the Wilderness* (Paris, Louvre; fig. 2), 15, *16*, 61, 128; *Saint Jerome in the Wilderness* (Verona, Castelvecchio), 60, 62, 130n3; Scuole commissions, 41, 47, 54n34; *Seven Lions and Three Stags* (Paris, Louvre; fig. 19), 61, *61*; sketchbooks, 15, 29, 43, 47, 53, 61, 82, 96, 97n16, 128
Bellini, Leonardo, 41
Bellini, Nicolò, 40, 53n17
Bellini, Nicolosia, 40, 41, 45, 66
Belliniano, Vittore, 50, 53, 97n16
Bellosi, Luciano, 39, 69, 74, 110
Bembo, Bernardo, 30
Bembo, Pietro, 14, 20, 30, 52, 124
Bencivenni Pelli, Giuseppe, 118
Berenson, Bernard, 34, 94–95, 110, 125n15
Bergamo, Galleria dell'Accademia Carrara: *Madonna and Child* (*Lochis Madonna*) (Bellini; fig. 11), 37, *38*; Orsetti collection, 92, 97n2; *Pietà* (Bellini), 44, 63
Berlin, Kaiser-Friedrich-Museum, 72
Berlin, Staatlichen Museen zu Berlin: *Resurrection* (Bellini; fig. 4), 12, 17, *19*, 106; *Saint Mark Healing Anianus* (Bellini; fig. 26), 78, *78*, 80
Bernardini, Giorgio, 110, 112
Besançon, Musée des Beaux-Arts et d'Archéologie: *The Drunkenness of Noah* (Bellini; fig. 17), *50*, 51, 52–53

Birmingham, Barber Institute of Fine Arts: *Saint Jerome in the Wilderness* (Bellini; cat. no. 1), 15, 29, 44, 45, 58–63, *59*, 128
Bissolo, Francesco, 50
Bocheta, Ginevra (later Bellini), 45, 47, 51, 54n56
Bode, Wilhelm, 70, 72, 115n8, 120
Bono, Pietro, 90–91
Bono da Ferrara, 58, 60
Borso d'Este, Duke, 81n11
Boschini, Marco, 11, 23n17, 72, 73, 94
Botticelli, Sandro, 17
Bouts, Dieric, the Elder: *Crucifixion* (Brussels, Musées Royaux des Beaux-Arts), 23nn29–30, 68, 82; *Entombment* (London, National Gallery; fig. 23), 23n29, 68, 69; *Resurrection* (Pasadena, Norton Simon; fig. 3), 17, *18*, 106; Venice altarpiece, now dispersed, 17, 23nn29–30, 68, 82
Brescia, Pinacoteca Tosio Martinengo, 78
Brussels, Musées Royaux des Beaux-Arts: *Crucifixion* (Bouts), 23nn29–30, 68, 82; *Crucifixion* triptych (Van der Weyden workshop), 85
Bruto, Pietro, 101–2
Bugatto, Zanetto, 91
Byam Shaw, James, 81n6, 96

Calò da Chioggia, Pietro, 58
Carpaccio, Vittore: Ancona, ties to, 100–101; Carità altarpiece panel, 72; *Meditation on the Passion* (New York, Metropolitan; fig. 44), 128, *129*; rabbits, depiction of, 130
Castagno, Andrea del, 43
Castiglione, Sabba, 14
Catena, Vincenzo, 50, 110, 112
Cavalcaselle, Giovanni Battista, 61, 70, 74, 94, 109, 110, 119, 125n17
Ceresara, Paride da, 52
Chiari, Giuseppe Bartolomeo, 86
Christ, iconography of, 44, 64, 82–85, 90, 104, 106, 114
Christ Blessing (Fort Worth, Kimbell; cat. no. 9), 17, 104–9, *105*
Christiansen, Keith, 21, 39, 44, 69, 81n11, 88, 90, 122
Cillenio, Giovanni Testa, 47
Cima da Conegliano, Giovanni Battista, 29, 94, 108
Colantonio, Niccolò, 48
Collenuccio, Pandolfo, 51
Colonna family (Rome), 86
Coningham, William, 108
Contarini, Taddeo, 20, 35n3
Contini Bonacossi, Alessandro, 70. See also *Saint Jerome in the Wilderness* (Florence, Uffizi)

Conversion of Saint Paul (from Pesaro altarpiece; fig. 29), 85, *85*
Copenhagen, Statens Museum for Kunst, 113
Coronation of the Virgin altarpiece. *See* Pesaro altarpiece
Correr, Teodoro. *See* Venice, Museo Correr
Corsini family (Florence), 86. *See also* Florence, Corsini Collection
Crowe, Joseph Archer, 94, 109, 110, 115n3, 119, 125n17
Crucifixion (Florence, Corsini; cat. no. 6), 84, 86–91, *87*
Crucifixion (Vicenza, Banca Popolare di Vicenza; cat. no. 8), 15, 18, 21, *56* (detail), 64, 84, 98–103, *99*, 129
Crucifixion with the Virgin and Saint John the Evangelist (Paris, Louvre; cat. no. 3), 70–75, *71*, 108–9
Crucifixion with the Virgin and Saint John the Evangelist (Venice, Museo Correr; cat. no. 2), *10–11* (detail), 17, 44, 64–69, *65*, 75

Dante Alighieri, 30
Davies, Martin, 95–96
Decembrio, Angelo, 58
Degas, Edgar, 119, 125n15
Della Robbia workshop, 55n109
Della Rovere, Federico, 92, 97n2
De Marchi, Andrea, 12, 73, 75
Denver, private collection, 108, 114, *114*
Diana, Benedetto, 73
Diletti, Giorgio, 32, 34
Donatello, 43, 52, 81n17
Dragonzino da Fano, Giambattista, 100
The Drunkenness of Noah (Besançon, Musée des Beaux-Arts; fig. 17), *50*, 51, 52–53
Dürer, Albrecht: Bellini's interactions with, in Venice, 51; on Bellini's skill as painter, 38, 107; and landscape painting, 14; *Saint Jerome in a Cave* (Washington, National Gallery; fig. 43), 126, *128*
Duveen, Joseph, 70, 72, 113

Eastlake, Charles Lock, 92, 110
Este, Leonello d', Marquess of Ferrara, 58
Eyck, Jan van: and Bellini's London *Saint Jerome*, 94; *Crucifixion* by follower of (Venice, Cà d'Oro), 67; *Saint Francis of Assisi Receiving the Stigmata* (Philadelphia Museum of Art; fig. 5), 17, *20*, 129

Facio, Bartolomeo, 58
The Feast of the Gods (Bellini and Titian; Washington, National Gallery; fig. 16), 38, *49*, 51
Feilding, Basil, Earl of Denbigh, 118
Feliciano, Felice, 38, 47, 102
Fioccardo, Alberto, 17, 103n5
Fisher, Richard, 70, 72, 108–9
Florence, Corsini Collection: *Crucifixion* (Bellini; cat. no. 6), 84, 86–91, *87*
Florence, Galleria degli Uffizi: *Annunciation* (Leonardo), 119; *Apostle(?)* (Belliniano), 97n16;

Crucifixion with Mary Magdalen (Signorelli), 103n12; *Judgment of Solomon* (Giorgione), 118–19, 121; *Sacred Allegory* (Bellini; cat. no. 11), 22, *36–37* (detail), 51, 116–25, *117*, *123* (detail); *Saint Jerome in the Wilderness* (Bellini; fig. 7), 17, 26–28, *26*, 94, *95*, 128; *Trial of Moses* (Giorgione), 102, 119, 121; *View of the Valdarno* (Leonardo), 80
Florence, Villa del Poggio Imperiale, 118
Fort Worth, Kimbell Art Museum: *Christ Blessing* (Bellini; cat. no. 9), 17, 104–9, *105*
Francesco di Giorgio Martini, 81n4
Francesco II Gonzaga, Marchese of Mantua, 14, 100
Francis of Assisi, Saint, iconography of, 19–20, 30–32
Fry, Roger, 34

Galeazzo Maria Sforza, Duke of Milan, 90–91
Gamba, Carlo, 98, 102
Gattamelata altarpiece (Bellini workshop), 41, 54n24
Genoa, Palazzo Rosso, 113
Gentile da Fabriano, 43, 54n36
Gentili, Augusto, 18–19, 20, 102
Gerspach, Édouard, 86
Giambono, Michele, 43
Giorgione: *Adoration of the Shepherds (Allendale Nativity)* (Washington, National Gallery; fig. 41), 119, *119*, 121; Bellini's artistic dialogue with, 38, 51, 102–3, 107, 113–14, 121; as Bellini workshop assistant, 38, 50; Castelfranco *Madonna*, 113, 115n20; *Concert* (Windsor, Royal Collection; fig. 39), *112*, 113; *Homage to a Poet* (London, National Gallery; fig. 42), 102, *120*, 121; *Judgment of Solomon* (Florence, Uffizi), 118–19, 121; and landscape painting, 13, 18; *Three Philosophers* (Vienna, Kunsthistorisches Museum), 20–21, 35n3; *Trial of Moses* (Florence, Uffizi), 102, 119, 121
Giovanelli family (Venice), 110–13, 115n2
Giovanni Andrea da Bologna, 58
Giovanni d'Alemagna, 43, 74
The Good and Bad Thieves, Dismas and Gestas (Newark, Delaware, Alana; cat. no. 5), 82–85, *83*
Granacci, Francesco, 101, 103n12
Grimani, Domenico (cardinal), 13, 126, 130n4
Gronau, Georg, 72, 90, 95, 112, 113
Guarino Veronese, 58, 69, 96, 97n21, 128
Guillaume de Deguileville, 121–22

Hamburg, Galerie Hans, 106, 109
Hamilton, James Hamilton, 1st Duke of, 118
Head of Christ (Ottawa, National Gallery; fig. 36), 106, *106*
Hinderbach, Johannes (bishop), 102
humanist thought: Bellini's affinity to, 38, 47, 51; of B. Bembo, 30; and Jews, 102; and *quadro* (painting on supports), 22; Saint Jerome as model of, 25–26, 58, 96

Isabella d'Este, Marchesa of Mantua, 13–14, 20, 30, 51–52, 108, 115n27, 123–24

Jacopo da Varagine, 58, 60
Jerome, Saint: and humanist thought, 25–26, 58, 96; iconography of, 25–29, 32–34, 58, 60–61, 92, 126–30; and Petrarch's *De vita solitaria*, 29–30; *Vita Pauli primi eremitae*, 122
Jews, persecution of, 101–2

Kann, Rudolf, 70, 72
Kaufmann, Richard von, 72
Kraus, Carl von, Baron, 85n6

Landino, Cristoforo, 30
landscapes. *See under* Bellini, Giovanni
Lanzi, Luigi, 118
Lauro Padovano, 72
Le Corbusier, 125n21
Le Hunte family (England), 76, 78, 81nn2–3
Lely, Peter, 76, 81n2
Leonardo da Vinci, 17, 43, 80
Leopold Wilhelm, Archduke of Austria, 118
Liphart, Karl Eduard von, 119, 125n18
Lippi, Filippino, 17
Lippi, Filippo, 43
London, British Institution, 70, 108
London, British Museum: Carpaccio drawing from Ancona, 101; *Crucifixion* (Mantegna follower; fig. 28), 66, 81, 84, *84*; Pietà drawing with verso child studies (Bellini), 80–81; sketchbook of J. Bellini, 43, 53, 61, 97n16; *Two Holy Women* (Mantegna), 78
London, Colnaghi gallery, 78, 81n5
London, Courtauld Gallery: *Nativity* (Bellini; cat. no. 4), 76–81, *77*; *Studies for a Christ at the Column* (Mantegna), 78
London, National Gallery: *Adoration of the Kings* (Bellini workshop), 120; *The Agony in the Garden* (Bellini; fig. 1), 15, *16*, 44, 63; *Assassination of Saint Peter Martyr* (Bellini), 121; *Blood of the Redeemer* (Bellini), 125n37; *Christ Blessing* (Antonello), 106; *Crucifixion with the Virgin and Saint John the Evangelist* (Antonello; fig. 30), 88, *90*; Eastlake as director of, 92, 110; *Entombment* (Bouts; fig. 23), 23n29, 68, *69*; *Homage to a Poet* (attrib. to Giorgione; fig. 42), 102, *120*, 121; *Madonna of the Meadow* (Bellini; fig. 35), 18, *95*, 101, 102; *Portrait of Doge Leonardo Loredan* (Bellini; fig. 14), 44, *48*; *Saint Jerome* (Bono da Ferrara), 58, 60; *Saint Jerome in His Study* (Antonello; fig. 9), 29, *31*; *Saint Jerome Reading in the Wilderness* (Bellini; cat. no. 7), 28, 80, 92–97, *93*; *Tramonto* (Giorgione), 121; *The Virgin and Child with Saints* (Previtali), 113
London, Sotheby's, 76, 81n6, 109
Longhi, Roberto, 11–12, 39, 75, 113, 125n31
Loredan, Leonardo (doge), 44
Lorenzi, Giuseppe Gallo, 92, 94, 97n1

Los Angeles, J. Paul Getty Museum, 23n29

Lotto, Lorenzo, 55n111, 113

Lovere, Accademia di Belle Arti Tadini: *Madonna and Child* (J. Bellini; fig. 20), 62, *63*

Lucco, Mauro, 39, 72, 73, 81n9, 106

Ludovico III Gonzaga, Marchese of Mantua, 45

Ludwig, Gustav, 72, 115n8, 121–22

Madonna and Child (Lochis Madonna) (Bergamo, Accademia Carrara; fig. 11), 37, *38*

Madonna and Child with Saints (Frari triptych) (Venice, Santa Maria Gloriosa dei Frari; fig. 15), *46*, 51, 53

Madonna of the Meadow (London, National Gallery; fig. 35), 18, 95, *101*, 102

Madrid, Thyssen-Bornemisza Collection, 60

Malamani, Vittorio, 72

Mansueti, Giovanni, 92, 97n2

Mantegna, Andrea: *Adoration of the Shepherds* (New York, Metropolitan), 67, 81n11; Bellini as influenced by, 15, 17, 39, 45, 62–63, 64–67, 75, 78, 82, 96; Bellini's work attributed to, or vice versa, 70, 78, 81n18, 109; biographical summary, 44–45; *Christ's Descent into Limbo* (Paris, École des Beaux-Arts), 66, 97n16; *Crucifixion* (from San Zeno altarpiece; Paris, Louvre; fig. 22), 17, 66, 67, 75, 84; *Crucifixion* by follower of (London, British Museum; fig. 28), 66, 81, 84, *84*; death, 53; Isabella d'Este, commission for, 13, 52; *Saint Jerome in the Wilderness* (São Paulo, Museu de Arte; fig. 18), 60, *60*, 62

Marcello, Jacopo Antonio, 44, 69

Marconi, Rocco, 50

Marcovich, Bartolomeo, 92, 94

Marostica (Vicenza), *95*, 96, 101

Mary, Virgin, iconography of, 44, 76, 118, 122

Mechel, Christian von, 118, 124n8

Medici, Ulderigo, 86

Mehmet II, Sultan, 49, 53, 55n119

Memling, Hans, 106

Michel, Émile, 70

Michiel, Giovanni (Zuan), 19

Michiel, Marcantonio: on Antonello's *Saint Jerome in His Study*, 29; on Bellini's Carità altarpiece, 72; on Bellini's *Saint Francis in the Desert*, 12, 27, 31, 35n3; and Bembo's art collection, 30; and landscape painting, 13, 17

Milan, Museo Poldi Pezzoli: *Imago Pietatis* (Bellini), 44, 63, 66, 89–90

Milan, Pinacoteca di Brera: *Pietà* (Bellini; fig. 12), *39*, 88, 90; *Saint Jerome* (Cima da Conegliano), 94; *Saint Mark Preaching in Alexandria* (Gentile and Giovanni Bellini), 53

Mocetto, Girolamo: *Resurrection* (Vienna, Albertina; fig. 32), 94, 96

Montagna, Bartolomeo, 49

Morassi, Antonio, 104, 108, 109

Morelli, Giovanni, 70, 110, 115n6

Mündler, Otto, 92, 110

Munich, Schloss Berchtesgaden: *Stories of Saint John the Evangelist and Drusiana* (Bellini; fig. 24), 72–75, *72–73*, *74* (detail)

Murano, San Pietro Martire (church), 34, 51, 96

Murray, Charles Fairfax, 70, 72

Naples, Galleria Nazionale di Capodimonte: *Transfiguration* (Bellini; fig. 6), 12, 17–18, *21*, 51, 98, 101, 103n5

Nativity (from Pesaro altarpiece; fig. 27), 78, *79*, 80

Nativity (London, Courtauld; cat. no. 4), 76–81, *77*

Nave, Bartolomeo della, 116, 118, 122, 124n1

Newark, Delaware, Alana Collection: *The Good and Bad Thieves, Dismas and Gestas* (Bellini; cat. no. 5), 82–85, *83*

New Orleans Museum of Art, 112

New York, Frick Collection: *Saint Francis in the Desert* (Bellini; fig. 8), 12, 17, 19–21, 27–28, *27*, 30–32, 35n3, 51, 102

New York, Metropolitan Museum of Art: *Adoration of the Shepherds* (Mantegna), 67, 81n11; *Design for a Wall Monument* (Francesco di Giorgio), 81n4; Granacci triptych, 101, 103n12; *Meditation on the Passion* (Carpaccio; fig. 44), 128, *129*; *Portrait of a Man* (Sustris), 113, 115n14; *Virgin and Child*, Davis (Bellini), 44; *Vulcan Building a Fence around the Mount of Venus* (Bellini's circle), 79, 81n10

Niccolini, Filippo, 3rd Marquess of Ponsacco and Camugliano, 98. See also *Crucifixion* (Vicenza, Banca Popolare di Vicenza)

Nicolò III d'Este, Marchese, 52

Nievo, Alessandro, 101

oil paints, 17, 38, 43, 48, 53n5, 54nn69–70, 106

Ojetti, Ugo, 113

Orsetti, Salvatore, 92, 97n2

Ottawa, National Gallery of Canada: *Head of Christ* (Bellini; fig. 36), 106, *106*

Oxford, Ashmolean Museum, 96, 97n13

Padua, Museo Civico, 67

Padua, Ovetari Chapel, Church of the Eremitani, 62

Padua, Papafava Collection, 94

Palma, Jacopo, il Vecchio, 113

Paris, Bibliothèque de l'Arsenal, 44

Paris, École des Beaux-Arts: *Christ's Descent into Limbo* (Mantegna), 66, 97n16

Paris, Musée du Louvre: *Crucifixion* (Mantegna, from San Zeno altarpiece; fig. 22), 17, 66, 67, 75, 84; *Crucifixion with the Virgin and Saint John the Evangelist* (Bellini; cat. no. 3), 70–75, *71*, 108–9; *Crucifixion with the Virgin and Saint John the Evangelist* (J. Bellini; fig. 21), *64*, 66; *Pietà* (Bellini), 78, 80, 81n9; *Saint Jerome in the Wilderness* (J. Bellini; fig. 2), 15, *16*, 61,

128; *Seven Lions and Three Stags* (J. Bellini; fig. 19), 61, *61*; sketchbook of J. Bellini, 15, 43, 53, 61, 82, 97n16, 128

Pasadena, Norton Simon Museum: *Christ Blessing* (Memling), 106; *Joerg Fugger* (Bellini), 48; *Resurrection* (Bouts; fig. 3), 17, *18*, 106

Pasqualino, Antonio, 29

Pavia, Lorenzo da, 123–24

Perugino, 52, 84

Pesaro altarpiece (Museo Civico di Pesaro): altarpiece reconstructed (fig. 13), *42*; and Bellini's artistic evolution, 12; Castle of Gradara depicted in, 14; *Conversion of Saint Paul* (predella panel; fig. 29), 85, *85*; execution of, in church of San Francesco, 47–48; *Nativity* (predella panel; fig. 27), 78, *79*, 80; and Saint Jerome's iconography, 128

Petrarch, Francesco, 26, 28, 29–32

Philadelphia Museum of Art: *Saint Francis of Assisi Receiving the Stigmata* (Van Eyck; fig. 5), 17, *20*, 129

Piatti, Piattino, 47

Piero della Francesca, 48

Pietà (Donà delle Rose) (Venice, Accademia; fig. 34), 15, 18, 100, *100*, 102

Pietà (Milan, Pinacoteca di Brera; fig. 12), *39*, 88, 90

Pino, Paolo, 13, 14, 52

Pisanello, 58, 96, 126, 128, 130

plague (Venice, 1427), 40, 54n22

Portrait of Doge Leonardo Loredan (London, National Gallery; fig. 14), 44, 48

Pouncey, Philip, 81n4

Prenner, Anton Joseph von, 118

Previtali, Andrea, 50, 110, 113

Puccini, Tommaso, 118

quadro (painting on supports), 22

Raphael, 15

Ravenna landmarks, depictions of, 14–15, 28, 100

Rennes, Musée des Beaux-Art, 80

Resurrection (Berlin, Staatlichen Museen; fig. 4), 12, 17, *19*, 106

Richter, Jean-Paul, 70, 74, 98

Ridolfi, Carlo, 48, 88, 109

Rimini, Roman bridge at, 15, 28

Rinversi, Anna, 39–40

Robertson, Giles, 37, 44, 72, 78–79, 88, 90, 102, 113

Rome, Galleria Borghese, 112

Rome, Palazzo Venezia, 130n4

Rondinelli, Niccolò, 50

Rowley, Neville, 52–53, 102

Ruskin, John, 53

sacra conversazione (genre), 12, 22, 47–48, 113–14

Sacred Allegory (Florence, Uffizi; cat. no. 11), 22, *36–37* (detail), 51, 116–25, *117*, *123* (detail)

Saint Dominic (Denver; fig. 40), 108, 114–15, *114*

Saint Francis in the Desert (New York, Frick; fig. 8), 12, 17, 19–21, 27–28, *27*, 30–32, 35n3, 51, 102
Saint Jerome in the Wilderness (Birmingham, Barber Institute; cat. no. 1), 15, 29, 44, 45, 58–63, *59*, 128
Saint Jerome in the Wilderness (Florence, Uffizi; fig. 7), 17, 26–28, *26*, 94, 95, 128
Saint Jerome Reading in the Wilderness (London, National Gallery; cat. no. 7), 28, 80, 92–97, *93*
Saint Jerome Reading in the Wilderness (Washington, National Gallery; cat. no. 12), 17, *24–25* (detail), 28–29, 32, 95, 126–30, *127*
Saint Jerome with Saint Christopher and Saint Louis of Toulouse (Venice, San Giovanni Crisostomo; fig. 10), 29, 32, *33*, 34, 126
Saint Mark Healing Anianus (Berlin, Staatlichen Museen; fig. 26), 78, *78*, 80
Saint Petersburg, State Hermitage Museum, 102–3, 121
San Gimignano, San Domenico (convent), 84
Sannazaro, Jacopo, 29–30
sansaria (broker's patent), 48–49, 50
Sanudo, Marin, 50, 53, 54n25
São Paulo, Museu de Arte: *Saint Jerome in the Wilderness* (Mantegna; fig. 18), 60, *60*, 62
Sebastiano del Piombo, 50
Seilern, Antoine, Count, 78, 79
Sforza family (Italy), 85, 90–91
Signorelli, Luca, 101, 103n12
Simon of Trent, 102
Speroni, Sperone, 14
Squarcione, Francesco, 44–45, 79
Squarzòla (Andrea Michiel), 104, 106
Stampart, Frans von, 118
Stories of Saint John the Evangelist and Drusiana (Munich, Schloss Berchtesgaden; fig. 24), 72–75, *72–73*, *74* (detail)
Strabo's *Geography*, 69, 96, 97n21
Stuttgart, Staatsgalerie, 100
Sustris, Lambert, 113, 115n14

Tempestini, Anchise, 98, 108
Teniers, David, the Younger, 118
Titian: artistic reputation of, vs. Bellini's, 53; Bellini's artistic dialogue with, 34, 38, 107, 113; as Bellini workshop assistant, 38, 50; *The Feast of the Gods* (with Bellini; Washington, National Gallery; fig. 16), 38, 49, 51; and landscape painting, 13, 18, 121; *Risen Christ* (private collection; fig. 37), 107, *107*; *sansaria* (broker's patent), 50; Santa Maria della Salute altarpiece, 35n30
Titulus Crucis (relic of True Cross), 101
Transfiguration (Naples, Capodimonte; fig. 6), 12, 17–18, *21*, 51, 98, 101, 103n5
Trissino, Gaspare, 98

underdrawing, 52, 62
Urbino, Galleria Nazionale delle Marche, 103n12

Vasari, Giorgio, 13, 48, 50, 51, 54n79
Vendramin, Franceschina, 40, 53n15, 53n17, 54n22
Vendramin, Gabriele, 13, 53
Vendramin, Samaritana (later Dominici), 40, 41, 54n22
Veneto countryside, 12, 15, 60, 114
Venice, Cà d'Oro, 67
Venice, Ducal Palace, 48–50, 75, 100, 123
Venice, Fondazione Querini Stampalia, 45
Venice, Gallerie dell'Accademia: *Martyrdom of Saint Mark* (Bellini and Belliniano), 53; *Miracle during the Procession in Piazza San Marco* (Gentile Bellini), 50; *Nativity* (Vivarini), 80; *Pietà (Donà delle Rose)* (Bellini; fig. 34), 15, 18, 100, *100*, 102; *Saint Jerome* (Basaiti), 92; San Giobbe altarpiece (Bellini), 51, 88, 90, 122; *Tempesta* (Giorgione), 121; *Virgin and Child*, Contarini (Bellini), 100; *Virgin and Child with Saint John the Baptist and a Female Saint in a Landscape* (Bellini; cat. no. 10), 14, 108, 110–15, *111*, 124
Venice, Giovanelli Collection, 110–13, 115n2
Venice, Museo Correr: *Crucifixion with the Virgin and Saint John the Evangelist* (Bellini; cat. no. 2), *10–11* (detail), 17, 44, 64–69, *65*, 75; *Pietà with Two Angels* (Bellini), 89–90; *Transfiguration* (Bellini), 63, 66, 75, 97n16
Venice, San Cristoforo della Pace (church), 126
Venice, San Giobbe (church), 51, 88, 90, 110, 113, 122
Venice, San Giorgio Maggiore (church), 94
Venice, San Giovanni Crisostomo (church): *Saint Jerome with Saint Christopher and Saint Louis of Toulouse* (Bellini; fig. 10), 29, 32, *33*, 34, 126
Venice, San Marco (church), 34, 41, 43
Venice, Santa Maria dei Miracoli (church), 95, 126
Venice, Santa Maria della Carità (church): *Crucifixion with the Virgin and Saint John the Evangelist* (Bellini; now in Paris, Louvre), 70–75; triptychs by Bellini workshop (under Jacopo), 17, 45, 74, 80
Venice, Santa Maria Gloriosa dei Frari (church): *Madonna and Child with Saints* (Bellini; fig. 15), 46, 51, 53
Venice, Santi Giovanni e Paolo (or San Zanipolo; church): Bellini's burial in, 53; *Madonna and Child with Saints Thomas Aquinas and Catherine* (destroyed), 47; *Saint Vincent Ferrer* altarpiece, 45, 73–74, 75
Venice, Santo Stefano (monastery), 109
Venice, San Zaccaria (church), 53, 128
Venice, Scuola dei Caleghéri, 80, 81n16
Venice, Scuola Grande di San Marco, 32, 41, 47, 49, 54n56
Vercelli, Museo Borgogna, 73
Verona, Museo di Castelvecchio: *Saint Jerome in the Wilderness* (J. Bellini), 60, 62, 130n3

Verona, San Zeno (church), 17, 66, 75, 84
Vianello, Michele, 14, 115n27
Vicenza, Banca Popolare di Vicenza: *Crucifixion* (Bellini; cat. no. 8), 15, 18, 21, *56* (detail), 64, 84, 98–103, *99*, 129
Vicenza, Santa Corona (church): *Baptism of Christ* (Bellini; fig. 38), 18, 97n1, 98, 103, 108, *108*, 114, 121
Vicenza Cathedral, 17–18, 98, 100, 103n5
Vicenza landmarks, depictions of, 15, 98, 100
Vienna, Albertina: *Resurrection* (Mocetto; fig. 32), 94, 96
Vienna, Kunsthistorisches Museum: *Three Philosophers* (Giorgione), 20–21; *Venus at Her Toilet* (Bellini), 51
Vienna, Stallburg, 118, 124n7
Vincent of Beauvais, 58
Virgin and Child with Saint John the Baptist and a Female Saint in a Landscape (Giovanelli *Sacra Conversazione*) (Venice, Accademia; cat. no. 10), 14, 108, 110–15, *111*, 124
Vivarini, Alvise, 50
Vivarini, Antonio, 43, 73–74
Vivarini, Bartolomeo, 80
Volpi, Elia, 70, 72

Waagen, Gustav Friedrich, 94
Washington, DC, National Gallery of Art: *Adoration of the Shepherds (Allendale Nativity)* (Giorgione; fig. 41), 119, *119*, 121; *Crucifixion* triptych (Perugino), 84; *The Feast of the Gods* (Bellini and Titian; fig. 16), 38, 49, 51; *Holy Family*, Benson (Giorgione), 102; *Saint Jerome in a Cave* (Dürer; fig. 43), 126, *128*; *Saint Jerome Reading in the Wilderness* (Bellini; cat. no. 12), 17, *24–25* (detail), 28–29, 32, 95, 126–30, *127*
Weinberger, Josef, 85n6
Weyden, Rogier van der, 85
Wilde, Johannes, 78, 80, 81
Windsor, Royal Collection: *Concert* (attrib. to Giorgione; fig. 39), *112*, 113

Zancaruol, Giuliano, 109
Zanetti, Antonio Maria, 72, 73, 75n11
Zeno, Battista (bishop), 100, 101
Zimmermann, Ernst, 94
Zoppo, Marco, 60, 73, 74
Zovenzoni, Raffaele, 47, 102

This publication accompanies the exhibition *Giovanni Bellini: Landscapes of Faith in Renaissance Venice*, on view at the J. Paul Getty Museum at the Getty Center, Los Angeles, from October 10, 2017, to January 14, 2018.

The exhibition was organized by the J. Paul Getty Museum and was made possible through the generosity of John J. Studzinski CBE, Maria Hummer-Tuttle and Robert Holmes Tuttle, Álvaro Saieh, and Fabrizio Moretti.

Published by the J. Paul Getty Museum, Los Angeles
Getty Publications
1200 Getty Center Drive, Suite 500
Los Angeles, California 90049-1682
www.getty.edu / publications

Nola Butler, *Project Editor*
Mary Christian, *Manuscript Editor*
Jane Bobko, *Proofreader*
Kurt Hauser, *Designer*
Michelle Woo Deemer, *Production*

Catalogue numbers 1, 2, 3, 6, and 8 were translated from the Italian by Alexandra Bonfante-Warren.

Distributed in the United States and Canada by the University of Chicago Press

Distributed outside the United States and Canada by Yale University Press, London

Printed in Italy

Library of Congress Cataloging-in-Publication Data

Names: Bellini, Giovanni, –1516, artist. | Gasparotto, Davide, editor. | J. Paul Getty Museum, host institution, issuing body.
Title: Giovanni Bellini : landscapes of faith in Renaissance Venice / edited by Davide Gasparotto; with contributions by Hans Belting, Keith Christiansen, Davide Gasparotto, Daniel Wallace Maze, Antonio Mazzotta, Susannah Rutherglen, Mattia Vinco.
Other titles: Giovanni Bellini (J. Paul Getty Museum)
Description: Los Angeles : J. Paul Getty Museum, [2017] | "This publication accompanies the exhibition Giovanni Bellini: Landscapes of Faith in Renaissance Venice, on view at the J. Paul Getty Museum at the Getty Center, Los Angeles, from October 10, 2017, to January 14, 2018." | Includes bibliographical references and index.
Identifiers: LCCN 2017009688 | ISBN 9781606065310 (hardcover)
Subjects: LCSH: Bellini, Giovanni, –1516—Criticism and interpretation. | Bellini, Giovanni, –1516—Exhibitions. | Landscape painting, Renaissance—Italy—Venice.
Classification: LCC ND623.B39 G56 2017 | DDC 759.5—dc23
LC record available at https://lccn.loc.gov/2017009688